# Reviews

## for

### Derivatives: The Wild Beast of Finance

"Dr. Steinherr has written a most valuable and badly-needed book on an important subject. Derivatives of all kinds are today a large part of an enormous international financial market which has no frontiers and which, thanks to modern means of communication, is not only world-wide, but also virtually instantaneous in its operation. The subject, therefore, has, not surprisingly, attracted a great deal of attention and this book is to date the most complete, comprehensive and searching description and analysis of derivatives and their markets. Indeed, I can think of no better manual as well as continuous reference work for anyone interested in the subject than this present work. He also has definite ideas of his own, which he expounds in this book fully. He regards, and this is very cogently argued, risk management as one of the most important developments in finance in recent years, and derivatives and the markets in which they are dealt with, including, of course, organised Stock Exchanges, as very important elements in the maintenance of stable financial conditions."

*Lord Roll of Ipsden*
*Senior Adviser, SBC Warburg*
*former Chairman of S.G. Warburg and Co. Ltd*

"Alfred Steinherr could hardly have picked a more topical issue for his book. A lot of nonsense has been said about derivatives, none of which has found its way into Steinherr's careful, but lively and very readable analysis."

*Alexandre Lamfalussy*
*former President of the European Monetary Institute*

"With deep understanding of the historical, social and technical forces involved, Alfred Steinherr pertinently extracts for the professional and lay reader the crucial elements of the financial revolution caused by derivatives in the last quarter century and alerts them to the further dramatic implications for banks, exchanges and regulators as the activity moves into the cyberspace world of the next millennium."

*Jack Wigglesworth*
*Chairman of LIFFE*

"A book full of ideas and written in a style that is both serious and entertaining. The policy proposals are fundamental for containing systemic risk and worth careful examination."

*Karl Otto Pöhl*
*Sal. Oppenheim Jr. & Cie*
*former President of Deutsche Bundesbank*

"Alfred Steinherr provides a lively and informative canter through the world of derivatives, including their history, implications—not least for regulators—and their future developments. While he stresses the overall benefits of derivatives in enabling risks to be measured, priced and hedged, his main proposal for limiting systemic risk is to encourage OTC business to be centrally settled, or even better exchange traded. This is a most valuable book for practitioners, officials and students alike."

*Professor Charles A.E. Goodhart*
*Financial Markets Group*
*London School of Economics*

"No economist or public policy official can nowadays afford to be without an intuitive understanding of derivatives—their potential for improving the efficiency of financial intermediation, and their scope, if abused for generating financial instability. Alfred Steinherr's book is a readable and entertaining introduction to the subject with much food for thought for the layman and insider alike."

*Andrew D. Crockett*
*General Manager*
*Bank for International Settlements*

"Alfred Steinherr has produced a lucid, authoritative tour through an arcane corner of modern finance that has emerged as a pillar of global capital markets. Senior executives in particular would be well advised to read this book if they want to know what their financial specialists are really up to."

*Professor Ingo Walter*
*Director, Salomon Center*
*New York University*

# Derivatives
# The Wild Beast of Finance

# Derivatives
## The Wild Beast of Finance

**Alfred Steinherr**

John Wiley & Sons

Chichester · New York · Weinheim · Brisbane · Singapore · Toronto

Published by John Wiley & Sons Ltd,
Baffins Lane, Chichester,
West Sussex PO19 1UD, England

*National*     01243 779777
*International*   (+44) 1243 779777
e-mail (for orders and customer service enquiries): cs-books@wiley.co.uk
Visit our Home Page on http://www.wiley.co.uk
                 or http://www.wiley.com

*Other Wiley Editorial Offices*

John Wiley & Sons, Inc., 605 Third Avenue,
New York, NY 10158-0012, USA

WILEY-VCH Verlag GmbH, Pappelallee 3,
D-69469 Weinheim, Germany

Jacaranda Wiley Ltd, 33 Park Road, Milton,
Queensland 4064, Australia

John Wiley & Sons (Asia) Pte Ltd, 2 Clementi Loop #02-01,
Jin Xing Distripark, Singapore 129809

John Wiley & Sons (Canada) Ltd, 22 Worcester Road,
Rexdale, Ontario M9W 1L1, Canada

*Library of Congress Cataloging-in-Publication Data*

Steinherr, Alfred.
  Derivatives : the wild beast of finance / Alfred Steinherr.
    p.  cm.
  Includes bibliographical references and index.
  ISBN 0-471-96544-8 (cloth : acid free paper)
  1. Derivative securities.   I. Title.
HG6024.A3S753   1998
332.64'5—dc21                       97–41436
                                    CIP

*British Library Cataloguing in Publication Data*

A catalogue record for this book is available from the British Library

ISBN   0-471-96544-8

Typeset in 10/12 pt Times by Dorwyn Ltd, Rowlands Castle, Hants
Printed and bound in Great Britain by Biddles Ltd, Guildford and Kings Lynn
This book is printed on acid-free paper responsibly manufactured from sustainable forestation,
for which at least two trees are planted for each one used

To Alessa and Adrian with the hope that they invest wisely in their future and hedge their bets.

To those I love and tired with this project, including Benji and Haiduc, always approvingly wagging their tails with infinite enthusiasm.

And to Furia.

# Contents

# Foreword

For the last 25 years derivatives markets have known phenomenal growth. Until 1995 the two segments of the overall market—the products traded on organised exchanges and those of the over-the-counter (OTC) market—grew in tandem. Since then, the growth of OTC products has continued unabated, while exchange products world-wide have seen much lower growth with notable regional differences.

The growth of derivatives products has fundamentally transformed financial institutions' risk-management and their customers have been able to lower their funding costs and structure risks to the desired level and configuration. This book brings together the experience of a banker and economist to identify the opportunities available to individual market participants and what it adds up to for the economy as a whole.

Of course, risk has been shifted and made less visible, not removed from the economy. And regulators have become increasingly concerned about off-balance sheet exposures to credit and market risk of large international banks. In the 1990s, a number of problems were highlighted in large, widely publicised crises: the problem with traditional accounting systems in the Metallgesellschaft débâcle; the lack of accounting transparency in the Mexico crisis on the dollar exposure of Mexican banks; concern about bank-internal risk-management in the case of the Barings' failure. All these cases, and many more, are carefully analysed and demystified in this book. These "teething pains" have contributed to regulatory actions undertaken, nationally and internationally, in recent years. We can now say that in 1998 the regulatory framework is much better adapted to the conditions of the global financial markets than at the beginning of the 1990s. The most recent significant regulatory breakthrough was the acceptance of banks' internal risk-management systems for market risks. However, it would be a gross mistake to think that there are no more grounds for concern. The rapid evolution of markets condemn regulators to always lag at least one step behind. And we can be sure that only experience will demonstrate remaining or new problems with the present regulatory approach.

Safe banking requires careful precautions in order to prevent the spread of individual bank problems. Measures such as the Basle Committee's capital standards and the reinforcement of payments systems are essential precautionary steps. They reinforce the financial infrastructure, but the question remains, and is posed in this book, whether they are sufficient.

Alfred Steinherr, while applauding the regulatory advances, makes the case that more responsibility should be given to market participants and that regulators should neither see their role in continuous surveillance of individual institutions, nor lock themselves into the uncomfortable moral obligation of saviour of last resort. His basic proposal is to re-engineer the financial infrastructure, within which market participants enjoy greater freedom, but also bear greater responsibility. The central idea is to isolate within a financial conglomerate the "monetary function" that is strictly regulated. Deposits should, therefore, be invested in liquid and safe tradable paper, while the rest of the financial conglomerate would be subject to standards of transparency and accounting, but left unrestrained in its activity.

This proposal deserves reflection, particularly as it deals with an issue, financial conglomerates, to which regulatory attention has already turned.

There are at least two important implications. First, the concept of a "bank" would lose its significance. What is important is the function discharged, not the name of the institution. This may sound evident, but it is a fact that in many countries regulations aim primarily at institutions, such as banks, securities firms, or insurance companies, although equivalent financial products are offered by all of them. Second, from the perspective of public policy, the concern should be with market failures. And since the major potential market failure is the contagion of financial crises, policy objective should not be to prevent the failure of any particular institution, but rather to safeguard the financial system from epidemic disease.

With respect to derivatives, this book emphasises the advantage of exchange-traded products from a risk-management point of view and argues that at least the plain vanilla OTC products should be managed through a clearing-house structure. This is already being done for certain swap products and there is scope for future developments that could effectively increase transparency and lower risk. The author uses a very catching metaphor when he compares clearing-house arrangements to an aquarium where all relevant parameters can be controlled, whereas the market for OTC products resembles the open sea.

From my present perspective as a stock market regulator, I am intrigued by the emergence of an integrated European capital market as a result of European monetary union. This exceptional historic event will profoundly change the efficiency and completeness of European financial markets—a major and too often forgotten benefit of EMU. The book has a discussion on derivatives exchanges in the integrated financial market that is both insightful and balanced.

One does not have to agree with all the views or proposals in this book—most people would, like me, disagree with at least some of them—to enjoy the rigour and clear treatment of a subject, which is of major importance from both a market and a regulatory perspective. Both practitioners and laymen will surely learn from this book and get a solid understanding of the subject.

*Tommaso Padoa-Schioppa*
*President, CONSOB*
*former Chairman of the Basle Committee on*
*Banking Supervision*

# Introductory Note

I read this book with infinite pleasure because three fundamental aspects of Alfred's personality converge in it, aspects that are also apparent in his daily work.

First of all, the humanist whose intellectual curiosity is aroused by the ramifications of economic activity, be they social or cultural, past or present. His "stories" at the beginning of each chapter make reading much more lively and represent an oasis for the traveller in the sometimes necessarily dry voyage through the panoramic desert of financial techniques. So we might be tempted to think "historia magistra vitae". This is, however, not at all the approach of Alfred Steinherr, who persuades the reader to approach every situation critically, independently of preconceived ideas.

The second element is his mathematical approach, even when no formulas are used. The reader cannot help but appreciate the continuous attempts to see market behaviour modelled behind the easygoing prose. The book is also impregnated with a resolute belief in technological progress and the need to master and exploit a full understanding of new financial techniques, so that society can benefit from them to the fullest degree.

But, in the end, Alfred is not a pure financier. He demonstrates that derivatives are, on balance, improving the allocation of resources, although he stresses the need for safer regulatory infrastructures.

Using a basically scientific and didactic approach, he manages to write a fascinating and entertaining text that, in reality, hides original models of thinking that combine the three aspects I outlined: the humanist culture, technological faith and deep economic understanding. In dealing with its current problems of slow growth, unemployment and relatively ossified structure, Europe is facing a major challenge. Dealing effectively with this challenge requires the very mental framework that I admire in this book.

*Massimo Ponzellini*
*Vice President*
*European Investment Bank*

# Acknowledgements

The starting point of this book was the essay "The Wild Beast of Derivatives: To Be Chained Up, Fenced In or Tamed?", which I wrote with David Folkerts-Landau. We set out together on this book and David wrote a large part of Chapters 2, 7 and 8, but, to my great disappointment, increased responsibilities prevented David from continuing with me to the end. My gratitude to him is commensurate with my regrets. I spent precious moments with him at the International Monetary Fund and benefited from the accumulation of experience and wisdom there.

Among the many people who have helped me with comments and discussion, is, above all, my former student and now colleague and friend, Eric Perée. Luis Gonzalez-Pacheco, Norbert Wuthe, Pascale Viala and Daphne Venturas have assisted in many ways. Maureen Thibaut-McCaw has helped me in carrying with tremendous efficiency the Sisyphus rock that was the many stages of the manuscript.

Nick Wallwork of John Wiley & Sons initiated the project and David Wilson provided excellent editorial assistance. Leo Gough provided editorial advice and my friends, Patrick Ventujol and Michel Heintz, helped with their artistic talents. To all of them I am eternally grateful.

# Introduction

Why the wild beast of finance? The increased use of derivatives, their potentially indomitable nature and devastation of the financial landscape is expressed in the following quote from *The Economist* (14 May 1994):

> "there are fears that derivatives fuel financial-market uncertainty by multiplying the leverage, or debt-based buying power, of hedge funds and other speculators—an uncertainty that could, if the things went wrong, threaten the whole of the world financial system."

This suggests brute force, lack of rational behaviour, lack of control—in short beastly danger. We might see, therefore, the sought-after legal and regulatory solutions as attempts to chain up, fence in or tame the beast (Folkerts-Landau and Steinherr 1994). At the same time, the greatest danger may not lie in the "brute force" (outstanding amounts), but in the interconnectedness of the global market where a small uncontrolled event could develop into a major financial crisis. No wild beasts are needed for that; as chaos theorists like to put it: "the fluttering of a butterfly in the Amazon could ripple through the dynamics of the world's ecology and cause an earthquake in Asia". This is precisely the point that motivated this book: the concern that somewhere in the interdependent global financial system, possibly in a carelessly regulated market, the high leverage provided by derivatives may lead to a financial "accident" that then magnifies as it ripples through the world's financial system.

The explosive growth in the global financial service industry during the last ten years has been one of the most far-reaching and consequential economic developments since the industrial revolution. Financial services—the raising and managing of funds, the structuring of balance sheets and of financial exposures, the engineering of financial solutions—are making a key contribution to economic performance in the post-industrial age. Not only have sophisticated financial engineering solutions become a necessary input for firms operating in the competitive global market-place, they are also becoming an indispensable input for firms of any size, as well as for the financial activities of households. For example, the difficult evaluation of stock options was one of the reasons for the spectacularly complex divorce procedures of Gary Wendt, Chief Executive Officer of GE Capital.

The growing reach of the financial service industry is readily apparent. It has facilitated the restructuring of industries through mergers, acquisitions and divestitures, and it has provided innovative solutions to massive privatisation programmes. It has internationalised the raising and investing of funds, expanded the sources and types of financing to support the emergence of new industries and it has facilitated the funding of economic development in emerging and transition economies around the world. The financial service industry is attracting the best and brightest minds to design a vastly expanded menu of financial instruments and techniques. It has greatly increased participation in global financial markets; in fact, the financial service industry is becoming the first truly global industry that has succeeded in pushing aside the strictures of national boundaries. The aggressive growth of this innovative global industry has significantly restricted the scope of freedom of discretionary government policy and as such it has made a significant contribution to the creation of a liberal global financial environment.

A central driving force of the globalisation of the financial service industry has been a revolutionary change in the ability to manage financial risk—with the help of derivatives. The demise of the Bretton Woods exchange rate arrangements, the liberalisation of the financial sectors around the world and the rapid internationalisation of economic life during the last twenty years have created new uncertainties. The risk-management industry has made it possible for participants in the global financial markets, from multinationals with sophisticated treasury operations to households with floating rate mortgages, to cope better with expanded financial risk—the risk of a change in commodity or stock prices, exchange rates, interest rates, or market liquidity. Indeed, the advances since the mid-1970s in the ability to identify and isolate the key financial risks commonly found in modern economies, together with the development of financial institutions and markets that can efficiently commoditise, trade and price such risk, are the crowning achievement in the evolution of modern market economies. At a fundamental level, it allows those who would like to reduce the economic uncertainty surrounding them to do so at a market-determined price, whilst those who are better equipped and willing to bear certain types of risk have vastly expanded opportunities.

The key contribution of the risk management revolution has been the successful use of derivative instruments (futures, options, etc.). The range of futures and options contracts traded on organised exchanges around the world has increased from a handful in the 1970s to a vast and increasing menu, and the volume of contracts traded has risen geometrically. At the same time, the over-the-counter (OTC) derivatives markets have exploded. For example, the volume of outstanding OTC interest rate swaps grew from US$683 billion in 1987 to US$12 810 billion in 1995. Currency swaps have seen a similarly explosive growth. Such growth rates are phenomenal and exceed anything observed in other domains of finance. But this success has also, and quite naturally, generated concerns: is this explosive growth not excessive? When will it settle down to a sustainable rhythm? What are the ramifications in the transformation of the financial industry and what are the new, still imperfectly understood, and perceived risks?

The increased ability to isolate key financial risks and to engineer financial instruments to trade and discover market prices for such risks completes the institutional evolution of market economies. For example, until recently, it would have been difficult to buy and sell financial exposure to certain interest rate differentials, to buy and sell the "volatility" of the Dow Jones index, or to sell exchange rate exposure thirty years into the future.

Financial risk has been a fundamental characteristic of economic life over the centuries, assuming a new dimension in today's global markets. Prices for goods and services, valuations of financial assets, and currency exchange rates are now almost all freely determined by international market forces as the world economy emerges from 5000 years of severe technological and policy restrictions on international trade and payments. A change in the expected fortunes of a firm is quickly reflected in prices and asset valuations, and developments in one part of the world are instantaneously transmitted across national boundaries. Although a global market economy offers vast new opportunities to create wealth, it also carries with it additional risks that have to be managed, and therein lies the challenge.

The economic benefits of managing these risks are not always obvious but they may be colossal. The ability to hedge the risks of changes in prices of goods and services and valuations of assets makes it possible to smooth income and to avoid consumption cuts. Hedges against certain adverse events also reduce the risk of costly bankruptcies. The pace of economic development and progress through the ages has greatly depended on the ability of entrepreneurs to confront and manage financial risks. The possibility of not realising expected gains, or, worse, the possibility of suffering losses that could result in insolvency has always had a dampening effect on investment, growth and development. To a large extent, economic growth has been driven by the willingness of entrepreneurs to venture forth to explore new territories and prospect for resources, to establish trading routes with distant lands, to introduce new production methods in agriculture and industry, and to build economic infrastructure that could support industrial development. The ability to finance such investments was key to the pace of discovery and innovation and the ability to manage the financial risk associated with such investments was essential to securing capital for economic development.

This is the background for this book. In trying to pull together the threads of innovation and structural change, it provides a perspective of financial intermediation that is both new and points to the challenges that lie ahead. These challenges concern the financial industry itself and its customers and the book demonstrates that a fundamental metamorphosis is unfolding.

Policy-makers will not be able to escape unscathed: their scope for intervention is increasingly restricted by the globalisation of the economy and the leverage derivatives provide to private market participants. As for financial regulators, they are in the process of losing their traditional well-defined national turf and their grip on markets through control of specific institutions, such as banks.

This book is, therefore, not narrowly focused on derivative products. Instead it investigates the role of derivatives in a wider process of transformation of the financial industry. This approach has the advantage of by-passing the technicalities of specific instruments, although it remains a complex enterprise to detect and analyse the widespread and important ramifications of the growing production and uses of derivatives on the financial industry and the overall economy. Because it is impossible to present a coherent analysis without knowing how certain risk-management techniques are designed or what specific instruments can achieve, I give frequent examples, wherever useful, instead of complicated technical demonstrations.

The book has four parts. Part I is an interpretation of the evolution of finance over the centuries in order to understand better where we are and where we are going. Chapter 1 shows that derivatives have been used for a long time. A revolutionary bang, however, has only occurred during the last twenty years with the development of organised derivative markets and even then only step-by-step. Why has it taken so long? Why now?

The derivatives business is dominated by a small number of major banks, predominantly the New York money-centre banks. This raises an obvious question: why? Chapter 2 provides an explanation and comes to the conclusion that the US financial system is designed in a way that puts pressure on performance and innovation and provides an environment in which all the major pieces of the puzzle for an open, competitive and transparent financial system are assembled—a system that has become a model for the rest of the world.

Any major new and fast-growing market receives careful attention, particularly when things go wrong as they necessarily do more easily at the infant stage. But in everything that goes wrong there are lessons to be learned. Chapter 3, therefore, analyses the major dramatic events of recent years involving derivatives. Discussing these cases also provides the reader with the basic information and the financial techniques involved in each problem case.

Part II turns to the basics of risk management and the role played by derivatives and discusses the organisation of derivatives markets. Readers anxious not to get too close to economics may prefer to skip Chapter 4. It is, however, clearly important to explain why, and under what conditions, derivatives can contribute to social welfare and to understand whether they serve mainly socially undesirable destabilising speculation or, more positively, contribute to market depth, better information and pricing and ultimately improved risk management. Such questions are answered in that chapter. The following two chapters identify the advantages and disadvantages of organised exchanges as compared to over-the-counter markets. The material in Chapters 5 and 6 is an important stepping stone for apprehending the future evolution of these markets and having a basis for the discussion of public policy issues in Part III.

Chapter 7 starts with an identification of the policy issues. What are the perceived risks and what kind of risks warrant regulation? The chapter emphasises the systemic risk in global markets with rapid and massive international transmission of local shocks. It shows how OTC derivatives have become the dynamite of financial crises and the fuse for international contagion.

Chapter 8 shows that the recent financial evolution has destroyed the classical paradigm of financial policy. This paradigm had emerged in the first half of this century strained by monetary instability. It consisted in central bank support of depositors and of banks when threatened with failure. In exchange, banking was tightly regulated and supervised. But modern financial engineering can easily transform any regulated operation into an equivalent unregulated one so that the classical regulatory equilibrium has become litter on the road to financial progress.

The chapter then scrutinises in detail the adequacy of existing regulatory frameworks and of proposals in public discussion to deal with the perceived risks of an already radically transformed financial sector. Although many of the recent regulatory innovations are positive steps, they trail market developments and at times create as many problems as they solve. What is really required is a totally new framework, which is developed in Chapter 9.

Chapter 9 makes the case for a different "financial infrastructure" based on one key idea and two concrete pillars. The idea is to rely much more than in the past on the industry's capacity to manage risk and to develop incentives for self-regulation. In this respect new territory has recently been explored with the regulatory approval of banks' internal risk-management tools for assessing the capital adequacy for covering market risks. One pillar is to channel derivatives from the OTC market to clearing-houses for better price transparency, mutualisation of risk and appropriate capital backing. The other pillar is ring-fencing of bank deposits in legally, but not organisationally, independent monetary service companies with low-risk, liquid assets. Financial conglomerates then stop being special and can be treated like any other company or industry. Central banks could then focus on monetary policy and, whatever regulations remain would be function-specific and not institution-specific. Self-regulation would gain in importance, assisted by rules concerning public disclosure, capital adequacy and so on.

Such an approach would be most successful if widely accepted in the global economy. For any remaining regulatory tasks acceptance of the "home" regulatory responsibility is gaining ground, that is, the regulator of the financial group's head office is responsible for the entire group worldwide, supported by an international network of supervisory exchange of information.

Chapter 10 attempts a look into the future. It suggests that what derivatives can achieve is much more than what we have seen so far, which is only the tip of the iceberg. Quantum jumps can be expected to come, some of which are already perceptible, others not yet. So far derivatives have dealt with financial risks, but not with "macro-risks", such as real estate, life-time earnings, business cycles, and the like. Even the corporation is unlikely to be the end of institutional evolution and very different organisations can already be imagined. As a result of these changes financial and non-financial firms will metamorphose dramatically, to the point of non-recognition. Among others, banks as we have known them will disappear. The driving force is technology and derivatives play a key role, but there are also other factors at work. To cite only some already visible trends: electronic money, the Internet as a market infrastructure and distribution mechanism and continued disintermediation (i.e., excluding banks as intermediaries from financial flows between ultimate borrowers and lenders) in an increasingly global market.

The main results elaborated in this book are regrouped in the Conclusions. A glossary at the end defines all technical terms to make the book self-contained.

To set the stage, each chapter starts with a story. Some are authentic, others fictitious. All have important messages and, I hope, contribute to the pleasure of reading this book. The book can be read as a general analysis of the growth and impact of derivatives markets and the regulatory issues they raise. Many examples are provided and more specific technical issues are contained in boxes so that the financially aware general reader will feel comfortable. The more technical aspects in boxes may appeal to readers who view themselves as financial experts. The book should be of interest to bankers, traders, regulators and students of finance and economics and, I trust, will increase the luggage weight of business travellers.

# PART I

# A LOOK BACK

# 1

# Evolution of Finance

*Venice, 4 April 1470*

Geramolo Foscati puts on his velvet cap as he is leaving la Chiesa SS Giovanni e Paolo. A mass had been celebrated this morning to solicit the Almighty's protection for the safe journey and return of the convoy of 238 galleys and canon ships. The ships will leave Venice today, now that the storms of the last few days have subsided, to sail to the Eastern Mediterranean and—if the Lord does not decide otherwise—return in about two months' time charged with Chinese silk, indigo, salt and oriental spices.

Geramolo looks worried as he eyes the early morning Venetian mist. Not many ships have returned safely recently, falling prey to the Turks or Arab pirates in the Aegean Sea or, as had happened on several occasions, along the Dalmatian coast. Geramolo is one of the wealthiest patricians of the Serenissima Repubblica. Like his uncle, Francesco Foscati, who was the predecessor of the present Doge, Cristofero Moro, he also has political ambitions. However, to maintain his chances of election to the Signoria, he must stop the accumulation of losses that have hit him recently. He still enjoys considerable wealth, but what the electoral college is looking for in the future leaders of this most successful, rich, admired and feared republic, is not only wealth, but also wisdom, prudence and sustained success.

Geramolo took a 10% participation in the costs of the allotted space for silk in the expedition, in return for an agreed number of silk bales. He had taken similar shares on previous occasions and he congratulates himself once more as he crosses San Marco square that he has never financed a ship all by himself. For the same amount of ducats he could take a 10% share in 10 expeditions and thus hope that at least some of the galleys would return.

When a ship returns, the profits often turn out to be fabulous. It is not just the gain that motivated Geramolo, but the admiration and, even more, the envy that is bestowed on successful merchants.

Because so few ships had returned recently after Venice's Captain-General Nicolò Canal lost Negropont—the brightest pearl in Venice's imperial crown—to Mehmet II, the price of silk now stands at 95 ducats per bale. If the convoy does not return overloaded with bales of silk, the price is bound to rise further, possibly as high as 120 ducats. If the galleys do return, the price is likely to fall. Geramolo discussed the matter with the other silk traders on the Rialto last Friday and the general opinion was that, immediately upon return, the price could fall as low as 70 ducats, still a good price compared to last year. Not selling his remaining stock immediately would preserve the chance of selling later at a higher price—if the difficulty of bringing ships back persists, which is not certain as the arsenal is now re-equipping ships with more powerful canons to strengthen their defence, and Pope Paul II, a Venetian and friend of his uncle, is desperately trying to store up support. The Pope has already declared a plenary indulgence for all those who took arms against the Turks, or financed a substitute for four months. Alas, with the exception of the old rival Genoa, which has lost the colony of Galata and her trading ports around the Black Sea to Mehmet II, Europe still refuses to lift a finger to help. In addition, interest rates are quite stiff due to the ever-increasing needs of the republic to build new ships which resulted last year in a forced loan of 20 000 ducats.

Geramolo's major customer is Piero Barchi, a Florentine merchant in Lucca who has recently expressed his dissatisfaction with the discontinued supplies, which disrupted production at his *officina*, and the unpredictable prices of silk, making it difficult to negotiate prices in advance with his customers.

He has discussed with Barchi a new sort of contract which he has already negotiated twice in the past. Barchi is willing to pay 6 ducats if he, Geramolo Foscati, delivered the silk bales to him at 50 ducats per bale, should the galleys arrive safely. In case of non-arrival, Geramolo would keep the 6 ducats and have no further obligations towards Barchi.

Barchi was expecting a reply today and Geramolo is having difficulties making up his mind. Were he more optimistic concerning the convoy's return, he would certainly not sign the contract. If the Lord did not wish to hear his prayers this morning, he would be happy to sign—as he had been with his previous two contracts, where the ships had not returned. Geramolo feels that there is, in fact, less than one chance in three that the convoy will return. In case of return, if the price really falls to 70 ducats, then he would be giving away 20 ducats by agreeing today to sell to Barchi at 50 ducats. But there is, at best, only one chance in three that the convoy will return, whilst Barchi's 6 ducats are certain. Of course, if the price did not fall to 70 ducats he would regret the contract. On the other hand if the price fell below 70 ducats, which he feels is quite possible, he would have proved his wisdom. Being a prudent man and considering that his participation in the convoy's costs amounted to 12 ducats per bale, he decides to send a messenger to Lucca to mark his agreement with Barchi's proposition.

After he has sent off his trusted servant, Giovanni, to Lucca, he ponders over why Barchi has offered this sort of contract. If Barchi held the same beliefs as he, Geramolo, then his gain would not be very large, as he had only one chance in three of realising a gain of 20 ducats, at the certain cost of 6 ducats, on which, in addition, he lost interest as he had to pay straight away. Surely, then Barchi must expect the price to fall less drastically than generally thought. Or he has some information that suggests that risks in the Aegean have subsided.

Leaning back in the leather armchair he acquired last year from a reputed crafts-man in Milan, and sipping a glass of expensive Marsala, he suddenly has an idea. At the Fondaco dei Tedeschi there are merchants offering silk bales for delivery in one or two months at a fixed price. For delivery in two month's time he heard yesterday a Flemish dealer quote a price of 103 ducats. If he bought at that price and the convoy did not return, he would make a profit, possibly as high as 17 ducats, as most merchants expect the price to increase to 120 ducats per bale. If the convoy did return and the price fell to 70 ducats, he would lose 33 ducats per bale, but what if the price were to fall below 70 ducats?

Geramolo retires to the oratorio of his palazzo to seek the Lord's advice and to find peace for his fatigued mind and wavering soul. Upon leaving he has decided not to pursue the matter with the Flemish merchant.

### Near Glasgow, 2 August 1990

From his terrace Calum McLaughlin, the owner of Scotland's biggest cargo shipping fleet, runs his gaze over the beautiful wild meadows, while appreciating the excep-tionally mild morning. He relishes this moment of tranquillity and success: he has managed to keep alive his reputation for being the "King of Cargo Fleets" which he inherited from his father, James McLaughlin. The honourable old man had been the first to build a fleet of vessels with a completely new transportation technology.

It is 10.56am when the phone interrupts his musing. His old friend from the harbour, Rory McCullon, alerts him nervously: "Listen, laddie, bad news from the Gulf: the Iraqis have invaded Kuwait this morning." Within seconds Calum's peaceful mood is washed away. If Saddam has attacked Kuwait, then the whole of the Gulf region will become a volcano that could virtually explode at any moment. And this means that oil prices will rocket. The cost of fuel accounts for around 15% of the cost of his shipping business—not exorbitant, but, besides wages, the only cost factor with which he could play in order to compete in the market.

What should he do? Price fluctuations have been relatively small over the last years and Calum has become used to buying his fuel spot whenever he needs it. Price offers to his clients, on the other hand, were usually made months ahead of the actual shipping. If a war broke out it could become impossible to stick to these offers. But how would oil prices develop? Would the Americans interfere in the Gulf region? And, if so, when and for how long would the fighting last? Would the USA be successful? How would other countries in that region react? And what about Russia? Too many uncertain factors with their interplay being equally unpredictable. But one thing is sure: there is a major risk of rising oil prices.

Calum has to be sure about future fuel costs and a quick decision has to be made— and "quick" means "now" if he doesn't want to risk the loss of some of his clients or, equally bad, the loss of huge amounts of money through using too low a cost factor for his fuel expenses. Calum grins all of a sudden. He picks up the telephone and places a call to John McGill, his banker in Glasgow. He asks for the futures price of crude oil, delivery in one month's time. What he hears from John confirms his fears. From last night to the first quotes this morning the price had increased considerably, from $US20.8 to $US21.95 per barrel. And, in the first trading hour, the volume of sales had already surpassed yesterday's end of the day total. Without hesitating for a single moment, Calum places an order: buy 1 000 000 barrels of crude oil for delivery next month. Not a perfect hedge as his ships are using diesel, not crude oil, but a very acceptable one for Calum, given the high correlation between crude oil and diesel prices.

John was already dialling the number of the bank's back-office at the London International Petroleum Exchange (IPE) whilst winding up with Calum. The other end of the line sounded like the deck on the sinking Titanic, making it difficult to transmit the order. A maddening bunch of pit traders seemed to be going berserk in a dumb-founding cacophony; one price quotation crossing swords with another in a chaotic stampede for an imaginary exit. The traders in the pit bid desperately for position taking, reflecting best whatever they made out of the new situation with all its un-knowns and uncertainties. Each time a new price was announced the traders bounced back with new bids or new customer orders. Only the trading-end chime of the clock later on in the day provided a short respite before the traders stormed out to the nearest pub to let off steam with floods of beer commensurate only with the day's order flows.

It is 11:24 when Calum finishes his last phone call to clients. He is quite satisfied with himself. From the moment the alarming news hit him, it has taken him only 28 minutes to get the whole situation under control. As a good Scotsman, he raises a glass of single malt to his father's honour and wonders what else this sunny day will bring.

One month later Calum could raise his glass for a second time: the spot price of one barrel of crude oil had reached the dizzy heights of $US30.

———————

Thales of Miletus: inventor of options?

"Deducing from his knowledge of the stars that there
would be a good crop of olives, while it was still winter
and he had a little money to spare, used it to pay
deposits on all the oil-presses in Miletus and Chios,
thus securing their hire. This cost him only a small
sum, as there were no other bidders. Then the time of
the olive-harvest came and, as there was a sudden and
simultaneous demand for oil-presses, he hired them
out at any price he liked to ask."

*Aristotle*, The Politics, *Book I, xi*

G ERALOMO Fosati was already very "modern" in managing his risks.
First, he diversified by buying shares in several ships. Second, he realised that this diversification had limited benefits as the Turks were after the
whole flotilla. Third, he was aware that the current price of silk was totally
irrelevant to him. He had to gather information about future prices. This was
difficult because there were no organised futures markets. McLaughlin in
1990 had it much easier: it only took seconds to obtain a price for oil delivery
in a month. Whether that forward price in the end turned out to be close to
the future spot price was irrelevant to him. He could cover his future needs at
a known price.

The historical snapshot of Venice in 1470 is a reminder that derivative[1]
products are not recent inventions, although their widespread use and the
development of derivatives markets are.

Derivative products have known a spectacular growth during the last
twenty years and have attracted a lot of attention from market participants,
regulators and politicians. Being relatively sophisticated products, they are
not easily understood outside a fairly small group of experts. As is typical of
new, fast-growing markets, there have been some major financial troubles and
many minor "teething pains" involving derivatives (Chapter 3), raising concerns about the risks to which the financial industry is exposed as derivative
products are increasingly used.

Of course, mishaps are typical of any new activity and stock markets have
had their own accidents, the most famous being the New York stock market
crash of 1929. The response was tighter regulation, not only of stock exchanges but also of banks through which the crash rippled. The lesson that
was drawn from that experience is that no major market can be fully understood in isolation. And, indeed, it is entirely possible that the development of
derivatives, of which so far we have only seen a modest beginning, will continue to generate spectacular failures before regulations catch up with market
developments. The risk is, of course, that regulations may either stifle the

growth of derivatives or distort competition conditions. Whatever happens on
the regulatory front, it is, however, safe to argue that derivatives will fundamentally transform the entire financial industry.

Before venturing into an analysis of the impact of the untamed evolution of
derivatives on the financial industry, it may be useful to review some lessons
of history to provide some perspective. Derivatives as a concept are not of
recent vintage; they have been known for more than two thousand years.
What is new is that during recent years they have become tradeable commodities so that their cost has declined, sparking off a rapid growth in
demand. Large markets have become available and their liquidity has pushed
costs down further, with a positive feedback on demand.

Financial intermediation has always been a risky business. Throughout history bankers have endeavoured to improve their grip on risk management.
Only recently, however, with the breakthrough of commoditised derivatives,
has financial engineering been able to separate financial risk from other business lines and control it extensively.

The organisation of this chapter is as follows. Section 1 discusses the basic
functions of finance which have remained constant throughout history, but
not their institutional roles. Sections 2 to 5 describe the evolution of risk
management: initially relying on collaterals and diversification, limited liability emerged in the late Renaissance, tradeable instruments in liquid markets, including derivatives, in the 17th century.

During this century the institutional evolution in the United States and
Europe diverged significantly. Section 6 explains this divergence to set the
stage for Chapter 2's discussion of the American model of finance. The major
difference has been the emergence of the risk-management industry in the
United States after 1970, discussed in Section 7.

To fix ideas, Figure 1.1 marks the most significant events on a time axis,
including a speculative view of the future, elaborated in Chapter 10.

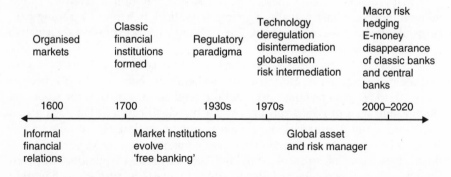

**Figure 1.1**   Time Line

# 1. THE FUNCTIONS OF FINANCE

### Six Basic Functions

Financial services are provided by *institutions*, such as money traders, banks or exchanges. Historians of finance have focused on institutions because they have changed over time. The basic needs they satisfy, or the *functions* they discharge have, however, remained remarkably constant throughout history. Any financial system—past or future—serves six basic functions[2]:

1. making *payments* to facilitate the exchange of assets, goods and services;
2. *providing resources* to fund large projects or enterprises;
3. *transferring resources* from savers to borrowers;
4. *managing risk*;
5. providing *price information* required for the co-ordination of decentralised decision-making;
6. creating *incentives* to borrowers to perform well, i.e. in the stakeholder's interest.

These six functions are obviously not independent of each other. For example, the transfer of resources through lending and investing depends on how well risk can be managed, whether performance can be properly assessed (for example, through the pricing system), and whether the incentives to perform well can be designed at low cost (through covenants, sharing in company results with call options, or other means). For that reason, it serves little purpose to discuss any of the six functions in isolation. The revolutionary *significance of derivatives* lies in the *extended scope*, *greater efficiency* and *lower cost* they provide for risk management, which in turn *opens up new activities* considered too risky without these tools. Derivatives also provide prices for future economic activity and expected volatility that facilitate rational investment and production decisions. And they help in providing proper incentives. These three financial functions—risk management, price information, incentives—are the ones most directly affected by the development of derivatives. They cannot be separated from the other functions (payments, pooling and transferring of resources) and, indeed, the ultimate benefit to society is derived from greater efficiency and innovation to which all six functions contribute.[3]

Banking is special because it intermediates in money and therefore treads on the turf of sovereigns. Bankers are called upon to finance the deficits of the public coffer, or to invest its surplus, to issue currency, or to share with the State the benefits of seigniorage.[4] For that reason, banking has rarely been treated like any other business and has been more controlled and confined to government agreed codes of conduct and scope of operations. Government involvement has solved some problems and created others, and innovations have frequently been driven by the need to overcome these problems. For example, a perennial financial problem is the debasement of money, a cheap way of refinancing the state's deficits, which few monarchs (or modern governments) could resist.[5] In 1272, Genoa pioneered the first gold coinage since Roman times and was quickly followed by Venice and Florence. Only city states which depended on their own commercial success and were ruled by an aristocracy of merchants, recognised the value of reputation and credibility and made sure that their gold coins retained their intrinsic value. In this way Genoa's genoin, the Florentine fiorentino and Venetian ducat remained "international" currency for centuries.

## Evolution of Institutions

Whilst throughout history financial systems have catered to the six primary needs, demand has become more sophisticated over time, putting pressure on the innovatory response of supply. For example, for a long time financial intermediaries have lent and invested their own resources rather than savings collected from the larger public. The major problem was, of course, that the public at large lived hand-in-mouth and every wealthy individual was his own merchant-investor-banker. It was the discovery of the New World and the Industrial Revolution that expanded the scale of financial needs in forms hitherto unknown (committed finance), and brought about the social changes that generated widespread savings. Capital markets took off, but banking was still unable to pool resources, essentially for lack of protection to depositors. Only in the 19th century, when governments had identified the need for pooling resources to finance industrial development and provided guarantees, did savings banks proliferate.

This development in banking also serves to illustrate that, whilst demand for financial products is driven by economic growth (and its social changes), supply responds with innovative new products (i.e., new packages of the basic operations) and new *institutional forms*.

To find the right institutional arrangement is by itself a major innovation, often hampered by the absence of an appropriate legal support (e.g., the absence of the legal concept of limited liability seriously hampered the risk management and resources pooling function until the 16th century), outdated regulations or laws, or inhibiting tax structures.

Because finance is special and therefore regulated, the institutional evolution has not only responded to economic needs but also to regulatory and legal changes. The fact that markets play much more of a role in the United States than in countries where banking dominates the financial industry is due to different legal and regulatory environments. As shown in Chapter 2, the Banking and Securities Acts of 1933–35 in the United States created the basis for well regulated, transparent financial markets. Needless to say, provision of the six basic financial functions is not comparable in market-based and bank-based financial systems. Whilst both offer payments services, pool resources and redistribute them, risk management, price information and performance incentives are far superior in the market-based institutional set-up, a point forcefully demonstrated in Chapter 2.

A final point to be noted is that the evolution of financial institutions is not strictly linear. Certain trends are an extension of geographical market size, greater sophistication of risk management in financial institutions, greater importance of market forces and therefore of liquidity and price information. Other trends are not. A good example is specialisation vs. institutional concentration. Medieval "bankers" were jack-of-all-trades, mainly traders of commodities running financial operations on the side and, above all, lending and money exchanging, like General Electric or Marks & Spencer today. The important difference is that modern financial operations are much more focused and their assets much more liquid. Until the 19th century, "bankers" could not easily take their pick in a financial operation, but usually had to accept a package deal. A recent trend has been to unbundle any kind of risk, or even the entire lending process, so that separate elements—assessment, financial transfer, risk, monitoring—may be sold off to different suppliers. For example, in US mortgage markets, origination is still the domain of banks (or specialised mortgage institutions) whilst most of these loans are sold and distributed by investment banks after repackaging into mortgage-backed securities. Mortgage servicing, which is a processing business driven by economies of scale, is carried out by specialised institutions. To a more modest extent, this also happened in the past. Lenders were sometimes able to sell the credit risk by obtaining a third-party guarantee. Or they sold the entire credit—such was the advantage of letters of credit—so that their value-creation was limited to origination.

Today the big question is, of course, whether this trend will not be reversed in the future by the formation of financial conglomerates.

**Technology as a Basic Driving Force**

Thus, modern banking and finance still deal with the same functions that have been around for millennia. What has changed is technology[6] and, in response, the institutional set-up. Technological progress has made the *world richer* so that more wealth is managed, creating economics of scale. Technology has lowered the *cost of communication*, transforming localised markets into national and, recently, into global markets. Technology has reduced the *cost of transactions* so that the volume of trading of any given financial instrument has increased and previously uneconomical transactions have become profitable. Technology has reduced the cost of *computing* and of *tracking* positions, making it possible to bundle previously separate activities into more and more sophisticated cocktails, or to unbundle previously amalgamated products. This financial engineering restricts risk and returns to suit the preferences of both investors and borrowers.

Just to get a feel of the importance of recent cost reductions which have made it possible to move from local economies to a global market, consider the following examples. In 1965, the cost of storing one megabyte of data (equivalent to a typical edition of the *Wall Street Journal*) in random access memory was about US$100 000. Today, it is about US$20. By 2005, it will probably be less than US$1.

In 1975 it cost US$10 000 to send a megabyte of data from New York to Tokyo. Today it costs about US$5. By 2005, it is expected to be about US$0.01. The cost of the processors needed to handle 1 million instructions a second has declined from US$1 million in 1965 to US$1.50 today. By 2005, it is expected to drop to a few cents.

## 2. THE FIRST STEP TOWARDS MANAGING FINANCIAL RISK: DIVERSIFICATION AND COLLATERAL

Banking was, of course, always a risky activity. But so was the business of traders and farmers. What made banking perhaps more risky was the "moral hazard" problem in the principal–agent relationship between lender and borrower and the "adverse selection" problem stressed by Stiglitz and Weiss (1981). Efforts to limit financial risk have always been at the heart of finance. Many of the main functions of finance evolved in response to the need to limit financial loss.

From the earliest times, bankers relied on the two ways still dominant today to reduce their risks: portfolio diversification and collaterals. Over time there was slow but continuous progress in perfecting both methods. Assets located in foreign lands (which until the formation of the nation-state meant outside city limits) enjoyed little value in case of need (sovereign risk), given the laws of the time (as today: what is a mortgage in Russia worth?) and the only guarantee in lending to sovereigns was their certain need for further finance in the future (again, what has changed?). The best guarantee was still provided by remittance of the merchandise that served as collateral, another reason why Renaissance bankers were banker-traders. Recent incarnations of the collateralised loan are repurchase agreements (repos)—selling and repurchasing a security at an agreed price at some future date—but the big difference is the existence of an organised market. A modern combination of collaterals and diversification are asset-backed securities, where assets can be mortgages, consumer loans, credit card loans, or other forms of loans.

Risk diversification relied mainly on lending to different parties, in different trades and locations. The diversification potential was unfortunately limited by the exiguity of economic life and the high cost of communication in international (i.e., beyond the city) business. However, what eased the transaction costs of international lending was the low foreign exchange risk of currencies based on gold.

Diversification of risk, sources of collateralisation and, more generally, risk management remained limited until very recently. Lenders covered their risk with fat risk premiums and refused to lend to anybody without collateral, which meant in reality, a very small group of economic subjects. This was the real and very substantial cost of underdeveloped finance. An important breakthrough was achieved in the 1950s with the development of modern portfolio theory, becoming the universal basis for managing diversification or the trade-off between risk and return.

## 3. THE SECOND STEP TOWARDS MANAGING FINANCIAL RISK: LIMITED LIABILITY, BANKRUPTCY LAWS, SENIORITY RULES, BALANCE SHEET STRUCTURE

For most of history, credit risk was limited by a legal environment that made borrowers personally fully liable for their debts—including the loss of their freedom. Polonius' precept "neither a borrower nor a lender be" (*Hamlet*, Act 1) was deeply imbued in the principles and practices of finance and commerce throughout the Middle Ages and into the early Renaissance. The prospect of spending time in a debtor's prison had, of course, a chilling effect on the willingness of entrepreneurs to finance ventures with borrowed funds. As the opening story indicates, it was possible to pool risks by participating in larger projects, such as trading ventures, and to achieve some diversification by investing in several such ventures.[7] But these "unlimited liability partnership" arrangements proved to be an unwieldy instrument to secure broad-based creation of financial wealth. Indeed, the one-sided allocation of credit risk to the borrower forced by the absence of a legal instrument limiting financial liability proved to be an important obstacle to financial development and to the further development of market economies well into the Renaissance.

### Limited Liability and Bankruptcy

The first important step in creating the legal and institutional environment that allowed for a more efficient allocation of credit risk was the establishment of corporate entities with a legal personality separate from the owners, such that *the liability of the owners of the corporation is limited to the size of their invest-ment.* Such entities existed already in the form of medieval corporations, such as universities and boroughs, which had an existence separate from their owners. This feature was then embodied in joint stock companies which were allowed to hold property and financial assets, incur debts, and undertake contracts on their own behalf. Equity ownership of a joint stock company vested control over the running of the firm and a claim to its revenue with its shareholders, but their liability for the corporations' financial obligations was limited to the nominal value of that capital subscription.[8] This represented enormous progress and impetus to entrepreneurial activity, but weakened the lender and shifted the need for further risk management means to him.

A complementary development which further shifted credit risk from the borrower to the lender was the emergence of *bankruptcy laws* that limited the financial liability of a borrower by protecting him from efforts of the creditor to collect on his debts. The emergence of various versions of bankruptcy laws, starting in the late Renaissance, gradually limited the liability of borrowers to their current possession, and later extended the protection to allow the corp-orate entity the possibility of a court-supervised debt workout. A personal borrower no longer forfeited his freedom and all of his future income if he failed to service his debts. As with the joint stock corporation, bankruptcy laws also had the effect of shifting risk away from the borrower to the lender. Although such a shifting of risk was clearly reflected in the interest charges on debt, it increased the willingness to fund investments with debt and thereby had the effect of increasing the rate of investment.

These two developments—growth of limited liability joint stock companies and bankruptcy laws—facilitated diversification of investments through parti-cipations in several ventures, while at the same time being able to limit max-imum losses and potential bankruptcy. These developments became the main vehicles that made it possible to secure broad-based funding for the industrial revolution in the 19th century. Although we tend to take these financial innovations for granted today, they have become the institutional means of limiting risk in modern market economies. The financial institutional arrange-ments of modern economic life, as we know it, would be radically different without the concept of limited liability.

**Hierarchy of Claims**

Once the liability of borrowers could legally be limited, it became possible to establish a *hierarchy of claims*, i.e., depending on the fortunes of the corpora-tion, debtors with the most senior claims would be paid, while the other lia-bilities would not be serviced. For the owners of a corporate entity, the introduction of limited liability created a hierarchy of claims in which debts had to be paid first—debt holders had seniority—and equity holders received the residual. Different levels of seniority among debt liability, in particular various forms of subordinated debt, also came into use during the last century. For example, debt owed to banks, or collateralised debt, generally had the highest seniority, followed by ordinary bonds, and then by subordinated debt. The introduction of these so-called "me first rules" was a key addition to the tool box used for risk management. The ordering of claims according to who is paid first—the first example of financial engineering—effectively created financial instruments with different risk and return characteristics, which was reflected in the pricing of these instruments. By separating its liabilities into different risk classes, the firm was generally better able to meet the risk/return demand from different investor groups and thereby lower its overall financing costs.

**Balance Sheet Structure**

Historically, the main method available to financial and non-financial firms to manage financial risk was to *structure their balance sheet* so as to minimise financial risk. In order to minimise the impact of interest rate changes, banks tried to match the duration of assets and liabilities, while paying due attention to the profitability of being mismatched. Non-banks matched the cash flow of assets with the cash flow of their financial and non-financial liabilities. In the same vein, the currency risk of foreign receivables was hedged with foreign borrowing. Early on, there were some off-balance sheet transactions, such as forward agreements and collateral, but the absence of organised markets limited their importance.

## 4. THE THIRD STEP TOWARDS MANAGING FINANCIAL RISK: CREATING TRADEABLE INSTRUMENTS AND LIQUIDITY IN ORGANISED MARKETS

**Tradeable Instruments**

One risk an asset holder faces is the inability to turn the asset into cash when needed. Risk management is, therefore, seriously limited when there is no market for an asset. Another consequence is the difficulty of assessing the value of such an asset and to make appropriate provisions. A major step forward was, therefore, the development of *tradeable* lending instruments and ownership rights and the subsequent development of organised markets in which fair prices were established.[9]

A *bond* is essentially a formalised, negotiable loan, whereas *credit* is a private arrangement between two or more parties. The first true bond was the "Grand Parti", issued by the French government in 1555. Bonds were also issued by firms from a relatively early date; for example, the Dutch East India Company had bonds outstanding in the 17th century.

At the same time, a truly financial revolution took place as the Dutch provinces shifted their borrowings from merchant banks to marketing negotiable *rentes* directly to wealthy individuals, thereby creating a rudimentary "capital market". Sophisticated instruments to suit the needs of market participants followed quickly, a striking resemblance to modern developments described in Chapter 2. Antwerp and Amsterdam also benefited from what in our time is called "Euromarkets" (originally Eurodollar markets). Italian bankers, and foreign lenders in general, were privileged lenders to the British and other crowns, because usury laws made borrowing from one's own subjects awkward. When the Tudors drove out the Italians, but not the Tudors' need for loans, they set up agents in Antwerp and Amsterdam to borrow money. In the 1960s and 1970s the Euromoney and Eurobond markets developed for exactly the same reasons—restrictive regulations at home.

### Early Examples of More Complex Instruments

In addition to equities and bonds, other types of securities were developed at an early date. *Convertible securities* (securities with an embedded option) have a long history. In continental Europe in the 16th century, certain equity issues forced the equity holders to convert their shares into debt at pre-specified conditions. In the 17th century, a number of English firms undertook conversions to benefit particular shareholders. For example, in 1631, King Charles I of England was allowed to convert his shares in the New River Company into debt when the company did not do as well as expected. Over the following years, the rights of conversion came to be specified more carefully at the date of issue, and the use of convertible securities gradually expanded.

*Preferred stock* is another security that was issued by firms at a relatively early date and has survived to the present day.[10] In the mid-16th century, English joint-stock companies started to give preference to certain classes of their stock. However, it was not until the late 18th century that preferred stock was widely used, first by canal companies and then in the 19th century by railway companies. In the English railway mania of the 1840s, in particular, preferred stock was issued in large quantities. The main reason for the popularity of preferred stock was the regulation that required companies in England to restrict their total loans to a third or less of their share capital. The proportion of total railway issues consisting of preference shares grew from 4% in 1845 to 66% in 1849. In the United States, preferred stock came to be used when industrial conglomerates appeared in the late 1880s and when the railroads were reorganised in the mid-1890s.

Both convertible securities and preferred stock are early hybrids of pure equity and pure debt. Much of the financial engineering of recent years has refined and generalised this cross-breeding. Furthermore, if conversion is a right, but not an obligation, then *it is a security enhanced by an option.*

## Development of Markets

As the number of joint-stock companies grew, the amount of equities outstanding increased steadily. Companies began to issue bonds as well as shares, so that the total value of securities grew significantly. In addition to the securities issued by firms, governments' need for finance led to a significant expansion in the amount of public debt. As the total amount outstanding became larger, *secondary trading* became commonplace, and financial markets became more organised. There was a considerable amount of trading of securities in Antwerp and Amsterdam in the 16th century and, in 1611, the Amsterdam Bourse was opened. Amsterdam was the most important exchange internationally for many years before London and subsequently New York took its place. Dealings in securities in London were not centralised until relatively late and the purpose-built stock exchange was opened only in 1802. Prior to this, the trading of securities mainly took place in coffee houses. The New York Stock and Exchange Board, which was the forerunner of the current New York Stock Exchange, was founded in 1817. Before that transactions were conducted in the streets, giving Wall Street its literal significance.

At the beginning of the 18th century, the smooth operation of European stock markets was severely disrupted by bouts of wild speculation. The most famous of these, perhaps, was the South Sea Bubble of 1720. The price of the South Sea Company's stock rocketed sky-high from 131% of par at the beginning of February to 950% by June 23 and then fell back to 200% by the end of the year. This speculation led to the so-called Bubble Act, which made it illegal to form a company without a charter.[11] It also prohibited companies from pursuing any line of business other than the one specified when their charter was issued. The result of this legislation was a severe restriction on the issuing of equities for the next hundred years or so. Although the stocks of existing firms were still traded, there was very little expansion in the number of firms. However, the securities markets continued to do well. Government debt expanded because 45 of the years between 1739 and 1815 were years of war, and there were heavy financing needs. Government bonds came to dominate the market—as they still do today in most countries.[12]

In the 19th century, the development of canals and railways led to the repeal of the Bubble Act and corporate securities again came to predominate in the London market. In 1860, British government securities had amounted to more than 50% of the total value of all securities, but by 1914 they had fallen to less than 5% of the total. During this period, the main innovations were concerned with different types of equity and preferred stock. The majority of English corporations had at least two types of equity and a significant number had more.

In the last half of the 19th century and the first half of the 20th century, the New York market grew in importance. The bonds issued during the Civil War and the active trade in them during the following decades had much to do with this change. In addition, the vast scale of railroad investment in the United States led to a large expansion in securities issued. During the First World War, New York finally replaced London as the most important financial market.[13]

After the Civil War, the market for *commercial paper* started to develop. This allowed corporations with a strong financial position to borrow short-term funds in the markets more cheaply than they could borrow at a bank. The commercial paper market faded after the Great Crash of 1929 and banks started to dominate the loan market in the United States, until commercial paper redeveloped in the 1970s. Another innovation that occurred at the beginning of the 20th century was the use of *warrants*, which experienced a renaissance in the 1980s. These were usually issued with bonds or stocks and essentially consisted of an option which allowed the holder to buy stock at a predetermined amount for a limited amount of time.[14]

## 5. THE FINAL STEP TOWARDS MANAGING FINANCIAL RISK: DERIVATIVES AND FINANCIAL ENGINEERING

The main characteristic of the risk management discussed so far was that it was all done "on-balance sheet", that is transactions were executed in the cash market. The important consequence was that risk management was not, and could not be, clearly separated from other balance sheet objectives. It required the development of the institutions capable of offering derivatives traded in liquid markets and custom-tailored derivatives for the particular needs of customers to get to the final stage of risk management.

Financial engineering is, essentially, the means of implementing financial innovations to find better solutions to specific financial problems. It proceeds with the *diagnosis* of a problem; *analysis* of the possible solutions (possibly a new financial instrument); *production* of the new instrument; *pricing*; and *customisation* when the solution is relevant to more than one client.

## What are Derivatives?

*Derivatives* are nothing particularly new. As the name suggests, derivatives are based on or derived from an underlying asset (or abstract performance indexes) and the way to evaluate derivatives is to value an equivalent structure of assets (or liabilities).[15] For example, a one-year forward purchase of foreign exchange, say Japanese yen against US dollars, is equivalent to borrowing for one year US dollars and investing them in one-year paper denominated in Japanese yen. In both cases no initial capital is required. In both cases there is absolutely no uncertainty as all prices are known at the time of contracting. And, abstracting from transaction costs, the returns are identical. In the forward contract the difference between the forward and the spot exchange rate is equal to the interest rate differential and the same is true for the alternative of borrowing dollars to invest them in yen.

Thus, conceptually, *all derivatives are redundant* because they can be replicated with a bundle of straightforward basic operations. In this sense they are nothing "new". Of course, this argument abstracts from transaction costs and this is the key. In the dollar–yen example it takes time to borrow the dollar amount and the lender will charge for transaction costs and a risk premium. Investment in yen also entails transaction costs and creates a counter-party risk for the investor. To close the position ahead of expiration is also more costly for the individual debtor/investor than for the banker dealing in the interbank forward market. Derivatives have one decisive advantage over the underlying bundle of assets and that is *transaction costs*.

A related source of confusion is due to the difficulty in distinguishing derivatives from other claims. Because any derivative can be replicated and, because any contingent claim, such as a bond, a share, a guarantee, can be looked upon as an option, the demarcation line is fuzzy.

It is not an uninteresting perspective to look at *stocks* and *bonds* as *primitive options*. Unlike rights in a partnership with unlimited liability, the maximum loss on a stock is the acquisition price and is hence known. The scope for gain is driven by the same parameters as the gain on an option. The underlying asset is the earnings potential of the firm. The major difference resides in the lower leverage of shares and bonds.

More precisely, a loan or a bond can be seen as a portfolio of a long position in a "risk-free" loan and a short position in a put option on the market value of the firm, i.e. a put option that the lender has sold to the firm's shareholders. In the language of Black and Scholes (1973, pp. 649–50): "Stockholders have the equivalent of an option on their company's assets. In effect, the bondholders own the company's assets, but they have given options to the stockholders to buy the assets back."

This interpretation also sheds a new light on third-party guarantees of a loan. If the guarantor is of impeccable quality (zero default risk) then the lender holds a risk-free loan and the guarantee is nothing but a put option, or in most recent terminology a "credit derivative". Since lenders have sought guarantees throughout history, it could be claimed that credit derivatives have been in use since time immemorial. They have been tailor-made products for which no organised market existed. Since few guarantors were default-free, however, lenders remained exposed to counterparty risk, i.e., guarantor non-performance, still a major problem for modern OTC products.

In this book derivatives are pragmatically considered as contracts whose payoffs are based on a continuously measurable underlying asset or performance index. Accordingly, an option on a stock is considered as a derivative, but not the stock itself.

## Early Examples of Derivatives

Derivatives have been known and used for a long time, although not many cases are reliably documented. The first option transaction is credited to the Greek philosopher Thales (Bernstein 1992, Millman 1995). From the opening quotation it is apparent that he knew his potential maximum losses from the beginning (the advance payment), whilst his gain was proportional to the amount of the crop times the price. The difference between this primitive option and modern traded options is again one of transaction costs and, in particular, of liquidity. It took Thales some time to seek out the owners of olive presses, pay them a visit, negotiate and settle on a price. Did he pay a fair price? Too much? Too little? It is difficult to know. Nor would it have been easy for him to sell his options before the harvest time at a fair price since there was no market to provide a competitive value.

As the introductory story of this chapter suggests, primitive forms of derivatives were extensively used in the high risk activity of maritime trade. In the 15th century risks were transferred from owners to financiers and diversified through loans called "bottomry", that only had to be repaid if the ship returned. These loans then evolved into maritime insurance.

Futures also have been around for some time. Money lenders often bought up future crops, when making their loan at planting time, at an agreed price to recover their loan. But these were illiquid bilateral agreements with a pricing that reflected the superior bargaining position of the lender, in rural areas often a local monopolist. The real breakthrough came when markets developed for futures. By the end of the 16th century herring were bought and sold before they were caught. De la Vega (1688) reports that options and futures (called "time bargains" or "*windhandel*" because buyers and sellers never saw real goods, but dealt in air) were used on the Amsterdam Bourse soon after its creation in 1611 for commodities, government bonds and shares. Options and futures were also extensively used in London by the end of the 17th century.

But the decisive institutional innovations to turn derivatives into the key instruments for financial risk management only took place during the last twenty-five years. Section 7 relates that tale.

## 6. THE EUROPEAN APPROACH TO RISK MANAGEMENT

Much of Britain's leadership during the Industrial Revolution is hardly imaginable without these advances in finance, especially the concept of limited liability, which was the precondition for making ownership a standardised tradable commodity. It is, however, difficult to identify cause and effect. Did the Industrial Revolution generate advances in finance or was it the other way round? Both hypotheses are supported by historical facts, which keeps historians busy and everybody else ignorant.

Whilst the United States developed its financial market very closely to British experience, the European Continent took another road. Germany, in particular, relied on the development of banks to finance its own industrial revolution in the 19th century. Banks became "universal", collecting the public's savings to finance retail and corporate loans, and taking care of all the financial and advisory needs of their customers. Whilst their unrestricted business scope allowed them to diversify credit risk close to the economy's average, they accepted the high risk of illiquid assets and of the most extensive maturity transformation imaginable.

Why did England and the United States follow a different road from the one chosen by Continental European countries? In my view, the main explanation is that the optimal configuration of the financial sector depends very strongly on the political organisation of society. To make this point *in extremis*, it seems fair to claim that in communist countries financial markets would not have flourished even if they had been admitted. In Continental European countries and Japan, the State was too involved in economic development to allow markets to make allocative decisions. Only in countries with a deep and long-standing commitment to free enterprise, could financial markets prosper. Even today, the weight and efficiency of the US and the UK financial markets are not comparable to those of any other country.

Financial systems are determined mainly by political factors, such as the role of state and of markets, which translate into the regulatory framework and by economic factors, such as the level of economic development. This suggests that there is no "optimal" regulatory framework for financial markets applicable to all countries. The options are restricted by different historical evolutions, the role of markets in a society and, by implication, the economic role of government and the public sector; the legal tradition in contract law and dispute settlements; and, finally, the level of economic development and the size of the domestic market.[16]

This view is inspired by the fact that financial markets are most developed in relationship to banking in the countries of Anglo-Saxon tradition where democratic principles have enjoyed the longest tradition and where property rights have remained unchallenged for centuries.[17] In all other countries there have been at least periods where the benefits of private ownership and of resource allocation through markets have been put into doubt.[18] The central role of financial intermediation in resource allocation has often motivated societies to control this activity more than others and reduce the scope of market forces.

This tendency to control financial intermediation for the public good is not totally unjustified at an early stage of the development process. Second-best theory suggests that government intervention can be welfare-enhancing in the presence of multiple distortions. And it is clear that major imperfections characterise financial markets particularly at an early stage of development: risk assessment is complicated by the macroeconomic or development uncertainties; collection and treatment of information are scant; markets are thin and therefore volatility "excessive"; markets (and institutional support and control) are incomplete so that risk cannot be diversified and idiosyncratic risk is generally not hedgeable. At this stage of development, the larger part of financial intermediation needs to be carried out by intermediaries rather than the markets.[19] Indeed, organised markets require standardisation of products, concentration of trading, a multiplicity of traders and a reliable and tested legal framework.

This interpretation suggests that as societies become increasingly democratic and market-oriented, the bank-based financial system will give way to the market-based system. Here is a first, very general, reason for the gradual decline of traditional banking in financial systems, a trend already observable now and, as I shall argue below, likely to become accentuated in the future.


## 7. COULD THE ACCELERATION IN FINANCIAL INNOVATION SINCE 1970 HAVE BEEN PREDICTED?[20]

The last twenty-five years was a period of exceptionally profound and prolific financial innovations. Many of today's standard financial products did not exist twenty-five years ago, although the concept and the basic ingredients existed in one form or another. As Miller (1991, p. 4) put it: "They were lying like seeds beneath the snow, waiting for some change in the environment to bring them to life."

Mark Twain was surely right in saying: "forecasting is always difficult—particularly the future". This can best be illustrated by the changes in the financial industry over the last twenty-five years, say, from the break-up of the Bretton Woods system to today, which in 1970 were either misjudged or not foreseen at all. Our predictive capacity turned out to be disappointing, despite the fact that much of the theoretical knowledge that underpinned the innovations in finance was already available at that time and had only to be refined for an expanding set of applications. Predictive failure was due to explosive changes in a number of factors, of which the most important was the interactions of technological progress in computation, communication and processing with exogenous events, such as the emergence of a new and little understood world monetary system, the promotion of an increasing number of countries to major actors in worldwide trade and finance and the response of markets and regulators. The major stage of this revolution in finance was the United States and its fascinating story.

## The Big Change: a New World Monetary Order

The first major event whose implications were grossly misjudged was the bankruptcy of the Bretton Woods fixed exchange rate system. Out of the ashes emerged a more diverse, complex and less rigid system. The US dollar started to float. Other currencies pegged to the dollar, to another major currency, or floated as well. Some countries changed their stand over time, either by decision or by the market's force. Most academics had prognosticated a world of flexible exchange rates in which exchange rates would smoothly adjust to prevent *real* exchange rate over- or undervaluation (misalignments). Exchange rate risks were thus seen as minimal, especially as exporters and importers are concerned with real rather than nominal exchange risks. This benign view was largely the result of a reasoning inspired by the historical experience of capital controls during the 1950s and 1960s, where capital flows were constrained to accommodate imbalances from international trade. This experience underrated the importance of capital flows as the driving force of exchange rates. As capital flows were increasingly liberalised, it became evident that trade flows are important for the longer run evolution of the exchange rate, but that in the short run (which can last several years, as shown by the US example of an appreciating dollar from 1981 to 1985 and a declining dollar and high volatility since then) the exchange rate is driven by expectations-based capital flows and positions in derivatives.[21]

Since 1970, market participants have, therefore, experienced vastly increasing exchange risks in both their international trade activities and as international investors. At the same time, and in fact as a driving force behind the increased exchange rate risk, was the sharp growth in international financial transactions, facilitated by exchange liberalisation around the globe.

Again not foreseen in 1970 was the market's reaction to increased foreign exchange risk: the *development of hedge instruments*. Foreign exchange futures were introduced in the Chicago exchanges (the International Money Market, IMM, which is part of the Chicago Mercantile Exchange or CME) on 16 May 1972 and on 10 December 1982 the Philadelphia Stock Exchange began to trade the first currency options. (For details, see Chapter 5.)

Of course, flexible exchange rates did buy some autonomy for national fiscal and monetary policies and, as a result, inflation and interest rates also became more volatile (see Figure 1.2). So not only was there more exchange rate risk, but also more interest risk in each country and interest rates across countries became less correlated. Few economists had expected such a result.

Exchange rate volatility increased dramatically after the demise of the Bretton Woods Exchange Rate Agreement, except for currencies in the European Monetary System (FF/DM). Interest rate volatilities generally increased, even if the graph suggests a relative stability for the United States and France. However, the starting period 1966–72 were for both countries exceptionally volatile by historic standards: Vietnam war expenditures and the pressure on the dollar explain high volatility during that period for the United States; social unrest, high inflation and a devaluation account for France.

**New Markets for a New World**

To cope with increased interest rate volatility, financial futures were started in Chicago by the Chicago Board of Trade (CBoT) in October 1975 with a contract on GNMA (Government National Mortgage Association) mortgage-backed securities. However, the contracts that were the most successful were the IMM's 91-day T-bill contract introduced in January 1976 and the CBoT's Treasury bond contract introduced in August 1977. When, in 1979, Paul Volcker allowed short-term US interest rates to fluctuate rather than maintaining government mandated levels, these contracts benefited substantially. In 1981, the Merc innovated in another major way by launching a hugely successful Eurodollar contract. This contract was the first cash-settled futures market and as such a precursor of cash-settled index contracts, such as the S&P 500. Cash settlement was necessary as Eurodollars, unlike the CDs or T-bills, are intangibles; they are just a rate of interest, which cannot be delivered. Over time, contracts were created for other maturities, other underlying cash instruments, and options were written on futures in the United States and other countries.

Futures markets, in fact, were not new. An organised rice futures market existed in 18th century Tokinawa Japan (the Osaka Rice Exchange) and

(a) Exchange rate volatility*

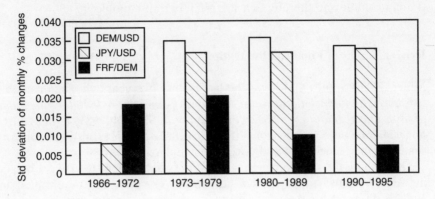

(b) Interest rate volatility*

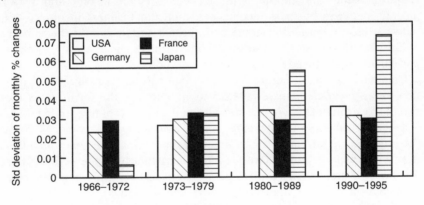

*Note*: *Standard deviation of monthly percentage changes
*Source*: IMF International Financial Statistics; author's computations

**Figure 1.2** Exchange and Interest Rate Volatilities Before and After 1970

futures markets for wheat developed in Chicago—the heart of agricultural America in the 19th century—by the mid-1800s. What was new was *financial futures* based on cash settlement rather than physical delivery.

The proliferation of organised market trading in currencies, equity and fixed-income derivatives during the last twenty-five years is unprecedented. Development in these markets in turn made possible OTC products such as swaps, many custom-designed to meet selective needs of issuers and investors. Mainstream financial institutions and pension-fund managers increasingly adopted quantitative techniques, such as computerised trading strategies, to better manage their portfolios. These changes have led to an explosion of trading volume and thereby to a sharp fall in transaction cost.


## Driving Forces of Financial Innovation

Miller (1986) argues that, over the last twenty-five years, the major impulse for *successful financial innovation has come from a desire to reduce the impact of taxes and regulations*. This is consistent with Silber's (1983) argument that financial innovations arise from efforts to reduce the cost constraints on corporations, and Kane's (1988) theory of dynamic regulation.[22]

The income tax system of virtually every country seeks to strike a balance between efficiency and equity considerations. The politically determined outcome is different tax rates for different sources of income—between income from capital and income from labour; between interest and dividends; between dividends and capital gains; between personal income and corporate income; between business income paid out and business income retained; between income earned at home and abroad; and so on. At the same time, securities can be used to transmute one form of income into another—in particular, higher taxed forms to lower taxed ones.

Changing the tax structure motivates innovation. Each successful innovation earns an immediate reward for its adopters in the form of tax money saved. Governments are in fact subsidising the process of financial innovation, just as they subsidise the development of new seeds or aeroplanes, but with the important difference that, in financial innovation, the government's contribution is inadvertent. There are cases, particularly in the politically sensitive housing area, where the US government has been the major pioneer of new financial instruments (mortgage-backed securities). In Europe, interest income taxed at source developed the Luxembourg financial centre and the German Bundesbank's prohibition of money-market funds caused them to blossom in Luxembourg for the benefit of German savers.

The same process can be seen at work in any financial area subject to government regulation, which is to say, still virtually everywhere. The pressures to innovate around profitable transactions not admitted by regulation, or around newly imposed interest-rate ceilings, are particularly strong. Even what purports to be deregulation, however, can sometimes trigger changes that go far beyond the intentions of the original sponsors.

The current vogue for swaps, for example, was set in motion in the 1960s by firms seeking ways to avoid British government restrictions on dollar financing by British firms, and on sterling financing by non-British firms. Other important innovations have involved the simultaneous inadvertent contributions of two or more countries. No single innovation epitomises so neatly the many strange and often unplanned elements that come together to produce a significant financial innovation, as the growth of the zero-coupon bond market.[23]

At times innovations arise out of very specific regulatory or tax environments. Some are significant in the sense of being permanent even when the original cause for its creation has disappeared (such as a response to particular regulatory and tax structures). The *Eurodollar market*, for example, owed its origin to Regulation Q. The regulation, among other things, placed a ceiling on the rate of interest that commercial banks could offer on their time deposits. Over much of the post-war period this ceiling was at least not drastically below the market clearing level. But that changed in the late 1960s and early 1970s with the rise in US and world interest rates. The US banks soon noticed that the restrictions of Regulation Q did not apply to the dollar-denominated time deposits in their overseas branches. They could and did bid competitively for short-term dollar denominated accounts; and they continue to do so on a huge scale today even though Regulation Q has long since become a dead letter.

The currently huge and rapidly growing *Eurobond market* was set off by a tax rather than a regulatory change. It sprang up initially in response to the US government's institution in the late 1960s of a withholding tax of 30% on interest payments on bonds sold in the United States to overseas investors. The locus of the market for dollar-denominated bonds for non-US citizens thereupon moved from New York to London and other money centres on the continent. The withholding provision has since been repealed, but the Eurobond market it promoted has continued to thrive.

**Portfolio Management**

The volatility of stock prices is a measure of their risk for which investors seek compensation through higher returns (the Sharpe ratio). Portfolio diversification can lower the risk whilst preserving the higher return. As the most complete diversification is obtained when a portfolio replicates an index of all traded stocks, it makes sense to buy such a portfolio, except if the investor has valuable knowledge about individual stocks. However, during the 1970s, research started to promote the "efficient market hypothesis" which says that prices incorporate all generally available information. Therefore, either the investor has some "inside information" and therefore gains from picking a particular stock, or he has not and then acts as if at a roulette table when choosing a particular stock. Rational investors without a gambling instinct (i.e., who would only accept a risk for an appropriate remuneration) would invest in a market index. This new insight had two unforeseen consequences. First, the development of *market index-based investment strategies* ("programme trading"). Second, the creation of options not only on individual stocks but also of *options on stock indexes*.

In fact, most stocks move with the general stock market: some very closely, some with amplification, and some in a dampened or even counter-cyclical fashion. This is the famous β-factor which measures the risk of a stock that is not diversifiable through the correlation of an individual stock's price with the market index. If a holder of a particular stock with a β < 1 adds a put option on the stock index to his portfolio, then he can expect to make money in a downturn of the market and preserve the full upside potential of his individual stock. (With β < 1 the investor might do better buying a put on the specific stock, if it exists. If such an option does not exist he can still hedge, but less precisely, with a stock index put.) Thus, through diversification and use of derivatives to hedge against specific types of risk, asset management made a qualitative jump of historical importance.

The development of options, which, as indicated above, existed for a long time, into a widespread, regularly used and traded financial instrument with applications in most financial domains, benefited tremendously from a *scientific breakthrough* achieved by Fischer Black and Myron Scholes in a rightly famous paper published in 1973 "The Pricing of Options and Corporate Liabilities" (see Chapter 4). The Black–Scholes formula is a benchmark for arbitrage operations and a basis for valuing a non-traded option. Without it, option products would not have achieved such an amazing success.

### A New World of Finance

What was perhaps the biggest predictive failure was not to foresee the fundamental new economic function that derivatives would assume and the economic benefits they would generate. During the last twenty-five years, the growth of derivative markets has made it possible to commoditise risk and hence to buy, sell, restructure and price risk in line with the investors' preferences, and separate from the underlying asset. This is truly a revolutionary innovation comparable to the creation of the equity exchanges in previous centuries.

The development of derivatives, in turn, has made possible a vast number of markets for combined products, such as a debt instrument with an option on equity or another currency denomination. The proliferation of customised combinations of basic instruments is infinite.

## 8. CONCLUSION

This chapter has outlined the evolution of key financial concepts. Drawing on a stock of basic financial transactions—as old as human civilisation—technological advances, economic development and internationalisation of economic relationships have been the perennial driving forces of change. But rarely, if ever, has something entirely unknown been invented. This chapter focused on salient events without any claim to completeness to give a sense of direction rather than of encyclopedic thoroughness.[24]

Whilst the basic financial functions have not changed with history, the institutional structure to perform these functions has evolved remarkably. Using a classification by Ross (1989), this chapter has shown that there appears to be a secular pattern away from "opaque" institutions (banks, insurance companies) to "translucent" institutions (mutual funds, pension funds) or "transparent" institutions (stock markets, futures and options markets). For example, loans preceded tradeable bonds, OTC derivatives preceded exchange traded products, deposits preceded money-market mutual funds, and so on. This suggests that there is intense competition between intermediaries and markets, providing greater transparency, liquidity and price information. This dynamic interaction is part of a "financial innovation spiral" pushing the financial system closer and closer to full efficiency.

Since 1970, financial innovation has accelerated markedly. A major motivation was to circumvent discriminatory regulations and tax laws. Another to deal with increased exchange rate and interest rate volatility after the end of the Bretton Woods fixed exchange rate system.

In my view, the most important financial innovation during that period has been the development of derivatives—the essential ingredient for modern risk management—a fundamental revolution whose significance is comparable to the industrial revolution. The story of Calum McLaughlin at the beginning of the chapter illustrates this point. As demonstrated in later chapters, derivatives change the way corporations and banks manage their business and transform the focus and structure of the financial industry. They also pose major challenges to financial managers, accountants and regulators.

Despite the fact that the circumstances that led to the innovations of the past quarter of a century—increased volatility, discriminatory taxes and regulation, technological advances—were present all over the world, all significant innovations have come out of the US financial system. In no other industry has the United States been as resolutely superior as in the financial industry. And in no other country has the financial industry been as radically transformed by these innovations. This is the puzzle to be resolved in the next chapter.

# ENDNOTES

1 For a definition of this and any other technical term, see the Glossary at the end of the book.
2 Crane and Bodie (1996).
3 A different classification serves to show that *any* financial transaction can be obtained from a combination of three basic operations: *safeguarding*, *lending* and

*exchanging*. The most primitive financial operation is *warehousing* (safeguarding), to ensure greater safety for transferable stocks of value. Today, still, depositing cash or securities with a bank is safer than hiding them under the mattress, a fact that provides the basis for banking all over the world. There is a natural step from depositing valuables to transferring some of the valuables deposited for payment of debt incurred. Should the valuables not be transferable for payment, then they can be used as collateral for obtaining *credit*, or for *exchange* into an asset more suitable for payment. With these operations (safeguarding, lending, exchanging) the major part of modern banking, namely deposit-taking, payments, lending on terms unrelated (a loan) or related (a share) to the borrower's future performance (with a possible maturity transformation risk), trading currencies or securities for customers out of own positions (market risk) or as intermediary are already covered.

4  Seigniorage is the income of the state that is obtained from the face value of currency in excess of the cost of production.

5  Henry VIII was a champion of this royal sport, originator of the "Great Debasement".

6  An early example of technological breakthrough is provided by the development of the double accounting system in 13th century Italy, itself facilitated by the replacement of the Roman numeral system by Arabic numerals. This must have had an effect comparable to the replacement of hand-written by computerised accounts. Similarly, the development of actuarial science in Europe in the late 17th and early 18th centuries, based on the work of Pascal, Fermat and Huyghens, was probably as important to finance then as the Black–Scholes options price theory is today.

7  In the 12th century, risky Venetian sea expeditions were funded through participations by various traders who spread their risks by participating in the funding of several voyages. Their contracts were like an option: for a price (their funding share) they secured the right to a high profit if the expedition was successful. Otherwise they lost their funding contribution.

8  The first joint stock companies with limited liability able to issue equity were granted that privilege in the interests of the Crown (e.g., the Russia Company of 1553).

9  Early progress in creating tradable instruments was achieved thanks to the running of trade fairs ("foires") in Europe in the late Middle Ages, which created markets where traders from various parts of Europe could meet. Bankers went international to follow traders and developed an instrument that made the risky and cumbersome transport of cash redundant. This was the letter of credit (bankers' acceptance), tradeable among bankers and merchants because standardised, and as good as cash as long as the issuing bank's reputation was beyond reasonable doubt.

10  Preferred and convertible shares were not the only types of option-enriched securities developed in the 16th and 17th centuries. Other securities were introduced at this time but have not proved as durable.

11  Repeatedly in history, market crashes provided the political push for tougher, if not more sensible, regulation. In this century the most important regulatory changes followed the 1929 crash. As argued in Part III, recent problems in derivatives markets have also sparked off regulatory fervour—only restrained by the lack of easy and workable solutions.

12  Another rediscovery emerged after the Congress of Vienna in 1815. British foreign lending started with Baring Brothers' financing of the French government's 700 million franc indemnity to allies.

13  A number of innovations occurred in the United States during this period. The first, *income bonds*, were issued by the Chesapeake and Ohio Canal Company in 1848. What distinguishes income bonds from ordinary bonds is that interest is paid only if

accounting earnings exceed a certain level. They were used frequently in the rail-road reorganisation of the 1880s and 1890s.

14 They were first used when the American Power and Light Company made an issue of 6% notes in 1911. After that they were used sporadically until 1925 when their popularity increased rapidly and they came to be widely used.

15 "Derivatives" are also called "contingent claims". Some use "contingent claims" to mean a class of assets (including derivative assets) whose payoffs are completely determined by a predefined set of underlying variables. If the underlying variables are the payoffs of an asset it is a derivative. If it is not but, say, an index (such as a consumer price index) then it would be a contingent claim. For simplicity we call both a derivative product.

16 See Steinherr and Huveneers (1994) for a more detailed discussion.

17 Anti-trust policy, inspired both by considerations of efficiency and democracy in the economic sphere, historically also played a much more important role in Anglo-Saxon countries. It was on such considerations that J.P. Morgan, at the time surely the most developed and powerful universal bank, was broken up and appropriate legislation was pursued. For the historical record and the concern with market power in the United States, see Benston (1983).

18 In Japan and most continental European countries, government relations with the economy, have alternated over time between waves of nationalisation and of denationalisation.

19 After the opening up of Eastern Europe, western experts hotly debated the question whether the former Socialist countries should create US-type financial markets or rely on German-type universal banks. My approach to this question, as outlined here and developed in more detail in Steinherr (1993) and Gros and Steinherr (1995) suggests that this debate is rather sterile: at their level of political and economic development, former socialist countries are not yet ready for market-based finance.

20 This section follows closely Miller (1991).

21 Moreover, the claim that flexible exchange rates free policy makers from external constraints also turned out to be exaggerated. At some level of the exchange rate the competitive disadvantage is such that the exchange rate can no longer be ignored. Domestic policies then have to be used to steer the exchange rate in the desired direction. This happened, for example, in 1985 when the dollar was over-valued to an extent that posed serious threats to US industry. The Plaza Agreement co-ordinated an international policy package to drive the dollar down.

22 There are two supplementary rationales for financial innovation. The first is that new securities may make markets more complete, that is they increase opportunities for risk sharing (Van Horne 1985). In a classification of the factors responsible for the introduction of 68 new types of securities, Finnerty (1988) lists tax and regulatory advantages in 27 cases and risk factors in 53 cases (some securities qualified for both). Another class of security innovation has resulted from efforts by managers to discourage take-overs.

23 The explosion in zero-coupon bonds by US corporates in 1981 was occasioned not strictly by a tax change, but by a technical flaw in the Treasury Department regulations that interpret the US tax law. Zero-coupon securities were already in existence, of course, notable examples being Treasury bills and even the Treasury's own Series E Savings Bond. But long-term deep discount instruments had rarely, if ever, been issued by taxable corporations until the Treasury's blunder was identified. So gross was that blunder—which permitted a linear approximation for computing the implicit interest and, hence, inflated the present value of the interest deductions—that a taxable corporation could actually come out ahead by issuing a zero-coupon bond and giving it away!

The Treasury reacted after a couple of years with legislation correcting the blunder and the supply of new zeroes by US corporations abruptly ceased. But the demanders for zero-coupon instruments that the first innovation had uncovered were still there begging for more. Much of this demand was sustained by the corresponding blunder of the Japanese tax authorities in treating all of the appreciation not as deferred taxable interest, which would have been advantageous enough to the holder, but as capital gains. And capital gains under Japanese law were exempt from tax. Zero-coupon bonds, moreover, were a clever way of blunting the force of Ministry of Finance restrictions on the value of foreign bond holdings by Japanese pension funds. Despite minor adjustments, these rules and the demand for zeroes they create, remained for a long time. Meanwhile, since the corporate supply dried up, US innovators have been busily creating a synthetic supply of zero-coupon bonds for Japanese buyers (and for tax-exempt domestic pension fund portfolio "immunisers") by stripping the coupons from US Treasury bonds and selling them separately as zeroes. Coupons due after the first year are used as one-year zero-coupon bonds; those due after two years as two-year zero-coupon bonds and so on. The principal, due at maturity, plus the last coupon are the longest zero-coupon bond obtained from stripping (Miller 1991).

24 For surveys of recent financial innovations, see Allen and Gale (1994) and Finnerty (1993).

# 2

# The Americanisation of Global Finance

─────

## *Minnesota Banc Corporation*

It is one of those very cold and windy January evenings in Minneapolis. The temperature is below −30°F, in stark contrast to the heated atmosphere in the board room of Minnesota Banc Corporation (MBC). The board has assembled to review the bank's policy in the light of the decline of MBC's share price from US$19 in May 1995 to US$18 on 6 January 1996, against an increase by 15% of a weighted index of US bank shares over the same period.

MBC has an excellent financial track record. Compared to the financial performance of the country's 20 largest bank holding companies since 1985, it has the second highest average return on equity, the fourth highest return on assets, and a Cooke ratio of 18.4% at the end of 1995. MBC has been able to increase earnings per share every single year for the last 20 years. This is all the more remarkable as MBC has pursued a strategy of very aggressive take-overs, transforming the local Minneapolis bank, ranked 274th in 1974, into a large supra-regional bank rated twenty-first in 1994.

Gary O'Brien, one of the most senior board members, has just finished his tough speech in which he attributed the decline of MBC's share prices to investor concern over MBC's very large interest rate derivatives portfolio. O'Brien even quoted two reports of equity analysts of Banc One Corporation, which in 1993 was in a very similar situation to MBC now:

> "The increased use of interest rate swaps is creating some sizeable distortions in reported earnings, reported earning assets, margins and the historical measure of return on assets . . . Were Banc One to include [swaps] in reported earning assets, the adjusted level would be 26% higher than is currently reported . . . Given its large position in swap[s], Banc One overstates its margin by 1.31% [and its] return on assets in excess of 0.20% . . . Adjusted for [swaps], Banc One's tangible equity-to-asset ratio would decline by 1.55%."
>
> (Pringle, 1993)

"Banc One's investors are uncomfortable with so much derivatives exposure. Buyers of regional banks do not expect heavy derivatives involvement . . . Heavy swaps usage clouds Banc One's financial image [and is] extremely confusing . . . It is virtually impossible for anyone on the outside to assess the risks being assumed."

(Salem, 1993)

Richard A. Freeman, MBC's chief finance officer, is now called by Jeremy M. Ringstad, Chairman and CEO, to explain. Given board members' lack of familiarity with hedging techniques, Freeman produces colour slides to present general risk-management principles.

A typical US bank's liabilities consist of floating-rate liabilities (such as short-term deposits or federal funds borrowings) and long-term fixed-rate liabilities (such as certificates of deposit, or CDs). Assets include floating-rate assets (variable-rate mortgages and loans, short-term securities) and long-term fixed-rate assets (such as fixed-rate mortgages and securities).

The need to manage assets and liabilities arises from a bank's strategic decisions regarding interest rate exposure. A bank could engineer its assets and liabilities to ensure that its earnings or market value would be unaffected by changes in interest rates. Alternatively, a bank could adjust its portfolio of assets and liabilities to profit when rates rose, but lose when they fell. It could also position itself to gain when rates fell, and lose when they rose. The selection of interest rate exposure is a major policy decision for financial institutions.

Most US banks typically have relatively more long-term fixed-rate liabilities than they have long-term fixed-rate assets. Banks that wish to better match the duration of assets and liabilities complement their loan portfolios with fixed-rate investments, such as Treasury securities, or borrow on a floating-rate basis rather than a fixed-rate one. These are called "natural" hedges.

As chief investment officer of MBC, Freeman has a staff of approximately 150 people, with 16 engaged in asset and liability management activities. They measure the degree to which the bank's assets and liabilities are matched and make investments consistent with the bank's policy of managing its interest exposure. As in most other banks, they have an official mandate to (i) invest funds in conventional investments and derivatives to conserve the funds' principal value yet provide a reasonable rate of return; (ii) keep enough funds in liquid investments to allow the bank to react quickly to demands for cash; and (iii) control the exposure of MBC's reported earnings to swings in interest rates.

In carrying out this mandate, MBC uses investments and derivatives. The main derivative instruments used are interest rate swaps. When it appears desirable to increase the share of fixed-rate investments, Freeman can sell a floating-rate investment and use the proceeds to buy a fixed-rate Treasury note. Or he can enter into a swap in which MBC pays a floating rate and receives a fixed rate of return. In terms of exposure, both operations produce identical results. But in terms of yield, credit-risk, capital requirements, transaction costs and liquidity, swaps often come out on top. For this reason MBC had a swap book of US$46.5 billion at end-1995.

To conclude his presentation Freeman argues that the reason for the large size of swap operations and the rapid growth of the swap book over the years is that swaps are very efficient and cost-effective instruments for lowering the bank's exposure to movements in interest rates. Somewhat emotionally he concludes:

> "Gentlemen, interest rate swaps are no longer exotic. As far as I am concerned, without these instruments banking would be thrown years back, exposing us to higher costs and higher risks. Why the stock market seems to penalise us for something that reduces our exposure to risk beats me!"

Gary O'Brien reacts quickly. Like other board members he feels reassured by what he has just heard, although, in the days when he was chairman of a bank, maturity transformation was banking by definition and nobody wasted time on asset-liability management. But there was another matter that bugged him: big New York banks have become frenetic dealers in derivatives and have generated more income from these activities than from lending. MBC has been one of the first regional banks to deal in swaps, forward rate agreements, inverse floaters, and to offer clients structured deals enhanced with options. He could understand why MBC was *using* swaps, but not why MBC was *dealing* in derivatives.

In his reply, Richard Freeman seemed upbeat, but somewhat less assured. The derivatives book at end-1995 had a notional value of US$27.6 billion. Not a large amount, Freeman argued, and insufficient to earn money, given the start-up and learning costs. The only strategic choice, in his view, had been to build up the derivatives book very substantially and not leave this lucrative market to the big boys from New York.

At this point a prolonged silence befell the board room. And in some people's minds an understanding of the recent dismal stock price behaviour slowly took shape.

---

> "Bankers Trust is a risk manager, not a bank.
> The acknowledged leader in the derivatives business,
> at once loathed and admired by rival firms,
> it has emerged from a decade-long metamorphosis.
> It began the 1980s as a mediocre money-sector bank;
> today it is a highly profitable specialist."
>
> The Economist, *April 1993*

THE example of Minnesota Banc Corporation's use of derivatives in managing its asset/liability targets provides a telling contrast with traditional bank practices of risk management.

In trying to understand the reasons for the fabulous proliferation of derivatives over the last twenty-five years, the significance of their widespread use and the impact on the evolution of the financial industry, one cannot look at derivatives in isolation. Their development is in part the result of exogenous events, such as the breakdown of Bretton Woods, but perhaps more significantly the symbiotic result of a deeper change in financial markets to which, in turn, derivatives contributed in a major way.

This chapter describes the evolution of this endogenous process which, in my view, originated and developed the momentum in the United States to result in the "American model of finance".

One of the more far-reaching and *consequential structural changes currently underway in the global economy has been the maturing of the American model of global finance* during the last twenty years and its success in recent years in exporting the institutions, practices, instruments, and financial infrastructure that comprise this model to the other major industrial countries. I will first discuss the evolution of the main features of the American model of finance— risk-management finance and a flexible supply of liquidity being its crowning achievements—and then argue that this model is destined to dominate global finance. Identifying the stylised features of the American model helps to see more clearly how the financial system in the other major industrial countries are likely to evolve, and how public policy can best respond.

There are six distinct features of the American model of financial intermediation that have been key to its success over the last twenty years—since the arrival of negotiated commissions on Wall Street on 1 May 1975—and that are now establishing its dominance in the other major markets. *First, competition-driven innovation has been the central force* of change. The aggressive application of advances in communications technology, data processing, and in financial modelling to generate new financial products and techniques is driven by highly competitive financial intermediaries who seek the economic rents that accrue to successful innovations. This characteristic has set the pace of evolution of the American model of finance and has kept it in the lead in global finance. *Second, the decline of relationship-based finance and the increasing commoditisation of finance*—in large part, through disintermediation from the banking system—has provided for near continuous and transparent price-discovery and valuation in a wide variety of highly liquid money-, derivative-, and capital-market instruments, and in an active merger and acquisition market for corporate control. It has made financial relationships more transparent and anonymous. The absence of lasting relationships has stimulated competition for intermediation business. It has also spawned the development of sophisticated market infrastructure: new trading systems, market-making methods, high-volume wholesale payments system. *Third, effective supervision* has ensured the relative integrity of markets by reducing market manipulation by insiders.[1] As a result participation in financial markets has been broadened and deepened. *Fourth, the growth of massive pools of institutional performance-oriented savings*—again, a product of competition—has provided a fertile ground for the profitable application of financial innovations. It has produced a shift from a buy-and-hold to an active arbitrage- and trading-driven approach to portfolio management.

There are two additional characteristics that are in many ways the crowning achievement of the American model. The first is the evolution of *risk-management finance*, i.e., the ability of the financial system to define and isolate a large variety of financial risks and to design instruments and adapt institutions (futures exchanges and money-centre banks that have evolved into risk-management institutions) through which such risks can be priced and traded in liquid markets. This development is the culmination of the earlier achievement of liquid money and capital markets. The other feature, without which risk-management finance could not have become such as prominent feature, is the development of a reliable mechanism to ensure continuous liquidity in money and capital markets. Such a *liquidity-supply mechanism* required the evolution of a new institutional structure, supported by an active central bank, to ensure that derivative, money, and capital markets remain liquid in adverse circumstances.

To clarify, Figure 2.1 contrasts the classical structure of financial intermediation with today's.

Its success on the home turf has helped the *American model of finance to make significant inroads into the major non-dollar financial markets.* Liberalisation—in part driven by loss of financial intermediation business to off-shore locations—has increased competition in the financial sectors of major European countries and in Japan. The UK financial sector is only a short step behind the American lead with similar brains, but less muscle. Its institutional arrangements and traditions are similar, its regulations more forward-looking and cosmopolitan and, as a result, it is host to the Eurodollar market with a major participation of US financial firms. On the continent, by contrast, much catching-up needs to be achieved. The inroads made by the American

(a) Classical view of financial intermediation

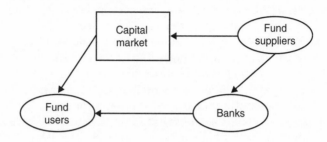

(b) Today's view of financial intermediation

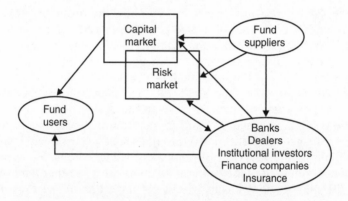

**Figure 2.1**   Classical and Today's View of Financial Intermediation

model into the major non-dollar currencies are already turning financial services into a major US export industry.

# 1. THE EMERGENCE OF THE AMERICAN MODEL OF FINANCE

**From Relationship Finance to Commoditised Finance: the Unexpected Benefits of Glass–Steagall**

The force that has propelled the evolution of the American model of finance has been the relentlessly competitive nature of this industry. Indeed, *competition-driven innovation has been at the heart of the evolution of the American model of finance* since the 1960s. The origins of the competitive nature of US finance are lodged in the banking legislation of the 1930s, the anti-trust legislation and in the aggressive application of these legal instruments.[2] The public policy towards the financial sector in the US has been a reflection of the general populist mistrust of concentrated financial power. US financial history since the 1930s has been shaped by the political aim to isolate financial power, to keep financial and corporate spheres of influence separated, and to do so irrespective of the perceived or real efficiency losses. Over time, this policy of creating a "fractured and segmented" financial industry has had the *unintended fortuitous consequence* of providing a fertile environment for the development of the most competitive and innovative financial system in the world.

Until the 1930s, US finance was similar to that of the major continental European countries today. Large banks were the primary sources of finance and they controlled the flow of funds. These banks built and maintained strong relationships with their main clients, like the so-called Hausbanken in Germany and the banks belonging to a *keiretsu* in Japan. They gathered and intermediated deposits to the corporate sector, and also underwrote debt and equity issues of their corporate clients, placing these obligations with institutional clients. Bankers served on corporate boards, financed corporate bailouts, and managed pension funds. Banks also managed corporate liquidity on their balance sheets, made short-term corporate loans and accepted short-term corporate deposits. Banks were thus at the heart of the flow of funds.

The dismemberment of the large US banking houses started with the congressional Pecora hearings, which led to the Banking Act of 1933, sponsored by Senator Carter Glass and Representative Henry Steagall (the commonly known Glass–Steagall Act) separating commercial banking from investment banking and brokering[3] (and creating federal deposit insurance). The bill was a reaction to the financial excesses of the late 1920s and the collapse of a large part of the banking sector in the early 1930s.[4] The argument was that involvement of banks in capital markets, particularly equity markets, had undermined sound banking and had been at the root of bank failures. But the link between the stock market crash and subsequent bank failures in the early 1930s is far from firm. Indeed, the Glass–Steagall Act was driven as much by the politics of the day—the need to find a scapegoat for the financial excesses and disasters—as it was driven by the need for sound reforms. In order to further weaken the influence of Wall Street banks, the Banking Act of 1935 created the modern structure of the Federal Reserve System and shifted power from the Federal Reserve Bank of New York—a traditional ally of the New York-based banking industry—to the Federal Reserve Board in Washington, DC.

The Glass–Steagall legislation is viewed today by the banking community, particularly the larger money-centre banks, and by academic observers, as having been ill-conceived and as having failed in its main aim of adding stability to the banking system. In addition, the restrictions on the activities are thought to have prevented US banks from exploiting the economies of scale and of scope available to foreign banks not subject to the restrictive separation of commercial and investment banking.[5]

However, the *Glass–Steagall legislation, together with the companion 1933 Securities Act and the 1935 Banking Act, has had a profound impact on the institutional evolution of the US financial system.* In particular, the segregation of commercial from investment banking facilitated the growth of the investment banking industry in the 1970s as a competition-enhancing countervailing force to the economic and political influence of the large New York-based banking industry. It laid the foundations for the evolution of one the most adaptive, innovative, and efficient industries of the second half of the 20th century. In the end, without this legislation and without the populist suspicion of financial concentration in the United States, it is likely that the financial sector in the United States today would look more like that of Germany or Japan.[6] It is highly doubtful that risk-management finance as we know it today would have been developed in such a system.[7]

### Disintermediation

A sustained increase in interest rates in the 1960s led bank customers to look for higher yielding instruments than the short-dated bank deposits that were subject to the regulatory interest caps. This provided the opening for the *money-market mutual fund revolution.* Money-market mutual funds became attractive alternative investments to bank deposits, particularly as the transactions technology of the accounts improved to the point where such accounts had all the intrinsic features of a deposit account except deposit insurance. The large New York banks responded by creating negotiable certificates of deposits (CDs) on which interest could be paid without restrictions, allowing money centre banks to buy deposits in wholesale markets. *The world of managed liabilities had arrived.*

Some banks, frequently small banks outside New York, with reserve deposits at the Federal Reserve in excess of legal requirements, started to lend such reserve deposits in an overnight market. Thus the growth of competitive markets in bank liabilities also led to the *growth of a liquid interbank market in reserve balances* held at the central bank, the so-called Fed funds market. Again a restriction, this time on interest rates, had induced the growth of a competitive market. The focus of banking gradually shifted from the banking floor to the trading room.

The elimination of fixed commissions on 1 May 1975 provided a strong impetus for further disintermediation from the banking system. The competition engendered by the ability to negotiate commission quickly led to shrinking margins and a restructuring of the brokerage industry that saw almost 300 brokerage firms disappear within the span of a year. The foundation for a rapid competition-driven decrease in cost of securities market transactions and an increase in transactions volume had been laid. Negotiated commissions allowed mutual funds aggressively to simplify their transactions cost structure.

As banks increased the issue of their short-term negotiable liabilities, the better-rated corporations soon discovered that they too could issue short-term instruments into a liquid *commercial paper (CP) market*. Since 1972, this market has increased in size from 23% of commercial and industrial bank loans to 92% in 1993. Much of the legal and institutional work necessary for the successful issue of commercial paper was provided by investment banks eager to capture what was viewed as a very big and profitable market. These firms were instrumental in bringing corporates to the commercial paper market. The development of the market for commercial paper was an important step in the bank disintermediation process. *Both sides of the bank balance sheet were now being disintermediated*: corporations replaced short-term loans with commercial paper, banks replaced short-term deposit liabilities with certificates of deposit, and savers replaced deposits, with money-market mutual funds. By 1980, the markets for commercial paper, Treasury bills, Fed funds, certificates of deposits, and money-market mutual funds had matured sufficiently to fully arbitrage yields, in other words an important aspect of the American model—the securitised, liquid money market—had come into being.

Furthermore, securities firms were instrumental in pushing the disintermediation process from the money markets into capital markets by bringing the better-rated corporations to the corporate debt markets. As the larger banks suffered from a decline in the quality of their assets, brought on by the less-developed countries (LDCs) debt crisis of the early 1980s, it became increasingly apparent that an AAA-rated corporate borrower was better off raising capital in the direct debt markets than going through an AA-rated banking intermediary.

This development gained further momentum when in March 1982 the Securities and Exchange Commission (SEC) enacted Rule 415—*shelf registration*. Instead of registering each security issue individually, borrowers could register a large block of securities and sell it in as many tranches as they saw fit over a two-year period. Now securities issues had obtained some of the drawdown flexibility offered by commercial loans. This development, including the availability of liquid money markets, in turn led corporates to set up more sophisticated treasury operations. Once such corporate treasuries had acquired the philosophy of minimising funding cost, and management had come to view the treasury operations as a profit centre, corporate treasurers became aggressive customers who played banks against securities houses. Such competitive pressures could not have developed in a financial system dominated by universal banks, as was the case in the United States until 1935 and is still the case in continental Europe. It is inconceivable that a universal bank would voluntarily undertake steps to put finance on a market footing by trying to persuade one of its corporate clients to by-pass the bank and issue short-term debt directly, even if the universal bank became the lead manager. As a result, money and capital markets in countries like Germany are only in their infant stage.

This competition-driven disintermediation from the banking system—particularly from wholesale banking—into securitised highly liquid money and capital markets was a key structural change in the US financial model. With the recent growth of OTC and exchange-traded derivatives, dollar-based financial intermediation became fully market-based. All types of borrowers are increasingly able to satisfy their liquidity, capital and risk-management needs directly in liquid securities markets. Not only are the various financial obligations and assets of financial and non-financial firms being traded in liquid markets, the main types of risks (and here derivatives enter the picture) are also traded and priced in the market. Spot, index and futures markets are fully arbitraged. Dealer-based money and capital markets offer a large choice of instruments and techniques, and the US government securities market has developed to be the only truly global 24-hour market—the world's benchmark fixed-income market. Financial claims, ownership rights and contingent obligations are increasingly taking the form of liquid securities. Formerly illiquid assets on balance sheets of financial and non-financial institutions—receivables, mortgages—are being securitised through the re-issue of asset-backed securities.

## From Relationship Banking to Commoditisation

*The most important consequence of the disintermediation from the banking system into liquid money and capital markets has been the shift from relationship finance toward the commoditisation of finance.* Until the 1960s, finance in the United States was largely based on relationships, as it is to a large extent in Germany and Japan. The marriage of certain companies to certain banks—consummated with the banker assuming a seat on the corporate board—was the central feature of financial relations until the mid-1930s. After that the system weakened somewhat, but banks and now securities houses still had close relations to loyal clients, who in turn had their loyalty repaid with guaranteed access to bank funding or with the commitment of investment banks to underwrite and expeditiously place their paper even in difficult market conditions. The key to relationship banking was that bankers came to share in their clients success and failures. When a bank or a securities house underwrote an issue, it felt responsible not only for the solvency of the firm but also for the performance of its management.

The shift toward commoditised finance began with the disintermediation from the banking system. Banks were obliged to replace deposits markets and became able to actively manage their liabilities, albeit at the cost of reduced margins in traditional intermediation business, culminating in a near collapse of commercial banking in the early 1990s.

In investment banking the client relationship began to weaken with the 1941 issue by the SEC of Rule U-50 which mandated *competitive bidding* for public utility holding company issues. Competitive bidding was, however, slow to spread to other industries, particularly the lucrative issues of railroad bonds.[8] Nevertheless, during the 1970s many of the blue-chip clients had started to place issues privately with institutional investors, such as insurance companies and pension funds. The other side of the coin was that the premier investment houses became less reluctant to underwrite issues of untested companies, and the houses would take less and less responsibility for the performance of the company. Instead, the credit rating function came to be performed, in part, by specialised rating firms rather than by investment houses or banks.

Relationship finance was further weakened by the introduction of shelf registration (Rule 415). The trading firms with a large capital base, like Merrill Lynch and Salomon Brothers, gained at the expense of the more traditional relationship underwriters like Morgan Stanley. The advent of the "bought deal" underwriting structure allowed securities houses to assume the full underwriting risk by acquiring the entire issue at a negotiated price, rather than go into the market to "build a book" and then pass on the price emerging from the book-building process to the issuer. The value of a long-standing underwriting relationship declined precipitously with the arrival of Rule 415, while capital strength and trading ability came to be more highly valued. The growth of liquid money and capital markets—fostered in part by disintermediation from the banking system—itself made relationship banking less important. Borrowers needed no longer to rely on banks to provide them with financing during difficult (illiquid) market conditions and worry about the proverbial rainy day.

The ultimate step towards commoditised finance is the growth of take-overs, mergers, acquisitions and leveraged buy-outs. Here it is not just a block of shares of the company that are for sale, but the whole or parts of the company. During the conglomerate wave of the 1960s more than 25 000 businesses vanished. However, unsolicited take-overs were still frowned upon in the 1960s. Merger work of investment banks greatly accelerated after the advent of negotiated commissions in 1975. Unlike underwriting, take-over business tended to antagonise at least one side in the transactions and so it further eroded relationship ties on Wall Street. Take-over business grew, however, because both commercial and investment bankers saw it as the answer to a deterioration in their respective core lending and underwriting businesses. With the help of junk bonds the take-over business moved into a new phase in the 1980s: previously banks and security houses had largely responded passively to requests for financing and advice with mergers and acquisitions. Now they began actively to suggest and sell transactions to the corporate sector, and, indeed, it did not take long before investment banks were taking major equity stakes in merged companies: merchant banking had been rediscovered. Most of the prominent investment banks set up sizeable pools of capital to finance risk arbitrage by taking positions in companies involved in take-overs, leveraged buyouts (LBOs), or merger battles. The "arbs" frequently joined forces with corporate raiders.

By the mid-1980s relationship finance in banking and underwriting was a thing of the past. The growth of deep and liquid money and capital markets had deprived relationships of their implicit insurance value. The decline of relationship finance made valuations more transparent and cost the key variable, rather than the less transparent and more mystical concept of "being there when the market dries up". The increase in transparency made financial packages easier to compare and thereby served to increase competition. An important consequence of disintermediation has been that investors' assessments of the changing fortune of borrowers were made immediately transparent and were fully reflected in securities prices, rather than being buried in the balance sheets of the banking system. *The immediate and highly visible market valuation has had a salutary effect on corporate governance and has, in fact, democratised finance.*

The breakdown of relationship finance and the ascendancy of commoditised finance brought with it an explosion of trading volumes in securities markets. Investment and commercial banks began to take proprietary positions in all capital and money markets (including foreign exchange). Profits from proprietary position taking and trading activity became a crucial source of income for commercial and investment banks.[9]

In addition, an arbitrage-driven approach to portfolio management generated large gross trading volumes in pursuit of trading profits. Dynamic hedging, with its voracious appetite for continuous trading, has contributed to these volumes. As a consequence, trading infrastructure has grown in sophistication: trading mechanisms have evolved to cope with increased volume; there has been a shift from the floors of stock exchanges to multi-location screen-based trading, which in some cases like Globex have become 24-hour global systems; settlement and clearing arrangements have been improved to cope with the increased volume.

**Creating Market Integrity: The Disappearance of the Insiders**

The creation of the SEC in the Securities Act of 1933 was an important step in the evolution of the American model of finance. This legislation too was another reflection of the populist undercurrent in American financial legislation and diminished the power of the insiders. Together with the transformation of relationship finance into commoditised finance, the SEC also democratised finance. Combined with US anti-trust statutes it provided the legal environment to keep markets competitive and informationally efficient. The requirement that organised markets report the last trades on a timely basis has further contributed to market efficiency. "Chinese walls" (with all their limitations) in investment and commercial banks are set up with the aim of ensuring that privileged information from clients is not used in the firm's proprietary trading or used in any way to the benefit of a third party. By ensuring the integrity of securitised financial markets it became less hazardous for issuers and investors to enter into the direct securities markets. Retail investors could count on getting their trades executed at prices that were close to the last reported trades—dealers could no longer "front-run" their trades—and they could be assured that there did not exist a group of insiders who profited at the expense of the general market participant. In other words, in the popular perception securities markets were no longer the domain of the "professionals in-the-know", but became a viable investment alternative to bank liabilities for the retail investor and small firms.

Through aggressive implementation of its legal instruments the SEC has created a market-place that is about as free of insider manipulation as can reasonably be expected in securities markets with a large number of diverse participants, practices and instruments.[10] The SEC has also been unwilling to recognise foreign listing standards; it has insisted on national treatment with regard to its rules and regulations.[11] The size of the US capital markets (more than half of global stock market capitalisation) has made it attractive for foreign firms to list in the United States. This has meant that foreign firms are adopting, albeit at a slow pace, US disclosure and accounting standards. They are arguably the most demanding and the most transparent. Lulled by the attraction of a listing on the New York stock exchange, foreign firms grudgingly accept to publish their accounts according to US Generally Accepted Accounting Principles (GAAP).

For decades, German companies, for example, had refused to come to the US markets for the very reason that they did not want to make the financial disclosures required under GAAP. The first German company to list on the NYSE was Daimler-Benz in 1994. The differences between the accounts according to German and US standards were such that it was difficult to imagine how the two versions referred to the same company. For the first half of 1993, Daimler-Benz made a group profit of DM168 million according to German rules, and a loss of DM942 million under GAAP. For 1993 as a whole the difference widened to DM3 billion.[12] The Daimler-Benz episode revealed the fundamental difference between a market-driven financial system and a bank-intermediated system.

The next significant step undertaken by a German company was the privatisation of Deutsche Telekom (DT), celebrating the dominance of US disclosure standards. The largest share issue in German history—and even Europe's largest ever—was entrusted to a global consortium, led by Deutsche Bank, Dresdner Bank *and* Goldman Sachs. The shares are listed on the Frankfurt, New York and Tokyo stock exchanges. With the help of two advisers (Coopers & Lybrand and Rothschild UK) accounts were only prepared on the GAAP basis to avoid discussion of differences in company evaluation generated by differences in accounting standards. In fact, a single prospectus was issued (translated from English into German). What better example of the "Americanisation of global finance"?[13]

In this area, as in others, the US and UK financial systems remain far ahead of the major industrial countries, many of which have only recently outlawed insider dealing and market manipulation.[14] Furthermore, although a number of countries now have insider trading statutes, enforcement leaves much to be desired. For example, much of the industrial/financial ownership structure, and the lack of effective segregation of fund management from other financial business, in continental European countries and in Japan would not be acceptable in the United States.

**Performance-oriented Institutional Investors: the Newest Players**

The institutionalisation of savings in the US since the 1950s has been a necessary condition for the development of the American model of finance. The demand for securities generated by institutional investors was the other side of the disintermediation coin. The growth of savings lodged in insurance companies and funded pension plans provided an important source of demand for securities.[15] But it was the explosive growth of the *mutual fund industry* from the late 1960s onwards that proved to be the driving force in stimulating broad-based participations in securities markets.[16] Mutual funds' demand for securities was not confined to equity and corporate bonds and became particularly important in money markets—the first segment that was disintermediated from the banking sector. The demand by money-market mutual funds for money-market securities stimulated the growth of the negotiable CD and CP market, as well as the growth of the treasury bill market. Mutual funds alone accounted for about US$3 trillion of private wealth in 1996, compared to US$4.2 trillion in assets held by US commercial banks. Although this sum is not as large as the assets managed by insurance companies and pension funds, mutual fund assets have increased at a much faster pace than have the assets of other institutional investors. In early 1997, there were more mutual funds available (5900) in the United States than stocks quoted on the New York Stock Exchange (NYSE).

One of the important factors underpinning this growth has been the competitive and performance-oriented nature of mutual funds, which has led to major advances in two areas. First, technological innovations in communications and data management technology have allowed funds to achieve significant reductions in the cost of securities transactions. The competitive pressures faced by mutual funds have translated into pressure on brokerage companies to reduce brokerage and research fees. Second, funds have continually increased the ease with which their customers can conduct transactions. There is now nothing unusual for a retail mutual fund investor to rearrange his portfolio at almost the same cost and speed at which a professional wholesale investor can rearrange his portfolio.[17] An important costs-saving for mutual funds and general brokerage services is provided by the Internet. Charles Schwab, the largest discount broker, conducts a rapidly rising share of its business over the Internet, offers cheque accounts, customer information and price services. The largest independent Internet broker in 1996 was Lombard Brokerage in San Francisco, bought in December 1996 by Dean Witter, Discover, subsequently merged into Morgan Stanley, Dean Witter, Discover.[18]

Institutional investors, particularly mutual funds, have been *important participants in derivative markets*. The major derivative markets, such as the stock index markets and the Eurodollar futures markets, have traditionally been significantly more liquid than the underlying cash markets. Thus when institutions need to make large portfolio shifts quickly they tend to make adjustments in their portfolio positions in derivative markets first, and then build the position in the underlying cash market gradually. Similarly, mutual funds have used derivatives to manage their position risks. For example, international diversification has led to the increased use of currency hedging instruments. Institutional investors are also the main users of dynamic hedging and portfolio insurance, relying heavily on derivatives. Underperformance with respect to an implicit benchmark has popularised benchmark-driven funds which can most cost effectively attain benchmark performance by investing in cash and index futures.

US *institutional investors have been a driving force in the globalisation of finance*. Their efforts to achieve an international diversification of their portfolios has been an important source of cross-border portfolio flows. For example, in 1993, a 5.7% foreign asset share in US pension funds translated into foreign security holdings by US pension funds of US$203.6 billion. With US mutual funds and insurance companies together holding roughly equivalent amounts, these three types of institutional investors in the United States alone control about US$400 billion in foreign securities.

US institutional investors have also been the agents of change in a number of issues of significance for the US economy, such as corporate governance, economic restructuring, and, more generally, the efficient use of capital. The funds have more aggressively used their proxy voting powers to work in the interest of their shareholders. It is likely that institutional investors will increasingly solve the problem posed by the fact that dispersed shareholders tend not to vote their shares in corporate matters.

## Some Problems Remain

Performance measurement, through the development of benchmarks, has made it possible for investors to compare easily the relative performance of funds, although risk exposures are much more difficult to assess.[19] Nevertheless, it remains a disturbing fact, established by the regular reports of firms that track funds' performance, that the majority of funds underperform relevant benchmarks over extended periods of time.[20]

Is the widespread use of risk-management techniques providing better protection for retail investors? The answer is generally positive with the exception of disasters created by incompetence, mismanagement and fraud. Financial markets, perhaps more than other industries, have always been subject to mismanagement and fraud. Technical Insight 2.1 gives a pertinent recent example.

**Technical Insight 2.1**   A case of mismanagement and fraud—among others

If one compares the stability of the banking industry with other industrial sectors, it is striking to observe that banking has known more débâcles than any other industry. John Law's Banque Royale in France under Louis XV, the failure of the Austrian Creditanstalt in 1931, entailing a general recall of US loans to Europe and thereby transmitting the US depression to Europe, the bank failures of the 1930s in the US, the Savings and Loans associations (S&L) débâcle of the 1980s, costing US taxpayers well in excess of US$100 bn or 3.2% of GDP (White 1991), the Scandinavian banking crisis of the 1990s, costing the Scandinavian taxpayers between 4% and 8% of one year's GNP, the Chilean banking crisis of 1981–85 with an estimated cost of 41% of GDP, the Mexican banking crisis of 1994/5 with a cost of 12–15% of GDP, and the pending crises of Japanese banking, to cite just a few.[21]

How is that possible, particularly in view of the regulations of the banking industry in all countries? There are several possible explanations, all of which are relevant in at least some cases if not all. The most important is surely that banks are often used as transmission mechanisms for policy objectives (lending to support political priorities). Another is that regulations reduce some risks but unintentionally create others. The best example is deposit insurance at undifferentiated premiums and restrictions on the diversification of the loan portfolio. As argued by White (1991) and others, that was the principle cause of the Savings and Loans association (S&L) débâcle, the lesson of which was to price risk premiums in line with the risk of particular institutions to augment controls but to deregulate lending activity.[22]

Managerial incompetence and fraud are arguably other important explanations for individual bank failures (John Law's Banque Royale, Michael Milken at Drexel, Burnham Lambert, Mario Conde at Banco Central, senior managers at Crédit Lyonnais, BCCI, Banca Nazionale del Lavoro, Prudential Bache Securities), to which can be added lack of close understanding by top management of the policies pursued and their risks (Barings), and blindly riding the wave of particular trends (junk bonds, foreign sovereign debt, derivatives, real estate).

It is instructive to look at a specific case in more detail.

How was it possible that the Prudential Insurance Company of America could have allowed its subsidiary, Prudential Bache Securities, to mis-sell more than US$8bn worth of risky financial products to hundreds of thousands of investors around the US? Limited partnerships, which pooled investors' money to buy assets like apartment buildings, oil wells or aircraft, were sold as products which promised high returns and big tax benefits. But above all, they were said to be safe and secure.

Nothing could have been further from the truth. By the end of the 1980s products which had appeared to guarantee high income were simply collapsing. And Prudential Bache was starting a vicious and largely unsuccessful campaign to ward off customers' claims.

There are many lessons in this story, which other large financial companies would do well to note.

The first is that Prudential diversified into a business which it knew nothing about. Impressed by the success of Merrill Lynch's Cash Management Account, it decided in the mid-1970s that brokerage firms were the path to the future, providing the cash management and lending services of banks. Like others, it was swept along by the fashionable concept of "womb to tomb" financial services.

Next, it bought the wrong company, and put the wrong people in charge. Bache & Company was no front-rank securities firm, and its recent history had been chequered. After the take-over, head-hunters scoured Wall Street to find a chairman capable of putting it on a new footing: they came up with George Ball, president of E.F. Hutton. Only later did it become clear that during his time Hutton had been involved in financial manipulation to boost its bottom line.

Prudential appears to have made little or no attempt to change the culture of its acquisition. In contrast to its own sober ways, executives in the securities firm continued with extravagant junketing. And Prudential was startlingly casual in the way it allowed its brand name to be used.

There is no doubt that the image of Prudential played a big part in persuading unsophisticated investors to hand over life savings in return for products which were too complicated for most to understand. More than that: a key selling point for some of the products was the heavily promoted fact that Prudential was backing them with its own insurance funds.

There was, perhaps, no reason for investors to be suspicious of products that promised to combine very large returns with a high degree of security. But Prudential should have known better.

The truth seems to have been that the limited partnership business was just too profitable for anyone to want to ask questions. According to one account, it brought in more than US$1bn in profits to the firm in the form of fees and commissions. At a time when many other parts of the securities business were reporting large losses, Ball did not want to know about problems with his one real success story.

This also explains why the firm's due diligence procedures were wholly inadequate. These were the systems which were supposed to put all partnership proposals under the spotlight, to make sure there were no hidden problems that might put investors at risk. But as sales of limited partnerships flooded in, Prudential Bache built its due diligence team largely out of young people straight from business school.

It was common knowledge on Wall Street that the individual in charge of the limited partnership department, and who was largely responsible for its explosive growth, had a dubious business history. So was the fact that an entrepreneur responsible for creating some of the biggest property partnerships was a convicted felon. But this was not the kind of thing you discussed at Prudential Bache if you wanted to stay in a job. In the threatening words of one executive: "It's my way or the highway."

*Source:* Adapted from Eichenwald (1995) and *Financial Times*
28 September 1995

## Hedge Funds

The most aggressive institutional investors, from the point of view of providing market arbitrage and speculative position-taking have been hedge funds (see Chapter 3 for a definition and historic origins). Hedge funds are dedicated to take speculative risk positions—they are the purest class of speculators in the markets today.[23] Although total assets of all hedge funds are estimated to be around US$300 billion, the possible positions taken by hedge funds tend to be much larger. This is because these investors are not constrained by the leverage restrictions of the Investment Company Act of 1940. In fact, some hedge funds committed to a particular investment opportunity may be leveraged between five and 20 times their capital. Factoring leverage into the net capital of hedge funds leads to the conclusion that they are a potentially important player in global capital markets.

The "macro," "opportunistic", or "directional" hedge funds are chiefly interested in the currency and bond markets, typically taking highly speculative, and highly leveraged positions through liberal use of bank loans, options, futures, and other derivatives. It is estimated that there are only fifteen or so of these macro hedge funds, but they appear to control a very significant portion of the industry's assets.[24] Although hedge funds invest globally, they tend to be largely a US phenomenon. It is difficult to obtain quantitative measurement of the impact of speculative hedge-fund behaviour on the performance of US markets. For a case study, see Chapter 3.

## 2. THE CROWNING ACHIEVEMENT: RISK-MANAGEMENT FINANCE

During the 1980s the US financial community brought a number of important innovations to the markets (some of which were discussed in Chapter 1). The balance sheet problems of the money-centre banks' losses on their Latin American loan books, real estate lending, the continuing migration of prime borrowers to money and capital markets, and new risk-based capital requirements, combined with a loss of cheap deposits eroded the intermediation margin and motivated the search for greater fee income from off-balance sheet activities. In fact, US commercial banks during the late 1980s, early 1990s underwent a serious crisis, some coming dangerously close to the brink of bankruptcy. What is, however, of greater interest today is that this crisis caused a fundamental self-examination, widespread reorganisation (mergers, acquisitions) of banks and focusing of their activities in line with their house-specific know-how. As a result, return on equity of US commercial banks increased to 15% in 1995, as compared to a low of less than 2% in 1987.[25]

None of the innovations and advances of the 1980s will be as lasting and have as profound an impact as the maturing of risk-management finance in the early 1990s. The impetus for the growth of risk-management finance came from three sources. First, the liberalisation of financial markets, including the increased flexibility of exchange rates, in the 1970s and 1980s permitted financial returns and prices to move freely, which in turn generated a *growing demand* for risk-management services. Second, money-centre and investment banks actively and persuasively marketed their highly profitable risk-management services as competition among underwriters had made straight underwriting less and less profitable. Third, all the *necessary conditions for the successful evolution of risk-management finance had been met*. These were the growth of highly liquid and efficient money and capital markets, active institutional investors, advances in transactions and information technologies, availability of the theory of pricing contingent contracts and high market integrity. These conditions all came together to create a fertile environment for the use of derivative instruments to price and trade financial risk.

The development of risk-management finance—the commoditisation of commonly found financial risks (with some notable exceptions, such as liquidity risk)—was a decisive step in the commoditisation of US finance. These risks can now be isolated and packaged as negotiable instruments, and priced in liquid markets. In some sense this completes the development of the American model of finance. Institutions (money centre banks specialising in risk-management and supplying liquidity to money markets, accounting standards for derivatives, legal enforceability of derivative contracts), markets (e.g., organised futures exchange, over-the-counter markets), and techniques (e.g., internal risk management) have evolved to sustain the development of new instruments to price and trade financial risks. *Financial innovation has become self-sustaining.*

The last twenty-five years has seen the evolution of *the two predominant risk-management institutions: the financial futures and options exchanges and the over-the-counter (OTC) derivatives markets*. Without these new institutions risk-management finance could not have prospered. A handful of money centre banks have come to dominate the OTC markets (see Chapter 6), both by acting as dealers in the OTC market and as users of exchange-traded instruments. In fact, money centre banks are increasingly transforming themselves from on-balance sheet lending institutions to off-balance sheet risk and liquidity management. Much of their human capital used to be concentrated on credit risk evaluation in their commercial and industrial loans and on their trading and funding activities. Today much of the credit evaluation function is focused on analysing the risks inherent in OTC transactions. These organisations have undergone a complete change in their corporate culture. Although largely driven by the declining profitability of their traditional activities, money centre banks have a comparative advantage in the risk-management field. Their advantage in risk management stems from their ability to generate liquidity as and when needed. OTC derivative markets rely entirely on the money-centre banks to keep the market for OTC instruments liquid. Their privileged access to the central bank is crucial in this regard.

**Benefits to the Economy**

The *benefits flowing from the American model* of finance, especially its capacity to manage risk, may be difficult to quantify precisely, but the ease with which the US economy, as compared to European economies, has adjusted to changes in technologies and demand, and to other changes that impact on the profitability of the corporate sector has much to do with developments in the financial sector. The industrial restructuring, including mergers, acquisitions and leveraged-buy outs (LBOs), that has taken place during the past twenty years, and the rapid pace of innovations, could not have occurred had it not been for the innovative financial and risk-management structures that were put together in the financial sector. Less tangible but probably of equal importance has been the impact of developments in financial markets on corporate governance. The possibility of hostile take-overs or leveraged buy-outs is likely to be providing discipline over managements. Also, the ability to price risk across a wide spectrum has ensured allocation of capital to a variety of activities, ranging from safe blue-chip companies to venture firms. Finally, the competitive nature of the system has benefited not only the financial wholesale sector but also the retail financial services. The financial sector in the United States has been one of the most innovative, adaptive, forward-looking ones, on a par with other high-technology sectors.[26]

Technical Insight 2.2 attempts to illustrate the economic gains from the financial sector's efficiency in monitoring the allocation of resources.

## 3. MAINTAINING MARKET LIQUIDITY: THE *SINE QUA NON* OF THE "AMERICAN MODEL"

The wholesale or *money-centre bank emerged as one of the key institutional players in the American model of finance.* Why? Why have insurance companies not become dominant in risk-management finance, or why has an altogether new type of institution not emerged to sell risk-management products? What is so special about the money-centre bank that has moved it to the centre stage in modern transactions-oriented, risk managing and liquidity-driven finance? Will this institution continue to supply the dominant players in the foreseeable future? For answers, it will be necessary to shed light on the importance of "liquidity" in modern finance, and particularly in derivative finance.

The *Achilles heel of the American model of finance is its reliance on highly liquid money and capital markets*—the essence of commoditised finance. One of its great accomplishments is that institutions have evolved to ensure the continued supply of such liquidity to its securities markets, even under adverse conditions. Many of the developments and innovations—the growth of

**Technical Insight 2.2**   The financial sector's contribution to growth

Whilst it is intuitively obvious that a more efficient financial system is good for economic growth and public welfare in general, it is difficult to put a precise figure on it. A very crude way to arrive at an approximation is to reason as follows. Every dollar invested in an economy serves to replace, upgrade or create production capacity. With a comparable degree of efficiency economies investing the same share of output should therefore exhibit the same growth performance. Of course, different business cycle fluctuations could upset a year-by-year comparison, but not longer term trends. The snag is in the proviso "with equal efficiency". Efficiency of resource allocation is certainly influenced by the financial sector as allocator and monitor of funds, but also by government policies and the institutional set up (social security, labour laws and regulations, and more). Nevertheless, the comparison of ICORs in the table below is too striking to be ignored. ICOR (incremental capital output ratio) measures the ratio between the share of investment in GDP and GDP growth. For example, during the decade 1965–74 every percentage point of growth in the United States required 2.44% of investment of GDP. Japan had about the same ICOR (2.47%). Hence investing nearly twice as much as the United States (in relation to GDP), Japan could grow twice as fast as the United States. Over time, it took more investment to generate growth, slightly more in the United States, strikingly more in Japan. Thus, in recent times, the United States grew more rapidly than Japan despite much lower investment shares. Germany's growth has not been higher than US growth, although Germany has consistently invested more. In a way, the United States can afford to save and invest little compared to other countries because it invests efficiently. How much of this is due to a vigorously efficient financial sector is anyone's guess, but not to give it some credit is clearly unwise.

Incremental Capital–Output Ratios

|  | USA | Germany | Japan |
| --- | --- | --- | --- |
| Average 1965–74 | 2.44 | 4.42 | 2.47 |
| Average 1975–84 | 2.35 | 4.04 | 4.29 |
| Average 1985–94 | 3.08 | 4.86 | 14.02 |

*Source*: IMF International Financial Statistics

A major study on capital productivity in these three countries arrives at similar conclusions: the economy-wide internal rate of return averaged over 1974–93 is 9.1% for the United States, 7.4% for Germany, 7.1% for Japan (McKinsey, 1996).

short-term money markets, the ascendancy of quote-driven, dealer-based securities markets, arbitrage-driven portfolio management, pricing of risk— require that the relevant markets remain liquid, i.e., produce continuous pricing, under adverse circumstances. This is particularly true for risk-management finance: derivatives can only be priced if the markets in the underlying instruments produce continuous prices (the equity market crash in 1987 demonstrates the problems when prices in the underlying instruments are not available for several business hours or make big jumps). The growth of exchange-traded derivatives relies heavily on the ability of market participants to generate intraday "good funds" (deposits at a clearing bank, T-bills) to meet potentially massive intraday margin calls that are required subsequent to major price movements. Similarly, dynamic hedging techniques rely on the ability to sell large volumes of securities into declining markets or to buy them in rising markets. The management of risk in the over-the-counter (OTC) derivative markets also relies heavily on liquid money markets (repurchase agreements or repos, T-bills, foreign exchange, interbank) and liquid exchange-traded derivative markets. *Liquidity in financial markets is the key requirement for the success of the new financial instruments.*[27]

A smoothly functioning dealer in effect provides the service for swapping one security for another. The swaps fund the dealer's operation, allowing the dealer to provide liquidity while avoiding the tapping of the dealer's bank line of credit. Nevertheless, only when handling very liquid instruments can dealers almost always avoid funding through banks. Dealers maintain credit lines in good funds (cash or near cash) and securities to finance peak load inventory acquisition or short positions.[28] Low capitalisation and high leverage are the essential characteristics of the securities dealers. They therefore tend to be undiversified, highly leveraged and vulnerable to failure.

**Money-centre Banks as the Penultimate Suppliers of Liquidity**

How is liquidity supplied to markets? In highly securitised financial systems, such as those of the United States, there exists an intricate network of short-term obligations connecting diverse financial institutions. Participants in money and capital markets rely on broker/dealers in their role as market makers to keep these markets liquid; broker/dealers in turn rely on the liquid repurchase markets to finance their securities positions. Corporate borrowers rely on the commercial paper market to satisfy their short-term liquidity needs. This is, therefore, a tightly connected system where failure of one element may break the chain.

The next link in the chain is the money-centre bank. In particular, non-bank financial institutions, such as broker/dealers rely on money-centre banks for lines of credit that can be drawn down when these institutions experience difficulties in rolling over their own short-term obligations in the repo market or elsewhere. Similarly, the corporate sector generally obtains standby credit lines with money-centre banks to assure access to funds in case problems occur in rolling over their short-term obligations and, as issuers of commercial paper, they must assure lenders that they can deliver good funds at maturity. A cash delivery can be assured only by buying a line from a bank. Finally, participants on organised futures and options markets, the heart of the last decade's development in financial engineering, make intensive use of bank lines because of the requirement of nearly instantaneous delivery of cash needed to satisfy margin calls. Credit lines are the only practicable method of assuring such delivery.[29] Thus *wholesale banks act as lender-of-next-to-last-resort through prearranged lines of credit.* Indeed, evaluating and managing the credit risk involved in these lines of credit and in their OTC risk-management positions has replaced the need to evaluate credit risk in the dwindling commercial and industrial loan book of banks.

Wholesale banks themselves rely on the interbank market to meet their end-of-day settlement obligations to the payments system. The vast interbank market redistributes liquidity in the banking system and is crucial in making it possible for an individual bank to have the ability to keep its promise to supply short-term cash-like credit to financial market participants. Liquidity stringencies first make their appearance in the Fed funds market—the inter-bank market for reserve positions at the Federal Reserve—in the form of sudden increases in the Fed funds rate. The banking sector has come to rely on the central bank to keep the market for bank liabilities liquid by smoothing the Fed funds rates and by standing ready to act as lender-of-last-resort to the banking sector. This is last link in the liquidity chain.

*Money-centre banks are unique among financial institutions because they are the cheapest source of liquidity in the economy.* This advantage is not derived from the special nature of individual banks but from the special nature of the banking system, which can mobilise good funds more easily than competing financial institutions. For example, a bank has access both to the banking system and to the liquidity services of the central bank. Such access to central bank liquidity facilities gives banks a comparative advantage in supplying liquidity.

Banks hold only a small percentage of their assets in good funds. Individual banks can make a credible statement about delivering good funds to their deposit customers and borrowers on demand because banks are part of a banking system, tied together by an interbank market and the clearing and settlement mechanism of a clearing-house. The interbank market acts to direct liquidity across the banking system. Banks experiencing a sudden and unexpected demand from borrowers drawing down their lines will turn to the interbank market. Members agree to lend to those who experience a drain on good funds on any particular day, i.e., to banks whose market-making activities in good funds cause them to have end-of-day net debit positions from large volumes of payments orders. Final settlement of payments among banks occurs with the delivery of good funds.

In contrast, in financial systems that are still bank dominated, such as in Germany, there has generally been a small number of large-bank players in the market for wholesale funds. Clearing of payments is effectively done internally to banking organisations or among a small group of tightly connected banks. Though banks are leveraged, their ability to obtain short-term funding is not impaired by sudden swings in the trading prices for securities. Few occasions will arise when large amounts of funds are demanded for unexpected settlements. Since much of the funding and lending of financial institutions involves end-users, financial flows through the interbank market remain relatively small. In the absence of major derivative markets, there is little need to deliver large volumes of intraday good funds. Because the failure of a financial institution is less likely to create a systemic disturbance, there is less need for the central bank to act as lender-of-last-resort.

The structure of financial markets is affected by the degree of liquidity. Certainly, bid-offer spreads are wide in dealer markets with scarce liquidity; but in addition, dealer markets may themselves be rare, with trading being undertaken instead through brokered markets. An illiquid system raises funding costs to smaller, less liquid potential issuers of securities by forcing them to compete with larger issuers for costly bank credit. Thus, the industrial structure tends towards larger entities that can readily throw off cash in the near term rather than toward smaller ventures with longer term, speculative payoffs.

### The Central Bank as the Ultimate Guarantor of Liquidity

An important element in the liquidity story is that liquidity is underwritten or backstopped by the central bank through its 'banking functions', intervening day-to-day in overnight markets to *"maintain orderly markets"*, providing credit in support of the *payments system* and *lender-of-last-resort* support.[30] For example, assuring end-of-day settlement in a wholesale payments system—directly through payments finality or indirectly through implicit guarantees—allows the pyramiding of intraday trades without credit risk or monitoring cost to the recipient of a payment. A policy of maintaining orderly markets prevents wide swings in overnight rates, which in turn reduces the liquidity risk and capital cost of short cash positions. Lastly, a policy of supporting banks that are "too large to fail" ensures continuous liquidity in the key markets for bank liabilities. Some of this central bank support was motivated by a desire to avoid a recurrence of liquidity disturbances, which had become more likely after financial innovations and changes in financial structure had taken hold. Some support—notably, the granting of large over-drafts in payment systems—was originally unintended but now difficult to eliminate. This role of liquidity supplier of last resort assumed by central banks has produced a fertile environment that supports the proliferation and survival of financial products through financial innovation.

### Maintaining orderly markets

During the last decade, the US central bank has increasingly intervened in open money markets (through repo markets or trades in short-term se-curities) to prevent extraordinary spikes and troughs in overnight rates. Al-though such intervention has theoretically been motivated by a desire to provide clear, noise-free signals as to the future path of monetary policy, it has become the most important source of liquidity for the financial system. In addition to the day-to-day liquidity management, the central bank also, on occasion, has to intervene more forcefully as the Fed did, for example, during the October 1987 equity market crisis, when it supplied all the liquidity re-quired to the Fed funds market.[31]

The Fed's intervention to smooth the Fed funds rate has made it the resid-ual supplier of liquidity on a day-to-day basis. If, for example, a disturbance in the commercial paper (CP) market forces CP issuers to have temporary re-course to bank lines, then banks will be bidding for Fed funds and the over-night rate will spike up without the Fed's intervention. As it is, the Fed supplies the needed liquidity in the course of maintaining the Fed funds rate in its target range. Such a reliable supply of liquidity has lowered the spreads and capital cover on the full spectrum of money and capital markets instru-ments, and indeed it has made possible certain OTC activities that rely heavily on liquidity in money and derivative markets.

### Payments system policy

Since payments are made on a continuous intraday basis, while settlement usually occurs at discrete intervals at the end of the trading day, there exists credit risk between settlement times. Such intraday credit exposure has to be monitored, and it is potentially the most important constraint on trading. Monitoring requires real resources and is made difficult in the payments system by the fact that it requires creditors to monitor not only direct exposure of a particular counterparty but of the counter-party's payees. For dollar-denominated interbank payments such monitoring costs are assumed by the US Federal Reserve, which guarantees interbank payments routed across Fedwire. Since CHIPS, the clearing-house for international dollar payments, is generally believed to be implicitly guaranteed by the Fed, the monitoring cost has been significantly reduced even for international dollar payments. It is, therefore, no surprise that most of Forex transactions are routed through the dollar.[32]

In addition to providing payments finality, some central banks also provide credit support to achieve settlement. For example, when a computer failure at the Bank of New York prevented the settlement of a day's transactions in this clearing bank for the government bond market, the Fed made good on the payments and took the bank's assets as collateral against an overnight loan, effectively doubling bank deposits at the Fed and expanding its own balance sheet by 10% overnight. Although the approach will differ, most major central banks will make sure that settlement can be completed since an unravelling of payments will certainly produce a systemic liquidity crisis.[33]

*Lender-of-last-resort support*

It has long been recognised that the central bank should expand its balance sheet to provide credit and its own deposit liabilities to the banking and financial system at times when demands for settlement in good funds surge. Such liquidity crises create externalities for claimants dealing directly or indirectly with entities that have shorted good funds, and they can generate costly bankruptcies. If, indeed, the entities experiencing such difficulties are otherwise solvent, the central bank can, at low social cost, expand the supply of good funds to meet the sudden demand.

Central bank intervention can also prevent liquidity crises caused by large price movements from becoming systemic. The central bank can supply emergency liquidity assistance to the banking system or induce the banking system to supply liquidity to the non-bank market makers. A large welfare loss is avoided by preventing the transformation of liquid into illiquid securities and needless bankruptcies among dealers, and ultimately among banking institutions. If such events are pure liquidity events, then intervention is costless in terms of central bank resources and price level stability.

However, in any credit operation that it undertakes in support of the payments system or as the lender-of-last-resort, a central bank will incur credit risk and potential losses, associated with the claims it acquires when expanding its liabilities to supply liquidity. Such losses will occur when the market value of the collateral is less than the amount of the loan or advance to the banks concerned.[34] Unless lending-of-last-resort is progressively costly, the lender-of-last-resort policy established to preclude a general liquidity crisis will inevitably provide an incentive for market participants to shorten their cash positions, since they no longer have to cover for this eventuality, and in so doing, they will increase the probability that liquidity disturbances may occur.[35] This is a real dilemma to which central banks respond in opposite ways. The Federal Reserve accepts that problem. The German central bank, and even more forcefully, the Hong Kong Monetary Authorities, have made it known that they would not act as lender-of-last-resort. In neither extreme circumstance has disaster been experienced so far.

## 4. GLOBAL FINANCE: THE RESULT OF EXPORTING THE "AMERICAN MODEL"

Global finance is a recent phenomenon. Its birth certificate was issued jointly by the narcissism of US regulators, pushing US institutions abroad in order to circumvent interest rate ceilings, reserve requirements and Glass–Steagall restrictions; and by the cosmopolitanism of UK regulations, embracing the returning pilgrims, vastly enriched in the meantime, and generously allowing them to develop the Eurodollar market. The superior efficiency of the US, a lowering of funding cost combined with flexibility in funding arrangements, brought on by innovations in techniques and instruments and by an expanded global investor base, did not escape the notice of large non-US borrowers. And as US corporations and financial institutions expanded their funding and investing in the Euromarkets, large non-US firms also saw an opportunity to benefit from moving a portion of their funding into the off-shore bond, and later equity, markets. In addition, foreign firms began to make use of the flexible short-term funding vehicles, such as Euro-note programmes and Euro-commercial paper. US banks and securities houses captured a major share of this foreign dollar and non-dollar underwriting business, and had it not been for the superior placement power of foreign institutions in their own markets, US institutions would have dominated this market from the beginning.

The availability of sophisticated money market transactions in the Eurodollar markets gradually attracted more money-market activity from the other major industrial countries—with more restrictive financial environments and less generous central bank support—to the lower cost offshore environment and, where redenomination was possible, into the more liquid dollar-denominated environment. For example, most foreign exchange trading uses the dollar as vehicle currency because of the lower cost of making wholesale international dollar payments and the lower cost of parking short-term funds in dollar money markets. Frequently, it is cheaper for foreign institutions to use the dollar money markets for their treasury operations—suitably hedging overnight foreign exchange positions and interest rate positions—rather than trying to implement such money-market transactions in their own insufficiently developed money markets.

US institutions operating out of New York, London and other financial hubs have also been successful since the late 1980s in capturing purely domestic financial business in the major industrial countries, particularly in the wholesale financial sector, such as treasury operations, including liquidity management, funding and risk-management transactions (see Technical Insight 2.3).

The greatest competitive advantage enjoyed by US institutions has been in the area of risk-management finance. This activity has provided the most significant opportunity for US financial firms to gain foreign market share. The global presence of the major US institutions has given them an important edge in global finance, such as global bond issues, international payments, global custody business. As institutional investors began to diversify their portfolios into foreign currencies, US financial intermediaries brought their fund and risk management expertise to bear in this area. US institutions have also benefited from the fact that the US government securities market—dominated by US houses—is the only truly global market, in which the trading book can remain open for 24 hours by being passed around the globe. A government securities market with round-the-clock liquidity has proved an important ingredient in global risk-management.

The evolution of the American model was driven by competition-induced innovation, supported and stimulated by a proactive public policy. In contrast, *the evolution of the financial sector in the other major industrial countries has largely been forced by competition from the outside*, i.e., by the threat of losing market share, and it has been supported by a public policy that has generally been reactive—with some notable exceptions, such as in France. The drifting of domestic financial business into off-shore markets and the growth of the market share of foreign intermediaries in domestic financial intermediation has led to a deliberate, albeit reactive in most cases, public policy of reform and liberalisation of domestic markets in the major industrial countries.

Competition from established international futures exchanges has forced most countries to support the establishment of a domestic financial futures market (Germany, France, Japan). A desire to increase participation in capital markets leads to public support for market integrity, which also tends to undermine relationship finance. The growth of fully funded pension funds creates more institutional investors (France, Netherlands, UK), and privatisation adds to the supply of shares. The more the central bank supports the budding money markets by back-stopping its liquidity supply, the faster the country will develop liquid money markets—including derivative markets. The logic of the evolution of the non-dollar financial markets is inescapable and the differences across countries are in emphasis only. Thus, the financial sectors in the major industrial countries are gradually assuming the main features of the American model.

**Structural Differences Still Exist**

However, the above trends notwithstanding, pronounced differences still remain in financial structure across major industrial countries. Specifically,

**Technical Insight 2.3**    The City of London: alternative or depository for the American model?

To see global finance as the result of the superiority of an American model may be shocking and unconvincing to observers of the City of London. London dominates the foreign exchange market, boasts the biggest international insurance market, the biggest market for swaps, and is the centre of the Eurodollar business. Its advisory capacity is legendary and its exchanges second only to Chicago and for some commodities the leading ones in the world.

Impressive as it is, it does not add up to a British model of finance, despite honourable traditions and numerous specificities. London surely benefits from centuries of financial experience and global relations. Its cosmopolitan past was certainly decisive in becoming the Eurodollar centre. Its time-zone advantage as a go-between for the two giants, Asia and the Americas, is also not negligible. Its market-based regulatory and legal framework made co-operation and adaptation to US standards easy.

Today, London is successful as a financial centre because it has adopted the American model. It has done so with a delay of about 10 years. LIFFE started futures trading in 1981, some 10 years after Chicago, and London's "Big Bang" trailed New York's by 11 years.

The "Big Bang" occurred on 27 October 1986, 11 years after fixed commissions were eliminated in New York. It flushed away trading cartels at the London Stock Exchange and in the market for British government bonds. Rules barring mergers between financial firms of different types were scrapped and foreigners were allowed to purchase members of the stock exchange. The old line between merchant banks, jobbers (market-makers) and brokers was removed. US firms bought up City stockbrokers and merchant banks (as did continental universal banks), although many US banks chose to build their own London business rather than buy. It was the US presence and their "transfer of technology" that promoted London to a leading financial centre in today's global market.

London has made the most out of its potential which is much more constrained than New York's or Tokyo's—but this is going to change. With the loss of the Commonwealth, Britain turned into a small, open European economy, more directly comparable to Italy than to Germany and France. Along with the Commonwealth and with the help of fiscal and monetary stop-go policies went the international role of the pound sterling—to the point that sterling was not even convertible for long periods after World War II. On all accounts Britain, the pound and, hence, British finance was no match for the United States and the dollar. Regulation had to protect rather than promote British finance.

The European Monetary Union (EMU) offers Britain a unique historic chance to enter into serious competition with New York/Chicago for the number one position (before HongKong/Shanghai take over in 10–30 years' time). EMU will give London all it lacks: an international currency with considerable attractions, such as full convertibility and predictability in its inflation stance; a currency area that is comparable in size to the US economy; and a continental capital market that needs to be integrated. London is superbly placed to become "the" European financial centre, given its strategic position, its cost advantage and its attraction to global institutions. What better proof of its potential than the transfer of some of the largest continental banks' (also in the top of a global ranking) investment banking activities to London?

Of course, the opportunity needs to be seized and, I am sure, will be seized. The United Kingdom should join EMU early rather than late and in the meantime some weeding could embellish London's regulatory landscape. For that a major step has already been taken in 1997: the transfer of bank regulation from the Bank of England to the Securities and Investment Board.

while sterling markets conform to the main features of the American model, the other major markets do not yet. For example, in Germany, a few large, universal banks continue to dominate the financial system, and private fixed-income securities markets have remained relatively illiquid, fragmented and of secondary importance. German universal banks enjoy close institutional ties to the corporate sector (in terms of equity stakes, proxy-vote control and their membership on corporate supervisory boards) and often play a major role in helping the corporate sector work out debt difficulties. They benefit from a large and still relatively loyal domestic retail base and, at least so far, have not had to confront the effects of a large-scale direct approach of the corporate sector to domestic credit markets, although Luxembourg branches of German banks do operate on very narrow spreads in some wholesale deutschemark (DM) banking markets. When firms need liquidity, they typically turn to their "Hausbank"; similarly, when they have excess liquidity, they deposit it there. Thus, in addition to longer-term credits, short-term wholesale payments also flow across the banks' balance sheets. Their considerable placement power allows universal banks to exercise some quality control over which potential domestic and foreign borrowers obtain access to the direct DM debt markets.

It is unlikely that any of these countries will in the near future produce as pure a risk-managing institution as some of the US money centre banks have become. The absence of Glass–Steagall type restrictions on bank activity will prevent a segmentation of the securities, derivatives and loan books into separate organisations, and hence the competitive pressure to innovate.[36]

The liberalisation and reform of financial markets in Europe and Japan, while motivated by a desire to reap the benefits of a more efficient market-based financial system, became more urgent with the growing loss of markets and activities in offshore markets and in dollar-denominated markets. A large and growing volume of capital market activities in the major currencies is being conducted and booked in London, DM wholesale banking markets are active in Luxembourg, the market for DM interest rate futures began on LIFFE— London's futures exchange. Reform efforts in the major countries concentrated on removing transaction and withholding taxes, including recently a lowering of minimum reserve requirements, on abolishing product restrictions and on improving market infrastructure (organisation of stock exchanges, clearance and settlement). The goal has generally been to establish domestic money markets (commercial paper, money-market mutual funds) and derivatives markets. In this area, the French reforms of market infrastructure have been among the most thorough and successful. Lagging reforms in Germany are the most telling example of reluctancy overcome only by external competitive pressure.

As liquidity-intensive money and capital markets activities in domestic non-dollar markets grow, central banks have found it necessary to become more supportive of these activities. "Maintaining orderly markets" through more frequent intervention in the money markets has become the norm (although in part with the stated aim of improving the reliability of monetary policy signals, rather than supplying liquidity). Most central banks now supply liquidity to money markets by smoothing overnight interest rates either through lending at a discount or Lombard window or through open market interventions.[37]

A rapid increase in wholesale payments traffic, denominated in non-dollar currencies, brought about by an increase in trading volumes in the emerging money and capital markets in these currencies, has made it increasingly clear that the unwinding of a day's trades is no longer a realistic option in case of settlement failure. Hence, it is now generally assumed by market participants that most major central banks would make discretionary credit available to the banking sector in case of a failure to settle a day's payments.[38]

However, despite the recent growth of domestic liquidity-intensive markets and activities, there has not yet been a need for central banks in the other major industrial countries to stand ready to provide lender-of-last-resort support as explicitly as in the United States. When a small number of large banks dominate the financial structure, as is for example still the case on the European continent, the central bank will be called upon to serve as lender-of-last-resort only in the most exigent circumstances.[39] Furthermore, the risk of failure of a bank can usually be dealt with by organising support from the banking industry, with minimal amount of central bank resources.

## 5. WILL NON-US CENTRAL BANKS BE FORCED INTO A MORE ACTIVIST ROLE IN FINANCIAL MARKETS?

The financial structure and practices in the major non-dollar countries have been changing at different speeds, and many structural differences have remained and in some cases have become even more pronounced. The United Kingdom has seen the fastest growth of liquidity-intensive markets and practices, while the development of liquid money markets is lagging in Germany. The Bank of England has actively managed liquidity and has provided lender-of-last-resort support, while controlling the risk of such support to the Bank's capital by careful regulation and supervision of the financial sector. Although the Bundesbank is increasingly intervening in the repurchase market to maintain orderly markets, it has generally taken a less interventionist approach to financial markets, preferring instead to concentrate its efforts on achieving its monetary policy objectives. With the completion of the single financial market in Europe and a single European currency, competition in financial services is likely to spread liquidity-intensive markets all over Europe and create a financial structure less dominated by banking institutions.[40] Arguably, the largest gain from European Monetary Union will be the creation of a large and efficient market-based financial system, close to the US system both in structure and size.

In general, *non-dollar central banks have three options to deal with the future evolution of their financial markets.* First, they can reduce the increased risk of financial disturbances arising from the growth of liquidity-intensive markets and activities by imposing restrictions to slow such developments. The risk with this option is that as a liquid environment is provided by a major central bank, such as the US Federal Reserve, willing to risk some of its capital in supporting the financial system, activities may shift into the US dollar markets. As the more liquid currency, the dollar would then remain the vehicle currency for third-party financial activities, thereby capturing even more international financial business.

The second option is to permit the growth of liquidity-intensive markets and practices and tolerate the higher risk of liquidity disturbances. With a credible no-support policy on the part of the non-dollar central bank, the holding of cash by market participants will increase, and there will be a need for intermediation spreads to increase in such markets. As long as liquidity is guaranteed in some major financial market (the United States), the end result will be that some activity will drift offshore or be redenominated into dollars, with a larger share of wholesale payments being made across the dollar payments system. At the same time the risk of liquidity disturbances will be higher in the domestic market. This option, therefore, contains the worst of both worlds—higher risk and a loss of financial activity.

As long as liquidity is central bank-supported in the United States, central banks elsewhere have little choice. They gradually need to assume a more activist role in providing liquidity support to their financial markets, as these markets become more liquidity-intensive. Such a broad approach to financial policy could be buttressed by a strengthening of supervision designed to limit the risk to the national central bank's capital. In this case the central bank will wish to assume a supervisory *and* regulatory role at the centre of its financial system, if it does not already do so, rather than leave such activities to separate bank supervisory agencies.[41]

There is, of course, a third option: the central bank provides liquidity and charges a price for it, but abstains from regulation as a *quid pro quo*. The risks from liquidity provision are weak justification for regulating banks. If the central bank is concerned with overall market liquidity, as it should be, and not with individual institutions, as it should not, then the link with regulation becomes even weaker. In history there is no case of general liquidity-enhancing central bank intervention which generated central bank losses. Losses are generated by support of insolvent institutions which can be properly identified by an independent regulator. In order not to create incentives for financial activity to move to a "lower cost" environment, pricing of central bank liquidity services would ideally be internationally co-ordinated. In reality, there is, however, little hope for achieving this. But, if priced liquidity support is compensated by a lighter regulatory burden, the risk of transactions emigrating may be small or non-existent.

These considerations are of particular relevance for the choices ahead for the European Central Bank. The Treaty of Maastricht, defining the rules of European Monetary Union (EMU), restricts the responsibility of the European Central Bank (ECB) to maintaining price stability. It therefore leaves the banking function to national central banks which form the European Central Bank System. As pointed out in Folkerts-Landau and Garber (1994), this gives too little weight to the liquidity-providing role which, if not amended, could place the future integrated European financial market at a competitive disadvantage in relation to the dollar market.

# 6. CONCLUSION

The 1990s have seen the completion of the basic architecture of the American model of finance with the development of risk-management finance and of a mechanism to ensure the liquidity in money and capital markets. The emergence of the American model of finance has been one of the most outstanding achievements of the US institutional history and US financial policy during the past 50 years. In this regard the rigorous enforcement of the financial legislation of the 1930s—the separation of commercial and investment banking, the establishment of the SEC, the anti-trust statutes—over time eliminated relationship finance and made finance more transparent. These characteristics then proved instrumental in unleashing the competitive forces that drove the evolution of the American model of finance.

The model that has emerged is robust, adaptable, flexible and largely free of implicit subsidies, rents or monopolies. It does, however, rely on the very active support of the central bank in the area of liquidity management. While the money-centre banks have become the penultimate suppliers of liquidity, which is their comparative advantage, the Federal Reserve has extended its role as the ultimate supplier of liquidity. This raises the question of whether the American model of finance becomes unviable without central bank support, and whether the public good aspect of modern finance warrants such active support. I believe that, at least for the time being, the answer is yes. The benefits flowing from the American model of finance—efficient credit intermediation in the wholesale and retail sectors, continuous price discovery in liquid money, derivative and capital markets, efficient pricing and allocation of wide variety of financial risks, disciplining corporate governance—together tilt the case in favour of active central bank support.

The US model has proved to be internationally competitive. The international expansion of the activities of US institutions—first into the Euro-markets and then into the domestic markets of the major industrial countries—has forced the pace of liberalisation elsewhere. In a world with nearly fully integrated financial markets, US firms are poised to make important further advances in the area of wholesale finance—money-market finance, Treasury management, corporate finance (including mergers and acquisition), funds management, global finance, global custody, settlement of international payments. The application of risk-management techniques has become the area of greatest competitive advantage of US firms in international markets, and it also remains the most profitable area of expansion.

International competition has inevitably led to a convergence of the non-dollar finance in the direction of the American model. Relationship finance is receding, liquid money, derivative and capital markets are growing, and commercial banking balance sheets are being disintermediated. The institutionalisation of savings is also underway. Legislation has been passed to improve market transparency. However, non-dollar financial systems have been slow to achieve the level of competition that drives the evolution of the US model, in part because the existing legal structure has made it possible for the financial sector to be dominated by a few large universal banking institutions.

As foreign financial systems converge to resemble more the American model, these systems also become more prone to liquidity-disturbances and hence they are placing greater demands on stabilising central bank liquidity policy. A key question facing financial authorities of the major industrial countries, therefore, concerns the proper balance between the gains from a liberal and liquid market environment and the cost of increased central bank support. In light of the cross-border dynamics of financial innovations, a policy decision to slow further evolution in the direction of the American model through a rigorous application of a more restrictive supervisory and regulatory framework would in all likelihood mean that financial structures and activity will drift towards the more liberal and more liquidity-intensive centres. Hence, there appears to be little alternative for the central banks of the major industrial countries but to support the evolution of their financial sectors by following the American model also in this area.

In this respect, the future organisation of the European capital market with a single currency in the making—the Euro—should absorb the lessons of the US lead. The United Kingdom had everything—the *savoir-faire*, a market organisation close to the American one, and, in fact, a more flexible regulatory framework—less the muscle provided by the size and wealth of the US economy. It had the initial advantage of a greater international orientation and became the centre of the Euromarket. But it trailed the United States in the development of financial futures markets and risk-management techniques by ten years.

Europe, with an economic weight equal to the United States, now has the historic opportunity to create a market, based on the Euro, second to none— if it can absorb the US lesson. The constitution of the European Central Bank, as embodied in the Maastricht Treaty, is designed for a different task. It will be fascinating to see whether, with today's efficient monetary markets, the American model of finance can blossom without extensive central bank support.

# ENDNOTES

1  In fact, insider trading became a prominent public policy issue only in the late 1960s when computer technology made it possible to routinely detect "unusual" patterns of trading activity.

2  A glance at the congressional hearings on the alleged abuses of financial power underscores this point: the Pujo hearings on money trusts in 1912, the Pecora hearings on the role of banks in the financial crash in 1933, the Nye hearings on war profits, the Wheeler hearings on financial control over railroads, etc.

3  For example, the House of Morgan was divided in September 1935 into J.P. Morgan, the bank, and Morgan Stanley, the securities firm.

4 In 1933 some 40% of the commercial banks had failed, reducing the number from 25 000 to 14 000. The governors of several states closed all the banks in their states, presumably to stem runs. As one of his first acts after taking office, President Roosevelt declared a national bank holiday. For more details see Benston (1996).

5 Empirical studies systematically fail, however, to detect in the data sizeable economies of scale or scope for banks. See Clark (1988), Shaffer (1988).

6 A taste of what that would have done is provided by the S&L crises of the 1980s—a disastrous regulatory failure. For a masterly review, see White (1991).

7 Until the 1960s, the financial sector legislation of the 1930s did not have much of an impact in practice. Banking houses that had been forced to spin off their investment banking departments, as part of the Glass–Steagall legislation, maintained close relations with their former colleagues. In effect the new investment banks resembled a retooled version of the securities departments of their banking parents with a variety of formal and intangible links remaining among the companies and their employees. Securities underwriting remained a clubby business and did not actively compete with the banking industry in the financing of corporate America. There always had been certain industrial sectors—railways, public utilities, large industrial firms, sovereign borrowers—that traditionally had relied to a large extent on capital-markets financing and such issues were underwritten by the securities industry, but the banking sector's commercial and industrial loans remained the main industrial financing vehicle. It was not until the late 1960s that disintermediation from the banking sector on the asset side was beginning to make itself felt.

8 For example, blue chip corporations continued to agree to exclusive issue relations with Morgan Stanley until IBM rebelled in 1979.

9 A good example is Bankers Trust which has moved far away from its traditional banking business. In 1993 loans accounted for only 16% of total assets, compared to trading account assets representing 48%.

For the 10 largest US commercial banks, trading account assets increased from 4.8% of total assets in 1986 to 10.3% in 1993 (*Federal Reserve Bulletin*, June 1996). Among the seven major US money-centre banks, interest income declined as a share of total revenues from nearly 80% in 1987 to less than 50% in 1993. During the same period, trading income doubled to 19% of total revenue.

10 As early as 1941, the SEC promulgated Rule U-50 mandating competitive bidding for public utility holding company issues (in 1944, the Interstate Commerce Commission enacted a similar ruling for railroads). Similarly, the Justice Department filed suit in 1947 against 17 investment banks and their trade group, handling about 70% of Wall Street underwritings, and charged them with conspiracy to monopolise underwriting in violation of antitrust laws. Throughout the post-war years the SEC has earned its credibility through tough enforcement actions and an unwillingness to compromise. Famous cases of insider trading involved Dennis Levine of Drexel Burnham Lambert, who had pleaded guilty in 1986 and helped to nail down Ivan Boesky, who was fined US$100 million and sentenced to three years jail. In March 1989, Michael Milken and two of his colleagues at Drexel were indicted on numerous counts of criminal racketeering, securities fraud and other crimes. Drexel paid a record US$650 million fine for securities fraud and other felonies, subsequently leading to its demise. More recent, spectacular SEC cases involve Nasdaq trading procedures and security sales to Orange County.

11 The SEC has proved to be unwilling, for example, to compromise on its capital requirements in its negotiations with the Basle Committee.

12 As a counterpart shareholders' equity in the Daimler-Benz balance sheet grew from DM18.9 billion at June 1993 under German rules to DM26.6 billion under US rules through market evaluations of "hidden reserves".

13 "Shareholder value" is slowly gaining importance in Germany. Daimler-Benz, Deutsche Telekom, Hoechst and other leading firms are accepting the "diktat" of US stock exchange evaluation and the requisite of transparency in accounting.

14 Germany and Japan in 1994 with, however, lesser penalties for offenders.

15 The first US pension fund to venture into equities was AT&T's in 1958. In the same year, the first American equity mutual fund was created, the US$221 million "One William Street Fund", founded by Lehman Brothers.

16 Total assets of the 300 largest US institutional investors rose from 30% of GDP in 1975 (US$535 billion) to more than 110% of GDP in 1993 (US$7.2 trillion).

17 Mutual funds are becoming more aggressive shareholders than, for example, pension funds, as illustrated by Fidelity, the biggest shareholder of Chrysler by end-1995 and the pressure placed on Chase Manhattan Bank from the mutual funds to break-up or merge before it merged with Chemical Bank. Mutual funds have become important players in the market for corporate control because they are under pressure to show short-term results and, more importantly, because the size of the larger funds makes it increasingly difficult simply to move into or out of investments without attracting attention and moving prices against them. They have been forced into the role of strategic investors, a role likely to grow over time.

18 In 1997 the newly formed financial service group announced the launch of a direct banking business over the Internet using the Discover credit card (48 million cardholders) brand name.

19 It is interesting to note that German commercial law prohibits advertising for mutual funds which involves comparisons of fund performance.

20 There are numerous studies to support this statement. A recent study by Gruber (1996) finds that standard common stock funds underperformed the market by 1.99% per year between 1989 and 1994.

21 In Venezuela the 1994–95 banking débâcle forced the government to take over 17 banks out of 41 and cost 18% of the country's GDP. In Argentina some 300 banks have been liquidated or rescued in the past two decades. The 1980–82 collapse cost 55% of GDP. Not one bank in Mexico has collapsed in five decades—at an unknown but certainly very high cost for the taxpayer (Caprio and Klingebiel 1996).

22 S&Ls obtain resources from short-term deposits and lend for long-term mortgages. When interest rates increase their funding costs increase, whilst, except for variable rate mortgages, their revenues only adjust to higher rates at the margin. To compensate for such losses as occurred during the early 1980s when interest rates reached historic levels, they invested in high-yielding junk bonds and Latin American loans (relaxation of regulatory constraints on asset allocation turned out to be a serious policy mistake). When both experienced problems many of the aggressively managed S&Ls went under. Had there been no deposit insurance, depositors would probably have monitored the lending practices of these institutions more closely.

23 Hedge funds are generally unregulated by the Investment Companies Act because they keep the number of investors below 100 or they are located off-shore. The vast majority of hedge funds have capital below US$100 million, and only about a dozen have assets currently exceeding US$1 billion. The largest hedge funds had assets between US$6 billion and US$10 billion in 1994.

24 Four well-known macro funds—Quantum Fund, Tiger Management, Steinhardt Partners, and Ardsley Partners—had net assets of almost US$25 billion mid-1994.

25 *Federal Reserve Bulletin* (June 1966, p. 483).

26 I do not wish to suggest that all is well with US finance. The social gains from fierce take-over battles are debated in the scientific literature. On a more pedestrian level, any foreign visitor who has tried to cash a non-US dollar cheque at any US bank is struck by a vision of incomprehensible inefficiency.

27 Trading strategies such as stop-loss sales or dynamic hedging rely on market liquidity for their success, that is, that there is always a counter-party for their buy or sell orders and that their order does not move the market price. For any one small player in the capital market, the assumption of a liquid market with price continuity is probably reasonable. When all the selling strategies are triggered simultaneously, however, they have proved to be unfeasible. Even the most liquid markets, like treasury bills, may experience pricing discontinuities. The rest of the market participants may have no knowledge of the existence of such traders because their call orders lie buried in the future. They will come to the market only if triggered by the proper contingency. When the time comes for those massive sales to occur, the sellers may find no buyers prepared to take the other side of the trade at the last reported price, and the price may suddenly collapse. A lack of liquidity in the market may cause a snowballing of sell orders. If the price falls dramatically below its fundamental value due to these liquidity problems, further sales may be triggered. Banks may make margin calls on their loans to security holders and dealers, and cancel lines of credit. This may either bankrupt the holders and dealers or force a sale of their securities, further depressing prices.

28 For a discussion of the impact of available dealer liquid resources on securities market spreads, see Grossman and Miller (1988).

29 The payment of fees for the use of such credit lines serves as compensation to banks for maintaining reserves and for satisfying regulatory capital requirements and other restrictions necessary to access their lines of credit to a central bank. Such payments are reflected in the market yields of money market instruments. Securities whose dealers or issuers rarely expect to draw on bank lines of credit to provide liquidity are most liquid, and this is expressed in relatively low market yields. Securities whose dealers expect frequently to use bank lines are relatively less liquid, and the higher probability of having to incur the costs of using the reserves of the banking system manifests itself in a relatively higher yield, or equivalently in the haircut in price, for such securities.

A liquid, securitised money market provides a perfect substitute for both bank liabilities and assets. It, therefore, allows a banking system to shrink or to expand its balance sheet so that reserve requirements are non-binding that is, banks hold the amount of reserves that minimise the total costs of effecting end-of-day net settlement of all the payments generated from inside and outside the banking system, including from the money markets.

30 Central bank *monetary policy* can be defined as activities that affect the supply and demand for the monetary base, with a goal to stabilise the price level, an exchange rate, or some other macroeconomic aggregate. *Banking policy*, on the other hand, comprises activities that involve changes in the composition of a central bank's assets and liabilities to provide funding that stabilises some class of asset values or yields through central bank funding. In addition, supervision and regulation and provision of clearinghouse and other technical facilities should also be considered under the rubric of banking policy. Thus, lender-of-last-resort operations that are sterilised in the open market are banking policy.

31 To take a less extreme example, in August 1991, US securities' dealers were forced to draw on their lines of credit with the money centre banks after the repo rate had unexpectedly risen to levels that could have impaired the solvency of some of the

dealers. The sudden increase in demand for funds sent banks into the Fed funds market, which drove the Fed funds rate above 30% and induced the Federal Reserve to lend in excess of US$3 billion through the discount window in order to preserve orderly markets.

32  Other countries, e.g., the UK. and Germany, have end-of-day net settlement systems. For some, market participants believe that there are implicit central bank settlement guarantees; others have an unwinding provision in case of a failure to settle. Many are now considering a switch to gross settlement with fully collateralised overdrafts, i.e., a system with little uncovered daylight credit—though it is not clear how compatible such a restrictive system is with the demands of institutions and practices requiring a high volume of payments. For example, TARGET— the future system for Wholesale Euro transactions (the future single European currency)—is a real time gross settlements system.

33  Careful recent analyses are provided by Borio and Van den Bergh (1993), Folkerts-Landau et al. (1996) and Rossi (1997).

34  For example, in a wholesale payments system with daylight credit and settlement finality, it may be possible for a bank to send a sufficient volume of payments messages to exceed the value of its assets.

35  Assuming the responsibility of lender-of-last-resort, of course, also entails major macroeconomic policy risks. If the central bank mistakes a fundamental decline of asset prices for a temporary liquidity problem and intervenes, it will either have to weaken the capital of the banking system; countenance price inflation; or absorb some loss itself. By erroneously adding liquidity to a market when the price of the security is higher than its ultimate level, the central bank expands reserves and pressures banks to lend against the securities. If the security price eventually falls as central bank liquidity is withdrawn, market makers will go bankrupt, leaving bad loans on the books of the banks and reducing bank capital. Depositors' confidence in banks will furthermore diminish, and banks will be less able to provide liquidity services in the future. To reduce the damage to the banks of this mistake, the central bank may decide not to contract reserves to their normal level. This leads to a permanent expansion in the money stock and to a rise in the price level and ultimately to a general welfare loss.

36  Large universal banks with a European or even a global vocation have picked up the challenge by transferring their market-related international business to London, where the largest Dutch, German and Swiss banks have acquired British merchant banks.

37  Indeed, from 1988 to 1991 average deviations from 30-day moving averages of overnight rates in the United States, Germany, Japan, and the United Kingdom were 14.4, 15.2, 8.2, and 30.9 basis points, respectively. It is noteworthy that the United States and Germany usually considered polar opposites in the extent to which the central bank supports financial market liquidity, display such similar volatilities in overnight rates. Kasman (1992, p. 21).

38  Reform efforts are currently underway in several countries to limit the central bank's exposure by developing continuous time gross settlement systems.

39  Large banks can, however, count on central bank support or bail-out by the ministry of finance, as amply demonstrated in recent years in France and Italy. The same is true in Japan except that the asset bubble of the 1980s and its bursting since 1989 have created financial fragility for the entire financial system.

40  Against this backdrop of the global dynamics of financial innovation and central bank policy, the European Community (EC) is in the process of uniting its national financial markets into a single financial and monetary area with the European

Central Bank (ECB) at the centre. Given the primacy attached to price level stability, the statute governing the role of the ECB seems to foresee a narrow role for the central bank in financial markets. In light of the convergence in EC financial markets towards structures prevalent in the dollar system, can such an aloof position be maintained over the longer run? Probably not. The EC will be confronted with the same difficult choice as other countries.

41 This is because the assignment of responsibility for the supervision of the banking system should avoid intra-agency conflict of interest. Such conflict would arise if the central bank puts its resources at stake, while another agency is responsible for establishing the solvency of central bank debtors. For example, the supervision of the banking system, i.e., the assessment of the market value of banking assets, could be subject to political pressure leading to a delay in corrective measures. An independent central bank with its own resources at stake is more likely to assess the solvency of potential borrowers sufficiently accurately to protect its own resources.

# 3

# Dramatic Events

## How George Soros sees it

*The following is a shortened transcript of testimony given by George Soros to the United States House of Representatives Committee on Banking, Finance and Urban Affairs, on 13 April 1994.*

I must state at the outset that I am in fundamental disagreement with the prevailing wisdom. The generally accepted theory is that financial markets tend toward equilibrium and, on the whole, discount the future correctly. I operate using a different theory, according to which financial markets cannot possibly discount the future correctly because they do not merely discount the future; they help to shape it. In certain circumstances, financial markets can affect the so-called fundamentals which they are supposed to reflect. When that happens, markets enter into a state of dynamic disequilibrium and behave quite differently from what would be considered normal by the theory of efficient markets. Such boom/bust sequences do not arise very often, but when they do they can be very disruptive, exactly because they affect the fundamentals of the economy.

The time is not sufficient to elaborate on my theory. I have done so in my book *The Alchemy of Finance*. The only theoretical point I want to make here is that a boom/bust sequence can develop only if the market is dominated by trend-following behaviour. By trend-following behaviour, I mean people buying in response to a rise in prices and selling in response to a fall in prices in a self-reinforcing manner. Lop-sided trend-following behaviour is necessary to produce a violent market crash, but it is not sufficient to bring one about.

The key question you need to ask, then, is: "What generates trend-following behaviour?" Hedge funds may be a factor and you are justified in taking a look at them, although, as far as my hedge funds are concerned, you are looking in the wrong place. There are at least two other factors which I consider much more relevant and deserving of closer scrutiny. One is the role of institutional investors in general and of mutual funds in particular; the second is the role of derivative instruments.

The trouble with *institutional investors* is that their performance is usually measured relative to their peer group and not by an absolute yardstick. This makes them trend followers by definition. In the case of mutual funds, this tendency is reinforced by the fact that they are open-ended. When money is pouring in, they tend to maintain less-than-normal cash balances because they anticipate further inflows. When money is pouring out, they need to raise cash to take care of redemptions. There is nothing new about this, but mutual funds have grown tremendously, even more than hedge funds, and they have many new and inexperienced shareholders who have never invested in the stock market before.

The trouble with *derivative instruments* is that those who issue them usually protect themselves against losses by engaging in so-called delta, or dynamic, hedging. Dynamic hedging means, in effect, that if the market moves against the issuer, the issuer is forced to move in the same direction as the market, and thereby amplify the initial price disturbance. As long as price changes are continuous, no great harm is done, except perhaps to create higher volatility, which in turn increases the demand for derivative instruments. But if there is an overwhelming amount of dynamic hedging done in the same direction, price movements may become discontinuous. This raises the spectre of financial dislocation. Those who need to engage in dynamic hedging, but cannot execute their orders, may suffer catastrophic losses.

This is what happened in the stock market crash of 1987. The main culprit was the excessive use of portfolio insurance. Portfolio insurance was nothing but a method of dynamic hedging. The authorities have since introduced regulations, so-called "circuit breakers", which render portfolio insurance impractical, but other instruments which rely on dynamic hedging have mushroomed. They play a much bigger role in the interest rate market than in the stock market, and it is the role in the interest rate market which has been most turbulent in recent weeks.

Dynamic hedging has the effect of transferring risk from customers to the market makers and when market makers all want to delta hedge in the same direction at the same time, there are no takers on the other side and the market breaks down.

The explosive growth in derivative instruments holds other dangers. There are so many of them, and some of them are so esoteric, that the risks involved may not be properly understood even by the most sophisticated of investors. Some of these instruments appear to be specifically designed to enable institutional investors to take gambles which they would otherwise not be permitted to take. For example, some bond funds have invested in synthetic bond issues which carry a 10 or 20-fold multiple of the normal risk within defined limits. And some other instruments offer exceptional returns because they carry the seeds of a total wipe-out. It was instruments of this sort which forced the liquidation of a US$600 million fund specialising in so-called "toxic waste", or the residue of Collateralized Mortgage Obligations that generated a selling climax in the United States bond market on 4 April 1994.

The issuers of many of these derivative instruments are commercial and investment banks. In the case of a meltdown, the regulatory authorities may find themselves obliged to step in to preserve the integrity of the system. It is in that light that the authorities have both a right and an obligation to supervise and regulate derivative instruments.

Generally, *hedge funds* do not act as issuers or writers of derivative instruments. They are more likely to be customers. Therefore, they constitute less of a risk to the system than the dynamic hedgers at the derivatives desks of financial intermediaries. Please do not confuse dynamic hedging with hedge funds. They have nothing in common except the word "hedge".

I am not here to offer a blanket defence for hedge funds. Nowadays the terms is applied so indiscriminately that it covers a wide range of activities. The only thing they have in common is that the managers are compensated on the basis of performance and not as a fixed percentage of assets under management.

Our type of hedge fund invests in a wide range of securities and diversifies its risks by hedging, leveraging and operating in many different markets. It acts more like a sophisticated private investor than an institution handling other people's money. Since it is rewarded on absolute performance, it provides a healthy antidote to the trend-following behaviour of institutional investors.

But the fee structure of hedge funds is not perfect. Usually there is an asymmetry between the upside and the downside. The managers take a share of the profits, but not of the losses; the losses are usually carried forward. As a manager slips into minus territory, he has a financial inducement to increase the risk to get back into positive fee territory, rather than to retrench as he ought to. This feature was the undoing of the hedge fund industry in the late 1960s, just as I entered the business.

I am proud to say that the Quantum Group of Funds, with which I am associated, is exempt from this weakness because the managers have a substantial ownership interest in the funds they manage. That is a key point. Our ownership is a direct and powerful incentive to practice sound money management. At Soros Fund Management, we have an operating history stretching over 25 years during which there was not a single occasion when we could not meet a margin call. We use options and more exotic derivatives sparingly. Our activities are trend bucking rather than trend following. We try to catch new trends early and in later stages we try to catch trend reversals. Therefore, we tend to stabilise rather than destabilise the market. We are not doing this as a public service. It is our style of making money.

So I must reject any assertion or implication that our activities are harmful or destabilising. That leaves, however, one other area of concern: we do use borrowed money and we could cause trouble if we failed to meet a margin call. In our case, the risk is remote, but I cannot speak for all hedge funds.

*Source*: Soros (1995), pp. 311–15
Reprinted by permission of John Wiley & Sons, Inc.

A s argued in Chapter 2, the Americanisation of global finance is a process influenced by many factors. But one central element of it is a more "knowledge" vs. relationship based approach, helping customers to achieve the best return/risk trade-off. In this respect derivatives play an essential role and this is where US institutions are particularly dominating.

Most people have become aware of the importance of derivatives only by reading the headlines of reports on major financial troubles involving derivatives one way or another. To build upon this awareness, this chapter draws lessons from a more detailed analysis of these famous cases, before embarking on a more structured and systematic presentation of derivatives in the next chapters.

Apart from drawing the lessons, this chapter also serves the important purpose of presenting a variety of risk-management strategies and products in a non-technical way and within the context of a real-life situation.

During recent years derivatives have hit the headlines of the financial press for essentially three reasons. The first is the extraordinary spread and growth of the market. In that process some banks have transformed themselves from traditional bankers to specialists with heavy involvement in derivative products. They, and a flurry of small, specialised boutiques, have at times reported phenomenal gains. Among specialised firms are "hedge funds", the most famous of which is the Quantum Fund run by George Soros. In the crisis of the European Monetary System George Soros staged a bet against the British pound using forward contracts that secured a gain of US$1 billion in less than a week, and an avalanche of criticism and jealousy.

The second reason is a series of spectacular losses made with derivative transactions and complaints by end-users about having been misled by their bankers. We should, however, be aware that spectacular losses are only the tip of the iceberg. Not making the headlines are millions of deals providing economic gains to hedgers or speculators fulfilling a private and social purpose as will be demonstrated in Chapter 4.

None of these "accidents" has led to a global financial crisis. In a sense, failures are normal in any fast-growing industry and especially in this one as derivatives can be used for (complicated) hedge operations *and* for speculation. Nevertheless, regulators and central bankers are concerned and this is the third reason for frequent headlines. Regulators are a large step behind the evolution of derivative markets and some of the débâcles demonstrated the need for greater transparency, better controls and international co-operation.

In this chapter I also discuss the major headline cases because they are full of lessons for the regulatory responses, examined in Part III. I chose the cases according to several criteria. First, derivatives must have been at the centre stage. This excludes the failure of Drexel, Burnham Lambert in 1990 which had more to do with junk bonds, insider trading and problems in the payment system.[1] Second, I only discuss major débâcles. This criterion excludes the myriad of firms making losses with derivatives without their existence being threatened. I, therefore, do not discuss the case of ABN Amro New York when in 1991 a trader hid his losses (in the end US$70 million) with OTC options (for which daily prices were not available) by manipulating a key input into option valuation, namely the volatility measure. (In 1997 a similar loss, amounting to US$125 million, affected NatWest Markets, National Westminster Bank's investment banking arm and contributed to a downsizing of the firm.) I include, however, the Procter & Gamble, Gibson Greeting Cards and Mead Corporation cases not so much because derivative losses threatened their existence, but because they illustrate the problems experienced by final users and because these cases threw another light on Bankers Trust, and seriously damaged its reputation as a first-class specialist. Third, a case had to be a recent one in order to provide information that has not yet become common knowledge. I, therefore, do not discuss the infamous Herstatt case of 1974. Herstatt had lost heavily in foreign exchange speculation, using forward contacts, created settlement problems in the payment system and caused substantial losses to a German and Swiss counter-party.

One strong lesson that emerges from several of these débâcles and that can no longer be ignored is that OTC derivatives pose very specific and huge problems. Neither the Bankers Trust, nor Orange County case would have arisen with exchange-traded instruments. I shall discuss this lesson seriously in Chapter 9.

# 1. THE 1987 STOCK MARKET CRASH

**The Facts**

Figure 3.1 shows the evolution of major equity indexes in real terms. From a historic record level in 1972, the deflated US index declined to half its value in 1982 before starting to increase again and reaching the level of 1972 in October 1987. However, in 1987 long-term interest rates were much higher than in 1972 and the difference between the yield on government bonds and on stocks increased steadily during 1987, as interest rates increased and equity yields declined due to rising stock prices. In early October, the yield on 30-year US government bonds rose above 10% for the first time since the end of 1985. A correction seemed unavoidable and, with interest rates rising, it could only come about through falling stock prices.

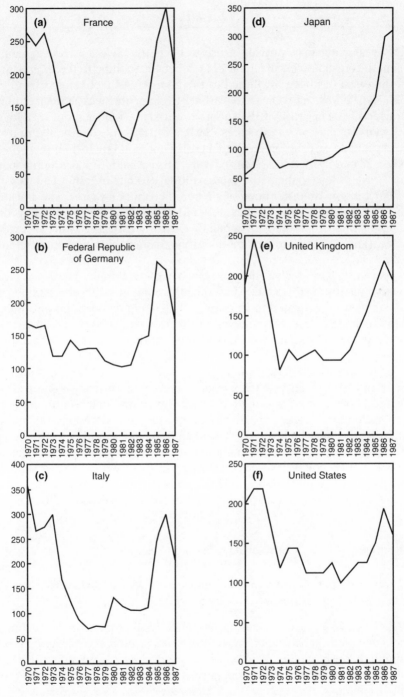

*Note:* Index of stock prices in local currency terms, deflated by composite GNP deflator, where composite deflators are averages for individual countries weighted by the average US dollar value of their respective GNPs over the preceding three years.

**Figure 3.1** Major Industrial Countries: Stock Prices in Real Terms, 1970–87
*Source:* International Monetary Fund

This reasoning may provide a useful background, but is too general to explain the crash that occurred on 19 October. In addition to these fundamentals, the crash has been attributed to the interplay of technological and psychological factors, as well as to various trading practices and institutional characteristics. The crash of 19 October resulted in a loss of about 28% for the stock markets in the United States (S&P 500). This was double the previous record of a 12.8% drop on 26 October 1929 and still larger than the two-day drop on 28 and 29 October 1929 of 24.5%. More than US$500 billion in paper value—a sum close to the entire gross national product of Italy—had vanished on 19 October in an order flood of a record 608 million shares. The crash was truly global. The United States suffered the largest single one-day drop among the major markets, but Japan dropped by 15%, the United Kingdom by 11% (and 12% on the next day) and the Sydney exchange plummeted by nearly 25%.

Apparently, large-scale selling in New York was initially limited to only a few large institutional traders. Subsequently, computerised programme trading systems were activated in an effort to hedge equity portfolio positions by selling stock index futures whenever prices in spot markets were falling. Stock index trading has been blamed for turning a "market correction" into a severe crash.

The role of stock index trading on 19 October remains a subject of controversy. Proponents of index trading stress the efficiency and speed with which markets process information. It thereby allows markets to find a new equilibrium more quickly, even if prices may be more volatile in the process. Critics argue that whenever stock prices crash, index trading can lead to a disruption of the price determination system. On 19 October, for example, such a situation could have occurred because there was an excess supply of stock to sell in futures markets. This excess supply led to a liquidity crisis, which in turn led to price discontinuities, creating further illiquidity.

**Did Futures Markets Cause or Amplify the Crash?**

In a report prepared under the chairmanship of Merton Miller (Miller 1991) the following conclusions were reached:

1. The crash of 19 October did not originate in the futures markets, but the selling wave hit the cash (New York) and futures (Chicago) markets simultaneously. The perception of a price decline preceding in the futures markets was due to the different procedures followed in the two markets at their openings. At the New York Stock Exchange (NYSE) the huge overnight imbalance of sell orders had delayed the opening of many of the leading stocks in the S&P 500 index. The prices for these stocks used in

calculating the publicly reported index value on the morning of 19 October were the last available quotes from the previous Friday's close. By contrast, the futures prices at the CME reflected the Monday morning information.

2. Whilst some pressure from the selling of futures contracts by portfolio insurers and other institutional investors was indeed transmitted back to the cash market by index arbitrage, the equivalent of 85 million shares was absorbed by participants in the CME.

3. Portfolio insurance selling played no significant role on 19 October. Price falls as large and rapid as those in the United States occurred in other countries (see Figure 3.1), where portfolio insurance and futures trading was much less important than in the United States. It is estimated that on 19 October portfolio insurance sales of futures represented between 20% and 30% of the share equivalent of total sales on the New York Stock Exchange (NYSE). Hence, it was not a dominant influence.

4. Index arbitrage programme trading was not responsible for chaotic market conditions. In fact, academic research is unanimous in failing to find a relationship between any measure of volatility and any measure of programme trading. The Brady Report concluded that the markets performed most chaotically precisely when the arbitrage link between them was broken.[2]

5. At times the margining process of the exchanges is seen as a potential policy tool. For example, the Brady Report suggested that the control of leveraged investments in stocks is necessary to curb speculative excesses.

   It is, however, noteworthy that on 19 October, the day that saw the largest one-day price crash ever recorded in the S&P 500 futures market, no trader suffered losses because of a contract default by a counter-party, no clearinghouse failed, and no futures clearing firm failed to meet its obligations to its customers.

6. It is also a fact, however, that liquidity was reduced during the key days. The difficulty experienced by US securities markets in processing the high volumes of trades caused by inaccuracies in the displayed prices of both individual stocks and stock indexes, resulted in price uncertainties which reduced liquidity of the futures markets. One piece of evidence is the larger-than-normal buy-sell spreads observed for these two days.

When the crash occurred the tendency for money centre banks to limit the provision of credit to securities firms threatened to force some of them into default and to exacerbate the crisis. The Fed's quick decision to make all the necessary liquidity available was certainly a key factor in preventing a sector-wide crisis.

At the time, margin calls were collected through four settlement banks in Chicago. Owing to the exceptionally large margin payments, the settlement banks were unwilling to confirm members' payments to the clearing-house until they had actually received funds from the New York banks with which the large clearing firms maintained their principal banking and credit relationships. At the same time, the New York banks were already concerned by rumours regarding the liabilities of their customers and had little time to fully understand the exposures that these securities firms had across their lines of business. Telephone calls placed by officials of the Federal Reserve Bank of New York to major New York City banks helped to assure a continuing supply of credit to the clearing-house members. This experience illustrates the argument of Chapter 2, that modern financial systems are liquidity-driven and therefore need an ultimate, unconstrained supplier of liquidity in emergency situations.[3]

## 2. THE EMS CRISIS AND THE ROLE OF THE HEDGE FUNDS

The European Union is a strongly and increasingly integrated group of 15 countries, with the ultimate goal of a confederal or even federal union. In 1993 a single market for goods and services came into being; people and capital can move freely throughout the Union equipped with an extensive legal, social and policy framework. It is the most advanced and ambitious project of economic and political integration in the history of independent states.

When the fixed-exchange-rate system of Bretton Woods ended in 1971, market integration in the Community of the six initial founders was already sufficiently advanced to make flexible exchange rates among member currencies unattractive. Experiments with several unsuccessful fixed exchange rate arrangements finally led to the creation of the European Monetary System (EMS) in 1978 under the leadership of French President Valery Giscard d'Estaing and Germany's Chancellor Helmut Schmidt.

The centrepiece of the EMS is a fixed exchange rate mechanism (ERM) with narrow intervention bands of +/− 2¼% prior to 1 August 1993. In theory, the EMS is centred on the ECU—an ex-novo currency based on a basket of national currencies of the Union—but, in practice, it is anchored to the DM. The problem of any fixed exchange rate system is that, apart from the anchor country, all other participants have to give up their monetary independence and must subordinate monetary policy to the exchange rate target. Failure to do so results in exchange rate misalignments and eventually in devaluation (or revaluation) of the exchange rate.

During the initial years of the EMS from 1978 to 1987 exchange rate adjustments were frequent. But by the beginning of 1987, convergence of inflation rates had progressed remarkably, although far from completely, and exchange rates were maintained stable until September 1992. In the meantime, some currencies which initially remained outside the ERM, such as the British pound, had entered the ERM. When Britain joined the ERM in 1990 at a rate of DM2.90 to the pound there was extensive discussion as to whether this was the right level. Independent economists had argued that a lower level, such as DM 2.50, would have better reflected the competitiveness of the British economy.

Italy, Portugal, Spain and Ireland managed to reduce their inflation rates, which remained, however, well above the German level, as did their interest rates. All these countries maintained capital controls to prevent capital out-flows. In fact, Spain and Ireland experienced substantial capital inflows as interest rates were attractive and as they were seen as catching up with the rest of Europe. Their external trade, however, suffered from the real appreciation brought about by higher inflation rates.

By 1992, the United Kingdom, Italy and Spain had visibly over-valued exchange rates, deteriorating foreign trade balances, sluggish growth and rising unemployment. The voices of those claiming a devaluation to stimulate growth became ever louder. The German Bundesbank was in favour of a realignment, but refused to revalue the DM against all other currencies in the ERM.

There were also the effects of German unification. Unification, by itself, did not necessarily require a revaluation of the DM. But many economists argued that it did, as Germany had to channel resources from its exporting activity to rebuilding East Germany and to do that a revaluation was seen as necessary. But this is far from certain. Who would expect the US dollar to *appreciate* if the United States were to take over Cuba or Mexico?[4] It was the Bundesbank's monetary policy that put pressure on the EMS. The Bundesbank saw the danger of increased inflation inherent in the refinancing of East Germany through sharply increased fiscal deficits. To stem that risk the Bundesbank increased interest rates, forcing other members of the EMS to follow suit. These countries now had overvalued exchange rates *and* higher interest rates. Those most successful in lowering inflation, to levels below the German inflation rate, experienced real interest rates far above those of Germany. The reasons for this were, first, because their inflation rate was lower and, second, because a potential revaluation of the DM forced a risk premium into their nominal interest rates which then remained above German rates.

Rising unemployment, high real interest rates and overvalued exchange rates represented political dynamite and the EMS rates were, clearly, not sustainable. Market participants started to wage against the most misaligned currencies, mainly using derivatives, following the Danish negative referendum on the Maastricht Treaty in June 1992. The Maastricht Treaty enshrined the goal of replacing national currencies in the Union by a single currency, at the earliest in 1997 and at the latest by 1999. This provided a sort of forward-looking anchor. When trouble arose in the ratification process, the EMS suffered even more in terms of political credibility because confidence in the single currency goal suffered.

The first reactions of defence were to increase short-term interest rates, already high as a consequence of the Bundesbank's determination to minimise the unification effects on Germany's inflation. Given that exchange rates were not in line with economic fundamentals, that interest rates were at unacceptably high levels and the overall economic situation needed policy stimulation, rather than restraint, policy-makers in the countries attacked by speculation did the right thing: they gave up the exchange rate peg.

In September 1992 the British pound and the Italian lira left the EMS and depreciated on the markets, whilst the Spanish peseta, the Portuguese escudo and the Irish pound remained in the EMS but were devalued. Speculation did not subside, however, after the first round of devaluations and lasted until August 1993—when the admissible fluctuation band around central parities was widened to +/– 15%.

Betting against an exchange rate parity is, of course, not very risky, as long as the fluctuation margin around central parities is small (it was +/–2.25% before August 1993). A speculator will lose at most the spread between the minimum and the maximum rate (4.5% in the old EMS) if he sells the currency at its floor and has to repurchase it at its ceiling—a rather unlikely event. The real risk taken is much smaller and often close to zero whereas potential gains are huge.[5]

The two major exchange market crises of the EMS turmoil, the one of September 1992 and the other preceding the widening of the intervention bands of 1 August 1993, were, however, of a very different nature. According to market participants, unlike in September 1992, the biggest demand in July 1993 came from institutional investors eager to protect their bond portfolios. The big hedge funds were not involved in July. Liquidity in the spot market was maintained except for the Friday (30 July) before the decision to widen intervention margins, whereas disruptions were severe in September 1992. Volumes traded had fallen in July 1993 and spreads widened from the normal 5 basis points on a large deal to 20–25 basis points.

In the derivative markets, volatilities rose in July 1993 and some problems of liquidity were reported, but the market remained far more orderly than in September. For example, in the September crisis option traders found it impossible to delta hedge at certain times because of gaping markets and dramatic rises in overnight interest rates (in excess of 1000% for several currencies).[6]

As shown in Figure 3.2, in September 1992 the market was taken by surprise and implied volatility (see Glossary) shot up from 11% to over 20%. By contrast, the August event was fully anticipated. End of July implied volatility rose gently and dropped back immediately after 1 August.

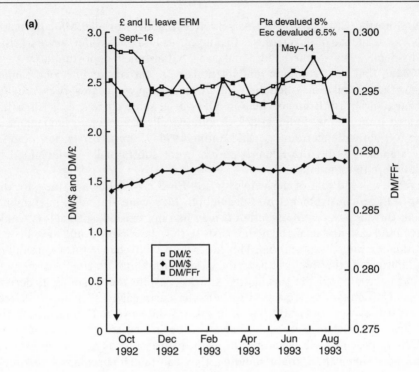

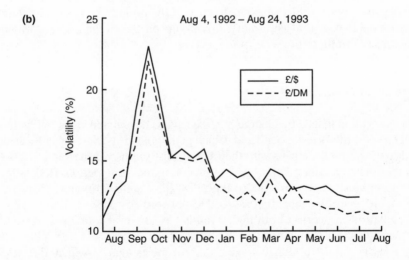

**Figure 3.2** (a) ERM: selected exchange rates, September 1992–August 1993; (b) 20-day implied volatility, 4 August–24 August, 1993

*Source*: mid- and end of month data; based on Risk magazine, Vol. 6, No. 9, Sep. 1993

Reproduced with permission

Before the EMS crisis the DM served as a hedge for all EMS currencies. The consequence of the crisis was that investors had to consider currency risks individually. This implied additional costs, but also new opportunities.

Given that the economic fundamentals were far out of line, one cannot argue that speculation killed the EMS. A correction was necessary even in the absence of a push from speculation. Of course, some currencies, such as the French franc, came under attack despite excellent economic fundamentals due to political uncertainties. And during 1994–95 some currencies, notably the Italian lira and the Spanish peseta, were substantially undervalued in relation to fundamentals.[7]

What was the role of derivatives in the EMS crisis? Because they are the most efficient instruments for speculation, they were the main instruments used. But they were not essential. If they had not existed, speculators would have used cash and incurred higher costs so that their gains would have been a bit smaller, but still substantial. The key fact is that exchange rates were out of equilibrium. If that had not been the case then mutual central bank support could have blunted the speculative attacks, despite the weapons of derivatives. The Bundesbank refused to help the currencies out of tilt, precisely because they were out of tilt. The Bundesbank did help the Banque de France because the exchange rate was judged to be in line with fundamentals. In addition, central banks can and do use forward agreements to support the currency. Given their credit standing, they can match speculators' volumes. But to do that and avoid an ultimate defeat with big exchange losses their strategy must be credible. Massive defence of the pound, the lira or the peseta would have lacked that credibility. Giving up on the exchange rate was the only sensible thing to do.

## More about Hedge Funds

A hedge fund managed by George Soros is said to have made US$1 billion from its bet against the British pound and gained great popularity. Subsequently, hedge funds have hit the headlines with their bet against the rise of the yen in 1994–95 and their bets on falling US interest rates during the same period. Both wagers were unsuccessful and some hedge funds lost huge sums of money. One of the largest, Steinhardt Partners (net assets US$4 billion), lost US$1 billion.

Regulators' concerns about hedge funds have several sources. High leverage through short-selling and extensive use of derivatives allegedly allows the larger hedge funds to launch wagers on currencies against which all but the most powerful central banks would be helpless. Moreover, given the dogged determination of hedge fund managers and their sophistication, they enjoy such a reputation as to be followed by herds of other investors, producing bandwagon effects. This allegedly allows hedge funds to drive markets. Whilst most of the time positions taken by hedge funds are not visible to market participants, major moves—such as George Soros' bet against the British pound—are too large to remain unnoticed. Moreover, at times the strategies pursued were even well advertised, such as Soros' move into the gold market and into the London real estate market.

Henry Gonzalez, the House Banking Committee Chairman, commented the reasons for holding hearings on the dangers posed by hedge funds as follows: "Hedge funds deserve extra scrutiny because their massive financial clout, fuelled by large credit lines from banks, is used for speculative purposes."[8] (Soros' views expressed at the hearings are contained in the introductory story.) The SEC has examined the management and trading activities of hedge funds to determine whether new regulations are needed.[9] And the Comptroller of the Currency increased scrutiny of national bank activities related to hedge funds.

The world's first hedge fund was launched some fifty years ago by Alfred Winslow Jones, a Wall Street investor. They have been around for a long time, but it was their recent growth that turned them into a power factor. Jones coined the term "hedge fund" because his investments were partly hedged. Hedging and leveraged position-taking has become much easier and cost effective with the development of derivatives. The rapid recent growth is depicted in Figure 3.3.

The typical hedge fund is, however, quite different from the few megafunds that have made the headlines. A typical hedge fund—of which there are over 3000 in the United States with an estimated US$160 billion or more under management[10]—is a private limited partnership, managing investments of

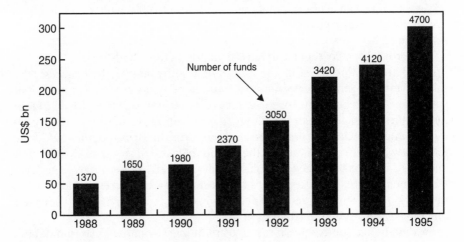

**Figure 3.3** World-wide hedge-fund assets
*Source*: Van Hedge Fund Advisers © *The Economist*, London

wealthy people. Minimum investments are on average US$375 000 and each partnership has no more than 99 investors, to escape SEC regulation. Funds are typically specialised. Most specialise in stock-picking, some in commodities or financial futures, other in leveraged bonds such as mortgage-backed securities, or currency trading. All use short-selling as a hedge (hence the name) and derivatives, either straight or embodied in leveraged securities. Fees charged to customers are more than handsome: typically management fees are 1% of assets on an annual basis and an incentive fee of 20% of profits (but no participation in losses). Some funds charge even more. Management invests their own funds for commitment. Their share is often as low as 3%, but can be considerably higher.

The earning potential has attracted some of Wall Streets' high-flyers into hedge funds, such as Leon Cooperman (Omega Advisors, net assets US$3 billion), a former research chief of Goldman Sachs and John Meriwether, a former star trader of Salomon Brothers (long-term capital, net assets US$2.5 billion).[11]

Under the partnership agreement, investors have to commit their funds for a minimum period of one to three years and can only sell at the end of each quarter. Therefore, hedge funds are not cursed with the problem of withdrawals in a declining market as are mutual funds, forced to unload stocks to meet redemptions by jittery investors and possibly accelerating a market plunge.

Interestingly, hedge funds have done best in declining markets due to their short selling via derivatives. The S&P 500 marginally outperformed the average of US hedge funds in the bull years of 1989 and 1991. By contrast, in 1990 when the S&P 500 declined and in 1992 and 1993 when returns were 6% or less, hedge funds generated 6% in 1990, 17% in 1992 and 23% in 1993.[12]

The most successful hedge funds have been the macro funds (betting on global trends of commodity, currency, bond and stock markets). During 1989–93 they achieved an average annual return of close to 40% with a probability of loss in any particular year of 2%. The worst performers were specialised short-selling funds with an average return of 6% and a loss probability of 40%.

Is there a specific regulatory problem for hedge funds? Since they are limited partnerships investing the money of wealthy people, their successes or failures may engender envy or pity, but there is no reason to curb their activities. Any regulatory concerns must rest on one of the following arguments. First, that the leverage they generate can move markets. This argument is unconvincing. George Soros did not force the British pound out of the EMS. It was the overvaluation of the pound that wetted speculators' appetites and Soros and his team saw that perhaps more clearly than others. Whenever hedge funds misread market trends they lost money and were unable to move the market into their direction. Speculation as such is not bad for economic outcomes, as is argued in Chapter 4.

Second, hedge funds rely on massive credit lines from banks so that default of a major hedge fund could push a bank into difficulties. So far, at least, no major problem of that sort has arisen, although that does not prove anything.

It can, however, be argued that the risks taken by these funds are being exaggerated. Even in his bet against the British pound, George Soros only put a very small fraction of his total assets at risk.[13] Moreover, since the Quantum Fund had some open positions in pounds sterling, at least part of the short-selling of pounds was a hedge and not a purely speculative operation.

Steinhardt Partners lost US$1 billion, a very large sum of money, but only 25% of their net assets. The hedge funds managed by David Askin collapsed (see below) and investors lost their funds, but banks did not suffer.

**An Unexpected Victim of the EMS Crisis**

A postscript to the EMS crisis of 1992–93 emerged in 1996 when it became known that, in an attempt to manage more actively Belgium's very high public debt (130% of GDP), a series of swaps had been concluded by the Belgian treasury with several American security houses before the EMS crises. The swaps (receiving interest in Italian lira, paying German interest rates) generated a substantial gain on interest rate spreads (about 400 basis points), but were exposed to exchange risk. As long as exchange rates were stable, these swaps were extremely attractive. But then came the EMS crisis, with a depreciation of the Italian lira of more than 50% with respect to the DM. The book loss became enormous on a maximum notional outstanding of close to US$2.5 billion. The civil servant in charge then sold dollar options to obtain premium income with which he acquired options to hedge his currency risk, as well as knock-out swaps and quanto swaps. In 1996 the marked-to-market loss of the entire position was over US$1 billion and a loss of US$150 million had already been realised. The Minister of Finance, one of the most experienced and respected in the world, had to respond to Parliament and the Court of Auditors on three charges: (i) the appropriateness of letting one single person take the responsibility for such operations, with simultaneous control over front- and back-office; (ii) the lack of any tool to assess or monitor risk; and (iii) inappropriate accounting of risks. This event was only one of many, but it created a serious political crisis.

# 3. METALLGESELLSCHAFT: IN THE RED OR IN THE BLACK?

**The Facts**

In late 1993 MG Corporation (MGRM), the US oil-trading subsidiary of Metallgesellschaft (MG), one of Germany's largest industrial firms (33.8%

owned by Deutsche Bank and Dresdner Bank, the two largest German banks), reported losses of US$1.3 billion on its positions in oil futures (more precisely, crude oil, heating oil and gasoline) and swaps. These losses exceeded half of MG's capital and only a massive US$1.9 billion rescue operation prevented MG from going into bankruptcy.

The losses were precipitated by MG's supervisory board's decision in December 1993 to liquidate MGRM's oil futures positions at a time when oil prices hit the bottom, and to liquidate the forward-supply contracts by waiving cancellation penalties and giving up (potential) unrealised gains that would have offset, at least partly, its derivative losses.

According to initial press reports and statements by MG board members, losses were interpreted as the result of massive speculation. This was, however, not the case, which makes the MG example all the more interesting.

MGRM sold forward-supply contracts that committed it to supplying about 160 million barrels of gasoline and heating oil over the next ten years at fixed prices (a total value of US$4 billion). These fixed prices were typically 3–5 dollars a barrel higher than prevailing spot prices at the time contracts were negotiated, independently of the length of the contracts.

Most of the forward delivery contracts were negotiated during the summer of 1993 when oil prices were low (US$17–19) and falling. End-users saw an attractive opportunity to lock-in low prices for the future and thus were willing to pay a premium of US$3–5, or 20% and more. Forward delivery contracts contained a cash-out option for counter-parties in case prices were to rise above the contractually fixed price.[14]

Fixed price forward delivery exposed MGRM to the risk of rising oil prices, initially eroding its premium and eventually causing severe losses. It therefore decided to hedge this risk with oil futures and swaps. Had MGRM been able to hedge its price risk successfully, it would have been able to generate a profit in excess of US$600 million (US$4 × 160 million).[15]

To assess MGRM's strategy, it is necessary to understand the risks faced by MGRM *even after hedging* the oil price risk:

- The contracts made with customers were for five or 10 years; futures contracts do exist up to 36 months, but the longer-dated contracts are illiquid. Most of MGRM's trading was in the near months. This made MGRM vulnerable to variations in the relative price of short and longer-term contracts.
- The strategy required MGRM to do a lot of trading. At its peak, MGRM's oil purchases equalled about 20% of the total open interest in the NYMEX crude oil futures contract. MGRM was heavily dependent on the continued liquidity of the market to roll over its position at reasonable costs.
- The oil products it was contracted to deliver were not identical to the products traded on the exchange. The company was at risk from variations in the prices of different oil products.

- Losses and gains on the future market appear as cash immediately; losses and gains on delivery contracts appear at the time of delivery. MGRM was vulnerable to fluctuations in funding costs.
- If oil prices fell (as they did), MGRM would be vulnerable to customers defaulting on their purchase commitments.

The strategy was, therefore, not free of risks, but, as I shall show, the concept was defensible.

The questions raised after the near-bankruptcy were: what was MGRM's hedging strategy?; what was the rollover risk?; was there a funding risk?; were alternative strategies available? I shall answer these questions in turn and then ask the key question: was the supervisory board's decision to liquidate the forward supply contracts together with the hedge position a rational one?

### What was the Hedging Strategy?

MGRM hedged the risk of rising energy prices with both short-dated oil futures contracts and swaps, entitling it to receive payments based upon floating oil prices while making fixed payments. Counter-parties were large swap dealers, such as banks. By the fourth quarter of 1993, MGRM held long futures equivalent to 55 million barrels and had swaps of 100–110 million barrels, virtually identical to its forward-supply commitments of 160 million barrels (a hedge ratio of 1).

As these futures and swap positions were in contracts with maturities of a few months, they had to be rolled forward periodically to maintain the hedge, less the amounts delivered to customers. Such a stack-and-roll strategy is only without costs if the price of oil for immediate delivery (nearby oil) is equal to the price of the futures contract (deferred-month oil), i.e., if the futures price curve is flat over the range of the hedge.

Markets in which nearby prices are above deferred-month prices are called *backwardation* markets. In such markets a strategy of continually rolling short-dated positions forward generates gains because old contracts are replaced by cheaper new contracts. A market in which nearby prices are below deferred-month prices are called *contango* market, which generate rollover losses.

The success of the rollover strategy—as compared to a perfect maturity match of forward deliveries—depends, therefore, on whether oil markets were going to be in backwardation or contango.

During 1993 oil futures markets went into a contango, causing losses for MGRM each time it rolled over its derivatives position forward. In addition, in late 1993 oil spot prices tumbled from US$19 per barrel in June to US$15, reducing the value of the derivatives position. Although this loss was offset by an increase in the (book) gains on the forward-delivery contracts, MGRM had to pay increasing margin calls. At this stage the MG Supervisory Board closed positions. A most unfortunate decision in hindsight, as already in 1994 oil prices increased and oil futures went into backwardation, as shown in Figure 3.4.

## Rollover Risk

MGRM suffered rollover losses because in 1993 oil futures markets were in contango, that is, every time an expired contract was replaced with a new one, a loss was realised. When deciding on the hedge strategy, they accepted that risk presumably because oil markets were historically more often in back-wardation than in contango, as shown in Figure 3.4 for the period 1986–94. Moreover, for that period, the average monthly rollover gain far exceeded the average rollover loss,[16] because there is no arbitrage-limiting boundary to restrict the amount of backwardation, that is, the potential gains, but available oil stocks provide a limit to potential losses.

Thus, on the basis of historical price patterns, MGRM could expect to make an additional profit by rolling its short-dated positions forward in time.[17] Of course, this is only true on average, not for limited periods of time. *The rollover losses of 1993 therefore stood a good chance of being offset during the remainder of the 10-year hedge strategy.* Thus, whilst MGRM's strategy was risky for any short period of time, it was defensible for a 10-year period and should have generated a net rollover gain.

There was, of course, the risk of failure during a protracted contango market and before the gains in a backwardation market could be obtained. Edwards and Canter (1995) estimate the standard deviation of the daily second-month basis for the 1983–92 period for oil at over US$0.80 per barrel, as compared to a mean rollover gain of US$0.25–US$0.45 per month—certainly a high risk. However, in terms of the price risk in its forward supply contracts, the rollover risk amounted only to about 15%.

Was the extended contango of 1993 predictable? Long contangos did occur in the past (see Figure 3.4), but what was unusual in 1993 was that *all* oil markets (crude oil, heating oil and gasoline) were in contango with high rollover costs.

In summary, past data provided reasonable support for the expectation of a rollover gain. However, for this expected result to materialise two conditions had to be satisfied. First, that the market structure be stable and that history repeats itself. Second, that MGRM be able to continue its hedging programme for a long enough period of time. This condition was perhaps the most critical one: continuation of the strategy was not only endangered by the losses of a prolonged contango, but also by the cash-out options in its forward delivery contracts, and by difficulties of funding.

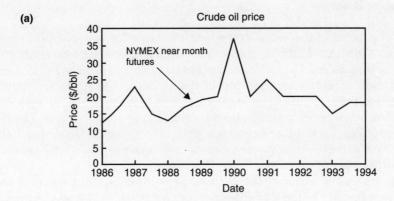

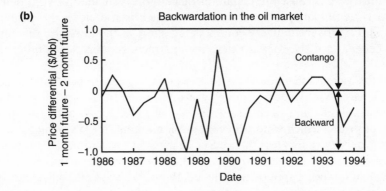

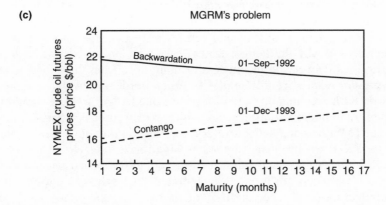

**Figure 3.4** Spot and future prices in crude oil market, 1986–94
*Source*: based on *Financial Times*, Finance 10 Supplement, 1997
Reproduced by permission of F.T. Pictures and Graphics

**Funding Risks**

Funding needs of the hedge strategy in 1993 arose for two reasons: to finance margin calls due to the decline in oil prices and rollover losses due to the contango markets. The two costs are not independent as falling prices are an indication of excess supplies and in the absence of spot market shortages contango price relationships are normal (see French 1986). The bulk of the funding needs arose, however, from meeting margin requirements. The financial problems caused by margin calls were exacerbated in December 1993 by NYMEX's decision to double the normal margin levels and to revoke MGRM's "hedge exemption".

As the fall in value of the derivatives position was accompanied by an increase in value of the forward-supply contracts, MGRM could, in principle, have borrowed against the collateral of its more valuable forward delivery contracts. A funding problem could only have arisen if either the unrealised gains in the forward delivery contracts fell short of the losses on the derivatives hedge, or if the forward delivery contracts contained a counter-party risk.

Did the increase in value of the forward delivery contracts match the derivatives losses? As the hedge strategy was one-to-one, such a result would only be achievable if there were also a one-to-one relationship between forward and spot prices, which is not the case in oil markets. A US$1 change in spot prices generally causes less than US$1 changes in forward prices, as contemporary changes in supply and demand have a larger effect on current spot prices than on future spot prices. Indeed, the volatility of more distant futures prices is considerably less than the volatility of spot prices. Therefore, the increase in the value of forward delivery prices was less (estimated by Edwards and Canter 1995 at 50%) than the loss on derivatives contracts.

Even if the changes in spot and futures prices were one-to-one, there is another reason why the hedge strategy was unbalanced. As the cash flows from forward delivery occur much later than those from the hedge position, their present values are different.[18] In other words, the hedge strategy was faulty on both accounts. Instead of a one-to-one hedge, MGRM should have adopted a minimum variance hedge with a hedge ratio significantly smaller than one.[19] With such a hedge strategy, the 1993 market downturn would not have produced any problems: net losses would have been close to zero; margin calls on derivatives and rollover losses would have been much lower. So why did MGRM opt for a one-to-one strategy? Clearly, a one-to-one hedge was optimal in the absence of any funding risk over the period of 10 years. Also, in a market of rising oil prices with backwardation, MGRM would have benefited from that strategy (so that a bit of speculation was added to the hedge strategy). Alternatively, MGRM could have achieved both a full cover for a decline and a rise in oil prices only by dynamically adjusting a less than one-to-one hedge towards one-to-one in a market of rising prices. Such a dynamic adjustment, however, could have entailed substantial costs.

Finally, did MG have a funding problem? As a preliminary, it is worth stressing the role accounting rules played. US hedge-deferred accounting principles do not require that either unrealised gains or losses on hedged positions be recognised. Under German accounting conventions, unrealised losses on open forward positions have to be recognised. Thus, MG had to recognise the unrealised losses on MGRM's derivatives positions, but could not recognise the unrealised gains on its forward-supply contracts. Its losses were thus exaggerated and dramatised as a result of "speculation" by inappropriate accounting rules, which might also have influenced MG's board decision. This is a valuable example of the feedback of modern risk-management techniques on accounting standards which need to be adjusted.

Did MG lack funds? The answer must be no. In fact, it had an *unused* DM1.5 billion credit line with 48 banks. Moreover, in December 1993, MGRM was offered financing on the basis of securitising its forward-supply contracts (Eckhardt and Knipp 1994). Finally, MG's dominant shareholders are the two largest German banks which have the resources to back-up a strategy considered as sound, and have inside access to information about the strategy. The possible non-transparency of the forward-delivery contracts could have been a deterrent to outside credit suppliers, but not to insiders. In the end, the MG board must have considered the hedge strategy as unsound.

**Were there Alternatives to the Hedge Instruments Used?**

MGRM had opted for a stack and roll strategy rather than for long-dated hedges.[20] A number of factors plead in favour of short-dated hedges: liquidity, which is higher in near-months contracts; the higher cost on longer-dated derivatives; and, related to lower liquidity in longer-dated contracts, the need to use OTC contracts.

Instead of using derivatives, MGRM could have hedged by buying oil and storing it until delivery. In principle, futures prices are determined by the arbitrage equilibrium with physical storage. However, forward-delivery prices were set at levels too low to cover the cost of storage.[21]

So why did MGRM not use (strips of) long-dated futures or OTC forwards with delivery dates close to those of its forward delivery contracts? As exchange-traded long-dated futures do not exist, the only alternatives were long-dated OTC contracts. But any OTC dealer offering such contracts would have had to hedge its position by using a strategy similar to the one used by MGRM, thus passing on to MGRM their expected rollover cost plus a risk premium for a possible MGRM default[22] and higher than expected rollover costs over a period of ten years. Both risks are quite high when accumulated over ten years. Apparently, MGRM preferred to accept the rollover risk rather than pay a high risk premium. Being itself a very large operator, it had no competitive disadvantage in managing its rollover risk. Furthermore, long-dated OTC contracts are generally illiquid and therefore costly and difficult to terminate in the event of MGRM customers exercising their cash-out option. Moreover, MGRM would have had to accept a credit risk as OTC dealers can default as well.

**What are the Lessons?**

The closure of MGRM's hedged forward delivery contracts brought MG close to bankruptcy. The first important lesson is surely that complicated hedge strategies pose difficulties of interpretation and understanding for top management (in this case, MG's board). The German accountancy rules, which have not been updated to properly cover hedge strategies, contributed to confusing the issues.[23] Closing the positions was clearly the least desirable decision, even if adverse market conditions had continued. In fact, they did not, so closure occurred at the least favourable moment. From the closure on 7 December 1993 to 8 August 1994 crude oil prices increased from US$13.90 to US$19.40 a barrel.

Closure did not pose liquidity or counter-party problems as contracts were short-dated and MG shareholders were on the paying side. A forced sale (for which there was no necessity) would not have posed problems for the futures contracts (which were serviced by margin payments), but could have put OTC counter-parties in difficulty.

MGRM's hedging strategy illustrates several other lessons. First, it is rarely possible to hedge every risk: price risk, counter-party risk, funding risk. MGRM opted for full protection against the risk of rising oil prices to which its long-term forward sales were exposed. It underestimated the risks of declining oil prices. Although its stack-and-rollover strategy can be considered as a textbook hedge example (Culp and Miller 1995), it was exposed to the risk of discontinuation. In other words, the hedge was not effective at every moment in time and required a sufficient length of life. Whether experienced traders—as MGRM strategists certainly were—had properly identified and evaluated all the risks cannot be verified. As the conflicting views of some of the top world experts[24] show, even *ex post* such matters are difficult to settle.

With hindsight, it appears that a one-to-one hedge was not optimal. A hedge ratio below one would have provided protection in a declining market, but management of such a hedge would have been more complicated. Futures contracts were the appropriate instrument for the hedge strategy. Whether MGRM was wise in offering hedged futures sales, given all the circumstances, is a question that cannot be answered.

# 4. BARINGS: VICTIM OF HIGH-LEVERAGED SPECULATION AND LOOSE CONTROLS

**The Facts**

Barings plc, the oldest merchant banking group in the United Kingdom (established in 1761) was placed in "administration" by the High Court in London on 26 February 1995, and was later taken over by ING, a diversified Dutch bank. Baring Futures (Singapore) (BFS), a subsidiary of Barings plc, suffered losses from large unhedged positions in futures contracts and options—exceeding the entire equity capital of the firm (estimated at US$860 million at the time). The final total loss was US$1.47 billion. Nick Leeson, general manager of BFS, was responsible for the trading strategies and losses of BFS. The fact that a relatively junior trader bankrupted a household name in banking attracted worldwide attention.

BFS engaged in unauthorised position building in futures and options, traded on SIMEX and Japanese exchanges. The *futures contracts* traded in 1995 were the Nikkei 225, Japanese government bonds (JGB) and Euroyen, with the former two accounting for virtually all the losses.

Figure 3.5 shows the cumulative loss (right-hand side) from the build-up of the Nikkei 225 position, which increased from 1080 March 1995 long contracts

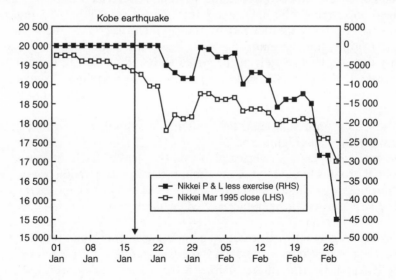

**Figure 3.5** Nikkei March 1995 close and cumulative Nikkei future P&L from 1 January 1995

*Source*: based on Inquiry Report (1995). Crown copyright is reproduced with permission of the Controller of Her Majesty's Stationery Office.

at 1 January 1995 to 61 039 contracts (55 399 March 1995 and 5640 June 1995 contracts) on 26 February. The cumulative loss over this period amounted to yen 48 billion.

A first major build-up of the long position occurred between 20 and 27 January 1995, presumably on the expectation that the market had overreacted to the Kobe earthquake and would recover. Another possibility is that Leeson expected that a position of that size could by itself move the market and thereby also protect the equivalent long position arising from the short option straddles which were written before this large future position (see Figure 3.5).

Leeson's *option strategy* can be described as "volatility trading", attempting to take advantage of what is regarded as mispricing. Options become more expensive when markets are volatile or are expected to become more volatile. Comparison of the computed historic volatility with the "implied" volatility and judgement are the basic ingredients for volatility trading.

Leeson must have expected that the Nikkei 225 would not move significantly from its trading range and that implied volatility was trading at unsustainable levels—which was not consistent with his futures positions. This is the only way his writing of "straddles" can be interpreted.

A straddle is constructed by selling a call option and a put option with the same strike price. The strikes will normally be at a level which corresponds to the price at which the underlying market is trading at the time the trade is executed. Where this is the case the straddle is described as being "at-the-money". So long as the underlying, in this case the Nikkei 225 index, remains within the range defined by the premium received, the writer will make a profit—the optimum outcome being where the underlying at the expiry date settles precisely at the strike and neither the call nor the put is exercised. In this event the writer retains the entire premium. If the underlying either increases or decreases significantly, the writer of the straddle loses money.

A graphical presentation of the profit and loss profile of a written straddle position is shown in Figure 3.6.

As with all options strategies involving the "naked" sale of options, the potential profit is limited to the premium received. The straddle is one of the most aggressive techniques used for shorting volatility and exposes the writer of the straddle to considerable risk when markets move in a sudden and unexpected fashion.

This risk is generally expressed by computing an equivalent futures or cash market exposure (known as "delta", see Chapter 4) for a given level of the underlying market (the futures market if the option is on a futures, the stock index if the option is on the stock index). Risk limits in options portfolios are often evaluated by reference to delta and its rate of change (known as "gamma"). In the case of a written straddle on the Nikkei 225, a fall in the index will cause the writer of the straddle to have the equivalent of a long

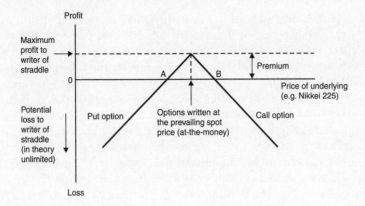

**Figure 3.6** Pay-off for a straddle

*Source*: Inquiry Report (1995). Crown copyright is reproduced with the permission of the Controller of Her Majesty's Stationery Office.

position in the Nikkei 225 because the sold put has moved into the money, whereas a rise in the index will cause the equivalent of a short position because the sold call has moved into the money (see Figure 3.6). Delta and its rate of change, gamma, tell the trader what the equivalent exposure is and how quickly it changes. In the case of an option on a futures contract like the Nikkei options traded by Leeson, these two key variables would be expressed in terms of equivalent futures contracts.

Most option traders will hedge their delta exposure by buying (when the market is rising) or selling (when the market is falling) in the underlying cash or futures market. Where a short volatility position is being managed, the profitability of the portfolio is determined by the extent to which the daily earnings of time value inherent in the option premium exceeds the costs of hedging. It appears that Leeson did not attempt to hedge his portfolio as the profit and loss swings show a very high degree of correlation to moves in the index.

A further significant element of risk in a trading position of this type is exposure to changes in the level of implied volatility, which also affects the calculation of delta and gamma risk. This is referred to as "vega" and is usually used to quantify the exposure of a portfolio to a 1% move up or down in the level of implied volatility.

Leeson had taken in a substantial amount of premium, apparently in the hope that the market would remain sufficiently stable over time to allow the options to expire close enough to their respective strike prices for his strategy to be profitable. The risk inherent in taking a position of this nature is a sudden and unexpected move in the market. The Kobe earthquake precipitated an 11% decline in the Nikkei 225, so that the put options were "in the money". At that time part of the unrealised losses on the put options were offset by the fall in value of the written call options. For a small movement in the Nikkei index (e.g., within the distance AB in Figure 3.6) this offset would have been substantial. For a large decrease, the offset became merely marginal, and the value of the position depended only on the value of the put options (for values of the Nikkei 225 to the left of point A in Figure 3.6).

The strategy Leeson followed is not inherently complex and is one with which experienced options professionals would be familiar. However, to manage an exposure of the size that Leeson constructed is demanding. Leeson did not apparently use a pricing model and did not seem to have a risk management system capable of calculating the sensitivities described above.

It is also likely that the options strategy, carried out according to "judgement" and without sufficient analytic support, was influenced by the overall position. As already mentioned, the large futures position was presumably hoped to move the market, thereby also correcting the loss on the short put options. To satisfy margin calls on the futures, Leeson sold additional options to collect premiums, thereby, however, leveraging his position further.

As of 31 December 1994 the options position had a marking-to-market profit, sustained until 22 January 1995. It all changed with the decline in the Nikkei 225 index following the Kobe earthquake. The option portfolio suffered both from the vertical fall of the index *and* a dramatic increase in volatility. The total number of contracts open at 24 February was 70 892, representing 37 925 call options and 32 967 put options. Leeson accumulated this position over many months extending back to January 1994. By 27 February the cumulative loss on the options portfolio amounted to yen 18.4 billion.

The collapse was triggered by BSF's failure to make margin payments so that SIMEX took over the positions. According to the Inquiry Report (1995), the final loss was as follows:

|  | (£ million) |
|---|---|
| Cumulative loss at 27 February | 827 |
| Additional losses to close out | 42 |
| Foreign exchange loss | 55* |
| SIMEX costs | 3 |
| Loss after liquidation | 927 |

(*Note*: Revaluation of the Sterling denominated cumulative losses equal to £19 million and £36 million due to the appreciation of the Yen against Sterling from 27 February until eventual closing out.)

### What Went Wrong?

Initial reports painted the picture of an individual trader, Nick Leeson, who had overstepped his authority and brought his venerable bank to its knees. In support of this interpretation, it was pointed out that BFS was extremely successful in 1994 and contributed on its own one-third of the overall profits of Barings. Leeson therefore enjoyed a considerable reputation within the bank as a man of financial genius. However, the amount of margin payments that had to be made needed the support of the main office, so that it is hard to imagine that Barings (London) did not receive signals of concern until the very end. Moreover, in 1994, head office controllers had already called attention to problems with Leeson's trading strategies. In retrospect, it would seem that head office granted Leeson excessive freedom of operation, given his presumed past successes, and failed to establish comprehensive controls and effective risk measurement and management.

Several organisational features were key to the role played by Leeson and serve as a serious warning to other banks.

First, Leeson, as general manager of BFS, was responsible for the back-office and as senior floor trader on SIMEX responsible for the trading strategies and their execution. The basic rule of separation of responsibilities for trading and back-office was ignored. SIMEX, in a letter to BFS of 11 January 1995 expressed concern that information required by the Exchange could not be provided in Leeson's absence.

Second, as revealed by the Inquiry Report (1995), Leeson had opened a special account (account "88888") in July 1992, as an error account for customer trading, for trading his own positions. All losses were booked on that account, although Barings' management was unaware of its existence. Despite huge positions and losses, this account quite incomprehensibly failed to attract attention. Account "88888" at end 1994 had already a cumulative loss of US$300 million. So much for Leeson's previous successes, which were to be rewarded by a proposed bonus for 1994 of £450 000.

Third, concealment of his futures and options trading was necessary because, excepting arbitrage operations, BSF was not authorised by Barings' management to transact futures or options in any capacity other than as an agency broker acting on behalf of customers.

Fourth, Leeson was authorised to conduct inter-exchange arbitrage operations ("switching") between SIMEX and three Japanese exchanges. According to the Inquiry Report (1995), Leeson manipulated trade prices and falsified accounts.[25] Between 1 January and 27 February 1995 the reported arbitrage profits were £18.6 million against an effective loss of £28 million (Inquiry Report 1995, p. 82).

It is noteworthy in this connection that over the last two years before the collapse a group of ex-Banker's Trust professionals headed by Ron Baker, had advanced into a dominant position within Barings and developed a new strategy. This strategy involved shifting the bank's trading focus into high margin areas, especially derivatives, proprietary trading, and arbitrage, and away from the bank's traditional emphasis on market-making and client business. As already discussed in Chapter 2, this new strategy has been common to the industry and was not special to Barings, as revenue from market-making, lending and traditional advisory services became squeezed by increased competition and disintermediation.[26]

**What are the Lessons?**

The first lesson is that, given the leverage of derivative products a single trader can bankrupt a large financial institution. The Barings' case may be an extreme, but it is far from being an isolated case. An increasing number of financial or corporate users of derivative products experience serious losses or go bankrupt due to highly leveraged, speculative positions taken by individual traders. Other known examples are ABN Amro New York, Kidder Peabody London, NatWest and many others.

The second lesson is that even experienced and large institutions fail to have appropriate risk management or (as in this case) control systems. The Basle Committee guidelines stress keeping trading settlement and compliance functions distinct both functionally and in terms of personnel. These distinctions were not made in Barings' Singapore office. Furthermore, UK law prohibits a bank from risking more than 25% of its capital on a single exposure. This compares to the ultimate loss in excess of capital. Had controls been in place at Barings, such extravagantly open positions could not have been built up. With proper controls, warnings would have been issued earlier.

Third, according to the Inquiry Report (1995), Barings plc had a state-of-the-art risk model, which reported a daily value for "money at risk" across the whole of the group. But models generate results from the data fed into them. Since the Singapore data were misleading, the output was misleading as well. This augurs ill for the "new approach to regulating" financial institutions on the basis of their own choice of models and control mechanisms.

Fourth, positions were unwound quickly and without undue stress because they were exchange traded so that margins covered counter-party risk. Proprietary positions were liquidated and client positions were transferred to other clearing members. Had positions been of an OTC type, liquidation would have proven complicated and loss coverage more difficult. There was no loss to the exchanges, members of the exchanges or their clients and hence there was no transmission of the Barings' difficulties to other market participants. Exceptions were limited to the relatively small OTC contracts.

Fifth, the Bank of England refused to bail out Barings because it estimated the risk of a domino effect as negligible. (A century ago Barings went technically bankrupt and survived only thanks to support received from the Bank of England.) This was surely the right decision, facilitated by the fact that Barings was not a commercial bank with many small deposits and that the derivative exposure was not in OTC products. However, the Bank of England was certainly not in the lead in identifying the problem in Singapore. Commercial counter-parties reacted more quickly and so did the Bank for International Settlements, commenting on Barings' exposure on 27 January. The Inquiry Report (1995) suggests that the Bank of England should extend its co-operation with the exchanges around the globe and collect information on subsidiaries of banking groups for which it is responsible. In 1997, the Chancellor of the Exchequer took a more radical decision, interpreted to have been at least partly influenced by the Barings fiasco, to discharge the Bank of England of regulatory duties. More generally, the Barings incident illustrates the shortcomings of national regulation. I shall return to this problem in Part III.

Finally, there is also a lesson for the exchanges. If SIMEX and the Osaka Exchange had swapped information they might have realised the extent of the position at an earlier stage and could have acted earlier. Moreover, SIMEX, like most other exchanges, has limits on speculative positions, but apparently it was impossible to classify Barings' position as a speculative one. This illustrates the practical difficulty of the timely distinction between speculative and hedge positions as this would require information on the group's asset and liability management. Such information could have been requested—but it was not.

However, SIMEX acting, like all exchanges, as a self-regulator, was the regulator acting with the greatest speed. It started the process of uncovering Leeson's manoeuvres. In December 1994 SIMEX required BFS to submit status reports on customer positions on a daily basis. Errors were noted in the report and written explanations were required. In January 1995, SIMEX required BFS to provide documentary proof that it was not financing customer positions and alerted BFS to the potential losses to which it was exposed in case of adverse market movements. It was this request that brought internal auditors to look more carefully into BFS operations.

# 5. BANKERS TRUST: CAVEAT EMPTOR

**The Facts**

Swaps are bilateral private agreements whose details are usually not public knowledge. Especially when the deal is innovative there is no incentive to give the secret away to competitors.

During nine days in April 1994, three well-known corporations made headlines by announcing big losses from swap agreements. Two features of these announcements turned them into a sensation: first, all three corporations claimed to have been ill-advised and misled by their counter-party to the swap agreements; second, the counter-party in all three cases was the same— Bankers Trust (BT).

BT is the money centre bank that transformed itself most radically from a classic bank into an institution driven by trading income rather than the intermediation margin. It made great efforts (see its Annual Report 1993) to create an image of a financial advisor and counter-party for state-of-the-art financial wizardry. BT was both admired for its innovations and criticised for its aggressive marketing of exotic derivative products to customers. Its reputation received a serious blow from the complaints raised against it.

Procter & Gamble, announced on 12 April that it had suffered a US$157 million pre-tax loss on two leveraged swap contracts. On 19 April, Gibson Greetings announced an additional charge against earnings of US$16.7 million on top of US$3 million realised loss on leveraged swaps. The next day paper manufacturer Mead Corporation announced a loss of US$7.4 million from debt-hedging operations, including a one-time loss on the close-out of a unique leveraged swap transaction.

All three companies filed suits against BT in the courts and with the regulatory authority (SEC). The Comptroller of the Currency issued new guidelines for customer protection, and the Financial Accounting Standards Board (FASB) proposed increased corporate disclosure rules.

To better understand what happened it may be best to start with an explanation of a "leveraged swap" and the "closing-out" process. The examples outlined below focus on just one end-user, Gibson, as all cases are very similar.

### Leveraged Swaps

A leveraged swap is an agreement the returns of which are a multiple of a similar plain vanilla swap.[27]

On 12 November 1991, Gibson entered into two fixed-for-floating interest rate swaps, each with a notional amount of US$30 million. Gibson's target was to lower its interest costs related to a US$50 million fixed rate borrowing at 9.3% completed in May 1991.

- *First swap*: Starting 1 June 1992 until 1 December 1993, Gibson pays fixed 5.91%, whilst BT pays 6-month LIBOR.
- *Second swap*: Starting 1 June 1992 until 1 December 1996, BT pays 7.12%, whilst Gibson pays 6-month LIBOR.

Thus, until the end of 1993, Gibson paid a fixed 5.91% on the first swap and received 7.12% on the second swap, thus receiving a net 1.21% per annum for 18 months. (Note that LIBOR-based payments cancel out.)

As the initial value of any swap must be zero, the expected value of the second swap for 1994–96 must have been negative, implying that LIBOR rates were expected to rise above 7.12%. The goal could have been to shift expected interest rate expenses from the immediate future to the more distant future, or to construct a hedge.

Gibson amended these two swap contracts in January 1992 and terminated them in July 1992, receiving a cancellation payment from BT of US$260 000. This payment reflected an increase in the value of those swaps to Gibson as interest rates were falling during the first half of 1992.

On 1 October 1992, Gibson entered into another swap, called a "ratio swap". This is a leveraged swap, based on the following formula:

$$\text{net payment} = 5.5\% - \frac{(\text{LIBOR})^2}{6\%}$$

If positive, net payment is made by BT; if negative by Gibson.

Figure 3.7 compares the interest rate sensitivity of the original swaps with the replacement swap. Under the new swap, the future net payments to Gibson would become negative more rapidly and the difference between the old swaps and the new would become greater as LIBOR increased.

This ratio swap was amended three times to shorten the swap term before being cancelled on 21 April 1993, with BT making a payment to Gibson of US$978 000. In one of the amendments, the termination date was shortened in exchange for entering into another, more complicated leveraged swap. Until 4 March 1994 Gibson entered into several additional swaps, all with complex leveraged structures.

When, at the beginning of February 1994, interest rates shot up sharply, Gibson had two outstanding swaps with BT and was thereby exposed to

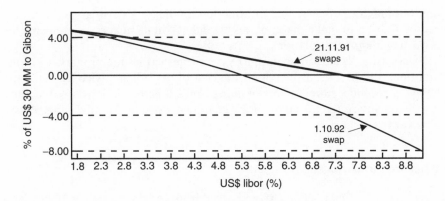

**Figure 3.7** Comparison of the interest rate sensitivity of the net cash flows on Gibson's original swaps with the swap that replaced them

interest rate increases. Instead of reducing the cost of its initial fixed-rate borrowing (the initial objective), Gibson added exposure to rising interest rates and got caught.[28] Eventually, BT and Gibson settled their dispute out-of-court. Instead of paying the full US$20 million it owed BT, Gibson only had to pay US$6.18 million. Also of interest, BT made US$13 million during the last 15 months selling derivatives to Gibson.

The Gibson case demonstrates a more general problem: structured deals can have implications that only profound experience and high-powered analytical tools can reveal. The benefit to corporate users can, under these conditions, be substantial. Otherwise corporations would be better advised to stick to more standard instruments.

**Regulatory Responses**

BT entered into a "Written Agreement" with the New York Fed regarding the future conduct of leveraged derivatives transactions (LDT).[29] This Agreement specifies that BT will seek to ensure that counter-parties understand the nature and risk of proposed leveraged swaps. BT also agreed to provide pricing information to counter-parties throughout the life of LDTs.

This Agreement must be taken by market participants as a signal of Fed policy. The price of leveraged—as compared to plain—derivatives transactions is likely to increase, especially for less sophisticated end-users, to cover more detailed customer information and the costs of potential legal suits. As such the Agreement raises concern about OTC derivatives and may increase the relative attractiveness of exchange-traded products.

The CFTC and SEC imposed jointly a fine of US$10 million on BT. The CFTC stated that BT had entered into an advisory relationship; the SEC argued that BT knew that Gibson would sustain unrealised losses from tear-ups, but failed to disclose that information to Gibson. It also argued that BT caused Gibson to make material misstatements on its financial statements by providing incorrect valuations.

By asserting its anti-fraud authority over transactions in this market for the first time, the CFTC has increased the cost of providing advice. Dealers are likely to respond either by maintaining arm's-length relationships and thus not giving advice to customers, or by charging explicitly for advisory services to cover the legal risk.

**What are the Lessons?**

There are least three lessons to be derived from the three cases involving BT.

The first is that OTC products can be complex enough to raise questions about how well understood they are even by experienced corporate treasurers. There is an associated uncertainty about the value of complex products for which there is no market. Dealers are at times tempted to input valuations that make the position look better and customers may find it difficult to evaluate their position themselves. They become, therefore, unduly dependent on dealers for pricing and management advice.

The second lesson is that banks find it difficult to impose a code of behaviour on their staff. Numerous cases, not only these three, but also the Orange County case (discussed below) and many others, show that the incentives for dealers are such as to make them overly aggressive in their marketing. Regulations are unlikely to contain that risk, barring the case where penalties would become so high as to make these products uncompetitive.

Third, these cases illustrate actual and potential problems with complicated OTC products and suggest that migration to the organised exchanges is one possible way out.

## 6. ORANGE COUNTY'S LEMON

**The Facts**

During the early 1990s, the manager of the Orange County Investment Pool, county treasurer Robert L. Citron, successfully invested his pool on the basis of his view that interest rates were bound to decline.[30] Investing in long-dated bonds and in structured notes, he achieved attractive results. From 1991 to 1993 his yields were above the 7% average of the bond mutual funds. This track record induced Orange County's municipalities to chip more money into the fund, raising the size of their deposits from about US$3 billion in 1991 to US$7.6 billion in 1994.

Above normal rates of return are usually a premium for the risk taken. It was, therefore, good fortune that helped to make high returns during 1991–93. However, the risk in the position was considerable. Already in October 1992 Merrill Lynch apparently recommended to Citron to reduce his risk exposure. Rather than following this advice, he appears to have persisted in his belief that interest rates would fall further and augmented his borrowings to increase his position. To the US$7.6 billion of his fund he accumulated a debt of about US$12 billion, collateralised by securities in the fund's portfolio.

The particular borrowing technique he used was reverse purchase agreements or repos (also known as matched sales-purchase agreements). Under a repo an investor sells securities to a dealer whilst at the same time repurchasing them at an agreed-upon price on a set future date. The sales proceeds are, in effect, a loan, at very favourable rates since fully collateralised. The lender has a double motivation to enter into a repo. First, to earn a small margin on a collateralised loan. Second, if he expects the price of the received securities to fall he will sell them and repurchase at a lower price before maturity of the repo. In fact, the repo market facilitates "short-selling".

To protect himself from a potential fall in the value of the collateral, the dealer will lend less than the market value of the securities, a difference known as the "haircut". Clearly, a repo exposes the investor (here, Robert Citron) to the risk that the price of the securities will fall below the price agreed for repurchase. It also locks him in until the date of repurchase, a risk that can be cut by unwinding the operation ahead of time—if he has the cash and is willing to pay a penalty. The cash is available if the loan received is invested in liquid short-term securities. This is not what Citron did and therefore his repos were unbalanced.

Moreover, when the value of the collateral falls below the value of the loan, the investor is required to put in additional funds (like a margin payment), or risks having his position closed out by the dealer. Citron used the loans to buy more securities which, in turn, were again repurchased out. Combining leveraged instruments and repos, he built up tremendous leverage.

The strategy foundered because Orange County invested the proceeds of short-term repos in much longer government agency debt, including inverse floating rate notes (see Technical Insight 3.1) with maturities up to seven years. It became increasingly difficult to negotiate new arrangements for this unmatched strategy at a time when Citron had to top up the collateral on longer-term repos as the value of the securities held by dealers were falling.

The main reason for the failure of the highly leveraged bet on falling interest rates was, of course, that interest rates went the "wrong way" and increased exceptionally sharply. On 4 February 1994 the Federal Reserve started to tighten interest rates and sent fixed-income securities into a grizzly bear market. By December 1994, the Fed had increased interest rates six times and the six-month LIBOR rate had risen from 3.6% to 6.8%.

On 6 December 1994, three days after Citron resigned and two months after the first rumours circulated, CS First Boston refused to roll over US$1.25 billion in repos and other dealers sold securities held against loans. The same day lawyers filed for Chapter 9 Protection (i.e., legally appointed administration) and the following day a former auditor general of the State of California was hired to oversee the restructuring of the portfolio. This "restructuring" was completed on 19 January 1995 with a final loss of US$1.69 billion.

**What do Derivatives have to do with it?**

Citron's investment strategy, speculating on lower interest rates and piling up short-term debt for longer-term investment created enough risk exposure for a potential disaster without derivatives. The use of derivatives was, therefore, not an essential part of the ultimate failure of the investment strategy. However, of the US$20 billion invested, about US$8 billion were invested in

**Technical Insight 3.1**  Inverse floaters

A typical inverse floater (also called reverse floater) promises a return based on the following formula:

$$\text{Return} = x - \text{LIBOR (six-month)} \tag{1}$$

where x is a percentage, say, 12%.

Hence if LIBOR decreases, the return on this formula increases, producing the term "inverse" floater. Investors are attracted by inverse floaters when they have strong views that short-term interest rates will decline. The inverse floater appears to provide the leverage necessary to realise capital gains from declining short-term rates. As demonstrated below, this intuition is wrong.

How do potential investors evaluate an inverse floater? Consider the following example of a one-year inverse floater when one-year interest rates are 8%, six-month rates are 6% and, hence, the forward rate for the second six-month period 10%. The inverse floater promises R as defined in the above formula, with x = 12%.

The investor obtains for the first six-month period 6% and on the basis of the forward rate he should expect to receive 2% for the second period. The investor will nevertheless choose this instrument if he expects subjectively that six-month rates during the second period will fall below 6%. In fact, the investor only makes money if the second period six-month rate falls below 2% so that the inverse floater yields at least 10% for the second half-year and 8% for the entire year.

This example shows that the value of the inverse floater depends crucially on the long-term (here the one-year) rate. Suppose that, one day after the issue, the one-year rate falls to 6% whilst the six-month rate remains unchanged. Then the forward rate for the second six-month period falls from 10% to 6% and the note becomes valuable if expected six-month rates are below 6% (rather than below 2% as with an 8% one-year rate).

In other words, the return on an inverse floater only depends on the long-term rate. With 8% interest on one year and 6% on the first six months, one can only consistently expect a rate for the second period of less than 10% if one expects the one-year rate to fall.

How does the issuing bank hedge its exposure? It invests the amount of the note in six-month paper receiving 6% and buys forward or on the future exchange the 10% return on the second six-month period. The income is therefore certain. Payments are 6% for the first six months and only exceed 10% in the second period, if the second period rate falls below 2%—a small risk to take in exchange for a high probability of gain.

Alternatively and more commonly, the issuer buys a fixed-rate bond at par and enters a swap agreement to receive a fixed rate and to pay LIBOR. The issuer receives therefore twice the fixed rate and pays LIBOR. This is the way of replicating equation (1):

$$
\begin{aligned}
\text{Return} &= \text{Fixed rate} + \text{swap} \\
&= 2(\text{Fixed rate}) - \text{LIBOR} \qquad\qquad (2)
\end{aligned}
$$

or $\quad$ PV $\quad = \text{PV}(2\,\text{Fixed rate}) - \text{PV(LIBOR)} \qquad\qquad (3)$

where PV = present value. Letting $\Delta$ denote change and using the approximation $\Delta\text{PV(LIBOR)} = 0$, one obtains from (3):

$$
\Delta\text{PV} \quad = 2\Delta\text{PV(fixed)} \qquad\qquad (4)
$$

Thus, the price sensitivity of the inverse floater is twice the one of a fixed rate bond, and short-term rates play only an indirect role.

Many investors in inverse floaters failed to understand the message of equation (4).

structured notes such as inverse floaters. Given their much higher interest sensitivity to changes in market rates (see Technical Insight 3.1), the corresponding loss when interest rates moved the wrong way was much higher than with plain securities. Derivatives amplified the risks taken and the ultimate loss.

## What are the Lessons?

The Orange County case shares a number of features with the Bankers Trust cases, but also presents different lessons. As was the case with numerous corporations using derivatives, the role of dealers acting as advisors, suppliers of structured notes and lenders appears in a shady light.

Merrill Lynch had a long-standing twenty-year relationship with Citron, advised him on derivative securities (on the day of bankruptcy 80–90% were supplied by Merrill Lynch) and lent money. It had become a leader in underwriting and distributing the security offerings of various Orange County municipalities. Merrill Lynch's income from underwriting and trading with Orange County in 1993 and 1994 is estimated at US$50 million.

The court filing against Merrill Lynch was based on the claim that, as principal long-standing advisor and dealer, Merrill Lynch was fully informed about the financial situation and policy pursued by Orange County and therefore fully aware of the breach of the law. The filing demanded that Merrill Lynch make good the US$1.69 billion in final losses; return the US$133 million in interest the County paid on reverse repo agreements and provide "substantial consequential damages".[31] Furthermore, there is again the question of whether complicated structured securities are transparent enough to allow end-users to fully understand them.

And, again, the regulatory void: laws and regulations deal with the problems of the past, prohibiting speculation by certain institutions in equity cash markets, but not explicitly in derivative securities. As with Baring, excessive risk-taking helped by derivative instruments created the losses, but inadequate supervision allowed these risks to be taken in the first place.

What distinguishes the Orange County case from corporate misfortunes is above all that public money was mis-invested. A corporation is free to speculate—at least if approved by shareholders. In the Orange County case, the savings of millions of citizens were at stake, triggering alarm in Washington.[32]

Jorion (1995) calls for greater and more detailed oversight of municipal funds. In particular, he proposes that municipal funds should be obliged to report market values on a regular basis. This way, the alarm bell will ring when funds first get into trouble, not when they are swamped by trouble. This would be a step in the right direction.


# 7. DAVID ASKIN: THE FALLEN STAR OF THE MORTGAGE-BACKED SECURITIES SKY

**The Facts**

In early April 1994 several hedge funds specialising in mortgage-backed securities (MBS), managed by one of Wall Street's darlings, David Askin, and patronised by prestigious investors such as the Rockefeller Foundation, were in the federal bankruptcy court. According to a trustee report of May 1994, Askin's downfall was as much due to his own strategies as to Wall Street's actions. Askin had built up an MBS portfolio excessively leveraged with loans from bond suppliers (as had Orange County) and made three serious mistakes. First, he gambled on falling interest rates, without any fallback strategy. Second, he lacked the most basic tools for assessing and managing the risk he was taking. For example, he had no way of telling how his turbo-charged bonds would react to shifting interest rates. Third, he apparently ignored the biggest problem with OTC products: his suppliers were the only arbiter of the value of some of the bonds in his portfolio. For example, just before the end, when interest rates were increasing sharply, he bought US$1.1 billion face-value of "interest-only inverse floaters" which only days later, in the hasty liquidation sale, turned out to be worth one-third less.

The trustee report identifies a number of problems that arose. When Askin started to make losses, Bear Stearns increased the "haircut, that is, the firm's margin of safety on its loans, from 10% to 20%. Overnight, because his bonds were worth less and the haircut had become 20%, Askin owed Bear Stearns more than the bonds serving as collateral were worth. Then, when Wall Street firms recovered the bonds that served as collateral for loans, price discounts changed abruptly by the hour. A number of firms resold the recuperated bonds immediately making hefty profits. Traders from Bear Stearns made back-of-the-envelope estimates of the bonds' worth (the "boys' price") which were seriously marked down. Nevertheless, Bear Stearns credited the Askin funds with US$18 million less than its own "boys' price" estimates.

The sharp increase in interest rates during 1994 not only caused the collapse of highly exposed and leveraged investors like Askin and Orange County,[33] but shattered the entire MBS market, conducting a stunningly expensive tutorial for seasoned and freshman investors alike. By mid-1994 cumulative losses ran into the tens of billions. The US$1.5 trillion market, third in size only to the US Treasury and corporate debt markets, stood out as a disaster area. (By end 1995 outstanding Federal debt was US$3300 billion, corporate debt US$1800 billion, and municipal debt US$1300 billion.)

**What are Mortgage-backed Securities?**

Although straightforward—simply bundle together a bunch of home mortgages and sell the package as a security—mortgage-backed securities (MBS) include some of the most complex financial instruments ever invented. MBS are an extremely useful financial innovation. Once, savings and loans associations (S&Ls) were the chief lenders to homeowners, and they kept mortgages at fixed interest rates until maturity. Pre-payment penalties could be stiff, whereas now they are virtually extinct in the US market. In addition, homeowners now obtain variable rate mortgages so that their costs are lower with positively sloped yield curves (the normal situation) and their interest payments closely track inflation. Faced with the financial stress of S&Ls, regularly provoked by periods of rising interest rates, which increased the cost of liabilities but left returns on outstanding loans unchanged, Congress set out to render mortgages tradeable and to expand the pool of investors in mortgages. It established Freddie Mac (and later Fannie Mae) to buy mortgages from S&Ls and combine them into securities that could be sold to investors. The securitised mortgages were enhanced by guarantees of repayment of interest and principal to make them more attractive.

Collateralised mortgage obligations (CMOs) were created in 1983 to make mortgage cash flows more stable and predictable. CMOs deal with the call option embedded in mortgages allowing the borrower to prepay or to lengthen the reimbursement schedule. To achieve greater stability of cash flows mortgages are split into time buckets of principal and interest payments, jointly or separate. One tranche might cover the first five years of their term, the next the following five years and so on. Prepayment risks were spread sequentially over the entire structure (implying higher risks for more distant tranches), and interest rates on the tranches varied accordingly.

To value the call option embedded in MBS, analysts developed sophisticated estimations and simulation models. That, in turn, led to an important innovation in the CMO market: planned amortisation class securities, or PACs. Designed to give investors more complete prepayment protection than the initial CMOs, as long as prepayments stayed within model-determined "bands", the PACs promised an attractive spread over Treasuries. To achieve that result, prepayment and extension risks were separated out into "support bonds". In the event that interest rates fell, prepayment exceeding the "band" would be absorbed first by the support bond. Similarly, if interest rates rose, extending the average life of the bonds, the support bonds would extend first.

PACs were attractive to a large range of conservative investors. The support tranches—also dubbed "toxic waste"—did not find similar widespread appeal. However, they were bought by insurance companies and banks to make bets on interest rates they were prohibited from making in straight derivatives.[34] In addition, the credit risk was reduced by agency guarantees.

During 1992–93, PACs were often designed to do well in a low-volatility environment at the risk of shortening or extending drastically once prepayments rose above or fell below projected rates. They behaved, in part, like support bonds and offered spreads of 130 basis points or more on regular PACs.

The reason for creating ever more complicated CMOs was Wall Street's quest for new profit opportunities. The dealers' ability to issue complex and lucrative CMOs was limited only by their ability to bundle excess risk into marketable support bonds. With increased competition, it was only by carving up CMOs into ever more complicated pieces that dealers could prop up diminished profit margins. In the early days of CMOs the dealer's margin was 1–2 percentage points; by 1995 margins were in the range of $\frac{1}{16}$ to $\frac{1}{8}$.

The greater the complexity of a creation, the greater the chance of profit for the dealer. As one dealer said, "all the profits are in toxic waste." At different times different instruments were fashionable: interest-rate only strips, principal-only strips, inverse floaters, support-tranche floaters, turbo floaters, and so on. By creating ultra-customised securities, liquidity was sacrificed. One victim of lacking liquidity was David Askin, among many others.

Another frequent mistake is to underestimate the volatility of CMOs. In highly leveraged CMOs the option components can exceed the fixed-income components, so that the key to pricing is the volatility assumption.

During the bond rally of 1993 some CMO investors got nasty surprises. As homeowners refinanced at unexpectedly high frequency, the duration of CMO bonds shrunk much more than assumed in the pricing model of dealers and investors gained less or even lost during the rally.

**Melting Mortar**

In February 1994, just before interest rates started to increase, investors held an estimated US$90 billion of extremely illiquid CMOs. When interest rates increased, average life and duration increased, sometimes dramatically so. Support bonds with an expected life of two years extended to a life of 20 years or more during 1994.

Substantial losses were made during the rising interest rate cycle in 1994 even by sophisticated investors and dealers like Kidder Peabody, Bear Stearns, Lehman Brothers and Nomura. Several investors, having lost one-half of their initial investments and holding illiquid paper, sued their dealers.[35]

The MBS market has declined from an origination of about US$1 trillion in 1993 to US$700 billion in 1994, concentrating on plain vanillas. Some growth is expected to come from securitising commercial mortgages, non-agency mortgage products and from developing MBS products abroad. A Bear Stearns' specialist has this formulation: "The mortgage market hasn't died and gone to heaven. It may be in purgatory. These types of dislocations are what opportunities are made of."[36]

**What are the Lessons?**

Hedge funds are sophisticated and, in general, successful investors. The Askin case underlines the fact that higher returns are obtained for higher risk. The losses of private investors in the Askin funds do not create a public policy issue, but the case forcefully illustrates the specific risks of OTC products. First, profit opportunities push dealers to construct products of such complexity that even sophisticated investors are unable to assess them. Modelling of the value of the prepayment options in MBS is extremely complex and the available models are far from reliable. Second, the leverage provided can be lethal if markets turn the wrong way. Third, during market turbulences liquidity disappears as all investors scramble for exit and there are no more buyers. Askin was unable to value his position during the critical days. The only way to sell was to sell his collaterals to his lenders—at their prices. He would have made big losses even in a liquid market, but he may have survived.

# 8. INSTABILITY IN EMERGING MARKETS: MEXICAN TEQUILA

During the 1990s several developing countries have successfully liberalised their economies and opened their financial markets, thereby gaining a promotion to the status of "emerging market economy". Attracted by their growth potential, substantial amounts of private capital have been flowing into these economies. The risk for foreign investors can, however, be quite high in view of the vulnerability of these countries to political changes and to a boom-and-bust economic cycle. The latter can be enhanced by foreign capital inflows, which at the first sign of adverse news may be withdrawn. Such flows are often dangerously large in relation to the size of the domestic market. Wary of such risks, regulators in emerging market economies attempt to ringfence national financial institutions by imposing limits on their foreign assets or liabilities and restricting the type or amount of assets that foreigners can acquire. Whilst investors and financial intermediaries have always found ways to circumvent such regulations, the 1994 experience in Mexico illustrates the role played by derivative products in circumventing regulations.

## The Build-up to the Crisis

On 20 December 1994, the Mexican peso was devalued by 15%. Two days later market pressures forced a free float and within months the peso had lost half its pre-devaluation value. Mexican financial markets only stabilised when a package of external assistance was put in place, together with a harsh adjustment programme. Before that, the crisis had already spilled over into several other Latin American countries and, possibly, even affected Thailand.

During 1990–93, Mexico received US$91 billion in net capital inflows, or about 20% of all net flows to developing countries. In terms of Mexico's GDP the inflows represented as much as 8% of GDP in 1994, a very large, but not unique, share in international comparison. In a truly integrated world capital market this would not have been a problem, but unfortunately there were other problems as well. About two-thirds of the capital inflows during that period were portfolio investments, only 15% were foreign direct investments. Much of the net portfolio inflows went into the equity market. As a result, the Bolsa index rose 436% in dollar terms over the period 1990–

93. The most important boom occurred at the end of 1993 and the beginning of 1994, as markets reacted to the ratification of NAFTA. As shown by Gilibert and Steinherr (1996), the price/earnings ratio increased from five in 1990 to over 20 in 1994. Under reasonable assumptions they show that only an expected earnings growth of close to 10%—never achieved on a sustained basis anywhere in Latin America—would have supported such price/ earnings ratios. Hence a severe correction was needed and was to be expected. In addition, a series of domestic and international events affected Mexico in 1994. Noteworthy among the foreign events was the increase in the US federal funds rate from 3% before 4 February 1994 to 5.5% by end-November. The initial Mexican response of sterilised foreign exchange market intervention maintained domestic interest rates and accelerated foreign fund withdrawals.

The crisis after the devaluation, resulting in a free float, was exacerbated by two factors. First, the value of Mexico's dollar-linked tesobono debt increased sharply in peso terms as the peso was devalued and then depreciated. Second, the depreciation of the peso and the rapid rise in domestic interest rates increased the amount of non-performing loans in the Mexican banking system. The crisis was contained when, on 31 January 1995, the United States announced a lending programme and, on 1 February 1995, the IMF approved the largest stand-by arrangement in its history.

I now wish to probe into the aggravating factors by showing the part played by derivative products.

# 9. THE ROLE OF DERIVATIVES

On-balance sheet operations are still the main instruments for circumventing regulation, but offshore OTC derivatives have facilitated that process. Mainly three types of instruments were used by Mexican banks to circumvent prudential regulations, which were considerably tightened after the 1991–92 reprivatisation of the Mexican banking system and accompanying financial liberalisations that included removal of credit controls and reserve requirements, free setting of interest rates and permission to offer US dollar accounts. These three instruments were tesobono swaps, structured notes and equity swaps.

When the Mexican situation became precarious at the end of 1994, the major actors—the Mexican authorities, the US Federal Reserve and the IMF—faced a very serious problem: to correctly assess the foreign debt situation of the Mexican banking sector. In addition to the usual problems of timely marked-to-market evaluation was the fact that Mexican financial intermediaries had used complex derivative products to circumvent national regulation and with the fall of the peso the market value of these derivative products turned rapidly against Mexican intermediaries requiring dollar payments in response to margin calls or to close-out positions.

Technical Insight 3.2 describes in detail tesobono swaps which were widely used by Mexican banks. Other derivative products contributing to a magnification of the turmoil included structured notes, equity swaps, equity repurchase agreements, Cetes swaps and Brady bond swaps. I focus on the most important instruments.

## Structured Notes

Structured notes are investment vehicles with coupon payments and principal repayments tied to other asset prices, including exchange rates, in such a way as to provide significant leverage on the initial capital investment. These transactions can, in most emerging-market accounting systems, be booked as cash investments, denominated in the currency of the prospectus. They therefore not only magnify the usual market risks associated with investment positions, but can also provide a ready method for avoiding prudential restrictions on currency positions or leverage.

Mexican financial institutions took large positions in structured notes during 1994 with investment houses in New York. Booked as claims with dollar principal and dollar payoffs, these notes were, in fact, currency bets that allowed Mexican banks to leverage their investment into a short dollar and long peso position to take advantage of the positive interest rate spreads between peso and dollar money markets.

These structured notes existed in many forms. For example, a Mexican bank might buy a note with a one-year maturity from a New York investment house for US$1 with coupon and principal payable in dollars. As an illustration, the coupon might be 85%, while the principal repayment might depend negatively on the peso value of the dollar, say $[1 + 5 (s_0-s_1)/s_1]$, where $s_0$ is the initial peso value of the dollar and $s_1$ is the value at maturity. If the peso has depreciated by 50% at maturity, from three to 6 pesos per dollar, the principal repayment will be $-US\$1.50$. The overall return is then $-US\$0.65$. Note that this is also the payoff structure of a position that is short US$3 at 5% per year and long 12 pesos at 25% per year. Effectively, the initial US$1 investment has been leveraged fourfold. On the books of the Mexican banks, this would appear as a US$1 asset. If the bank had borrowed the initial US$1 for the investment, it would officially have a balanced position in dollars. In fact, however, it would be effectively short US$4 and long 12 pesos.

Mexican banks are subject to Comision Nacional Bancaria regulations that restrict net foreign exchange positions to a maximum of 15% of capital. According to the regulatory definitions of what constituted foreign exchange—an asset or liability the principal or coupon of which were

**Technical Insight 3.2**   Tesobono Swaps

*Tesobono swaps* are offshore derivative operations that were used by Mexican banks as a means of leveraging tesobono (Mexican treasury bills denominated in peso) holdings. These operations facilitated circumvention of the regulations forbidding holding financial assets on margin in Mexico. It is estimated that about US$16 billion of tesobonos were used in swaps at the time of the devaluation.

The leverage involved in tesobono swaps can be most readily examined by considering first the nearly equivalent tesobono repurchase agreement. Consider a New York investment firm that is willing to lend dollars for one year against tesobono collateral. The firm will engage in a repurchase agreement with a Mexican bank to buy tesobonos at their current value and to resell them in a year at the original price plus a dollar interest rate. Suppose the dollar rate is LIBOR plus 100 basis points. In 1994, the typical tesobono repo had a maturity of one year and required between 10% and 20% margin, producing a leverage up to nine to one. The Mexican counter-party would, for example, buy US$500 worth of tesobonos in Mexico and sell them to the New York firm for US$400. The tesobonos would be delivered to the New York firm through its custodial account, usually with Citibank Mexico.[37] The gain to the Mexican bank is that it pays LIBOR plus 100 to finance tesobonos that may pay the equivalent of LIBOR plus 300. The gain to the US lender is that it gets to place dollar funds at LIBOR plus 100.

In the crisis the dollar market value of tesobonos suddenly fell. This resulted both indirectly from rumours that capital controls might be imposed and through the failed auction of January in which the government accepted an unfavourable yield. The fall in market value reduced the value of the collateral and triggered margin calls to deliver dollars or close out the position.

Suppose, for example, that the typical tesobono fell by 15% in dollar value, to the extent that they could be valued at all. For the tesobono repo in the example above, collateral is now insufficient to the extent of US$75. The Mexican bank must now either go to the exchange market at the depreciated peso exchange rate to acquire the US$75 or close out the position. To close the position requires the delivery of US$400 in cash. The scramble for dollars to cost such margin calls and positions close-outs was associated with the currency turmoil of January and February 1995.

*Source:* Garber (1996)

denominated in a foreign currency—the US$1 that was originally paid to acquire the structured note would enter the books as a long US$1 position, even though its payoff was equivalent to a short US$4 position. In addition, some banks could count it against their liquidity coefficient because of its short.

If the bank borrowed the initial US$1 used to purchase the note, it would have a balanced net forex position for regulatory purposes. However, when the exchange rate was devalued in December 1994, the dollar value of its structured note declined, leaving the bank with an unbalanced dollar liability. In seeking to cover this imbalance, the Mexican banks had to sell pesos, contributing to market pressure on the peso.

After losing the principal and coupon on the note, there were no further loss implications for the Mexican bank. The New York counter-parties, however, then had only the long peso-short dollar position used to hedge the original note. At this point, the New York houses too started taking losses.[38]

This type of structured note was a financial engineering device created to avoid prudential restrictions. Only the principal is booked in accordance with value accounting principles. The positions implicit in the payoff of the structured note are not booked—they are off-balance sheet items. That is the accounting trick: one can alter the effective nature of the booking through the payoff formula. Accounting regulations for the determination of forex positions will need to be changed towards more accurate risk accounting, so that the position is classified as unbalanced if it generates potential gains or losses from the movement of the exchange rate.[39]

**What are the Lessons?**

Mexico, like a number of other emerging markets, has been able to attract major capital inflows to boost its stock market and, with fixed exchange rates and high domestic interest rates, obtained substantial foreign lending in local and foreign currency. When the economic fundamentals cracked, the foreign currency commitments far exceeded what market participants and official bodies had expected. Off-balance sheet derivatives are responsible for that. Market participants were, thus, basically misinformed and so were policy-makers. This is the first, and very disconcerting, problem. The second is that Mexico was bailed out for fear of spillover effects into other countries. Any emerging country can now reasonably expect a similar bail-out should it run into Mexico-type problems. In 1997, Thailand, Indonesia and Korea encountered such problems and received substantial international assistance. Other countries are bound to follow soon. Systemic risk is visibly not only a theoretical concern. Unfortunately, countries can now behave like major banks: they can even take excessive risks because they are too important to be allowed to fail.

## 10. CONCLUSION

Since 1983 investors have enjoyed one of the greatest bull markets in history. In the United States there were temporary corrections such as the 1987 crash and the 1989, 1990 and 1994 downturns. The Tokyo stock exchange achieved record, uninterrupted growth until 1989 when the bubble burst. The 1987 correction for technical reasons overshot and tested the implications of programme trading. While the long-lasting bull market wetted appetites for speculation and fostered demand for leveraged products, the market corrections stimulated demand for derivatives that provided downside protection.

Volatility on equity exchanges was at times surpassed by volatility of commodities, fixed income securities and foreign currencies. Hedging needs, as well as regulatory constraints (access to many foreign markets, restrictions on investments vehicles), provided impetus to market developments.

While most of this dynamic evolution enhanced efficiency and provided widespread welfare gain there were also notable problems raising regulatory concerns. Indeed, the very biggest speculators were banks (and S&Ls), reassured by the empirically tested conviction that in times of crisis tax payers would be there to bail them out. When the S&Ls' imprudent speculations in leveraged real estate turned sour at the end of the 1980s, it was the government bail out that generated the opportunity for speculators to earn astronomic returns by riding the yield curve in 1992 and 1993, which led in turn to the bond-market débâcle of 1994. It may even be the case that the Fed's reluctance to act more vigorously in 1994 was attributable in part to fear of toppling the fragile banking system.

From this survey of problem cases, certain lessons emerge. First, OTC derivatives have reached a level of complexity that makes it difficult even for sophisticated end-users to fully understand the characteristics of the derivative strategies or instruments. They rely on dealers to explicate the risk-return characteristics, failing to recognise that dealers are trained to close deals, not to provide optimal risk-management strategies to clients. Second, speculation becomes much more powerful through the leverage for derivatives. Failure of a bet whose downside risk is unhedged can result in hefty losses. This risk is not always fully comprehended by top management as it does not appear on the balance sheet. Third, price information is often lacking and in times of emergency the unwinding of a position may be difficult or very costly for lack of liquidity in the customer designed OTC market segment. Fourth, regulations are seriously lagging behind market developments and have a major job to accomplish in catching up.

But here, as with all half-empty bottles, there is also the other half. In all these disasters no significant social cost was involved.[40] For any derivatives contract, the loss of one party is the gain of another. A social cost only arises when some capital is destroyed (the Baring's case comes closest, as the *savoir-*

*faire* of an old merchant bank disappeared), or when socially valuable activity is discouraged (the decline in futures activity in 1995 is sometimes attributed to the Baring disaster, but this is far from proven), or when innocent third parties are affected (as in a bank-run). But this has not happened—so far.

Miller (1996) argues that all these derivatives disasters ought to be more properly renamed "management disasters". In fact, most of the disasters would have disappeared and even generated gains if enough time had been granted: Metallgesellschaft was hedged; by May 1995 the Japanese stock market had increased 30% above its post-Kobe lows in February; interest rates had fallen dramatically during 1995 and 1996.

Two dramatic events discussed in this chapter concerned macroeconomic crises: the EMS exchange rate turmoil of 1992–93 and the Mexican crisis of 1994–95. Hedge funds, despite their impressive leverage, cannot be held responsible for the break-up of the EMS the fundamentals of which were out of tilt. But derivatives allowed Mexican banks to circumvent national regulations and to build up a foreign exchange position outside of official statistics and unknown to policy-makers and a large part of market participants. When the crisis arrived the surprise unfolded and turned a crisis into a catastrophe. Here is a problem with which regulators in emerging markets and international agencies still have to come to grips.

## ENDNOTES

1 Drexel, Burnham Lambert was a member of several major exchanges, but, given the strict rules of those exchanges, no third parties suffered any loss. Drexel, Burnham Lambert lost, however, substantially on its own derivatives book.

2 On 20 October, the New York Stock Exchange (NYSE) considered stopping trading, a decision supported by the White House. Beryl Sprinkel, Chairman of the Council of Economic Advisors is reported to have objected in the following terms: "Mr. President, that's crazy. If you close the markets down, you will lose the ability to interpret what they are telling us. The markets must be left open." It was the support received on the demand side from the corporate buy-back programme that kept the NYSE open.

3 The settlement sum on the CME for 19 October was a record total of US$2.53 billion, as compared to US$120 million on a normal trading day. That is, as a result of the crash, the longs owed the shorts. Only by keeping Fedwire, the Federal Reserve secured banking payments system, open all night could the balances be settled by 7:17 am the next morning—three minutes before the opening of the currency markets.

4 For a fuller discussion of this point see Gros and Steinherr (1991).

5 A speculator who benefits from a 5% devaluation, even when selling the currency at its floor, makes a gain of 2.75% (5 – 2.25 = 2.75), assuming that after devaluation market prices are close to central parity at which rate the currency is bought back. If this position is held, say, for one week, the annualised return would be 326%.

6 In July, liquidity was normal and volumes were significantly higher than normal in forwards, FRAs, interest rate products and options.

7  Those in favour of flexible exchange rates tend to attach little importance to over-shooting, a phenomenon inherent in flexible exchange rates. In tightly integrated economies such as the European economies, overshooting destroys the essence of a levelled playing field.

8  As quoted in *Business Week*, 25 April 1994, p. 117.

9  Hedge funds in the United State are in principle regulated by the CFTC as they are profligate users of futures contracts. Most funds receive, however, a waiver from the CFTC that allows them to make only limited reports to the agency.

10 Some funds, such as the largest hedge fund which is George Soros' Quantum Fund (net assets US$10 billion) are offshore funds to escape regulatory and fiscal author-ities and can only be sold outside the United States. Some exploit market imperfec-tions in emerging markets, or invest in new high-tech firms or a portfolio of near bankrupt firms. The most intense derivative users are macro funds (see below) and "market-neutral" funds, i.e., funds that can generate profit independently of how the market moves.

11 Meriwether was one of the three top officials forced to resign in August 1991 after Salomon Brothers disclosed having made a series of improper bids at several US Treasury note auctions.

12 Data produced by International Advisory Group, Inc.

13 Had the pound not been devalued Soros would have lost transaction costs and a small spread, in all likelihood not more than US$100 million.

14 MGRM counterparties could choose to sell their forward obligations back to MGRM for a cash payment of one half of the (positive) difference between the prevailing near-month futures price and the contractually fixed supply price.

15 Assuming an average premium of US$4 on 160 million barrels.

16 The reason is that the amount of contango loss is limited by arbitrage to the cost-of-carry. The reversal of cash-and-carry arbitrage is restricted because a shortage of the physical commodity makes it costly to borrow the physical commodity.

17 As oil markets experience frequent seasonal shortages, there is a convenience yield embedded in futures prices for these periods. Futures prices reward a synthetic storage hedging strategy by permitting hedges to avoid the full cost of storage.

18 Adjusting the hedge ratio for differences in the financing of cash flows is known as "tailing the hedge". It is well known that failing to tail the hedge can force the premature liquidation of an otherwise sound hedge strategy.

19 Edwards and Canter estimate that a derivatives position of 61 million barrels (for forward deliveries of 160 million barrels) would have been appropriate.

20 As argued above, an alternative to the one-to-one hedge would have been a dy-namically adjusted minimum variance hedge. But could MGRM have relied on other instruments?

21 Storage space is limited so that the marginal cost is misleading for storing ad-ditional oil of very large quantities. Edwards and Canter estimate the potential cost of carry for MGRM at US$0.24/barrel per month, whilst the break-even point is estimated at 7–8 cents.

22 This risk could have been eliminated by a margining requirement which would have left a funding risk for MGRM.

23 In fact—highlighting the risk of legal or accounting standards trailing financial innovations—one could argue that if MGRM were owned by US shareholders (such as an experienced money centre bank) its temporary problems would have never hit the news and the strategy could have been profitable in the end.

24 Culp and Miller (1995) and Edwards and Canter (1995) disagree on issues such as (i) whether the hedge was self-financing; (ii) the riskiness of rollover; (iii) and the final decision to liquidate. Culp and Miller argue that the programme was sound

and was killed off prematurely by the unfortunate and precipitous liquidation. Edwards and Canter are more reserved. Culp and Miller put the net loss during 1993 from the marketing/hedging programme at no more than US$170 million. That loss would have been more than recouped in 1994, 1995 and 1996 when oil prices bounced back!

25 For example, Leeson instructed the settlements staff to break down the total number of contracts into several different trades and to change the prices to cause profits to be credited to "switching" accounts and losses to account '88888'. Thus, whilst the cross trades on the Exchange appeared to be genuine and within the rules of the Exchange, the records of BFS reflected pairs of transactions adding up to the same number of lots at prices bearing no relation to those executed on the floor.

26 A former executive recalled: "It was absolutely staggering to see how much the bank was transformed over a very short space of time. The transformation was huge. The focus shifted completely from the traditional product line to Baker's products, which seemed to bring in amazing amounts of money" (IFR, 4 March 1995, p. 5). According to the *Financial Times*, July 22/23, p. 9, Baker admitted that "his [own] lack of experience in exchange-traded equity derivatives" contributed to the bank's collapse. But his experience was apparently enough for a £880 000 bonus for 1994.

27 In the written agreement between BT and the New York Fed, a leveraged derivatives transaction is defined as a derivatives transaction:
- where a market move of two standard deviations in the first month would lead to a reduction in value to the counter-party of the lower of 15% of the notional amount or US$10 million, and
- for notes or transactions with final exchange of principal, where counter-party principal (rather than coupons) is at risk at maturity;
- for coupon swaps, where the coupon can drop to zero (or below) or exceed twice the market rate for that market and maturity; and
- for spread trades that include an explicit leverage factor.

28 A full description of the 29 swap transactions between Gibson and BT can be found in Overdahl and Schachter (1995).

29 According to the Banking Code (12 USC/8/8), a banking regulator may take various enforcement actions (e.g., penalties) against a bank if the bank fails to adhere to the terms of a "written agreement".

30 In his 22 years in charge of local finances the Orange County fund earned a respectable average annual return of 9.4%. This was far above the investment record of the California state fund (Jorion 1995).

31 Orange County had filed a US$3 billion law suit against Merrill Lynch, its principal advisor, alleging breaches of the Securities and Exchange Act, the California Constitution and the California Government Code. Californian state law prohibits investment of public funds in ordinary shares considered as too risky. Clearly, Citron's investment strategy was considerably riskier. The California Constitution imposes a mandatory debt ceiling preventing county treasurers from incurring debt greater than the county's annual revenue. The California Government Code requires that a county treasurer "keep safely all money belonging to the county". Deals which break these laws are declared *ultra vires* and must be rendered null and void. To avoid a penal lawsuit Merrill Lynch settled out of court for US$30 million.

32 This alarm is all the more justified as Orange County is only the most spectacular case. Morgan Stanley has been fighting a West Virginia County Court judgement that the firm knowingly violated state laws by entering into reverse purchase

agreements with the West Virginia Board of Investors. In 1992, the court ruled that the bank should pay US$32.6 million in losses and a further US$4.9 million in damages. Morgan Stanley appealed.

Other cases involve San Diego County, Escambia County in Florida and public institutions in Texas. In all cases derivative securities were used to gain greater leverage in bets on movements in interest rates. In all cases substantial losses were incurred.

33 Piper Jaffray, a sophisticated manager of mutual funds, lost an estimated US$800 million by betting on a drop in interest rates and engineering high leverage through investments in principal-only strips and inverse floaters. According to some estimates 75% of the total portfolio was invested in these MBS. In Hong Kong the US$1 billion First Investment Ltd. Leveraged US Government Bond Fund suspended trading in August 1993. Paine-Webber, J.P. Morgan, Morgan Stanley, Japan's Kokusai Investment Trust Management, and Yamaichi Securities all made substantial losses with MBS investments in 1993–94.

34 Until Congress passed the Tax Reform Act in 1986, banks invested heavily and profitably in municipal bonds as the interest rate expense on the financing of municipal bonds was tax deductible. Once that tax favour was eliminated they turned to MBSs for high yield although they had to accept the prepayment risk. By way of example, one of the most successful and prudently managed banks, Banc One, in the early 1990s held two-thirds of its investment portfolio in CMOs.

35 For example, City Colleges of Chicago sued for recession of the sale of a principal-only CMO and demanded US$50 million in damages.

36 As quoted in Carroll and Lappen (1994).

37 The tesobonos would then be held in the "foreign address" category, although their ultimate holder had a domestic Mexican address.

38 In preparation for the likely exercise by the Mexican bank of its put option, the New York investment house would normally have wanted to delta hedge by shorting the peso, but it was difficult to take a short position in the peso. Market participants argue that a close substitute was then to short "Mexico like" currencies, such as those of Argentina and Brazil. Shorting other currencies that would behave similarly to the peso would provide some cover, though there would still be basis risk.

39 A market in *equity swaps* also existed to avoid financial market regulations: the regulation that prohibited buying securities on margin and the regulation that limited the possibility of short selling. Market participants have characterised the market in offshore equity swaps as very large.

40 For more details see Miller (1996).

# PART II

# DERIVATIVES AND THEIR MARKETS

«...... MARGINS ON PLAIN VANILLA SWAPS ARE EVAPORATING, SO I WORK ON SUPER-POWER-EXOTIC-TOXIC SWAPS NOBODY WILL BE ABLE TO FULLY UNDERSTAND»

# 4

# The Revolution in Risk Management

### Farming for the Future

In November 1994, more than 300 people attended a Washington conference on risk management in US agriculture, sponsored by the Farm Foundation and the Commodity Futures Trading Commission (CFTC). Traditionally, farm profitability has been determined more in the capitals, whether Washington or Brussels, than in the fields. Increasingly, participants learn, cuts in subsidies and plans to end emergency payments from Washington will force farmers to protect their profits with insurance and hedging.

Congress, with its new Republican majority, is expected to abolish many of the costly agricultural price support programmes. Although these have been steadily reduced since 1985, farmers have not faced such potential for radical change since the subsidies began in the Great Depression.

Risk management in US agriculture
Rodney Gangwish, a Nebraska corn farmer, manages his risk through an agricultural hedging programme from Merrill Lynch. He uses two advisers to instruct Merrill Lynch over whatever share of the crop he enters into the programme. "Marketing is even more important than a combine because the marketing determines your profitability", he says. "It is the most important aspect of managing a farm today."

Gary Hellerich, who grows soya beans in Nebraska and won the top marketer award in the National Soybean Marketing Challenge in 1994, says he relies on the University of Nebraska for his approach to the market. He attempts to market 25% of his projected crop in a futures contract on the CBOT in May. During the season, he says, the market typically jumps, and he tries to catch that jump with another 25% of expected production. The remainder of his crop is sold on the "dead cat bounce", typically between two and 12 weeks after the harvest.

Tom Young, a South Dakota wheat grower, uses Finpac, a computer programme from the University of Minnesota offered through his county extension board, to create a marketing plan in January. He uses forward contracts with his local granary (elevator) for a price near his break-even point and futures contracts or options from his commodities broker to enhance his crop price.

The Alto Dairy Co-operative in Waupun is contracting for 800 000 pounds of milk per month from several members, effectively offering them a forward contract on raw milk and then hedging its risk with Cheddar cheese and non-fat dry milk futures contracts on the Coffee, Sugar and Cocoa Exchange in New York. This way small producers can have access to the same risk-management tools as the larger producers.

Increasingly, farmers are combining crop insurance and hedging, selling forward insured crops and, in several cases, collecting full payments even when their farmland is under 10 feet of water in the 1993 Midwestern floods and they haven't harvested a bushel. New crop-yield insurance futures and options contracts on the CBOT, which began trading in 1995, offer insurance companies, rail and barge transporters and trading companies a way to hedge their risks.

European Common Agricultural Policy—risks still borne by society
On the other side of the Atlantic, the European Common Agricultural Policy (CAP) has been pursuing two objectives through its programme of price fixing: to raise the incomes of European farmers and to reduce uncertainty. As a result of prices fixed above world market levels, excess production developed which had to be stocked, destroyed or exported at prices below cost. The budgetary cost of the CAP absorbs two-thirds of the European Community's budget. In addition, and more important, are the losses resulting from a subsidised resource allocation, borne by consumers who have to pay higher prices.

Although the social costs result only to a lesser extent from price stabilisation and, more importantly, from stabilisation of levels above world market prices, the CAP is an example of risk management by making the whole society (and even outsiders) bear the cost. A cost that European society is less and less inclined to bear.

Therefore, in Europe, as in the US, decades of waste, fraud and absurdity are (slowly) coming to an end as the system of support for agricultural prices is gradually dismantled. European farmers, like their US cousins, are turning to the futures markets.

They are actively encouraged by their bankers who have a concrete interest in helping farmers to manage their risks. Lending to farmers is highly concentrated in a small number of large banks set up for that purpose, together with a large number of small rural banks. "A fundamental change in lending assumptions, such as deregulation of prices or changes in tax rules, is what frequently causes a banking crisis", says John Leonard of Salomon Brothers International in London. "In Europe, reform of the CAP is just the sort of change to facilitate a banking crisis."

European agricultural futures and options
Agricultural futures and options are traded in London and Paris, and are taking hold elsewhere. Wheat futures are in the pipeline in Amsterdam, Hannover and Paris.

In Valencia, Spain, futures contracts on oranges have been trading since 8 September 1995 on a new electronic exchange known as Futuros de Citricos y Mercaderias de Valencia (FC&M) (oranges had never received much support from the CAP). Every contract enables the buyer or seller to determine the price of five tonnes of navel/navelina oranges over the next six months. Trading volume has built steadily from 100 to over 300 contracts per day.

Citrus prices typically vary by 16% to 23%. So far FC&M executives are satisfied that cash and futures prices are moving in step as agricultural co-operatives become more involved. The new Valencia exchange was established in Spain's major citrus growing area. The country is the world's fourth largest, and Europe's largest, citrus producer with five million tonnes per year, half of it oranges. Futures on another type of orange, Valencia Late, and others involving tangerines and possibly lemons are in the pipeline.

In Frankfurt and Hannover, plans to open Germany's first agricultural commodities futures exchange are moving apace. The blueprint outlined in a confidential report to the German Commodities Association favours a computerised exchange dealing initially in future contracts based on pork, wheat and possibly potatoes.

As in Valencia, the decision to opt for an electronic exchange is in keeping with the decentralised nature of agriculture. The pork contract, in particular, is expected to be used by breeders in neighbouring Denmark, where prices are already denominated in DM. A computerised exchange can also be cheaper than a US-style trading floor in terms of transaction costs, and it makes market surveillance easier.

Derivatives can help more European farmers to minimalise price instability. Like many continental countries, Spain and Germany need to diversify their financial sectors with new types of activity. The agricultural derivatives business would probably migrate to the USA should Europe's regulators prove too heavy-handed.

Agriculture untouched by the financial markets
There are, of course, many farmers in the world, like Ounko Kuramba in Tanzania, who can neither benefit from a government price stabilisation programme nor hedge their risks by selling the crop on futures exchanges. Ounko grows maize which the government buys up at a fixed price, but which is below his production price, and he fears payment arrears. There is, of course, a corn (maize) futures contract in Chicago, but Ounko has never heard about it and even if he had he would receive no support from his local banker. Like his father and grandfather before him, he manages his risk through diversification: a few vegetables, a couple of animals—enough to keep his family from starving, but sometimes only just enough.

*Source:* Adapted from *Risk Magazine*, Vol. 8, No. 2, February 1995

> "Along with the decline in the rate of productivity
> increase [in the 1970s and 1980s in the United States]
> went a strong movement into finance. The phenomenon
> is not new: Italian city-states moved from trade and industry
> into finance; Bruges, Antwerp, Amsterdam and London
> did so as well. American interest in banking was early:
> Michel Chevalier noted in 1834 that in settling a new town,
> Americans built first an inn with a bar, next a post office,
> several houses, a church, a school, a print shop and then
> a bank, this in communities that were still populated
> by bears and rattlesnakes."
>
> *Kindleberger 1996, p. 182*

THESE examples from farming illustrate well the role of derivatives in making the uncertain everyday economic life more manageable.

Derivative markets are controversial because they are not well-known outside a small group of specialists. Most people look at them with suspicion and focus on their role of highly effective instruments for speculation. And, indeed, given the leverage they provide, fortunes can be made or lost in the wink of an eye. How can they possibly do any good for a society's welfare if they only produce speculative orgies but no tangible goods, like wheat, coffee, copper or oil, or services like air transport or money management? Clearly, derivatives do not "create" anything, but, in the first section, I endeavour to show that the benefits are substantial, although indirect, as are those of many other financial services without which the cost of producing wheat, coffee, copper or oil and many other goods could be much higher and therefore the quantities available smaller. The first task is, therefore, to show what gains derivatives can provide not only to individuals or firms, but also to society as a whole.

How much would you be willing to pay for information of what the interest rates, the exchange rates, the price of oil, etc., will be next year? Some people would pay a fortune for that information, thereby putting a price sticker on its value. Futures markets do not provide this information, but for a risk manager these markets make that information redundant. This means there is tremendous value in the information provided by futures as individuals are ready to pay a price for reducing some unwanted risks. Traditionally, they have done so by taking insurance or shifting the risk to a trading partner (and paying for it!), or diversifying their activity or investments. Unfortunately, cost/benefit analysis of such strategies is murky and, in any case, it is often impossible to clearly define the nature of the risk within the context of the whole financial activity being undertaken. This results in the necessity to accept that in-depth knowledge of risk is "fuzzy" and haphazard.

A clear reflection of the fuzzy nature of risk is the fact that own funds are the most important source of finance for companies. Why do owners endow firms with large amounts of equity despite the higher cost (historically the cost of own funds exceeds the cost of borrowing by 3–6%)? Own funds are a buffer against any form of risk, a cover for all seasons. If through the use of derivatives, firms can isolate and cover specific risks (such as foreign exchange, refinancing, input prices, output prices) then their need for expensive capital as cover for general risk declines and rare and precious resources can be used elsewhere. A substantial economy-wide gain!

Of course, in order to reform this function successfully, specific risks need to be isolated, analytically treated and repackaged for trade. For this to be possible the tremendous progress in technology over the last twenty-five years has been crucial as it has increased computing power exponentially with an equally impressive fall in costs. This has allowed substantial improvement in risk measurement and the development of pricing models. The next step was to unbundle economic activity and separate out the risk component as a separably tradeable "thing". But to make these products attractive the price had to be right and for that a liquid market was necessary. Once such markets existed risks became "things" like commodities—tradeable at any moment at the right price. With the increase in volume the cost of transaction went down which in turn stimulated demand and in this way a virtuous cycle was generated.

This decomposition into the most basic components was necessary to commoditise risk. Once achieved different basic elements could be recombined to create products that allow users to determine exactly over which price range they are willing to take some losses (or none) and at what price they wish to preserve potential for gains.

Most people would agree that a world in which one can take out insurance against fire, theft, car accidents or bad health is preferable to one where no insurance exists. For the same reason, a world with derivatives is better than one without. This is not because risk is lower; quite the contrary. If insurance or other risk-hedging possibilities did not exist, many risky activities would not be carried out, or only on a smaller scale (and at a higher price). So the existence of derivatives increases in all likelihood the risk exposure of the economy—and its output. The above quote of Kindleberger refers to the deep structural crisis of the United States during the 1970s and early 1980s and the concomitant decline in productivity growth. The fundamental changes in the financial sector made, however, the economy-wide restructuration possible and turned the US economy of the 1990s into one of the most competitive on a global scale, creating more employment than all other OECD economies combined.

In addition, derivatives ease the distribution of risk at a fair price so that nobody has to bear a risk burden unwillingly. It is difficult to quantify the extent of the social gains, but at least we can be sure that such gains exist and are extensive. Everything, however, is not perfect. Prices of exchange-traded derivatives are certainly fairer—because commoditised—than the ones I, a very prudent driver, have to pay for my car insurance. On the other hand, derivatives may be used for activities such as speculation, an activity seemingly lacking in nobility.

Section 2 examines the economic benefits of price discovery through liquid derivatives markets. Because speculation is always seen as something undesirable, I look at the question more carefully and make the point that speculation provides a useful and even necessary economic service. Hence, there is no ground for policy-makers to constrain derivatives because they make speculation easier and more potent! But, as this section shows, certain derivative instruments may contribute to excess volatility.

One particularity of derivatives, the co-existence of two different market organisations—organised exchanges and over-the-counter—will be discussed in later chapters. Section 3 elaborates the economic background.

After the cost-benefit analysis of derivatives in Sections 1 to 3, the remainder of the chapter focuses on risk management (why?, how?) and the role of derivatives.

Section 4 argues that managing risks in any economy is better than ignoring risks, especially in very uncertain environments. Whilst risks have always been around, they have increased for economic decision-makers in a deregulated and liberalised environment that evolves towards an increasingly competitive and global economy. In such an environment risk management is not an ancillary but an essential, if not the most essential, activity of corporations in the brutish battle for economic survival.

Recent developments in integrated risk management, notably value-at-risk models are discussed in Section 5, and Section 6 illustrates these with concrete cases. Of course, risk management would have risen to stardom even without derivatives, the same way that the entertainment industry would have gained in importance even if movies and TV did not exist. But just consider the difference.[1]

## 1. WHAT CAN DERIVATIVES ACHIEVE?

Consider an Australian farmer confronted with the choice between planting corn or using his fields as additional pastures for his horses. The price of wheat in a year's time will crucially depend on economic and weather conditions all over the world, but especially in Russia, China, Canada and the USA. If, as he has already experienced in the past, the world market price for wheat is low, our Australian farmer might prefer not to plant wheat. By contrast, if the world market price for wheat is high, he would definitely make good money out of wheat. Not knowing what next year's price of wheat will be, a risk-averse farmer may well decide to do nothing. If, however, there is a futures price for wheat in one year's time, he can make a decision on the basis of a known price at which he can sell his not yet planted crop. Never mind whether this futures price will be close to the actual cash price in a year's time or not. At the time of planting, a farmer unwilling to take risks can make a rational choice based on the known futures price. This is clearly a significant economic gain.

As futures markets for agricultural products have been around since the middle of the 19th century, this example has well-known benefits. The same benefits can be realised whenever efficiently priced and liquid instruments exist to manage risk. A US firm competitive in the German market at a current spot exchange rate of, say, DM1.50 to the dollar, but no longer competitive at an exchange rate above DM1.70, may not be willing to bid for a long-term contract in the German market, or expand its production facilities in the United States for goods intended for the German market, if it cannot hedge the exchange risk. Similarly, German firms like Siemens or Daimler-Benz, which export more than half their domestic production, would have made gigantic losses during 1994–95, when the dollar depreciated to as little as DM1.38, shattering their existence, had they not hedged part of their currency risk.[2]

Or consider the potential gains if derivatives existed for professional skills: given the possibility of a future excess supply of physicians, would it not be a great advantage to a student wavering about going to medical school to sell part of his future income as a physician in the futures market, or buy a put option?

There are, of course, good reasons for the non-existence of futures markets even for activities where risk is substantial. In all cases the reasons boil down to the difficulty of a well-defined measure of the underlying product (what is a "physician"?, what is a "physician's income"?), the cost of transaction and the difficulty of establishing a liquid market.

## A Theoretical Benchmark: the Arrow–Debreu Model

Theory can abstract from such practical considerations and provide a benchmark vision of a world where all risk can be traded. This is done in the Arrow–Debreu model,[3] where the future (a collection of periods extending into infinity) is fully described by an exhaustive set of states of nature for each period.[4] For each state of nature in each future period there is a price for every economic good or service. Prices are therefore contingent on the state of nature (and the probability of materialisation of such a state). This is a perfect solution not only for our Australian farmer but also for his helpers whose salaries are obviously also contingent on the state of nature, as are the cost of capital, the rental of land, the prices of inputs, such as fertilisers, and the prices of the goods to be consumed out of the incomes generated.

Modelling the unknown future as probabilistic states of nature is a clever device. In fact, it can be shown that identical results can be obtained by a sufficiently large set of securities which are like options (if a particular state materialises, the buyer obtains one dollar but obtains nothing if that state does not materialise). Thus, the existence of complete economic optimality requires the existence of derivatives for a sufficient number of states of nature to span the universe of all possible outcomes.

Despite the dramatic advance of derivatives during recent years, the real world is still a far cry from the Arrow–Debreu benchmark. And, although derivatives will contribute to moving the real world closer to the theoretical ideal, it will always remain far removed. The reasons were already suggested in the example of a prospective student of medicine: the objective difficulty of sharply defining and measuring the underlying risk, and creating a sufficiently liquid market through standardisation. Theory abstracts from transaction costs—and this is not a trifle but rather key. However, over time as technology reduces cost of communication, of back-office and trading operations, as analytic advances open new applications and demand generalises from a few specialists to a larger segment of the population, more and more contracts will become economically viable.

And there are massive synergies between risk management and overall economic activity. Certain investments only become attractive if risk can be hedged, so that supply of one increases demand for the other. For example, an issuer of an option or a manager of a return-targeted investment has to hedge dynamically (i.e., to readjust continuously as time passes or prices change). This is made easier by the availability of exchange-traded futures. Again, supply of one increases demand for the other. Availability of futures reduces the cost of dynamic hedging, the growth of which increases demand for futures.

There is another fundamental point which requires attention. Whilst we can observe volatility and consider more volatile assets riskier than less volatile ones, we cannot fully describe future states of the world and the probabilities of their occurrence. As was illustrated in Chapter 1, few of the innovations in finance during the last 25 years were foreseen in 1970. And the same is true of oil crises, political upheavals or new products that have appeared on the market since then. In other words, today's prices of derivatives only reflect *known risks*—approximated by past volatility, plus a subjective evaluation by market participants of future happenings. The most important, and typically rare, future events are most likely to be totally unanticipated today. Therefore there is no hedge for them.

An illustration of this difficulty is provided by the difference between today's rate of, say, foreign currency for delivery in a year and the actual spot price in a year's time. Today's price reflects all available information, but the spot price of next year will also be determined by unanticipated events, such as earthquakes, changes in government, and so on.

Frank Knight has made the distinction between *uncertainty* and *risk*, reserving the use of the word "risk" to events for which there is an empirically observable probability distribution.[5] Pursuing this differentiation it is clear that markets can only deal with risk, but not with uncertainty. That is, futures prices reflect the statistically comprehensible part, but not the surprise part, of uncertainty.

Where uncertainty dominates there is no scope for efficient markets. For example, the probability of bankruptcy of a particular firm over a given time horizon cannot be established statistically, and can only be "guessed" with a complex and inconclusive analysis of the markets in which the firm operates, its competitive position and its balance sheet and cost structure. This is precisely what rating agencies and bankers do all the time. Traditionally, there were no markets on which the bankruptcy risk of the firm could be traded. However, the risk of bankruptcy can be lowered through diversification and statistical properties can be applied to a large pool of firms. This is what insurance companies are doing all the time. Recently, however, a new derivatives market for individual credit risks has been developing (see Chapter 6). Thus, not all uncertainty can be traded away, only a small but expanding subset. For the remainder risk can be lowered through diversification and can then be traded.

**Can Derivatives Reduce Risk?**

It is sometimes argued that derivatives do not produce a net gain for society, as risk is only *redistributed* but not *reduced*. This is certainly correct from a *static* angle: the availability of a wheat futures contract does not affect the probability of bad weather. But because someone else is willing to buy the risk of lower wheat prices next year our Australian farmer is producing wheat, whereas otherwise he might not be. Hence redistribution of risk results in a different and superior production outcome—at least if futures prices are determined in a competitive market. The conditions for markets to be competitive are described below.

We should not forget, however, that any activity, particularly during its infant stage of development, creates risks of its own. In the learning process of the institutions offering new services errors are made; and end-users must become familiar with new products, as we saw in Chapter 3. Even beyond the infant stage there are risks inherent in the new markets. For example, as long as markets are suppressed by governmental policies and prices perhaps controlled, volatility is low. That does not mean, however, that risk is low. It just means that somebody else (the government or society at large) is footing the bill and that sub-optimal decisions are being made (price controls usually result in excess demand or supply) based on false price signals. The argument that greater use of derivatives has increased volatility is—barring exceptional circumstances—therefore not valid. We show below that it is a "spurious correlation", due to the fact that derivatives develop when volatility is high.

More serious is the point that new derivative products deal with some risks but create new ones. For example, in all derivatives contracts there is considerable credit and liquidity risk (which would not exist if there were no derivatives contracts). But, again, the importance of this argument is limited. If the credit risk in such contracts is not underpriced due to implicit government guarantees, then that risk *must* be smaller than the risks hedged through these contracts. What is to be corrected is not the contract but the implicit subsidy. This is precisely what I propose in Chapter 9.

In most hedge strategies it is extremely difficult to eliminate *all* risk, although it is always possible to trade-off *some* or *most* of the risk. Take, for example, an investor holding corporate bonds of a certain risk class. There is no futures contract for the same type of bonds and therefore the investor may hedge with Treasury futures. When interest rates increase both the value of the corporate bonds and of the Treasury bonds will decline, but not by exactly the same percentage. This is called "spread" risk. If, however, the interest rates sensitivities of the long investment and the short futures are well known and stable then their correlation can be used to set the hedge ratio such that most of the spread risk will disappear.

Akin to spread risk, another important source of risk is "basis risk",[6] explained in Technical Insight 4.1.

### The Costs of Untradeable Risks

As long as specific risks are not tradeable commodities—most are not yet—unfocused risk management has an incisive influence on economic decisions; decisions that show up as inefficient detours when markets for risk are available. We already gave an example at the beginning of this chapter: the extensive use of own funds as a buffer for all seasons. But economic life abounds with such inefficiencies: where foreign exchange risk cannot be hedged foreign trade and investment is likely to be lower; where the future cost of capital is uncertain investment is likely to suffer. Even the structure of economic activity is distorted by non-tradeable risk, as a clever example by Robert Merton illustrates. Suppose a company owns oil reserves and a distribution network, but no refinery. To secure its sales of unrefined oil and purchases of refined oil for distribution, an obvious strategy is to build a refinery. And, indeed, traditional oil companies are vertically integrated from oil drilling to distribution, despite the fact that oil refining is not the most profitable activity. When futures markets for unrefined and refined oil exist, our hypothetical

**Technical Insight 4.1**   Basis risk

Even for futures of exactly the same specification as the underlying asset, there is a risk, called "basis" risk. To see this define the basis at time t for a contract expiring at time T as:

$$\text{Basis}_{t,T} = \text{cash price}_t - \text{futures price}_{t,T}$$

Consider the example of a gold contract. Arbitrage ensures that the futures price is equal to the cash price plus the financial cost of keeping a stock of gold plus the storage cost. If the futures price were higher then an investor could borrow money, buy gold, stock the gold until delivery and cash-in a riskless profit from having sold a gold futures. If the futures price were lower than suggested by the above relationship, called the "general cost-of-carry relationship", then a similar arbitrage argument can be made.

The case of a negative basis (since futures prices are normally higher than cash prices) is called a *contango*. If the basis is positive, then the market is said to be in *backwardation*.[7] Such market conditions can and do occur (see the Metallgesellschaft example in Chapter 3). A necessary condition is that the cost-of-carry relationship described above does not hold. How is this possible? The major reason is a shortage of the physical commodity limiting arbitrage possibilities. Typically, when commodities are in short supply, cash prices are rising and this is when markets may be in backwardation.[8]

Most futures contracts exist for several expiration dates, although rarely for periods longer than two years. If an investor wishes to hedge for longer periods, he must roll the hedge forward. But even when longer dated futures contracts do exist, it is not obvious that they are more appropriate than shorter dated contracts. The shorter the contract the more futures and cash prices are correlated and hence the smaller is the basis risk. Using a more distant contract typically increases the basis risk but reduces the frequency of rollovers and hence transaction costs. Most hedgers prefer short (near month or near quarter) contracts and as a consequence liquidity is much higher for short than for long contracts. This is also the reason why very long-dated futures do not trade.

company can create a "virtual refinery": sell forward unrefined petroleum and, with a time lag, buy forward refined petroleum. The outcome is identical to physically owning a refinery, but allows the company to specialise in the physical activity where it is best.

# 2. PRICE DISCOVERY AND LIQUIDITY

## Price Discovery

The ability of futures markets to provide information about prices is a major economic gain: it makes the economic system more efficient. Just suppose there were no futures prices at all. It would then be difficult to make decisions about whether to buy certain commodities now or to wait, whether to produce now or later, and so on. People would have to make decisions on the basis of their own subjective beliefs.

Of course, for economic efficiency it is not enough to have prices for future delivery. These prices have to accurately reflect expected relative costs of production and benefits from consumption as is the case for spot prices. Moreover, as shown in Technical Insight 4.1, spot and futures prices are linked so that they must be inter-temporally consistent. It would be impossible to achieve an efficient set of spot prices in the absence of futures prices: to obtain efficient spot prices it is necessary to dispose of efficiently set futures prices.

Efficient prices can only be obtained in liquid, competitive markets. This is because full information, price transparency and instantaneous dissemination are required—exactly what trading on organised exchanges provides. Typically, several futures contracts on a commodity or asset are trading simultaneously, each calling for delivery at a different time in the future. These prices are the result of competitive trading on the exchanges, reflecting all current expectations about future supply and demand. These prices are continuously disseminated throughout the world by elaborate exchange-supported price-reporting systems.

## The Role of Speculation

It is intuitively obvious that cash prices affect futures prices. Does causality also run the other way, that is, can future prices affect cash prices? Suppose the futures price for immediate delivery is higher than the cash price. Then arbitragers will buy the commodity in the cash market, thereby pushing up the cash price, and sell futures contracts until the two prices are equal. In this example there is no need for speculation. Technical Insight 4.2 shows that in more realistic cases speculators are playing a useful and necessary role.

Is the view of speculation developed in Technical Insight 4.2, i.e., that speculators, on average, stabilise prices, too benign? Critics would argue that if speculators do not act on the basis of fundamentals, but follow the herd, they contribute to irrational price movements. Whilst this argument is not restricted to futures and other derivatives markets, its pertinence is

**Technical Insight 4.2**   Hedgers and speculators

Assume all participants in a futures market are hedgers and there is therefore no speculation.

In the graph, hypothetical demand and supply schedules are drawn for a specific futures contract. It is also assumed that market participants hold a view about the future spot price (this is the weak part of the story: where does such an expected price come from?), denoted $EP_{t+k}$.

The demand schedule of long hedgers is downward sloping until the expected price is reached, and the supply curve is upward sloping until the expected price is reached. When future prices are much above expected spot prices, long hedgers will be reluctant to seek cover, since they will pay more than they expected to pay in $period_{t+k}$. As the price declines demand goes up until all positions are hedged at $Q$. Beyond $Q$ the demand curve becomes vertical. The supply schedule indicates the quantity of futures contracts that short hedgers wish to sell. Short hedgers are reluctant to hedge when futures prices are much below the expected price, because their expected spot price is more attractive. At or above the expected future spot price they hedge fully (see Figure 4.1).

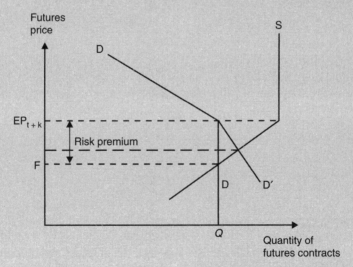

**Figure 4.1**   Speculation reduces the risk premium

As shown in the graph, the differences between the equilibrium price F and the expected price $EP_{t+k}$ is a *risk premium*. The example in the graph depicts a net short hedging imbalance. At other times there may be a net long hedging imbalance with the future price above the expected price.

Independently of whether short or long hedgers pay a risk premium the cost of hedging is increased and the market price is a bad predictor of expected spot prices. The price discovery gain of futures markets is at stake.

Such a sub-optimal outcome as in the above graph is the result of having constrained market participation to hedgers. What happens if speculators are admitted?

Speculators observing the difference between expected spot and futures prices in the graph will purchase futures contracts at price F, sell at the expected price if it indeed materialises and pocket the gain. (Of course, *ex post* the spot price may be quite different from the expected spot price, hence speculation is risky.) Their purchase will shift the demand curve to D' and drive up the futures price, thereby reducing the risk premium and hence the cost of hedging. Future prices then become better predictors of expected spot prices. Thus, more speculation makes futures markets more efficient at performing their hedging and price discovery function.

An open question remains, however, whether speculation succeeds in eliminating the risk premium (i.e., in reducing it to an undiversifiable threshold) or, more modestly, only contributes to reducing it.

*Source:* Edwards and Ma (1992)

particularly pronounced here, as derivatives are the most efficient (and leveraged) vehicles for speculators. The price discovery function would be seriously impaired by herd behaviour; speculation would increase volatility which would lead to higher risk premiums and necessarily less efficient prices.

The issue is thus both a theoretical and an empirical one: does speculation result in irrational price movements and increased price volatility? As the empirical literature has failed so far to produce conclusive evidence, I concentrate on the theoretical arguments.

## Do Derivatives Increase Volatility?

Theoretically, it is fairly obvious that if market participants are rational, derivative markets tend to stabilise prices for the reasons outlined in Technical Insight 4.2. If, by contrast, they are irrational, this positive result disappears for the obvious reason that anything is possible if people are irrational. This is, therefore, not a very interesting observation, neither easy to prove nor disprove empirically, except that market participants cannot all be irrational all the time.

More interesting is the question of whether volatility could be increased by derivatives markets even if people behave rationally. Technical Insight 4.3 surveys the literature and concludes that this is indeed possible in the presence of market imperfections. The effects of destabilising behaviour depend strongly on the nature of market imperfections and can, in specific cases, be corrected through appropriate regulatory actions.

**Examples of Added Volatility**

The line of reasoning discussed so far has consisted of treating derivatives as an instrument for making speculation more powerful and checking whether speculation was a bad thing. This approach is not entirely satisfactory because derivatives by themselves may pose specific problems, such as easing circumvention of official regulations, distorting traditional data of bank balance sheets or the balance of payments as in the Mexican débâcle discussed in Chapter 3.

One specific problem—but there are others—attracted attention in 1995 when the US dollar moved from a value of 101 yen in early January to 80 yen in mid-April and back to 104 yen in mid-September. This was widely interpreted as a substantial overshooting and, despite many macroeconomic explanations for the extreme volatility of the dollar/yen rate, market specialists were not convinced that the dollar's decline could be explained with market fundamentals. They pointed to the role played by derivatives in the depreciation of the dollar against the yen, in particular the role of "knock-out" exchange rate options. Technical Insight 4.4 provides details. The magnitude of the effect of these options on the dollar/yen spot rate is difficult to estimate. But since options prices were directly affected, and implied volatilities at times doubled, the spot market must have been affected. So certain types of derivatives do add to price volatility, i.e., market instability, purely on account of their technical construction.

## 3. ORGANISED EXCHANGES vs. OVER-THE-COUNTER: WHY DO DIFFERENT MARKET ORGANISATIONS CO-EXIST?

Most of the arguments developed so far pertain to all derivatives. What requires explanation is why two forms of market organisation, OTC markets and organised exchanges co-exist. For example, why is there an interbank market for forward contracts *and* a futures market? Both serve to insure against price risk, but the key to understanding their difference is *liquidity*. We have already seen that price discovery is a major social gain of derivative markets, but a necessary pre-condition for meaningful prices is that markets

**Technical Insight 4.3**  Are derivatives markets stabilising spot markets?

"Destabilisation" can refer to two quite different processes. The one most people have in mind is "excessive volatility", that is where the standard deviation of prices is larger than some benchmarks. Another notion of instability is where prices diverge from one equilibrium to another.

Several researchers have been able to identify specific conditions ("market imperfections") which lead to market destabilisation in the first sense. Genotte and Leland (1990) distinguish between informed and uninformed investors. The latter interpret a price movement as a reflection of a change in fundamentals and therefore sell (or buy), thus reinforcing the price movement. By contrast, informed investors distinguish between supply shocks and changes in fundamentals (Black 1988, Grossman 1988). If there are few informed investors, then markets are illiquid and prices excessively volatile. In markets where informed investors dominate, uninformed investors cannot generate excess volatility (Cutler et al. 1989, Hart and Kreps 1986).

Brennan and Schwartz (1989) have shown that portfolio insurance by itself is not enough to explain excess volatility. In conjunction with the presence of misinformed investors, portfolio insurance does, however, contribute to temporary excess volatility. Moreover, the spot market operations required for portfolio insurance are non-linear functions of prices, generating the possibility of multiple equilibria and hence catastrophes (jumps from one equilibrium to another).

Artus (1994) examined a specific market imperfection: restricted access to credit. His analysis shows that in combination with limited information or noisy signals, destabilisation in the second sense cannot be excluded.

Bowman and Faust (1995) give another example of destabilisation in the second sense. They show that the addition of an option market may lead to sunspot equilibria[9] in an economy which has no sunspot equilibrium before the option market is introduced. This phenomenon occurs because the payoff of an option contract is contingent upon market prices which are exogenous for each agent, but not for the economy as a whole. One implication is that option markets, instead of helping to complete markets, may in fact increase the number of events against which agents need to insure. The intuition behind this result is the following. A movement in the price of an asset on which an option is written would not change the return of a state-contingent security of the Arrow–Debreu model, but it will change the return of the option contract and thereby reallocate wealth across agents. This wealth reallocation will change excess demand and can help support the price change as a new equilibrium.

**Technical Insight 4.4**   Knock-out options on dollar/yen rates: is the messenger distorting the message?

Knock-out options are used to hedge only against moderate fluctuations in the price of the underlying assets, but not extraordinarily large movements and are cancelled when spot rates reach a specified "knock-out" level. Such partial hedges became popular because they are relatively inexpensive. These option contracts can exert a disproportionate influence on the underlying exchange rate, under market conditions similar to those in early March 1995.[10] Large volumes of knock-out options were purchased by Japanese corporations during the previous 12 months to partially hedge the yen value of expected dollar receivables against the possibility of a further modest appreciation of the yen. For example, a corporation would pay a fee up front for the right to sell dollars against yen at, say, 90 yen and also specify that in the unlikely event the yen appreciates all the way to, say, 85 yen, the option would be "knocked-out"; it would become useless to the corporation, while the options dealer would earn the full premium.

In late February 1995, the major dealers apparently had on their books a substantial quantity of these knock-out options with knock-out values between 90 Yen and 80 Yen.[11] When the yen appreciated in early March toward the knock-out levels, dealers had an incentive to push the value of the yen up through the "knock-out" levels and thereby eliminate their obligations under the options contract.[12] In addition, some dealers, who had dynamically hedged these contracts, had positions requiring the sale of dollars after these "knock out" levels had been reached.[13] Moreover, the original customers were exposed to an appreciating yen as the "knock-out" level was approached and their currency-risk protection removed. They, too, would be inclined to purchase more dollar put options or sell dollars. Under the circumstances prevailing at the time—a bunching of limit orders, spot prices approaching the knock-out levels, momentum from technical analysis—it is likely that trading by major dealers influenced the spot exchange rate for a short period around a specific knock-out value. This provided additional pressure on the exchange rate to move to the next lower knock-out value, and so on.

*Source:* IMF 1996, pp. 42–4

are liquid.[14] In what follows we first show why organised exchanges thrive on liquidity and how liquidity sets up a virtuous cycle by reducing transaction costs which in turn generate higher liquidity. For simplicity of exposition we limit the reasoning to futures and forward contracts.

### Comparing Futures and Forwards

All futures contracts of the same specification are perfect substitutes for each other. By contrast, all forward contracts of the same specifications are not perfect substitutes because the parties to the contract matter and may be different from one contract to another. As a futures contract is a product of an organised exchange, its validity is independent of the buyer and of the seller. Thus, by design a futures contract is *fungible*. Note the similarity between a futures contract and currency and between a forward contract and a cheque: money does not smell, that is, we do not care from whom we receive cash, but the quality of a cheque depends on the quality of the issuer.[15]

But if liquidity is so important, why is it that futures contracts trade at different maturities, despite the fact that liquidity would be maximal if trading were restrained to a single contract? The only single maturity date that would remove the necessity of renewal is infinity.[16] In markets, where delivery is desirable, finite maturities are necessary and so is a trade-off between liquidity gains and other desirable properties. Consistent with this view is the fact that the maturities available for futures contracts are rather limited and set so as to accommodate the most frequent maturity demands, even if maturities in some markets (such as Eurodollar) extend up to four years.

Pursuing the comparison with currency, a futures contract acquires the same advantages over a forward contract as trade settled by money has over barter trade. This attribute of money makes futures contracts a temporary store of purchasing power.

In futures markets there are increasing returns to liquidity.[17] One should, therefore, expect that the same contract is only traded on more than one exchange if the volume of trade is very large so that increasing costs offset the benefit of greater liquidity, or if there are other advantages such as trading in different time zones. Most of the time when similar contracts are traded on different exchanges they are, indeed, not strictly identical.

### Price Variability is Essential for Futures

Two features are key in determining the suitability for trading on an exchange: the *number of potential users*[18] and the *price variability*. OTC contracts have a definite edge over futures when demand is limited either in total or due to differentiation. Differentiation may be demand induced or an artefact. In the latter case, standardisation pays by yielding higher liquidity and eventually tradeability on the exchanges.

The benefit of organised futures trading increases with price variability. As long as prices exhibit only small variability (as has been the case in European agricultural markets due to EU price support policies), there is little hedging needed or speculatory potential except for periods of crisis. Therefore there is little sustained demand for futures trading and OTC contracts may satisfy the temporary needs during exchange market crises. Daily liquidity on the exchanges can only be sustained by permanent price variability (risk).

This association between price variability and futures trading has often caused confusion—inverting the causality just suggested: some observers argue that futures trading increases price variability when, in fact, price variability is a pre-condition for the emergence of futures trading.

Total costs of a futures contract (the commission per trade and margin payments) depend on the volume of trade and the size of open commitment. Liquidity has therefore two opposite effects on total cost: more transactions require higher costs, but as liquidity increases with volume and the standard deviation of the distribution of market-clearing prices goes down, costs decline. The net effect depends on which argument dominates. At a high enough volume of trade the liquidity gain becomes small, but at low volume the liquidity gain dominates.

This suggests an evolution driven by a "virtuous circle". As price variability in a market increases (as was the case in currency markets after abandonment of the Bretton Woods system), demand for futures trading goes up. The greater volume increases liquidity, which tends to lower marginal costs so that commissions and margins go down. In response, demand for futures contracts goes up, further increasing liquidity, which in turn . . .

Of course, if price volatility declines for a particular commodity (as was the case with inflation due to the Fed's restrictive monetary policy after 1982) the circle becomes vicious and may lead to the extinction of a futures contract trading (as was the case with the consumer price index (CPI) contract introduced in 1985).

## 4. IS RISK MANAGEMENT A FUNDAMENTAL CORPORATE OBJECTIVE?

Excess return is either a reward for genius (innovation) or for risk-taking. But whilst some risks are in the nature of a specific activity and are willingly taken, others are not. For example, a firm has to accept the risk of shifts in the demand for its product. Yet it does not have to accept and may prefer not to take the risk of increasing prices for its inputs, or of unforeseen increases in its financial costs, or of losses in export sales caused by exchange rate variations.

There are various ways of getting rid of such undesirable risks. Derivatives are one type of instrument among others, but they are often the ones that offer most flexibility and cost effectiveness which explains their wide and growing use as hedge instruments. Indeed, according to various sources, most derivative end-users employ derivatives for hedging and only a minority for increasing their risk exposure (speculation).[19]

## Should Corporations Hedge?

Some 25 years ago risk management was not very topical. The reason is not only that financial derivatives were not available. The logic also works the other way round: risk was less important and, therefore, so was the need for derivatives as hedging instruments. Risk was less pronounced because under the Bretton Woods system exchange rates were much more stable and so, therefore, were interest rates. Liberalisation and deregulation of economic and financial activities fostered internationalisation and finally globalisation of economic activity, thereby increasing the risk exposure to exchange and interest rate movements. As for financial institutions, price competition between banks was restricted by deposit rate regulation and in some countries by cartel practices so that market risk was limited. As illustrated by the introductory story, the reduction of government intervention in certain non-financial markets, such as agriculture, has also increased price risk and hence the need for hedging.

Whilst it is clear why our Australian farmer would like to hedge the price risk of his future crop, it is not so evident why a large corporation (financial or non-financial) would want to hedge. The *shareholders* of a corporation typically own a diversified portfolio. Indeed, the corporate form of organisation was developed precisely to disperse corporate risk among many investors. If that is so, it is difficult to see why corporations themselves also need to reduce risk? For example, a US investor holding Ford Motor Company shares who does not wish to be exposed to the risk of a higher dollar in terms of yen, which would lower Ford's profits, could offset that risk himself by adding to his portfolio Toyota shares which would gain from the higher dollar. Over time, hedging transactions sometimes make money and at other times lose money. Hedging cannot systematically make money and on average should just break even. So why hedge at corporate level?

This question is at the heart of a paradigm of corporate finance and goes back to a ground-breaking article by the Nobel prize winners, Merton Miller and Franco Modigliani.[20] The key insight of Miller and Modigliani was that value is created on the assets side of the balance sheet when companies make good investments in plant, products and know-how. How companies finance these assets—through debt, equity or retained earnings—is totally irrelevant.

It only has implications for the distribution of gains among different providers of funds, but not for the overall value of these investments.

If this view is accepted, then it follows immediately that risk management at corporate level is irrelevant. And so is our argument that risk management reduces the need for expensive own funds because their assumptions *equalise the cost of own and borrowed funds*. However, the Miller–Modigliani benchmark only holds under a very restrictive set of conditions which are far removed from the real world.[21] For corporate financing and hedging to increase the firm's value in the real world requires at least one of the following conditions to be true: that they reduce the likelihood or cost of financial distress; that there is "inside" information; that they reduce "agency" costs, that is conflicts of interest between management, shareholders or creditors; and that financial markets are less than perfect!

Most people would readily agree that those conditions are generally applicable. Financial markets are certainly not as perfect as postulated and some forms of financing are cheaper than others. Typically, companies prefer to fund investments with retained earnings over debt issues and are most reluctant to issue equity. Empirical research also suggests that companies frequently reduce their investment spending when they lack sufficient internally generated cash flows. By the end of the day, and despite the insights of the Miller–Modigliani breakthrough, there is a solid empirical basis for risk management at the corporate level.

Once it is recognised that capital markets are not perfect, it can be argued that volatility disrupts investment because it forces business to both reduce the amount of capital devoted to a new project and seek external resources at times of low profitability. However, due to capital market imperfections, external financing is more costly than internally generated funds. These added costs result in under-investment in low profitability periods. Recognising this, the company would gain from volatility-reducing strategies. One way to achieve lower earnings volatility is to shift into low volatility activities or to diversify. Given the specific know-how of a company, it is unlikely that such a strategy is optimal. The other way of achieving lower volatility is to maintain activities chosen in recognition of the company's competitive advantage and reduce earnings volatility through hedging.

There is an additional argument that goes beyond the Miller–Modigliani context. The Miller–Modigliani argument is confined to diversifiable risk, that is, risk that can be eliminated by suitable diversification. For example, by investing in shares of the Ford Motor Company a loss may occur either because the Ford shares underperform the overall stock market or because the stock market falls and so do Ford shares. The first type of risk is *diversifiable*, the second is *undiversifiable*.

There is a fundamental difference between these two concepts of risk. Diversifiable risk does not have to be borne by anybody if not desired. By contrast, undiversifiable risk has to be borne by somebody, but any particular economic agent has the possibility of transferring it to somebody else. The role of risk management is precisely to keep risk at a level and in a form judged acceptable and the choice of instruments is dictated by the need to reduce the cost of transferring risk. As such, each individual agent will gain even if economy-wide undiversifiable risk is not reduced. By not being hampered by an unnecessary risk burden the individual corporation or financial intermediary can use its resources more effectively and can assume more of the entrepreneurial risks.

### Governments, too, can Benefit from Hedging

It is not only corporations, but also governments, that can derive benefits from hedging future tax revenues or financing costs. Shortfalls in government revenues can generate a downward spiral of reduced public sector spending, lost jobs and further tax revenue losses. In fact, hedging of tax revenue has been tested by the state of Texas, where that state's revenues depend heavily on oil prices, given its oil-based economy. In 1992 Texas took experimental measures to stabilise the budget and protect the value of oil resources. The state treasury allocated US$2.5 million to purchase oil options with the aim of providing a hedge.[22]

## 5. RISK MANAGEMENT—SCIENCE OR FAD?

The difficulties many firms are experiencing in setting up reliable risk management systems—some of which were discussed in Chapter 3—have created the impression that risk management and the use of derivatives is perilous, difficult to control and, perhaps, best avoided. On the other side of the equation, the incomes of dealers and risk managers are such as to suggest that what they do requires sheer genius. This seems astonishing to those who are familiar with the brain power and organisational sophistication needed to develop, produce and market aeroplanes or any other high-tech product. Why is there a sheer impenetrable myth around risk management?

### Risk management: Change of Guards

To insiders the major reason is that now is a period of transition where risk management techniques and products are new and unfamiliar to most senior managers, who often have to trust and rely on younger specialists. Rapid technological progress also makes catching-up on the learning curve extremely difficult, so that the generation gap at times widens instead of narrows. This is, perhaps, the most fundamental reason. In addition, other risks with which we are familiar, such as engineering risks, can rely on extensive testing in a physical environment that is controlled. Not many surprises can affect the oscillation of a metallic object once all the physical factors, such as temperature, atmospheric pressure, friction, etc., have been controlled. But oscillations of interest or exchange rates are, to a large extent, the result of combinations of exogenous events. Past influences and performance are only a guide to the future if historic patterns repeat themselves. Major economic crises are unpredictable. Therefore, there is always room for surprises. Moreover, only rarely can a risk be completely hedged; there is always the possibility that the residual risk (a counter-party risk, rollover risk, basis risk, stability of historic correlations) may misbehave.

But with time, as tested structures and methods of risk management become standard and as the technological revolution is absorbed in top management's '"cultural" revolution, the structural-managerial uncertainty will settle down.

**Principles of Risk management**

Any risk manager has first to decide what kinds of risks he is ready to accept and what kinds he does not wish to accept. After this very general definition of acceptable types of risk, the corporation's risk tolerance has to be established, reflecting the maximum risk over a chosen time horizon in relation to the firm's capital, presumably contingent upon the risk–reward trade-off. Once risk tolerance has been defined, management must proceed to measure risk exposure, monitor risk and decide how to achieve these targets. It is only at the last stage of risk management that derivatives play an important role, notwithstanding the practical difficulty of risk management and monitoring when complicated derivatives (e.g., options) are on or off balance sheet.

A satisfactory risk measurement system covers the entire corporation, not only specific profit centres, such as the treasury, foreign sales or subsidiaries, and takes into account the correlations that may exist among different assets and liabilities.

So far, however, there is no system that can deal with all types of risk and aggregate them meaningfully. The most developed systems are those dealing with *market risk*, that is, the risk that the evolution of interest rates, exchange rates, or other financial market prices will affect net worth negatively. Product risk or counter-party risk are more difficult to assess, still more difficult to aggregate with market risk and, worse, may not be independent of market risk. To appreciate this difficulty, consider the financing of a real-estate investment through a fixed-rate mortgage with interest-rate risk hedged with a fixed-rate/variable-rate swap. If the counter-party in the swap is always able and willing to pay, the hedge is fully successful. However, when market interest rates increase, the counter-party's obligations rise and the incentives for the counter-party to default increase as well.[23] Counter-party risk in a derivatives contract is particularly difficult to assess as it is correlated with the underlying risk which is to be hedged. Moreover, the nature of the correlation is endogenous to the contractual arrangements (e.g., maturity of the contract, settlement contingent on specified events such as downgrading by independent rating agencies).

It is against this background that state-of-the-art risk-management models need to be seen. The currently most favoured measure of corporate risk is "value-at-risk", which has become the standard for financial firms.

## Value-at-risk

Value-at-risk (VAR) is an estimate of the "maximum" loss in the value of a portfolio or financial position over a given time period with a certain level of confidence. This level of confidence is represented by the probability that the actual loss will not exceed a pre-specified "maximum". The probability is usually referred to as the confidence interval. The Basle Committee's 1995 Accord allows banks to use proprietary models and sets a capital charge which is the higher of:

- the previous day's value-at-risk
- three times the average of the daily value-at-risk of the preceding 60 business days.

Basic requirements are that VAR be computed daily, using a 99% one-tailed confidence interval; that a minimum price shock equivalent to ten trading days (holding period) be used; and that the model incorporate a historical observation period of at least one year. Under these standards, a US$100 million value-at-risk means that there is only a 1% chance that the loss in the portfolio value over a ten-day period will exceed US$100 million. Specifying value-at-risk as the standard risk measurement is like specifying a common unit of measurement.

Value-at-risk can be, and currently is, estimated by using various techniques. The so-called asset-normal approach is commonly used and assumes that asset returns are jointly normally distributed.[24] Under this assumption, the probability distribution of the rate of return of a portfolio can be estimated easily and quickly, which facilitates the calculation of value-at-risk. The main disadvantage of this approach is that the value-at-risk calculation might not be accurate if the normal distribution does not offer a good description of the underlying price data. Furthermore, the asset-normal approach cannot easily deal with option risk, as the value of an option relates to the cash price in a non-linear fashion. Technical Insight 4.5 provides examples for the computation of value-at-risk and discusses the problems posed by options.

Even after adopting a given value-at-risk model, choices of empirical implementation lead to vast differences in results. Also not to be forgotten is the

**Technical Insight 4.5** Computation of value-at-risk

Two parameters are essential for VAR computation. The selected time horizon T and the confidence level C. The Basle Accord retained T = 10 days to reflect a trade-off between cost of frequent monitoring and benefits of early detection. From a business perspective, however, the choice of time horizon is dictated by the nature of the portfolio analysed (trading vs. investment portfolio, for example). The confidence level of the Basle proposal is 99%. This choice is determined by a trade-off between the safety of the financial system and the adverse effect of capital requirements. The choice is also important for model validation.

*Example 1*:
A bond portfolio valued at US$100 million, has a duration of 3.6 years. (Duration is defined as the price sensitivity of a bond with respect to changes in relevant market interest rates; Section 6 discusses duration more fully.) If the worst increase in interest rates over the next ten days at the 99% level is 1.23%, then the worst dollar loss is:

$$VAR = 100 \cdot 3.6 \cdot 0.0123 = US\$4.43 \text{ million}$$

For normally distributed returns the computations of VAR become particularly straightforward. The confidence level C corresponds to a value $\alpha$ that can be read from a cumulated normal distribution function. For C = 0.99 one obtains $\alpha = 2.23$. For an initial value Vo of a portfolio VAR with respect to the mean is:

$$VAR(mean) = \alpha\sigma \sqrt{T}Vo$$

and with respect to zero:

$$VAR(zero) = (\alpha\sigma \sqrt{T} - \mu T)Vo$$

where $\sigma$ is the daily standard deviation, $\mu$ the daily mean return and T the chosen horizon.

*Example 2:*
The daily standard-deviation of a portfolio is US$16.2 million. Then

$$VAR(mean) = 16.2 \cdot 2.33 \sqrt{10} = US\$119.36 \text{ million}$$

*Example 3:*
Consider a portfolio of two assets to show the importance of correlations between the various assets in a portfolio. Call the share of asset 1 in

the initial portfolio Vo $w_1$, and its standard deviation $\sigma$. Same for asset 2. Call the correlation coefficient between returns of both assets $\rho$. (For standard assets all $\sigma$ and $\rho$ can be obtained, daily, from RiskMetrics.) Then:

$$VAR = \alpha(w^2_1 \sigma^2_1 + w^2_2 + 2w_1w_2\rho\sigma_1\sigma_2)^{1/2} \sqrt{T}Vo$$

Clearly, when $\rho = 0$ the term in parenthesis can be much smaller than average variance. With $\rho < 0$ the variance is further reduced. In general, except for $\rho$ close to (plus) one there are gains from diversification.

Suppose $w_1 = 0.8$, $w_2 = 0.2$, $\sigma_1 = 2.6$, $\sigma_2 = 4.9$, $\rho = 0.4$, $\alpha = 2.33$

Then:
VAR (asset 1) = $2.33 \cdot 2.6 \cdot \sqrt{10} = 19.15$
VAR (asset 2) = $2.33 \cdot 4.9 \cdot \sqrt{10} = 36.10$
VAR (portfolio) = $2.33 (0.8^2 \cdot 2.6^2 + 0.2^2 \cdot 4.9^2 + 2 \cdot 0.8 \cdot 0.2 \cdot 0.4 \cdot 2.6 \cdot 4.9)^{1/2} \sqrt{10} = 19.36$

The VAR of a portfolio with investments in both assets is about the same as for an investment in the low risk asset, thanks to diversification.

*Example 4:*
Consider a forward contract which, as was seen in this chapter, is equivalent to a short position in a domestic bond (borrow at r) and a long position in an asset acquired at price S and receiving yield y. VAR can be computed as in previous examples with the help of the standard deviation. Alternatively, VAR of a forward (or any other linear contract) can be viewed as the VAR of a portfolio of exposures on risk factors. Indeed, fluctuations in the value of the forward contract can be written:

$$df = \frac{df}{ds} ds + \frac{df}{dr} dr + \frac{df}{dy} dy$$

The VAR of the contract can now be established by evaluating separately the three terms on the right-hand side.

An approach that can be used to compute the value-at-risk of a portfolio with options and other derivative instruments is the so-called delta normal method. This approach treats an option as a position equal to the market value of the underlying asset multiplied by the delta of the option. Whilst conceptually and computationally easy, it ignores the effect of a change in the delta of an option (the gamma risk). More importantly, since the linear approximation only works for small changes of the underlying asset prices, the approach can produce a significantly biased estimate of value-at-risk when large price changes occur.

The "delta gamma" approach is an extension of the delta normal approach. It incorporates both the delta and the gamma of an option to construct an approximation of the option position. Whilst this approach can yield more accurate results, it is also computationally more intensive and still leaves out the "vega" risk.

An approach that has become very popular among the sophisticated derivative houses is the so-called model-simulation or Monte Carlo approach. This approach directly assesses the value of a derivative asset by evaluating its price for a large number of simulated price paths for the underlying asset, which are generated according to a particular dynamic model. An advantage of this approach is that it can be used for any kind of derivative contract. Furthermore, provided that the assumed price dynamics are correct, this method would produce more accurate estimates of value-at-risk because it does not rely on approximations of any kind. This method, however, introduces model risk into the calculation—the risk that the underlying model of price dynamics might not be correct. Moreover, because banks make different assumptions about price behaviour, the same Monte Carlo approach can produce very different estimates of value-at-risk.

*Source:* IMF (1995)

fact that easily implementable, standard models cannot deal with what concerns users most, namely the rare occurrence of major market disturbances. As some risk managers have pointed out, the assumption of normal distribution of returns (no "fat tails") implies that events such as the stock market crash of 1987 or the EMS débâcle of 1992 are not apprehended by such models. "Risk management is not a formula", commented Patrick Brazel, managing director of SunGard's global risk division. "We think we know more about risk management than anyone, including J.P. Morgan. RiskMetrics must be handled with care. Under RiskMetrics' value-at-risk calculation, the 1987 crash would only happen once every 20 million years."

This is certainly an exaggeration, but George Soros has stated that he is not interested in using value-at-risk models because they assume away precisely what interests him most, namely, the "dynamic disequilibrium" of markets. Whilst his views may not be directly relevant for institutions with different lines of business, they are a useful reminder that actual risk-management models are ill-equipped to deal with exceptional and high risk cases. VAR models are state-of-the-art. But they are models, nothing more. They cannot replace control systems, and, above all, judgement. A useful complement is stress-testing (catastrophe scenarios).

# 6. RISK MANAGEMENT: SOME EXAMPLES

Risk-management models are of recent vintage. Specific needs require specific data, research and modelling. This section focuses on the problem of managing *market risk* in financial institutions.

## Asset-liability Management

It was only during the 1980s that financial institutions started to build general asset-liability management (ALM) systems and only during the 1990s have most institutions started to operate some ALM system.

The purpose of ALM is to assess the overall market risk exposure of an institution. As a financial intermediary typically has a mismatch (this could even be the traditional definition of banking) between the maturities of its assets and its liabilities—traditionally banks had longer average maturities for assets than for liabilities—an *increase* in interest rates shrinks the replacement value of assets by more than the replacement value of liabilities and hence diminishes net worth. If the average maturity of assets is shorter than the average maturity of liabilities—as is nowadays often the case with banks that lend on a variable-rate basis and re-finance with fixed-rate CDs—then a *drop* in interest rates would hurt net worth. For example, consider a very simple balance sheet where the only asset is a 10-year government bond and the only liability three-month certificates of deposit. Initially, equity is zero. If interest rates increase, the market value of the bond declines more sharply than the market value of the CDs. Now equity is negative. If interest rates decline then equity would become positive. The balance sheet is thus exposed to significant interest rate risk. ALM deals with that risk.

Of course, maturity is not the right concept. To see this, just remember that the cash flow and hence interest-rate sensitivity of an equal maturity bullet bond (periodic coupon payments and repayment of the principal at maturity) and a zero-coupon bond are very different. The proper measure is "duration", which is a present-value weighted average maturity of all cash flows, and as such captures the theoretical price elasticity of a financial instrument with respect to changing interest rates.[25]

Duration is easily computed and aggregated. It facilitates the institution-wide interest rate risk management and makes the inefficient matching of individual assets and liabilities superfluous. A duration of, say, five years means that if interest rates increase by one basis point, value would decrease by five basis points (or 0.05%).

This is, of course, highly valuable information for management. If management is concerned with the possibility of rising interest rates, or has a firm view on the matter, then it may wish to reduce the equity duration. If it holds the opposite view on interest rates, then it may wish to lengthen the equity duration. Or, if management wished not to gamble on interest rates it could decide at any time to reduce equity duration to zero and keep it there forever and thereby "immunise" the equity value.

Needless to say, to increase or decrease equity duration according to market views and risk preferences or to maintain equity immunisation is not achievable by restructuring the loan book or liabilities by traditional means. Only derivatives provide the flexibility and cost effectiveness of achieving set management targets.

This description of ALM is, of course, grossly simplified. Duration only gives a good measure of interest rate sensitivity for parallel shifts of the yield curve. Such shifts are, however, the exception rather than the rule. One way to deal with non-parallel shifts is to create duration "buckets" (e.g., 0–3 months, 3–6 months) within which shifts are approximately parallel.[26] Technical Insight 4.6 illustrates the ALM methodology using duration buckets with a concrete ALM report of an international financial institution.

Simple ALM models are "what if" models: what happens to the replacement value of assets, liabilities and equity if interest rates change by a certain number of basis points in one direction or the other? The next step is to superimpose a probability for particular interest rate scenarios to develop (as in Example 1 of Technical Insight 4.5). Such probabilities can be generated by Monte Carlo studies or by the other approaches explained in Technical Insight 4.5. The most widely used package is J.P. Morgan's RiskMetrics.

**Technical Insight 4.6**   Asset-liability Management in the European Investment Bank

The European Investment Bank (EIB) is the world's largest multilateral financial institution in terms of annual disbursements (in 1996 ECU23 billion or about US$27 billion). It specialises in financing of projects, making funds in various currencies available at fixed or variable rates for periods of 20 years or more. Refinancing occurs through the EIB's issues on capital markets.

This activity has a simple financial structure, but is potentially exposed to major market risks. The EIB's basic objective is to provide finance to worthwhile projects at the finest conditions without taking risks other than project risk. Three sources of unwanted risk are particularly prominent. The first is currency risk. To minimise currency exposure the EIB re-finances its lending in the same currency. The second source of risk arises in the timing discrepancy between loan disbursements and borrowing operations. As disbursements are priced according to market conditions at the time of disbursements, whereas refinancing typically occurs at an earlier date, so that collected funds are parked in the treasury, a decline in market rates during that interval would cause losses. To avoid that risk the EIB uses DRS (deferred-rate settings) arrangements, swaps or futures.

The third and major source of risk is embodied in maturity, or more precisely duration, mismatches. To match average maturities of assets and liabilities is problematic for several reasons. First, as the Bank's loans are amortisable, whereas borrowings are typically bullets, maturity-matching would imply a negative duration gap. Second, duration matching immunises the gearing ratio (the ratio of liabilities to assets), but not equity. The EIB, therefore, developed a comprehensive asset-liability management (ALM) system as early as 1988.

One advantage of a comprehensive ALM system is that attention is focused on the overall risk situation. Before the existence of the present ALM the EIB was reticent to make available long-dated fixed rate loans in currencies where it could not issue bonds of similar maturity. Similarly, variable-rate loans were refinanced with variable-rate borrowings. The integrated ALM approach has the advantage that the mixture of long-dated loans and of variable rate loans generates an average maturity that can be matched or exceeded by available bond issues.

A synthetic ALM report of a typical international financial institution like the EIB is produced below. It shows that equity at risk at that particular time was quite high as, by definition, the value of loans exceeds the value of borrowings, and their duration was also longer.

The present value of all assets—treasury holdings and loans—is ECU107.8 billion and the present value of all liabilities is ECU92.3 billion, leaving an equity of ECU15.5 billion. The balance sheet is "asset-sensitive" so that equity will suffer from an increase in market rates, as can be seen from the average duration of assets, equal to 3.3 years, as compared to an average duration of liabilities equal to 2.9 years. Equity duration is derived from the following identity:

$$D_E = (A/E) \, D_A - (L/E) \, D_L$$

where D stands for duration and A, L and E for assets, liabilities and equity respectively.

The equity duration is 5.5 years as the longer asset duration is, in addition, weighted by assets which exceed liabilities in volume.

The Bank's equity is therefore exposed to considerable risk, as illustrated in the table below showing the effects of a 1 basis point increase of interest rates (BPV = basis point value). Equity would fall by close to ECU8 million or a 100 basis point increase in interest rates would destroy ECU800 million equity.

Management decides whether it is comfortable with that risk, given its views on the evolution of interest rates. If not, equity durations can be reduced by reducing the duration of assets or increasing the duration of liabilities, typically through swaps (paying fixed, receiving floating rates).

If the institution wanted to "immunise" its equity it could achieve such an objective by increasing the duration of liabilities above the duration of assets according to the identity above.

There is, of course, a price tag attached to lowering equity exposure: if it is believed that the yield curve remains positively sloped, average equity return correlates with equity duration.

International Financial Institution: Summary Interest Rate Risk Position at 30 September 1995

| Assets | Present V (ECU m) | Duration (years) | Liabilities | Present V (ECU m) | Duration (years) |
|---|---|---|---|---|---|
| Sh.T.Treasury | 3 337.73 | 0.060 | Short Term | 454.49 | 0.069 |
| Inv.Portfolio | 2 447.00 | 4.060 | Float R.B. | 16 638.40 | 0.205 |
| Float R.L. | 15 534.26 | 0.198 | Fixed R.B. | 74 710.60 | 3.498 |
| Fixed R.L. | 86 260.80 | 3.894 | Total | 92 282.49 | 2.880 |
| Total | 107 748.43 | 3.248 | Equity | 15 465.94 | 5.447 |

Effect of an Increase of 1 basis point of Interest Rates

| | on the NPV of Total Assets (ECU) | on the NPV of Total Liabilities (ECU) | on the NPV of Total Equity (ECU) |
|---|---|---|---|
| Up to 3 months | −334 841 | −250 882 | −83 962 |
| 3 to 6 months | −130 611 | −227 610 | −96 999 |
| 6 to 12 months | −489 407 | −365 339 | −124 070 |
| 1 to 2 years | −1 899 012 | −1 737 939 | −161 077 |
| 2 to 4 years | −6 801 354 | −6 546 813 | −254 539 |
| 4 to 6 years | −7 804 001 | −7 083 434 | −720 565 |
| 6 to 8 years | −5 960 168 | −5 311 300 | −648 867 |
| 8 to 12 years | −7 188 250 | −2 435 343 | −4 752 906 |
| more than 12 years | −2 175 085 | −974 568 | −1 200 516 |
| Total | −32 782 726 | −24 933 225 | −7 849 501 |

## ALM Targets

Duration targeting is, of course, not the only possible focus for risk management. Some institutions may prefer to target (or immunise) the gearing ratio, cash flows and net income streams. In general the choice depends, among others, on the nature of an institution's activity. A money market fund or pension fund is more likely to be interested in protecting cash flows or returns. Often, when objectives are activity specific, the optimal approach to risk management may be quite specific as well. A well-known example is portfolio insurance for asset managers. Technical Insight 4.7 illustrates this.

**Technical Insight 4.7** Portfolio insurance applied to corporate pension plans

In the United States changes in the value of pension assets relative to pension liabilities can affect reported earnings. If the value of assets falls below the value of liabilities companies are required to post a balance sheet liability (FAS 87).

To avoid a balance sheet liability, the pension plan needs a floor on the value of its assets equal to the present value of its liabilities. These floors will vary, because interest rates vary and, therefore, the present (discounted) value of pension obligations. For a portfolio insurance strategy to work under these conditions, it needs a variable floor. The difference between the value of the portfolio and the floor is a safety cushion. As the cushion decreases, risky assets have to be sold to reduce exposure; as the cushion increases, risky assets are added to capture more of their appreciation.

The simplest way to explain the hedging strategy developed by Fischer Black and Robert Jones (1988) is to assume that the portfolio consists of a risky asset and a reserve asset. The reserve asset has an acceptable minimum rate of return that should move closely with the value of the floor. A good choice for the reserve asset is a security (or package of securities) that has the same sensitivity to interest rates, i.e., duration, as the accumulated benefit obligations. A typical accumulated benefit obligation has about the same interest rate sensitivity as a long-term Treasury bond, which therefore serves well as reserve asset.

One way to avoid posting a balance sheet liability is to invest an amount equal to the accumulated benefit obligation in long-term bonds. But this will have only a small share of the portfolio in stocks.

The portfolio insurance strategy works as follows. Choose an initial exposure, i.e., the amount in the active asset. Exposure divided by the asset (i.e., portfolio value minus floor) is called the multiple.

As the cushion changes, either because of changes in asset values or changes in the accumulated benefit obligation, trade in order to bring exposure back to the multiple times the cushion. As the cushion approaches zero, allocation to bonds approach 100%. Thus, the cushion will become negative only if assets fall sharply relative to liabilities before there is a chance to trade.

As the cushion rises, exposure may reach the maximum for stocks. At that maximum there are no longer any trades.

Choosing a high initial exposure implies a large multiple. The higher the multiple, the larger the participation in a stock market rally. But if stocks are very volatile the strategy implies frequent trades, buying high and selling low. The higher the multiple, the larger the risk of losing in volatile markets.

To limit the costs of frequent trading, it is desirable to specify a tolerance for the drift of exposure away from its target value before trading to restore the relation between exposure and cushion.

These arguments and simulations performed with this strategy suggest that portfolio insurance helps most when the market goes straight up or down in relation to the floor. The worst performance is achieved during periods when the market and floor finish close to where they started, but had large fluctuations in-between.

A particularly attractive feature of this approach is that no complex mathematical models or computer programmes are needed, underlining the basic simplicity of portfolio insurance.

*Source:* Black and Jones (1988)

Complete risk hedging is unappealing to most individuals and institutions. Few are totally risk averse, although it is not easy to define risk tolerance precisely. Managers' risk tolerance evolves in line with market views, cash flows and returns already obtained and so does their acceptable return-risk trade-off. It is, therefore, important to have access to hedging instruments that are flexible enough to cover some risks, but not all, to preserve earning potential, and that can be rapidly unwound or readjusted in the light of management's changing views. Technical Insight 4.8 illustrates techniques that enhance yield at the cost of capping the maximum gain. A second example is provided to show how potential gain can be traded against downside risk so that ultimately, without spending cash, an investor obtains a hedge structure that preserves precisely defined earning potential.

**Technical Insight 4.8**   Derivatives used for yield or safety enhancement

Derivatives are used by many institutions as a form of yield enhancement. The most common are "covered calls". Institutions sell calls to help finance a stock position up to a level at which they are prepared to sell the stock. For example, an investor is bullish on company A stock which he has recently purchased at 100. He believes that over the next 12 months the price may climb to 110 at which point he will feel it is overvalued and will sell. In addition, to a capital gain, the stock provides dividends of 4. The investor sells his banker a one-year call option on the stock, struck at 110 for which he receives 4.3. His break-even on the upside if exercised is 118.3%, a return of 18.3%. On the downside, he has 4.3% of protection against capital losses, plus his dividend. Effectively, this strategy caps the return for a higher yield (see Figure 4.2).

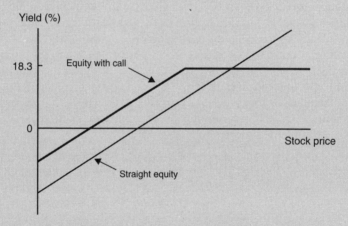

**Figure 4.2**   Yield enhancement

Zero Cost Hedges are used by many institutions to lock in pension surplus, or to hedge substantial gains in underlying positions for a particular period of time. Pension surpluses are a case in point. Many funds in surplus have chosen to protect their gains using creative variations of the Zero Cost Hedge. The basic form of the Zero Cost Hedge involves the investor purchasing a put option on the target portfolio, and selling a call option on the same portfolio such that the premiums from the two transactions offset. This results in the zero cost. The put option provides the hedge against any erosion in the current value of the portfolio. The call option is used to finance the cost of the put. The key to optimising the Zero Cost Hedge is to identify the level and maturity of protection desired, and then to work out the least onerous call to sell to pay for that protection. By skilful structuring of the call using "knockout" options, "capped options", "all or nothing options" among others, the investor can achieve downside protection and still participate in some upside gain.

Adjusting the duration of puts and calls can also produce attractive risk/reward characteristics. For example, a fund this year may be willing to lock in its gains until next year using an overlay strategy of derivatives. An alternative may be to buy a put with a three-year maturity whilst selling calls only to year end. The structure still gives a zero cost and provides full protection, but for a substantially longer period, which means that more upside is given up this year.

These are examples of static strategies. Potentially better results can be obtained with dynamic strategies which require, however, greater sophistication, frequent trading and acceptance of more risk.

# 7. CONCLUSION

This chapter has attempted to answer the fundamental question whether, and in which way, derivatives generate economic gains to society. Answers are not straightforward as the gains are indirect, like all gains from financial instruments. It has been shown that derivatives markets provide precious information for today's decision-making; that many risky, but economically gainful activities would suffer from the absence of hedge instruments, among which derivatives figure prominently. Even economic structure is profoundly influenced by the availability of derivatives: in their absence firms are exposed to unwanted risks, with the likely consequence of under-investing, and have to accumulate excessive amounts of own funds to hedge adverse events. Risk markets allow firms to divest unwanted risk and focus on their core activity, the production of goods and services. Even strategic decisions such as vertical integration may often reflect a cumbersome attempt to reduce risk.

For any economic decision the key information is the price. Just imagine a shopping trip to a supermarket where no price tags are attached to the goods. But this is precisely the problem for people investing in a profession, of farmers planting for next year, or for airlines publishing fares for the next season without knowing next season's price of kerosene. Experience is useful for making an educated guess, but a futures' price is a certainty, making intertemporal decisions easier.

Nothing is perfect, including derivatives markets. Yes, they allow an economy to accept more risk—for a reward. Yes, they make speculation easier and more leveraged. But not all speculation is bad and by far the greatest use of derivatives is for hedging risk.

The low cost, transparency and continuous tradeability of exchange-traded derivatives have generated a new industry, affecting all walks of life: professional, focused risk management. It is still lacking maturity and many institutions have suffered from spectacular or relatively minor teething problems. This is typical of any new activity, especially one as pervasive and fundamental to the life of a corporation as risk management. But it allows firms to focus on the primary business they are good at and lay to rest their worries about exchange rates, interest rates and input and output price fluctuations. In Chapter 10 we will go a step further and muse about the changes derivatives will bring to business organisation in the future.

In principle, any derivative product can be replicated by a judicious combination of the underlying asset and of borrowing/lending cash. In this sense derivatives are redundant. This chapter has shown that derivatives are useful for individual users and provide substantial gains to society. But the question remains: why are they needed if they are conceptually redundant?

The simple answer is one of cost. To replicate an option on a stock with the stock and cash requires *dynamic hedging*, i.e. continuous management of the position, absorbing time and requiring a large number of transactions. It also creates new risks (a sudden jump in stock prices or interest rates) and counter-party risks (on the borrowed or invested cash). The liquidity of the underlying may be (and usually is) inferior to the exchange-traded derivative and price information on the replication unreliable. The redundancy of derivatives is therefore only theoretical; in practical terms they are irreplaceable.

# ENDNOTES

1 This chapter draws on material in Rubinstein (1987), Edwards and Ma (1992), Telser (1981), Allen and Gale (1994), and IMF (1995).
2 Paul Samuelson, whose basic textbook *Economics* educated millions of Americans for nearly two generations, in the 9th edition of 1973, expressed concern about a world "in uneasy limbo" after the United States went off the gold standard in August 1971. He only gradually warmed to the idea of flexible exchange rates, especially *as futures markets* developed (pp. 724–25).
3 Arrow and Debreu (1954).
4 A state of nature is a long list of possible realisations for each uncertain exogenous event. Together, all possible states of nature fully describe any possible future unfolding of uncertainty.
5 Knight (1921).
6 Here the narrow definition of basis risk is used. In practice, any risk arising from a difference in price behaviour between the asset to be hedged and the hedge is referred to as basis risk.

7 Backwardation is also used when the basis is negative, but less than what the cost-of-carry relationship would suggest.

8 In late 1995 the gold market moved into backwardation as Central Banks limited their gold loans to cover short positions.

9 A sunspot equilibrium is defined as an equilibrium in which there exists at least two states in which endowments and preferences are the same, but prices are different.

10 George Soros, when testifying before a US Senate committee, likened the destabilising impact of knock-out options to the destabilising impact of portfolio insurance during periods of rapid equity price movements, which would put downward pressure on prices in a declining market and upward pressure on them in a rising market. Portfolio insurance was thought to have contributed to the US stock market decline (Black Monday) in 1987.

11 Malz (1995) notes that, "transactions in knockouts had increased to between 2 and 12 per cent of all currency options trading by early 1995 from a negligible share just two or three years ago".

12 To the extent that dealers, themselves, had built up short dollar positions in order to influence the price, they would have to repurchase dollars after the "knock-out" level was breached.

13 Although knock-outs are difficult to hedge and many dealers rely on a diversified portfolio of these options for protection, some dealers hedge by selling more put options close to the "knock-out" level together with buying a put at the strike price. As the spot rate goes though the "knock-out" level and the option is cancelled, the dealer is exposed to losses from further declines in the spot rate on the sold puts used as the hedge. Either the dealer needs to buy back the put options sold for the hedge or sell dollars in the spot market. Often dealers establish stop-loss orders at these levels to facilitate the unwinding of these positions. These actions drive up the price of put options with strikes at the "knock-out" level and exert pressure for a further dollar spot rate decline.

14 Chapter 3 reports on OTC cases where end-users must rely on the suppliers of the contract to obtain price information which is not available continuously and may lack reliability.

15 Telser (1981).

16 This can be done. Chapter 10 suggests contracts based on the present value of indefinite future income streams for GDP.

17 Telser (1981) shows that the standard deviation of equilibrium prices decreases with the volume of trade. A 1% increase in the volume of trade results approximately in an 0.5% decrease in the standard deviation.

18 Here again the comparison with money is compelling: despite a poor record in terms of price stability the US dollar is the most important international currency because it acceptably spans the globe.

19 According to a survey carried out by Price Waterhouse (1995), of 386 leading companies in 16 countries, more than three-quarters of the companies use derivatives to manage their risk. However, less than half apply the control standards considered necessary to manage these activities. More companies are requiring their Treasury departments to provide a profit contribution by actively managing the underlying financial risks rather than simply fully hedging the exposures. Some 25% of the corporations in the survey pursue a fully hedged approach to risk management aimed at eliminating risk, and only 1% took on risk unrelated to any underlying business exposure—that is, to speculate. In more than 30% of companies, the board of directors did not formally approve policy. In more than 50% of cases, the board did not receive regular information on Treasury activities; and in almost half the companies the treasury function operated without adequate limit controls over its risk-management activities.

20 Modigliani and Miller (1958).
21 See Fama (1978). There is extensive literature aiming at a better understanding of the observed use of debt and equity by firms. Myers (1984) sums up the literature: "How do firms choose their capital structures? . . . the answer is 'we don't know'."
22 The Texas experimental programme is two-fold. At the beginning of each month, the treasury bought put options on the next month's contract. The aim was to buy 50 000 barrels of the less expensive out-of-the-money puts with a low delta, for example, a delta of 0.25—so that if oil prices fell by US$1 the put option would increase in value by US$0.25.
   The state's second approach involves the purchase of option contracts based on market movements. If future prices start to fall, the state legislature can approve the purchase of put options extending out three months, thus reducing the losses due to the state's natural long oil position. If oil prices rise above the budgeted level, the state legislature can sell its put contract, thus locking in the high oil price.
23 This was indeed one major difficulty in the Metallgesellschaft case discussed in Chapter 3.
24 The asset normal approach is the method employed by J.P. Morgan's highly publicised RiskMetrics, risk-management system. Under this distributional assumption, the standard deviation of portfolio returns can be computed from the standard deviations of the asset returns, their correlations, and the individual weights of the assets in the portfolio using a standard statistical formula. The value-at-risk under a 99% confidence interval is simply the level of loss corresponding to a 2.32 standard deviation drop in the value of the portfolio.
25 More rigorously: $\Delta B/B = -D\Delta Y/(1+Y)$ where B = bond price; $\Delta$ = change; D = (Macaulay) duration; Y = current yield on the bond.
26 Another approach is to simulate the impact of various interest rate scenarios.

# 5

# Mutualisation of Risk on Exchanges

## Chicago's Other Side

In 1967, like millions of other Americans, Leo Melamed read Milton Friedman's articles in *Newsweek* magazine about his vain effort to sell the British pound sterling short. Melamed was shocked, but at the same time he smelled a great business opportunity. "Here was a great economic mind told he could not do something in the market. I was flabbergasted. I was looking for viable instruments of trade, and you didn't have to be a genius to figure out that if Bretton Woods did come apart, it would create a big era of volatility in currency and interest rates. It seemed you needed a futures market to give an opportunity to everyone to take part in the movement of price," he recalls.

By early 1971, when Leo Melamed began to put together the world's first futures market in currencies, the strains on the Bretton Woods system were unmistakeable. In August of that year, President Nixon stated that the US government would not exchange gold for dollars, officially closing the "gold window" and pulling a plug on the Bretton Woods system.

The time was ripe. Currency chaos would provide the perfect environment for a flourishing futures market in currencies. At the time, the futures industry was almost completely unregulated, and no government authority could refuse permission for the Merc to begin trading currency futures. But nothing of the sort had ever existed before, and Melamed had two worries: either that no one would take him seriously enough to use the exchange or that central bankers would take him very seriously and demand that the market be shut down.

In 1971 Melamed and the president of the Merc, Everett Harris, made a pilgrimage to the idol's summer residence in Vermont to enlist his support for a paper demonstrating the economic benefits of a market for currency futures. As Melamed recalls the meeting, Friedman replied, "I like your idea and I'll write the paper for US$5000."

Melamed wasted no time sending the paper to Nixon's treasury secretary (later Ronald Reagan's secretary of state) and former Chicago professor, George Shultz, who agreed to meet with him. About the idea of a futures market in foreign exchanges, he said, "I read the paper from Milton Friedman that you sent, and if it's good enough for Milton, its good enough for me." Arthur Burns, chairman of the Federal Reserve Board and a former teacher of Milton Friedman, also endorsed the idea.

On 16 May 1972, the world's first futures market in international currencies officially opened for business. The Merc built a pit for currency trading, just like the pits where traders standing on concentric stairs shouted bids and offers for eggs, butter and livestock futures. But at first, hardly anyone shared Melamed's zeal for currency futures. Wheedling, cajoling and twisting arms, he managed to persuade a few experienced traders to stand in the currency pit, but they weren't dedicated to the trade. A good commodity trader could make a living trading cattle and hogs, but who ever heard of trading deutschemarks? No one. Exchange traders don't just trade with each other. Much of their business depends on executing orders for customers outside the exchange who have a reason to buy or sell futures contracts. Since the currency exchange was brand-new, outsiders weren't yet using it. Nor were they eager to begin. In fact, the big New York and London banks, which held most of the world's money and bought or sold currencies for their clients, laughed it off.

Melamed knew that the absence of traders could kill off his creation. What if outsiders tried to send orders to the exchange but there were no traders in the pit to take their orders? Word would quickly get around that the Chicago market lacked liquidity; that is, it could simply not handle orders to buy and sell. So he first persuaded the exchange to establish a new category of cheap, limited memberships and then swept the streets for cab drivers, steelworkers, discontented lawyers, or just about anyone who had always had a burning desire to make a fortune playing the commodity markets but couldn't afford to buy a full exchange membership. "We sold these memberships for only US$10 000, and then there were 150 traders committed to the currency market, because they couldn't get into the cattle pits," he recalls. With a true promoter's instinct for the grandiloquent phrase, Melamed decided to call these new members the International Monetary Market (IMM). Starting with these traders, and capitalising on the tremendous instability of currencies in the post-Bretton Woods era, the IMM would emerge as one of the most powerful international financial institutions in the world. During the 1980s, when the full force of market power hit the economies of the world like a tidal wave caused by an undersea volcano, evening news shows in places as remote as the Missouri Ozarks would carry reports of currency values on the IMM.

Meanwhile, a young professor from the University of California was at work on a project that would rescue the fortunes of the other exchange, the CBoT—a project that would change the way every home buyer in the USA bought a house, and permanently rearrange the power structure of the banking industry.

Richard Sandor had spent the late 1960s teaching economics on the front lines of the US's cultural revolution: Berkeley. His finance faculty colleagues included a Tibetan Buddhist meditator named Barr Rosenberg, whose research on randomness and volatility led him to start a program trading operation that eventually managed

US$9 billion for investors, who put up a minimum of US$75 million each, and made him the "pope" of program traders everywhere. There was also Hayne Leland, a finance professor best remembered for inventing portfolio insurance, the program trading technique that two decades later would be blamed by US Treasury secretary, Nicholas Brady, for contributing to the great stock market crash of 1987. Out on the campus, minding his own business, quietly hurrying past the demonstrators on his way to finance class, was a sedulous, clean-cut young student named Michael Milken.

Sandor taught the first futures course ever offered in a business school. At most universities, if futures classes were offered at all, they were part of the agriculture curriculum. Sandor was also one of the first academics to look into the question of whether futures could be used for something completely different. He applied for a grant to study the possibility of a futures contract in mortgages. After all, they were something like crops. It took three months for a loan officer to handle all the paperwork—that was something like the time it took to grow a crop of beans. Prices changed too, as interest rates moved. A mortgage loan made at high interest rates would be worth more if interest rates went down three months later. The changes in interest rates were as unpredictable as the changes in corn prices. Also, the more money the government printed to finance the war in Vietnam, the more likely it was that inflation would break out. When that happened, the Federal Reserve would have to raise interest rates again, and when interest rates eventually went up, anyone who had invested money in mortgage loans would be in trouble because the loans would be worth less. So it seemed to Sandor that a futures market made sense for banks and S&Ls to hedge against interest rate risk.

Yet after sorting through the loan portfolio of a large California-based S&L, he decided that a futures contract couldn't work for mortgages. Unlike corn, beans, pork bellies, or any other commodity that can be sorted into grades and bought or sold by the truckload, mortgages were full of idiosyncrasies. People repaid them at different rates depending on what neighbourhood a house was in, on whether the owners were married or single or divorced, on income levels, and on many other factors. Mortgages didn't have enough in common to turn them into a commodity. Sandor published those findings in 1971.

They were almost obsolete as soon as they were printed. The government was on its way to turning mortgages into a commodity, as it had become clear that money for mortgages could no longer come primarily from local bank depositors. Institutional investors like insurance companies, pension funds, and investment banks were buying bonds issued by government agencies and the government agencies used the proceeds to buy mortgages loans. It was a natural step when, in 1970, a government agency issued a security called a Ginnie Mae. This security was really an ownership interest in a pool of mortgages: an investor who bought a Ginnie Mae received the right to principal and interest payments from mortgages in the pool. Ginnie Maes helped connect Wall Street more closely with Main Street. Since Americans now held so much of their savings in the form of insurance policies or pension funds, it made sense to tap that source of capital for mortgages.

Ginnie Maes were reasonably successful, and they solved the problem that had vexed Sandor. Assembling mortgages in a pool and issuing government-guaranteed securities based on them meant that mortgages could now be as standardised as any other commodity. Shortly afterward, the management of the CBoT approached him with an offer to set up an economics department at the exchange. He told them about his idea for a futures market in mortgages. They liked it. Sandor took a sabbatical from Berkeley and joined the CBoT for what he expected to be a one-year stint.

It lasted a lot longer. Sandor worked out the idea of a futures contract in mortgages and went to call on big New York banks to see if they would use it. "I got thrown out of a lot of places," he says, "They looked at me and said, 'Berkeley, free speech, drugs, Vietnam War, student activists, and you're from the Chicago exchange' ". Bankers presumed that he was not only weird but provincial. They dismissed futures as something that might work for corn, beans, or wheat, but was as out of place on Wall Street as a herd of Holsteins.

Then there was the government. When Sandor began his work, futures markets had been regulated by a small group in the US Department of Agriculture. In 1974, a regulatory reshuffle rolled the regulatory authority into a new agency, the Commodities Futures Trading Commission (CFTC). At first, the CFTC still had an agricultural mindset. "They sent out their standard form, and they asked how much storage space there was in Chicago for these Ginnie Maes. We said we didn't need silos or barns or anything like that, its just pieces of paper," he recalls. It took time for the agency to outgrow its agricultural roots.

By 1975, Sandor had finally assembled from financial institutions enough support for the new contract to make it worthwhile to try trading it. But his problems weren't over. "Twenty-four hours before Ginnie Mae started trading on 20 October 1975, the SEC sought an injunction to stop the CBoT from trading the securities," he says. A turf war had broken out between the SEC and the CFTC. A higher court ultimately overturned the injunction, and trading began—but the jurisdictional dispute continued to simmer.

Sandor's timing, like Melamed's three years earlier, couldn't have been better. By the mid-1970s, everybody could see that the economy was falling apart and interest rate charts were beginning to look like an electrocardiogram of a heart attack victim. Sandor started to work on other interest rate products. Treasury bills futures began to trade in 1976, and then treasury bonds futures.

Of all these new products, bond futures were the toughest to sell. Dominated by the most Wall Street elite, the long-term bond market was a white-shoe club. The prestigious money lords in New York didn't favour the idea of the Chicago outpost meddling in their affairs. So when long-term bond futures began to trade in 1977, they got off to a slow start. Then in 1979, Paul Volcker, the new Federal Reserve Board chairman, made an announcement that Wall Street remembers as the "Saturday Night Massacre". Abandoning a decades-old policy of controlling interest rates, Volcker said that the nation's central bank would focus its attention instead on controlling the money supply. In that year, interest rates started a stratospheric ascent that soon would carry the prime rate to an astonishing 20%.

Wall Street used to be a cosy warren of old boys from the right schools, relying more on the nod and the wink than on any substantive economic analysis. It had changed little since the days when periwigged traders lifted glasses of port to toast the health of US Treasury secretary, Alexander Hamilton. Then the Chicago futures markets established a second centre of financial power, where nothing mattered except the price. Now maths and physics PhDs relied on the prices set by futures traders to craft new equations and economic models that could be run only with another new tool, the computer. Futures and options became the basic building blocks of a whole new genus of financial products, called derivatives—financial abstractions, their value mathematically derived from changes in the value of interest rates, commodities, stock prices, currency exchange rates, and other factors. Suddenly, on Wall Street, "who you know" became less important than "what you know". By 1990, at the top of the big financial houses, chairmen and presidents and directors noticed that most of their revenues were coming from a business they did not really understand. Although the old boys had grand titles, they didn't really control their businesses. Power had passed them by.

> "To qualify as most significant,
> an innovation must be important,
> not only in and of itself, but must
> have stimulated substantial further
> innovation as well. It must have
> set off a chain reaction . . .
> By this standard, my nomination for
> the most significant financial innovation
> of the last twenty years is financial futures
> —the futures exchange style trading of
> financial instruments."
>
> Miller 1991, p. 9

CHICAGO achieved a substantial international reputation and standing with the creation of financial futures and options markets in the early 1970s. It is a good illustration of the American entrepreneurial spirit and drive. Unexpectedly, this innovation has profoundly transformed the financial industry.

The evolution of exchange-traded financial derivatives is presented in Section 1. Section 2 then explains in some detail the organisation of the exchanges and the functions of clearinghouses. Section 3 examines what makes a successful exchange-traded contract and Section 4 surveys new product developments in the pipeline. Section 5 reflects on the strategies of the main exchanges to lower costs and gain market shares by choice of technology (open outcry vs. electronic trading), and to serve customers worldwide through an international presence in a global economy. A particular event is the challenge of a single currency in Europe.

## 1. EVOLUTION OF EXCHANGE-TRADED FINANCIAL DERIVATIVES[1]

This section first provides perspective by analysing the past development of exchange-traded financial derivatives. As futures are the most important products on the exchanges in terms of turnover, they receive particular attention in the discussion.

The Chicago commodity futures exchanges in their drive to diversify had, by the late 1960s, developed their interest in new kinds of contracts, building on their accumulated expertise in commodities. In view of higher currency volatility after the demise of the Bretton Woods fixed exchange rate system, the idea of foreign exchange contracts was particularly attractive and contract design was seen as exceptionally easy as foreign exchange is a perfectly standardised commodity.

The International Money Market (IMM) was inaugurated in 1972 as an offshoot of the CME and the era of financial futures trading began,[2] although few people at that time appreciated the historic significance. See Miller (1991) pp. 11–12. The expectation that a futures contract could substantially lower the costs of managing foreign currency exposure proved to be justified by events. Thanks to the post-Bretton Woods floating exchange rates, the price volatility and hedging demand shot up so that the IMM attracted a substantial volume of trading virtually from its inception.

Figure 5.1 shows the phenomenal growth of trading activity on US futures and options exchanges. From 1972 to 1994 the number of contracts traded increased nearly fifty-fold.

Compared to the New York-style stock markets, the symmetry of futures contracts for short and long positions in commodities had always been one of the standard claims for advantage of the Chicago-style futures markets. No costly borrowing and escrowing of securities were needed to go short in Chicago; no uptick rules had to be observed before a short sale could be executed. A short in Chicago was just the negative of a long and the cost of hedging markedly lower.[3]

Exchange trading for foreign currencies did not, of course, displace the interbank (over-the-counter or OTC) market. Big trades—in excess of US$100 million—are still routed through the interbank market. The IMM's comparative advantage is in the handling of smaller trades—another contribution to the US democratisation of finance. The benefits from futures trading are, however, not limited to direct participants in the futures market. Empirical studies confirm that spreads in the big-player spot and forward markets are significantly smaller when there are futures markets. At the other end of the order-size spectrum, even small users are benefiting. Dealers' spreads would have to be larger if they did not have access to reasonably low-cost hedging for their own inventory. This is important because the financial futures are not typically products that individuals consume directly. They are essentially "industrial raw materials" (Miller 1991).

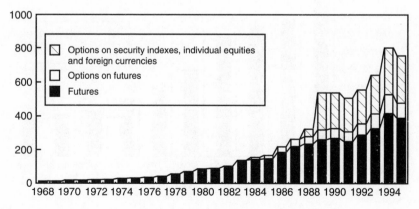

**Figure 5.1**  Volume of futures and options trading on US futures and securities exchanges, 1968–95

It is obvious enough with hindsight that the same conditions that opened the niche for foreign currency futures were also present in bond markets. In 1975 the CBoT introduced GNMA (Government National Mortgage Association) futures—a contract that some regard as the first true *financial* futures in the strict sense of the term. Shortly after the GNMA, the CME introduced Treasury bill futures,[4] a contract still very successful unlike the GNMA contract.

From short-term T-bills, it was a logical step to long-term Treasury bonds (although the practical step was far from trivial because of the greater difficulty of standardising instruments with different coupons and maturities and with less regularity in the infusion of new supplies). Long-term T-bonds have become one of the leading financial futures contract in terms of daily trading volume, only recently surpassed by three-month Eurodollar futures. From Chicago, government bond futures trading has spread to foreign money centres where its impact in lowering transaction costs was even greater than it was in the United States, given lower volumes and the more heavily cartelised trading structures there. In fact, financial futures must surely be given some of the credit for the wave of deregulation and decartelisation that subsequently swept through the European and Asian money and capital markets.

The most important markets outside the United States are the London International Financial Futures Exchange (LIFFE), which was started in September 1982, some ten years after their debut in Chicago; Brazil's BM&F and the French financial futures market, the MATIF (Marché à Terme des Instruments Financiers), was established in 1986 and has also proved to be very successful. Of more recent date, but growing fast, is Frankfurt's Deutsche Terminbörse (DTB) with its electronic trading system. As with other financial innovations, Europe and Japan trailed the United States by a considerable

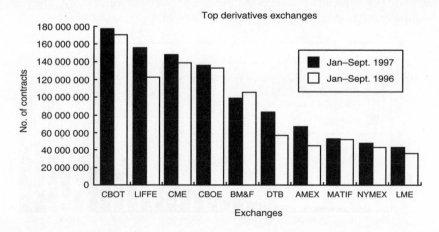

**Figure 5.2**    Top derivatives exchanges
*Source: Futures and Options Week*, 10 November 1997

margin. But Europe is catching up rapidly. In 1997 (January to September) LIFFE has overtaken CME; DTB ranks sixth and MATIF eighth. On all markets trading futures and options ranging from interest rates, foreign exchange, and equities to exotic products, the greatest volumes materalise in interest rates futures.

Table 5.1 summarises turnover by contract category on the world's derivatives exchanges. Between 1986 and 1995, annual turnover has grown about four times from 315 million contracts to 1210 million contracts, with a slight contraction in 1996 to 1162 million contracts. While in 1986 over 90% of trade was carried out on US exchanges, in 1996 the rest of the world had caught up to trade more than 60%. The lion's share of non-US trading takes place on European exchanges. Interest rates futures (nearly 60% of total trade in 1994 and more than 50% in 1996) have known the most impetuous growth, increasing sevenfold since 1986.

Impressive as it is, the growth of exchange-traded derivatives does not render full justice to their real importance. Major banks and securities firms that serve as market-makers for securities and OTC derivatives need exchange-traded derivatives to balance their risk positions. They work on the assumption that markets for exchange-traded derivatives will provide sufficient liquidity to offset their risk exposures, even during episodes of major price swings when other markets may become relatively illiquid. During periods of exceptional market volatility the volume of activity on derivatives exchanges can rise dramatically, for certain days up to 10 times the average daily turnover. As stated by BIS (1997, p. 1) : "When markets are already under stress, the loss of an exchange's market liquidity or a delay in the completion of exchange-related payments or deliveries could well lead to systemic disturbances, the liquidity of other financial markets could be seriously impaired, and payments systems and other settlement systems could be disrupted." For example, the largest ever daily settlement in relation to the average daily settlement in 1995 reached a factor of 15 on the MATIF (21 December 1994), a factor of 8 on the Tokyo International Financial Futures Exchange (TIFFE) (17 August 1995), a factor of 16 on the Swiss Options and Financial Futures Exchange (SOFFEX) (18 August 1995), a factor of 9 on the Board of Trade Clearing Corporation (BoTCC) and on the Chicago Mercantile Exchange (CME) (October 1987) (Source: BIS 1997, p. 116).

Before the range of futures could be significantly extended in the 1970s, two innovations proved necessary: cash settlement and index contracts.


**Cash Settlement**

"Cash settlement" in lieu of physical delivery was another quantum leap to futures markets. The first contract with cash settlement was a Eurodollar

**Table 5.1**   Annual Turnover in Derivative Financial Instruments Traded on Organized Exchanges Worldwide[1] (in Millions of Contracts Traded)

|  | 1986 | 1988 | 1990 | 1991 | 1992 | 1993 | 1994 | 1995 | 1996 |
|---|---|---|---|---|---|---|---|---|---|
| Interest rate futures | 91.0 | 156.3 | 219.1 | 230.9 | 330.1 | 427.1 | 627.8 | 561.0 | 612.2 |
|  | 16.4 | 29.4 | 70.2 | 84.8 | 130.8 | 161.0 | 282.4 | 266.5 | 283.6 |
| – 3-month Eurodollar[1] | 12.4 | 25.2 | 39.4 | 41.7 | 66.9 | 70.2 | 113.6 | 104.2 | 97.1 |
| – 3-month Euro-yen[2] | — | — | 15.2 | 16.2 | 17.4 | 26.9 | 44.2 | 42.9 | 37.7 |
| – 3-month Euro-deutschemark[3] | — | — | 3.1 | 4.8 | 12.2 | 21.4 | 29.5 | 25.7 | 36.2 |
| Futures on long-term interest rate instruments | 74.6 | 122.6 | 143.1 | 146.1 | 199.3 | 266.1 | 346.1 | 294.5 | 328.6 |
| – US Treasury bond[4] | 54.6 | 73.8 | 78.2 | 69.9 | 71.7 | 80.7 | 101.5 | 87.8 | 86.0 |
| – Notional French Govt. bond[5] | 1.1 | 12.4 | 16.0 | 21.1 | 31.1 | 36.8 | 50.2 | 33.6 | 35.3 |
| – 10-year Japanese Govt. bond[6] | 9.4 | 18.9 | 16.4 | 12.9 | 12.1 | 15.6 | 14.1 | 15.2 | 13.6 |
| – German Govt. bond[7] | — | 0.3 | 9.6 | 12.4 | 18.9 | 27.7 | 51.5 | 44.8 | 56.3 |
| Interest rate options[8] | 22.3 | 30.5 | 52.0 | 50.8 | 64.8 | 82.9 | 114.5 | 225.5 | 151.1 |
| Currency futures | 19.9 | 22.5 | 29.7 | 30.0 | 31.3 | 39.0 | 69.7 | 98.3 | 73.7 |
| Currency options[8] | 13.0 | 18.2 | 18.9 | 22.9 | 23.4 | 23.8 | 21.3 | 23.2 | 26.3 |
| Stock market index futures | 28.4 | 29.6 | 39.4 | 54.6 | 52.0 | 71.2 | 109.0 | 114.8 | 119.9 |
| Stock market index options[8] | 140.4 | 79.1 | 119.1 | 121.4 | 133.9 | 144.1 | 197.9 | 187.3 | 178.7 |
| *Total* | 315.0 | 336.2 | 478.3 | 510.5 | 635.6 | 788.0 | 1142.2 | 1210.1 | 1161.9 |
| United States | 288.7 | 252.2 | 312.7 | 302.7 | 341.4 | 387.3 | 513.5 | 455.0 | 428.2 |
| Europe | 10.3 | 40.7 | 83.0 | 110.5 | 185.0 | 263.5 | 397.3 | 353.3 | 425.8 |
| Asia–Pacific | 14.4 | 34.4 | 79.18 | 85.8 | 82.8 | 98.4 | 131.9 | 126.5 | 115.2 |
| Other | 1.6 | 8.9 | 3.9 | 11.6 | 26.3 | 43.7 | 99.4 | 275.4 | 192.7 |

*Notes*:

[1] Traded on the Chicago Mercantile Exchange–International Monetary Market (CME–IMM), Singapore Mercantile Exchange (SIMEX), London International Financial Futures Exchange (LIFFE), Tokyo International Financial Futures Exchange (TIFFE), and Sydney Futures Exchange (SFE).
[2] Traded on the TIFFE and SIMEX.
[3] Traded on LIFFE and since 14.1.1997 on DTB.
[4] Traded on the Chicago Board of Trade (CBoT), LIFFE, Mid-America Commodity Exchange (MIDAM), New York Futures Exchange (NYFE), and the Tokyo Stock Exchange (TSE).
[5] Traded on the MATIF.
[5] Traded on the TSE, LIFFE and CBoT.
[6] Traded on the TSE, LIFFE and BCoT.
[7] Traded on the LIFFE and the Deutsche Terminbörse (DTB).
[8] Calls plus puts.

*Source*: Bank for International Settlements, IMF (1996)

contract, now the most successful contract globally. The typical commodity futures contract gives the holder the right to demand delivery of the commodity at the agreed-upon price and the times, places and quality grades specified in the contract. In practice, relatively little physical delivery actually takes place. 98–99% of long (short) contracts are liquidated by offset—that is, selling (buying) in the market an equivalent contract.[5]

Why has the delivery option not been dropped in favour of cash settlement long ago? In part, and particularly for the traditional agricultural commodities, spot prices were not deemed sufficiently tamper-proof to serve as an accepted basis for settlement. But that surely was no longer an argument for instruments such as foreign exchange or T-bills, where large and active spot markets exist.

What initially prevented cash settlement in financial instruments was a provision of law. In many of the states in the United States, notably Illinois where the big exchanges are located, a contract settled by delivery, if only in principle, was a futures contract. But a contract that could be settled only in cash was a wager. And in most states wagering was illegal.

These restrictive state laws were superseded in 1974 by the federal regulatory statute that set up the CFTC (the Commodity Futures Trading Commission) as sole regulator of futures markets. Since there was no federal prohibition of gambling, legal barriers to cash settlement evaporated.[6] Once the CFTC had removed the major obstacles to this innovation two major steps forward soon were taken by the industry.

**Index Contracts**

In terms of current volume of trading (see Table 5.1), the most important innovation was a futures contract in a whole portfolio of individual stocks. Since the settlement for the portfolio of stocks was to be in cash rather than by physical delivery, it was natural to focus on those portfolios most relevant for possible hedging purposes for institutional investors: the major market indexes (and later also industry sub-indexes) of the kind already widely used in performance evaluation, such as the Dow Jones, S&P 100, S&P 500, and so on.

Index futures have become among the most successful contracts.[7] But they also created some unforeseen practical problems. For example, the problems associated with contract close-outs under the delivery system re-emerged in a different form. The close-out on expiration days for cash-settled contracts no longer sees the shorts desperate to deliver the spot commodity to the longs, but the so-called "programme traders" scrambling to unwind their arbitrage positions. On some days—the so-called "triple witching days"—the actions of the programme traders were sometimes reinforced by the similar arbitrage-related actions of the options converters, and big fluctuations occurred in the prices of some of the underlying stocks.

The next step in financial evolution was to use indexes that were closer to being measures of abstract concepts (for example, inflation index) than to deliverable bundles of commodities. The major developments are still to come, as argued in Chapter 10.

### Options

Like futures, tailor-made options have been around for a long time. But in view of the specific needs for which they were used, they could not be traded. In 1973 the Chicago Board Options Exchange (CBOE) introduced standardised options with the aim of creating a liquid secondary market. The CBOE was immediately successful and by 1984 it had become the second largest securities market in the world, second only to the New York Stock Exchange.[8]

Initially the options traded on exchanges were all options on individual stocks. In the early 1980s options on other instruments were introduced. The first was an options contract on CBoT Treasury bond futures started in October 1982. Subsequently options on other debt instruments were initiated, including options on specific Treasury bonds, notes and bills. In December 1982 the Philadelphia Stock Exchange introduced currency options and this was followed by a number of other exchanges. Options on indexes began in March 1983, when the CBOE offered an option on the S&P 100 index. This and other index options have proved very popular and are widely used.

The top individual contracts, futures and options, are listed in Table 5.2.

## 2. ORGANISATION OF THE EXCHANGES[9]

A key feature of exchange-traded derivatives is their high degree of standardisation, which allows for a multilateral netting of positions among counterparties (already a very substantial efficiency gain). Institutionally, the credit risks of multiple counter-parties are ultimately substituted with the single risk of a *clearing-house* (the second major efficiency gain). In general, clearing-houses become the opposite party to every exchange-executed trade.[10] In becoming the opposite legal party to all derivatives contracts listed on the associated exchange, clearing-houses always have a balanced position—an equal number of long- and short-listed contracts. Having a perfectly matched portfolio of contracts, clearing-houses isolate themselves from market risk but remain directly exposed to the counter-party risk of their clearing members, and indirectly to the counter-party risk of the clearing members' customers. Currently, each of the 13 US futures exchanges has an affiliated clearing-house, organised either as a division of the exchange or as a separate corporation.

**Table 5.2** Top contracts

| Position | Contract | Exchange* | Jan–Sept 1997 | Jan–Sept 1996 | % change |
|----------|----------|-----------|---------------|---------------|----------|
| 1 (1) | Eurodollar | CME | 73 828 187 | 71 503 606 | +3 |
| 2 (3) | US T-bond | CBOT | 72 644 098 | 63 946 651 | +14 |
| 3 (9) | Bund | LIFFE | 34 970 000 | 29 753 178 | +18 |
| 4 (8) | US $/Real | BM&F | 34 299 625 | 33 663 196 | +2 |
| 5 (10) | Euromark | LIFFE | 30 429 520 | 27 457 296 | +11 |
| 6 (7) | 1d Int rate | BM&F | 29 043 750 | 40 152 303 | −28 |
| 7 (5) | S&P 100 (o) | CBOE | 28 632 923 | 43 641 609 | −34 |
| 8 (11) | 10-yr Notional | MATIF | 26 423 116 | 26 115 170 | +1 |
| 9 (18) | Dax (o) | DTB | 24 674 553 | 18 386 113 | +34 |
| 10 (16) | US T-bond (o) | CBOT | 22 422 182 | 19 533 940 | +15 |
| 11 (–) | Bund | DTB | 22 162 651 | 11 844 872 | +87 |
| 12 (21) | Eurodollar (o) | CME | 20 248 173 | 16 712 169 | +21 |
| 13 (17) | S&P 500 (o) | CBOE | 18 930 660 | 19 043 332 | −1 |
| 14 (19) | Crude oil | NYMEX | 18 579 972 | 18 142 304 | +2 |
| 15 (14) | Euroyen | TIFFE | 18 217 600 | 23 030 583 | −21 |
| 16 (20) | 10-yr T-note | CBOT | 17 551 328 | 16 829 294 | +4 |
| 17 (25) | BOBL | DTB | 17 198 812 | 13 579 237 | +26 |
| 18 (26) | 10-yr Notional | MEFFRF | 16 817 009 | 13 111 201 | +28 |
| 19 (–) | Aluminium | LME | 16 136 798 | 10 440 592 | +55 |
| 20 (–) | Sterling | LIFFE | 15 071 309 | 11 380 001 | +32 |

*Source: Futures and Options Week*, 10 November 1997

There is a long history of clearing member defaults and near defaults in the exchange traded futures markets.[11] However, it is important to note that most problems occurred at new or small exchanges, in countries with under-developed regulatory frameworks, and that losses of members of major exchanges did not result in putting the clearing-house at risk or in losses of final users. (Barings did not jeopardise SIMEX.) In well-regulated (i.e., self-regulated) markets, such as the United States, there has never been a default by a clearing-house.

Some of the factors affecting counter-party risk exposures relate directly to the financial integrity of clearing-houses, including: membership requirements, credit surveillance, and monitoring of members; adequacy of margining system and reliability of processing systems; procedures in the event of member's default, or market emergency; financial resources of the clearing-houses and its ability to withstand the default of major members; regulatory environment and government support in times of financial distress; and systemic linkages between clearing-houses and risk exposures connected with them.[12]

Clearing-houses perform critical functions for the integrity of exchange-traded derivatives contracts by regulating, monitoring and guaranteeing the obligations of their members. One of the main functions clearing-houses perform is the clearance and settlement of exchange-executed trades. The execution of a trade is the transacting of an order on an exchange floor, while clearing is the subsequent process of recognition (matching, confirmation, recording and guaranteeing) of the transaction by the clearing-house and the actual cash settlement.

Once a customer's order is executed by a broker on an exchange floor, it is subsequently transmitted to the clearing-house by clearing members acting on behalf of the parties to the trades, or acting on their own behalf. All clearing of trades must be done by clearing members. Modern clearing-houses settle all transactions that are made on affiliated exchanges by *offset*, that is, the clearing-house substitutes itself as a counter-party to each trade. Before accepting a trade for clearance, the clearing-house compares the reports of trades submitted by buyers and sellers in order to "match trades". Unmatched trades or "out-trades" must be resolved before the next trading day. Only then is the trade confirmed by the clearing-house to its clearing members. Prior to this confirmation, the counter-party's risk is to the clearing member and not to the clearing-house. Trades are then recorded in a trade register. At this stage the clearing-house guarantees each trade, and interposes itself as the counter-party to both sides of every transaction. The direct relationship between buyer and seller is thus replaced by the clearing-house that matches longs and shorts to settle member positions.[13]

After an order is executed on the exchange floor, the clearing member must post acceptable collateral (cash, government securities, letters of credit from highly rated banks, etc.) that is called *initial margin* with the clearing-house. The clearing member collects this margin from its customers.[14]

All US clearing-houses, except CME and NYMEX, use *net margining systems*. In such a system purchases and sales of the same contract by different clients of a clearing member offset each other in the clearing member's customer account and the clearing member is not required to post initial margins on his gross position. The CME and NYMEX use *gross* margining systems in which initial margins on both short and long positions have to be posted.

The margining process, however, does not end there. Acceptable margin levels must be maintained, called *maintenance* or *variation* margin. Depending on how markets move, the amount of margin that must be maintained can vary daily. This process is called *marking positions to market*, and it is one of the main safeguards clearing-houses use to protect themselves against customer default. All margin funds are held until the contract is closed by either offset or delivery. The clearing-house calculates margin requirements throughout the day using its risk analysis system, and it has the flexibility to re-evaluate margin requirements in stress situations. Clearing-houses can also require the posting of increased margins as additional protection against credit exposure.

Commercial banks (in some countries the central bank), referred to as *settlement banks*, are an integral part of the clearing process. Settlement banks transfer cash, extend credit lines to market participants and provide letters of credit to be used as partial payment for margins. This is a very smooth process, but, because clearing-houses have different settlement and payments systems, a settlement bank may have to pay out funds to one customer prior to collecting funds from the other side of the position. Such technicalities, together with a general liquidity problem, caused serious settlement difficulties during the crash of 1987.

Leo Melamed (1996) recalls in his book the drama of settling trade discrepancies and receiving settlement payments on 19 October 1987 (a total of US$2.3 billion, compared to US$120 million on a normal trading day). The CME managed just in time to square the accounts: on 20 October at 07.17 am, three minutes before the opening of the currency markets!

Clearing-houses may become vulnerable to weaknesses in money settlement arrangements, as illustrated above in the 1987 example. Clearing-houses that use central bank funds in settlements avoid the risk of settlement bank failure. Nevertheless, the clearing-house could receive a provisional payment from a clearing member early in the day and have the payment unwound later because the clearing member could not cover a short position at the central bank. When commercial banks are used as settlement banks the clearing-house is exposed to settlement bank failure from the time its account is credited until the payments system achieves finality. Two steps can mitigate these risks. One is to enhance intraday risk management through frequent trade matching and settlement of margin deficits during the day. This poses no problem for exchanges employing screen-based trading which have true real-time information on members' open positions and variation losses. The other step is to strengthen money settlement arrangements by utilising payment settlement systems, such as real-time gross settlement (RTGS), that provide real time or at least intraday finality of fund transfers. For more details see BIS (1997).

## Regulation of Clearing Members

To clear trades, a firm must become a *member of a clearing-house*. Clearing-houses can have a wide range of members, including banks, securities brokerage houses, commodity merchants, futures commission merchants, specialist-clearing firms, commodity trading firms, and individuals. Some clearing-houses have different categories of clearing members with different clearing privileges.

To qualify for clearing membership, an applicant must be a *member of an affiliated futures or options exchange*. Exchange members who are not members of a clearing-house must then clear through a clearing member.

Clearing-houses impose financial requirements and reporting obligations to ensure the solvency of their members. Most clearing-houses have minimum capital requirements for their members, which vary considerably from one clearing-house to another. Clearing members are frequently subsidiaries of large financial institutions, but few clearing-houses require parent company guarantees.

Prudent membership standards and the need to attract members require a careful trade-off. For a large bank or securities firm, it would be unacceptable to risk its entire capital by guaranteeing a clearing subsidiary. In general, trading is tempted to migrate to exchanges with looser standards and lower capital and margin requirements. Clearing-house solvability is a public good that is certainly recognised by members, but probably not at full value as most public goods. The ability of a clearing-house to dictate tougher membership standards depends on the importance of its contracts, the stringency of local regulators, and the presence of competing exchanges.

In the United States, clearing-houses require members to report large customer positions. Outside the United States, clearing-houses may have access to information on large customer positions although few require active reporting. Most clearing-houses *limit the size of speculative positions* in a given contract. No limits are imposed on hedge positions on many exchanges as profits or losses on the hedge and the underlying position should cancel each other out, thus decreasing the overall price risk of the counter-party.

In order to circumvent position limits, customers may seek to accumulate positions in a given contract through several different clearing members at the same exchange, or similar contracts at different exchanges. Moreover, customers' OTC positions are invisible for clearing members and clearing-houses, making the monitoring of customers' overall exposures very difficult. Defaults on OTC trades could cause losses sufficient to trigger a default on exchange-listed positions. This illustrates the need for information on overall exposure of clients, beyond their positions on (possibly several) exchanges.

Globalisation of derivatives markets, competition between exchanges, and lack of patent protection for successful contracts induces exchanges to replicate the successful contracts of their rivals. This makes it harder to monitor proprietary or customer positions of member firms that clear through several clearing-houses even where such reporting requirements exist. Consequently, the need to meet margin calls on the same or correlated contracts at several clearing-houses simultaneously may increase the risk of member or customer default. Currently, many clearing-houses cannot monitor their members' margin calls at other clearing-houses, but co-operative efforts are underway to improve exchange of information. The importance of communication between clearing-houses and the inability of contract limits to prevent financial disasters was well illustrated by the collapse of Barings plc (see Chapter 3).

An increasingly important credit issue is the monitoring of affiliates of clearing members. Sudden losses at the parent level or at other affiliates could affect a clearing member's ability to honour contract obligations. In 1994, the CFTC adopted rules designed to prevent financial stress at multipurpose US conglomerates.[15]

Clearing-houses require only that clearing members post margins and, within some constraints, leave members to set margins and other requirements for their own customers. Exchange-imposed customer margin requirements are directed at regulating this potential gap. Minimum customer-margin requirements aim at keeping competition among clearing members from pushing initial customer margins to levels at which customer defaults would be unacceptably high. Preventing customer default decreases the likelihood of members' defaults and contributes to the financial stability of the clearing-house.

In general, all clearing members are subject to initial and ongoing credit surveillance. Monitoring of clearing members for maintenance of segregation of customers' accounts (and other safeguards of customer funds) is an important clearing-house function. However, the Barings case also highlights the practical limits to oversight of clearing members.

Some clearing-houses have more stringent membership requirements than others, and the quality of member surveillance appears to vary widely. In setting membership and margin requirements, clearing-houses face competitive pressures to relax standards. In the course of their operations, they make daily judgements about the financial strength and integrity of clearing members that could have significant financial repercussions for clearing members and non-clearing counter-parties alike.[16] On the regulation of clearing-houses, see Technical Insight 5.1.

**Margin Management**

Having a perfectly matched portfolio of contracts, clearing-houses manage to isolate themselves from market risk but remain exposed to credit risk—a clearing member may fail to perform on a call for additional margin due to the inability to collect the required collateral from his customers, due to losses from his own trading or other activities, or due to problems at affiliates.

Clearing-houses have built multiple layers of protection for counter-party risk exposure. The most important layer consists of the collection and maintenance of security deposits, or margins, on the contracts that clearing members trade. Margin requirements are *not* designed to fully collateralise a clearing-house's exposures to its members in *all* market conditions. They reflect a balance between the risk reduction benefits of greater

**Technical Insight 5.1** Regulation of Clearing-houses

In 1995 there were more than 44 futures and options clearing-houses around the world that are regulated by various regulatory bodies. In Europe and in the Asia/Pacific region, some clearing-houses are under the direct supervision of their Ministries of Finance. Others are under the regulation of national securities regulatory agencies.

In the United States, the federal regulation of commodity futures and options markets is based on the Commodity Exchange Act ("CEA"). Originally enacted in 1936, the CEA was subsequently amended by the Commodity Futures Trading Commission Act of 1974; the Futures Trading Acts of 1978 and 1982; and the Futures Trading Practices Act of 1992.

Futures and options clearing-houses in the United States, with the exception of the Options Clearing Corporation (OCC), operate under the regulatory jurisdiction of the CFTC. The powers of the CFTC include the approval of a futures exchange to operate, its overall rules and regulations, and the trading rules for each "designated" contract. Clearing-houses, like exchanges, are subject to inspection and rule enforcement reviews by the CFTC.

Originally created as a wholly-owned subsidiary of the CBOE, the OCC is now jointly owned by the CBOE, the New York Stock Exchange, the American Stock Exchange, the Philadelphia Stock Exchange, the Pacific Goods Exchange and the National Association of Securities Dealers. The OCC operates under the jurisdiction of the Securities and Exchange Commission (SEC) because it clears US listed options—contracts that are characterised as securities and not as commodity contracts.[17] By-laws and rules of the OCC must be approved by the SEC, as must the rules and regulations of the exchanges or markets on which the options issued by the OCC are traded. The SEC also requires the issuance of a prospectus and options disclosure documents describing the obligations of the OCC, the types of options, and the responsibilities of clearing members.

collateralisation and the opportunity costs entailed. Most clearing-houses set margins that cover 95% to 99% of potential losses from movements in market prices over a one-day time horizon—as in VAR procedures (see Technical Insight 5.2).

Clearing-houses require lower margins on various offsetting positions (e.g., spreads and straddles). Margins on speculative positions are usually higher

**Technical Insight 5.2**   Fixing of margin requirements

Clearing-houses have been pioneers in developing risk-management systems. They use various systems to calculate the margin requirements, which can be divided into two categories: risk-based margin systems and margin systems based on a fixed percentage of the contracts' values. All CFTC-regulated markets, the London Clearing-house, and the SIMEX use the Standard Portfolio Analysis of Risk (SPAN) system developed by the CME. The Options Clearing Corporation has developed its own risk-based system—the Theoretical Intermarket Margins System (TIMS)—which is also used by Trans Canada Options, Deutsche Terminbörse, the Hong Kong Futures Exchange, and the European Options Clearing Corporation. Many European clearing-houses (such as MATIF, OM Stockholm, OMLX London Securities & Derivatives Exchange, ÖTOB Clearing Bank, and the Norwegian Futures & Options Clearing House) use their own, proprietary risk-based margin systems. The majority of the clearing-houses in the Asia/Pacific region use margin systems based on a percentage of the contracts' values. These systems are less sophisticated and more arbitrary than the risk-based systems.

The risk-based margin systems simulate the effect of changing market conditions and use options pricing models to calculate the overall gains and losses for each clearing member's overall portfolio. For example, SPAN calculates many standard scenarios of price and volatility changes for all contracts each day. The parameters of the system, such as price and volatility range, choice of theoretical option-pricing model, and so forth, are variable and are set by the respective clearing-houses. SPAN calculates dollar values for each position scenario, and the largest potential loss becomes the required margin for that position.[18]

The models underlying clearing-houses' risk-based margin systems, like any model, may not be foolproof. When setting initial margin levels, a clearing-house may assume that the probability distributions of different contract prices are independent of one another. In this case, a margin imposed on a customer who trades futures on US Treasury bills would be the same, whether or not he is simultaneously (in the same account) trading futures on the S&P 500 index. Historic volatilities and correlations may be poor predictors of future relations and, during periods of crisis, volatilities can increase by a high multiple (is this not the definition of crisis?) and correlations may deviate significantly from their historic pattern.

As clearing houses may only experience serious difficulties in extreme market crashes, "stress" testing is essential. Such tests can be used to identify and limit exposures to individual clearing members and to gauge the adequacy of the clearing house's financial resources (in the G10 countries perhaps half the clearing houses currently have stress testing programmes).

Liquidity considerations are often not incorporated into the margin calculations. Even liquid contracts under extreme conditions may become illiquid. Therefore, a more conservative approach to calculating margin levels might be to use price changes over more than one day as input data points. But there is clearly a limit to conservatism: to the extent that architects do accept a non-zero risk that under extreme stress a building may collapse to avoid excessive costs, clearing-houses, again for cost considerations, also have to accept some residual risk for extreme cases.

than margins on hedge positions. Although clearing members at some clearing-houses must specifically report that positions are for hedging purposes, it is unclear whether clearing-houses can accurately determine at all times which position is which. Customers usually report to clearing members whether their positions are for hedging or trading purposes. Clearing members, on their part, report their positions to the clearing-house as hedges or for trading. But there is no inspection mechanism to assure the accuracy of these self-reporting procedures. The Barings case illustrates this problem: SIMEX, apparently, could not identify the speculative character of Barings' positions.[19]

What happens if a clearing member fails to post the required margin after a variation margin call? Given daily resettlement (marking-to-market) on the contract, the clearing-house would try to close the position by entering into an opposite trade, and by using the posted margin to cover any resulting loss. The clearing-house would also attempt to transfer the member's non-defaulting customer accounts to another clearing member in order to protect them.[20]

**Risks to Individual Customers**

Most clearing-houses stand between clearing members, not between individual customers. As principal to contracts, clearing members are fully responsible for performance, regardless of the situation of their customers. For example, even if a non-clearing counter-party fails to post the required variation margin with its clearing member, the clearing member is still responsible for posting a variation margin with the clearing-house. The 1985 failure of

Volume Investors, a CFTC-regulated futures broker and clearing member of the Comex Clearing Association Inc., illustrates this point.[21]

The Volume Investors case also brings up another credit issue—that of account segregation. There are three ways that a clearing-house segregates accounts. The most common one is to segregate only proprietary from customer accounts, but aggregate all customer accounts into one account. Alternatively, a few clearing-houses outside the United States segregate all accounts from one another, including setting up individual customer accounts.

Most clearing-houses follow the first method, that is, they segregate accounts into one proprietary account and one customers' account. In this case, default could be triggered by losses in the proprietary activities of the clearing member, or by losses of a customer. If proprietary trading of a clearing member is the cause of default, customer funds are protected because the clearing-house cannot use them to satisfy the clearing member's obligations. However, if the clearing member defaults on a margin call on a customer's account, the clearing-house can use the clearing member's own proprietary margin account to make up the deficiency.

When all accounts—proprietary and individual customer accounts—are segregated from one another, customer protection is greatest. Inversely, the degree of customer protection is least where no segregation occurs.[22]

Third-party custody of margin and the use of letters of credit in lieu of cash or securities to meet margin requirements could reduce the assets under the control of the clearing-house and clearing member. Some clearing-houses, for historic or local market conditions, accept only cash as collateral (for example, Manila International Futures Clearing House and Sydney Futures Exchange Clearing House); others accept a variety of collateral, including bank guarantees and letters of credit. The ability and willingness of banks to honour these contracts is an important risk element for non-clearing counterparties and clearing members, as well as for clearing-houses themselves.

That not all is perfect on the exchanges has been demonstrated by several "market squeeze" attempts at the London Metal Exchange. Technical Insight 5.3 reports on the latest episode, the Sumitomo case. It is important to note, however, that similar manipulations for financial products are much more difficult and, indeed, market squeezes have not occurred on financial exchanges.[23]

There is still scope for increasing efficiency of the exchanges: joint back-offices, sharing of a clearing-house (as in London), and co-operation for (global) electronic trading. This will take time (it took the CBoT and the CME 15 years to combine their clearing operations), but competition ensures that it will come. Given the economies of scale for the exchanges and clearing-houses, the theoretical optimum configuration would comprise only a small number of exchanges/clearing-houses in the global economy. The path to such an optimum is still a long one.

**Technical Insight 5.3**   The London Metal Exchange (LME) and Sumitomo

The LME is the world's biggest and most liquid base metals market. Its turnover has grown seven-fold during the last seven years—an extraordinary success. In 1995 contracts traded represented more than 1 billion tonnes of metal valued at over US$2500 billion. More than 95% of the LME's business comes from outside the United Kingdom, a degree of openness which is astonishing even by London standards.

The LME's design differs from most other exchanges because it is based on the needs of metal producers. Nearly 5% of its trading results in physical delivery, a far higher proportion than for any other commodity exchange, and, therefore, the LME has 380 authorised warehouses in 42 locations around the globe. The role of investors (speculators) has been increasing in recent years and 20–25% of trades are estimated as speculative.

There is no variation margining in cash at the LME. Profits and losses are not realised until the contract expires. This suits metal producers or users whose cash flows are limited to the physical market. But it creates additional risks.

The LME has been faced with difficult situations more than once recently. In 1985 LME members lost some US$600 million when 22 governments refused to pay up after their tin market price support scheme collapsed. The LME narrowly survived.

There have been market "squeezes"[24] and there have been "rogue" traders. Codelco, the Chilean copper firm made a loss of US$175 million—enough to be concerned, but nothing compared to the "Sumitomo affair". On 13 June 1996 Sumitomo revealed that Mr Hamanaka, its chief copper trader, had lost US$1.8 billion (a loss which finally totalled US$2.6 billion), mostly in trading copper futures and options on the LME.

Earlier in 1996 regulators had already investigated what appeared to be a squeeze in the copper market (about 70% of the world's exchange traded copper is traded on the LME)—that is, an attempt to force up the spot price by restricting copper supply. The chief support was Sumitomo, since it controlled a large amount of copper supply. Nevertheless, and excepting a modest increase in copper's future price at end April/early May, the price declined from about US$2800 per tonne at the beginning of the year to US$2000 in June. During this period Mr Hamanaka built up long positions, believing that prices would increase and trying to prop them up with his own purchases.

It is alleged that hedge funds contributed to the rapid price decline in June from US$2300 to US$2000 per tonne. If so, this would be an example of speculators helping to restore prices to a level dictated by underlying fundamentals, and counteract market manipulation.

Some observers have pointed out that if daily margins had to be settled in cash the Sumitomo affair would not have occurred. But it is also a fact that the exchange did not incur any losses—other than for its reputation. Volatility during the first six months of 1996 tripled to reach a historic record—not only because of market fundamentals alone, but also because of the actions of one trader.

The Securities and Investment Board's (SIB), the UK financial watchdog, investigation acquitted the LME of any responsibility in the Sumitomo affair, but listed a number of suggestions to improve internal management rules and transparency.

It is generally expected that there will not be a major overhaul of the LME's operating rules despite recent criticism. Stricter rules for membership would not have avoided the Sumitomo affair as Sumitomo is not a member.

## 3. WHAT MAKES A SUCCESSFUL EXCHANGE-TRADED CONTRACT?

Some insight has already been gained as to what constitutes a successful exchange-traded contract in this chapter's review of past contract innovations and in Chapter 4's discussion of the economics of futures. As is clear from Chapter 4, the number of successful futures contracts should be fairly limited by three economic factors: the underlying risk, the need for a homogenous product definition and the necessary liquidity. Beyond these basic features there are five broad characteristics of importance: those specific to the underlying instrument; those of the contract itself; complementarity with other dimensions of the exchange activity; the competitive aspects of the introduction of a new contract on an exchange; and the regulatory restrictions. As we shall see, no single criterion by itself will assure the success of a contract.

### The Underlying Instrument

A *deep and liquid cash market* for the commodity or instrument underlying the potential futures contract is of key importance, given the tight connections of cash and futures markets. Related to the "deep and liquid" cash market is the notion that the underlying commodity or instrument ought to be a *homogenous good*.[25] A homogenous good facilitates low cost transactions and parties to a trade do not have to negotiate its qualities with each trade. In other words, it must be sufficiently standardised so that trades can be completed without inspection or extensive oral or written documentation so that market participants focus on the price not the quantity or quality. One major reason for the failure of various attempts to trade real estate futures is the difficulty of standardisation of "real estate". In addition, the greater the standardisation, the greater the deliverable supply (or the easier the definition of the "deliverable" in cash settled contracts). A large deliverable supply means that manipulation is less likely to occur.

As argued in Chapter 4, one of the major reasons for the existence of a futures market is the efficient allocation of price risk. Thus, a successful contract is aided by *high price volatility in the cash market*. With low price volatility, potential hedgers may find that the cost of hedging outweighs the benefits. As noted in Chapter 10, the failure of the CPI futures contract in 1986 has been attributed to the (temporary) decrease in the volatility of inflation rates in 1986.

Price volatility is usually associated with a free market. In particular, if prices of the underlying commodity are fixed or price movements limited by governments or a cartel the likelihood of having sufficient hedging demand is diminished.[26] For the same reason socialist economies had no need for futures markets, although the economies, but not individuals, faced the same risks as capitalist economies. Or, conversely, as illustrated by the reaction of farmers to price deregulation in agriculture, when prices are deregulated market participants turn to futures markets for risk hedging.

**Product Design**

Delivery characteristics are among the critical design elements of a futures contract. They determine the convergence between the cash and futures prices as the futures contract approaches expiration. The ability to arbitrage and hedge is based in large part on the delivery specifications. For commodities, it is important to structure the delivery system so that the relation between the quality and location of the various deliverable units conforms to commercial practices. Many financial futures contracts specify the delivery of cash-based contracts on a final settlement price and the procedure for arriving at the settlement price is therefore crucial.

Alternatively, the delivery system for non-perfectly homogenous financial products must be designed to allow different units to be delivered at "adjusted" prices. For example, the US Treasury Bond contract permits many bonds to be delivered. Similarly on the MATIF, the "notional contract" is a theoretical bond issued by the French government, with a maturity between seven and ten years,[27] a coupon of 10%, payable "in fine". Deliverable are all fixed rate French government bonds in French francs with a residual maturity between seven and ten years and issued amounts in excess of FF5 billion. The value of each bond to be delivered, its invoice price, is determined by multiplying the final futures price by a "conversion factor". The conversion factor is meant to make every bond look as if it had a coupon of 10% and a maturity between seven and ten years.[28] Because the seller of the futures contract decides which Treasury bond to deliver, and will therefore deliver the cheapest one available, the futures contract "tracks" the cheapest-to-deliver bond. This means that the delivery system does not necessarily have to make every unit equivalent as long as there is a consistent relation between the units that market participants can understand.

Another aspect of contract design that is important is that the *pricing of the contract be easily understood*. Successful contracts attract both hedgers and speculators. If hedgers have exposures both as buyers and sellers of the underlying instrument, one basic role of speculators, namely the one of creating counter-parties to allow a futures market to function, is less essential.

### Complementarity with Other Contracts

When contemplating the design of a futures contract, an exchange needs to examine the *currently available cross-hedges*.[29] Hedgers may be unwilling to switch to a new contract unless the precision of the hedge is enhanced enough so as to offset the lower transaction costs (higher liquidity) of the existing cross-hedge. Usually the product used to cross-hedge has enough liquidity so that the bid/ask spread is small. However, the cross-hedge may not provide very precise offsetting price movements to those for the underlying commodity or instrument. That is, there is a low correlation between the prices of the future contract and of the hedger's instrument so that the basis risk is high. The hedger will be willing to move to the new contract if the basis risk is low enough to offset the higher transaction cost of a new contract. An example was provided in Chapter 3. Before the EMS crisis of 1992, the DM/dollar contracts were used as a cross-hedge for other EMS currencies. After the crisis new contracts have been created because the market realised that the cross-hedge had become unsatisfactory for trading.[30]

### Competitive Aspects

At times exchanges do attempt to invade another exchange's product line by trading a similar, but not strictly identical, contract (see Table 5.2, which provided a list of the major contracts and the exchanges on which they are traded). If the contract specifications of the new contract better meet the needs of potential users, the new contract may win volume from the older, more mature contract, or may establish another liquid market. In general, however, contract reapplications fail most often because they lack a sufficient, distinct advantage to compensate for being second.[31]

An interesting case is the German government bond contract, traded on LIFFE and Germany's DTB. It is LIFFE's most successful contract (followed by the three-month Euro-Deutschemark contract), trading in recent years about double the volume of the long gilt contract. LIFFE was first to launch the contract and when DTB created its own in 1990, volume on LIFFE was already close to 10 million contracts a year. DTB only started to surpass that level in 1994, trading about one-third of the volume on LIFFE. In 1997, market shares of both exchanges were converging. Contract differentiation is insignificant. What differentiates the two contracts is the underlying trading technology: pit-trading on LIFFE, electronic trading on DTB. This example has rightly become famous because it provides two important practical lessons. First, any national market has a certain natural attraction for trading local products. Although being late, DTB could capture a rising share of the market. Second, the national exchange is not the inevitable market leader. LIFFE dominate the contract solidly. This is perhaps the most unexpected practical result. Being first with the right trading environment seems more important than being located in the currency zone of the contract.

**Regulation of New Contracts**

In the United States, the Commodities Futures Trading Commission (CFTC) must approve all contracts prior to their listing. The proposing exchange must demonstrate that the contract conforms to commercial practices, can be used effectively for hedging, has an adequate deliverable supply to preclude manipulation, aids price discovery, and is in the "public interest".[32]

The futures industry, however, has argued for many years that approval delays and costs are seriously impeding the exchanges' competitivity with OTC products. Most of the rules were, indeed, put in place when the majority of clients of the exchanges (then limited to agricultural products) were farmers rather than professional investors.[33]

The CFTC brought about a storm of protest when in July 1995 it declared void some of Metallgesellschaft Refining and Marketing Inc. (MGRM) swaps (see Chapter 3) on the grounds that they were illegal, off-exchange future contracts. This was a rather bizarre decision: as stated in Chapter 3, futures contracts differ from forwards only in that they are traded on an exchange. The 1936 Commodities Exchange Act makes the trading of "off-exchange futures" illegal. This law was designed to concentrate futures trading on organised and regulated exchanges. But it failed in its mission because, as was argued in

Chapter 4, futures contracts have no economic attributes that distinguish them from forward contracts or swaps (which is merely a package of forwards) other than trading on an exchange. Unfortunately the law is unclear about what exactly constitutes a futures contract, so that the unfortunate CFTC decision has created consternation and uncertainty. Merton Miller in the *Wall Street Journal* (17 August 1995) has firmly called to "rein in the CFTC".

In 1997 this seemed to be happening. Bills are being discussed in both Houses of Congress that would relax the regulatory regime for professional traders on US futures exchanges—the so-called "pro-exemption". A pro-exemption would strip the CFTC of much of its existing power and would also end the CFTC's ambition to draw OTC contracts into its orbit.

## 4. NEW PRODUCT DEVELOPMENTS ON THE EXCHANGES

The exchanges are under constant competitive pressure from OTC markets and other exchanges to innovate. The most successful contracts are copied (and slightly differentiated) by other exchanges around the world. Innovations are concentrated on new products, new management and dealing systems and wider distribution of established contracts through mergers of exchanges and co-operative agreements.

Strategies of new product development can be seen in three dimensions: new products in areas where some products exist already; more flexible product designs; and products for new applications. The first is to identify demand for a new product. Very often this demand is perceived from cross-hedges, that is, hedges with a basic risk. New products are created for shorter or longer maturities along the treasury yield curve or for different credit classes (Euro-contracts, commercial paper contracts, mortgage-backed securities). A successful contract then may be replicated in another currency (e.g., bunds on LIFFE). The next step is to create options on the cash instrument or on futures. In currency markets the first futures and options were on dollar/DM or dollar/yen rates; the next step was to expand the set of dollar rates and the final step was to create cross-rate contracts (e.g., DM/yen).

A particularly interesting new product, volatility futures or VOLX, was launched in 1996 by OMLX in London. These futures are based on the price volatility of the reference market (stock market indexes). Since the price reflects current and expected volatility, such contracts create a "volatility term structure". They serve to hedge vega and gamma exposures, difficult to hedge otherwise, and long-dated options positions.

A more classical recent innovation was the launch of a futures on the Dow Jones Industrial Average on the CBoT and an option traded on the CBOE. Both exchanges launched the new products with a record US$50 million promotional budget. The contracts are targeted for retail investors and, although the Dow Jones is no longer an index reflecting overall market developments, it is the best-known index.

A second dimension consists in making the standard design more flexible, either in terms of expiration dates (LEAPS are long-dated options on corporate shares) or in terms of major contract specifications (flexi-options). This is one way of competing head-on with the flexibility of OTC products. Chapter 9 explores this avenue in greater length.

A third dimension is to explore entirely new areas where risk is prevalent but not appropriately packaged yet.[34] *Basis trading*, or exchange for physicals, are common methods of trading by OTC players. These allow the simultaneous purchase or sale of a bond, for example, in the cash market and offsetting purchase or sale in the futures market. More recently the principle of basis trading has been adopted by the exchanges. LIFFE in London set up its Basis Trading Facility (BTF) to enable traders to cross trades in the bund futures and cash market.[35] In Germany, DTB launched a similar scheme for its "bund and bobl" (*bundesobligation*) futures.

Among the most interesting recent contracts for entirely new purposes are insurance derivatives. The potential is so impressive that these contracts warrant a closer look.

## Insurance Derivatives

One major new area promising significant advances are *insurance derivatives*. Some experts believe that insurance derivatives could become a source of explosive growth, citing capital constraints in the insurance industry, changing demographic patterns, the ballooning costs of health care and of natural disasters. This area is therefore explored in some detail.

At present the US insurance industry boasts some US$175 billion of primary capital. There is some US$25 billion in reinsurance capital, and around US$15 billion at Lloyd's of London. This has to support a US$7 trillion US economy with all its associated product liability, medical and legal malpractice, environmental, property and other insurance claims.

Until recently the only way insurers could hedge their underwriting risk was through reinsurance. Although they were able to use financial derivatives to hedge their asset portfolios and interest-rate sensitive liabilities, there were no traded instruments available to cover the increasing claims arising from losses in property and casualty lines of insurance. Demand for such instruments was heightened by the growing costs of catastrophes and the consequent effect on reinsurance available.

Buying put options can be thought of as taking out an insurance policy. This analogy has now come full circle, with options and futures contracts poised to replace conventional insurance and reinsurance activity. Exchange-traded *catastrophe insurance derivatives* (cat futures) were launched by the CBoT in December 1992, followed by insurance contracts for the agricultural sector.

Before insurance risk can be securitised, however, it must first be standardised. In the case of the CBoT's catastrophe insurance contracts, this meant devising an index on which to base derivatives. Unlike the equity, bond or commodity markets, the insurance market has no obvious, continuously updated, underlying cash price. The solution chosen by the CBoT is the loss ratio index, calculated by the Insurance Service Office, which uses data from at least 25 designated reporting companies. The loss ratio is the dollar value of reported losses incurred in a given quarter (the loss quarter) and reported by the end of the following quarter (the run-off quarter) divided by one fourth of the dollar value of premiums collected in the previous year. The contract value is US$25 000 times the loss ratio.

As the premiums are known and constant throughout the life of the contract, changes in the futures price are caused solely by the market's changing expectations of the amount of losses for the loss quarter that will be reported by the end of the following quarter.

Although activity in these contracts got off to a slow start, volumes have risen rapidly in the past years. The novelty of the concept and the conservatism of the insurance industry were obvious obstacles, but an additional handicap was the fact that initially Illinois was the only state to allow its insurers to use these instruments. Approval has since been obtained from New York and California, the other major states with large numbers of insurance companies. Technical Insight 5.4 explains the use of insurance derivatives.

The next major innovation from the CBoT—*crop insurance derivatives*—should find a far more receptive audience, as the exchange has been trading grain futures since its creation in 1848 and crop yield is a far simpler concept than the loss index ratio. Crop insurance is the first major innovation in agriculture in 20–25 years. It is an obvious candidate for derivatives, as the crop yield is an insurable, commoditisable risk.[36] The US Department of Agriculture estimates that the Federal Crop Insurance Act would increase participation in crop insurance from about 33% of eligible land at present to 80%. Total insurance premiums are predicted to rise from US$750 million in 1993 to more than US$2 billion by 1999. The mid-West floods of 1994 cost some US$4 billion in disaster relief and crop insurance payments, and total crop insurance liabilities are about US$13 billion.

It is unlikely that the traditional insurance and reinsurance industry could meet such a dramatic increase in demand. Private insurers have hitherto been loath to commit much capital to crop insurance because systemic weather shocks mean a high correlation between yield from different farms and thus prevent insurers from minimising their risk by diversifying their policies across large numbers of farms or a variety of crops. Options and futures based

**Technical Insight 5.4**   How insurance futures work

An insurer who wants to hedge against a possible excess of losses over a given quarter will *buy* a futures contract. If severe catastrophes occur, the gain generated by each long position in a futures contract will offset the high amount of claims to be paid.

A more popular hedge than a long futures position is a call spread. A "cat" call spread, like any other, involves buying a call at a strike price $(k_1)$ and selling a call at a higher strike $(k_2)$, both calls having the same maturity. Where it differs is that both calls are written on the futures contract: $k_1$ and $k_2$ are called loss ratio attachment points. A long position in a call spread gives coverage, once the premium is paid, between two loss ratio attachment points.

Call spreads are more heavily traded than the futures contracts for obvious reasons. The amount of risk at stake, whether taking a short or long position, is much more limited, a desirable feature for a new instrument and for insurers who are not familiar with derivatives. Also, the pay-off profile generated by a cat spread bears a striking similarity to that for a layer of reinsurance, so that insurers and reinsurers have an idea of what the "fair price" of a call spread should be.

Turning to the sellers of cat futures and call spreads, these tend to be construction companies which benefit from catastrophes, some reinsurance companies and speculators willing to take risks in order to make profits.

The increasing popularity of cat call spreads can be explained by the additional capacity of reinsurance they give the market-place, the low transaction costs, the possibility of unwinding a position and the financial integrity of the CBoT as a counter-party. OTC hybrid insurance derivatives, such as foreign exchange Cats, are now being offered by a number of financial institutions.

on crop area yield could be the answer. These are proven tools for hedging risk and would attract fresh sources of capital. The existing catastrophe insurance contracts would not be suitable for hedging crop loss because they are based on an index of property liability claims.[37]

Another advantage of the crop yield contracts is that there is already an OTC derivatives market in this area. The lack of OTC business was a significant handicap for the catastrophe products in their early days. Present estimates of OTC business in catastrophe insurance derivatives range from 10 to 20 times as big as the exchange-traded market. Many OTC deals are based on the CBoT indices, with customisation of the underlying region, as well as maturity dates and contract sizes.

*Medical insurance*—a major preoccupation of the Clinton administration—is another candidate for derivatives contracts. The CBoT has seen the potential in this trillion-dollar market and has already won CFTC approval to trade futures and options on health insurance. The trading unit would be based on the ratio of total claims paid to total premiums earned on all policies in a defined underlying insurance pool during a predetermined period.[38]

The time is ripe for radical innovation in Europe. The European Union's recently issued "Third Life and Non-Life Insurance Directive" is expected to encourage many insurers to increase their use of financial derivatives for investment and hedging. Capacity constraints are just as pressing as in the United States, and the discredited Common Agricultural Policy is prompting calls for cuts in government subsidies to farmers.

## 5. EXCHANGES FOR A GLOBAL MARKET

Alliances between the world's exchanges have become increasingly fashionable, as exchanges step up efforts to distribute products more widely to gain from the underlying economies of scale. The trend has been highlighted by a number of recent developments. One is the creation of global electronic trading systems, such as Globex (set up by the CME with Reuters and co-owned with the CBoT for a few years, later joined by MATIF and SIMEX), or Project A (after the CBoT withdrew from Globex) with overnight sessions to cover other time zones (CBoT and Bloomberg).[39] The other is co-operative agreements among the exchanges. Two deals in 1995 have connected LIFFE to markets in other time zones. In late 1995 LIFFE concluded an agreement with the Tokyo International Financial Futures Exchange (TIFFE) allowing it to trade TIFFE's three-month Euroyen contract in London when trading closes for the day in Tokyo. In early 1995 LIFFE and CBoT announced an agreement allowing LIFFE traders to deal in the CBoT's Treasury bond contracts in the London morning. In turn, Chicago traders deal in LIFFE's bond contracts after the London close. Since then many more product exchange agreements have been concluded.

Separately, the electronic link-up agreed in the autumn of 1994 and abandoned in 1996 (before a new agreement was reached in 1997) between France's MATIF and Germany's DTB highlights the use of new computer-based trading technologies and the difficulties encountered in co-operation. The exchanges planned to trade a select number of products over a common electronic network and were examining the expansion of the agreement to cash equity markets.

There has been a plethora of other connections. European and US exchanges have made a number of initiatives to link up with smaller but rapidly growing Asian exchanges, and a number of the world's commodity derivatives exchanges are seeking connections with the bigger financial markets.[40] In

1996 LIFFE merged with the London Commodity Exchange (LCE), which had discussed merger with the New York Coffee Sugar and Cocoa Exchange and the International Petroleum Exchange.[41]

These link-ups are happening for a variety of reasons. The world's largest investment banks and securities houses—which own and control a number of exchanges—are tending to exert greater influence, and demanding much greater co-operation between the markets. These banks are increasingly offering *integrated global services* to their customers, ranging from trading to settlement and clearing activities. With banks and investors taking an integrated approach to financial markets, the traditional lines dividing different kinds of commodity exchange and financial markets are seen as increasingly artificial.

At the same time, with trading volumes stagnating since 1995 and costs rising, dealers are becoming conscious of the need to cut costs. The major players have all the infrastructure in place but are not operating at full capacity and want to reduce costs. Of interest in this regard is the agreement between the CBoT and the CME to establish a common *banking facility* to provide joint clearing and delivery of contracts. Independently of co-operative agreements among the exchanges, economies of scale suggest that the fewer clearing-houses there are, the lower the costs. For historic reasons, many exchanges have their associated clearing-house. The new trend is to share clearing-house facilities to save costs. A model in this respect is the London Clearing-House, clearing four exchanges: LME, LIFFE, IPE and the electronic stock exchange, Tradepoint.

The move towards alliances also reflects the maturity of the domestic markets for financial derivatives, such as bond futures and options. Over the past twenty years, sales of the world's biggest financial contracts have grown at rates which cannot continue and some market participants even think that the great period of contract development of financial futures may be over.

The costs of marketing and researching new products is rising and the exchanges are faced with an increasingly expensive burden of regulation, which is inhibiting their ability or willingness to devote scarce resources to product development. The immediate product range has been exhausted so product sharing arrangements are in the ascendant. There could be a dearth of big-selling new products at least in established product ranges until the markets of China and Russia and Eastern Europe come on stream.

As a result, exchanges are eager to examine channels through which they can sell more of their existing products or earn a commission by selling products listed by other exchanges.

One channel in emerging markets is to set up exchanges with local investors (prominent examples are Brazil, Mexico and Taiwan) for the commercialisation of local products and home products. Chicago-based exchanges have a clear competitive advantage for reasons of expertise and cost, but also because their dollar-based products are demanded worldwide and they can market to their own market, the largest financial community in the world, products from their emerging market subsidiary (joint venture).

In this global competitive battle two issues are of specific interest: one is the trading technology and the other the creation of a single European capital market.

## Trading Technology

A much debated problem is the technology of futures trading. Is Chicago's, London's or Paris' colourful open-outcry of futures trading just a relic of the past? Or is it rather an efficient way of supplying the service of "immediacy" in those inventory-propelled or arbitrage-driven futures markets, where the demand for speedy executions of trades is high? Opinions are divided, but around the world more and more exchanges opt for electronic trading.

For more abstract products, such as indexes, there is not much demand for immediacy—not enough, at least, to justify a group of traders standing around all day in the pit waiting to handle urgent incoming orders. For financial futures in these abstract products to succeed, electronic trading must replace pit trading which has its comparative advantage at higher ends of the volume and urgency scale. Trading of low urgency contracts pose problems in terms of efficiency and over time competition will cast its verdict. As there is less room for "market makers" on the futures exchanges, the "order-matching" of electronic trading is perfectly suited for the immediacy of order execution, transparency, and instantaneous recording.

The industry is still far from unanimous about the relative merits of the two basic trading systems. DTB firmly believes in electronic trading, whilst the Chicago exchanges, LIFFE and MATIF still bet on pit-trading. For that (and other) reason(s), the planned co-operation between DTB and MATIF floundered. Some exchanges combine open outcry and electronic trading by offering services of the latter once the pits are closed.

Moreover, the distinction between pit trading and electronic trading is increasingly losing its sharp edge. The New York Stock Exchange already collects 80% of its customer orders via computer. The two Chicago exchanges have a joint project, TOPS, to deliver orders electronically to the floor clerk. Computer screens can be installed in the trading pits, themselves, dispensing with clerks entirely. But for the time being, the order is first transmitted to an exchange member who phones his floor clerk. Depending on the contract, the floor clerk uses his hands to signal the order to the trader or asks another clerk to deliver the order. The results are often chaotic, especially on a busy day, delaying execution of customer orders. Paperwork also creates mistakes. In 1993, 8% of CME's trades did not match with customer orders; this was reduced to 4% in 1995. Electronic transmission or order execution have the advantage of speedier execution and of less frequent mistakes.

Except for Brazil's BM&F and MATIF, all new derivatives exchanges built since 1986 are fully automated. However, less successful so far have been efforts to exploit the co-operative potential of electronic trading to span the globe. For example, Globex in 1995 only accounted for 1% of Merc's total volume, although it accounted for 8.7% of MATIF's volume, a clear sign of encouragement.

One of the leading experts who virtually grew up in the pits, but was also the champion of Globex, CME's honorary chairman, Leo Melamed, has a very decided vision of electronic trading:

> "The low level of screen-based transaction volume on after-hour exchange systems gives testimony to a lack of understanding by many futures exchanges that—like it or not—a screen-based transaction process is in their members' future. While it is comforting to know that the mass of futures liquidity is still on the trading floor today, it represents a false security blanket. Foreign exchange, a market institutionalised by futures exchanges, offers a stark and sobering comparison between electronic-driven volume and open outcry . . . the turnover figures for major Forex centers in cash markets between 1992 and 1995 shows whopping increases of between 30 and 60 per cent. However, CME foreign exchange contracts did not benefit from their growth . . . Whilst admittedly some of this OTC volume can be attributed to exotics not traded on the exchange, one must accept the fact that OTC screen-based technology is an extremely attractive medium for FX market transactions.
> . . . While I do not advocate turning off the lights on existing trading floors— that could be unforgivably stupid—it is equally suicidal not to seriously prepare for a technological tomorrow.
> . . . In almost every critical area of advanced technological competence, exchanges with trading floors have fallen behind. For instance, LIFFE is the only exchange with real-time clearing capabilities. Futures exchanges are far behind securities exchanges in automatic order routing" (Melamed 1996, p. 450).

Electronic trading has a number of particularities, beyond the obvious advantage of integrating fully by design order matching, order execution, recording, settling and risk-management—without delay, mishandling, or misunderstanding. For one, the precise location of the exchange loses in importance. For instance, the fact that DTB is located in Frankfurt is irrelevant for most traders, who, equipped with a terminal can be anywhere in the world. Whilst during the first years most traders were, indeed, located in Frankfurt, DTB is making efforts to win traders located all over Europe and even overseas. It has already located terminals in six other European countries and more are planned. In March 1996 the CFTC granted permission to open terminals in the United States.

## The Single European Capital Market

One of the greatest events in financial history will occur early next century: the emergence of a unified European capital market. Today there is only one efficient, liquid and relatively complete financial market in the world and that is the US market. European countries on their own are simply too small. In addition domestic regulations have stifled the development of capital markets, so that national markets—even in Germany, the largest European economy—are illiquid and offer only a limited menu of financial products.

The European Union has already taken the necessary steps to create a single passport for banks and securities firms under a common regulatory framework. What still segments national markets are national currencies. When in 1999 the Euro is due to be launched, a fully integrated Euromarket[42] will develop, over time spreading all over Europe. The weight of the European economy, Germany's insistence on conservative monetary policy and UK's financial expertise will combine to create the second largest capital market, as liquid and as complete as the dollar market.

Today there is a derivatives exchange in virtually every European country (a new futures exchange was opened in Portugal in 1996), 23 in total. All of them are faced with a very uncertain future (e.g., in August 1996 the Irish Futures and Options Exchange closed down). The only business they are likely to retain is equity derivatives (at least some of them), as long as stock exchanges are surviving in each country (for more details see Steinherr 1998); interest and exchange contracts will either disappear or migrate.

The exchange market presents a rather easy case. All contracts involving one or two European currencies will disappear and the only futures contracts will be dollar/Euro and yen/Euro contracts. Their trading volume is, however, likely to match or exceed the sum of the existing contracts. Where these contracts will be traded is to be seen—on LIFFE, on overseas exchanges and on electronic exchanges, such as the DTB. In any case, most foreign exchange deals are over-the-counter, so that the impact on the exchanges is relatively marginal.

More interesting is the future of interest rate and bond contracts. In the EMU, short-term interest rates will converge so that short-term Euro contracts will replace existing short-term contracts. Exchanges are already preparing their claim on short-term Euro contracts by adding to their existing arsenal contracts that are expected to evolve into Euro contracts.

For longer maturities convergence is not expected to be as complete. Even with a single currency, national government bond prices are expected to reflect different risk premiums. This then opens up the possibility, unknown so far in any other market, of liquid government benchmarks for different risk classes. The outstanding government debt (to be converted into Euro) of Austria, Germany, France and the Netherlands (and, one day, the United Kingdom) would form an AAA Euro-benchmark with a volume of about one-third of the US government debt. Belgium, Ireland, Italy, Spain and Sweden could form an AA+ or AA Euro-benchmark with a volume of one-fourth of US government debt. Figure 5.3 compares outstanding public sector debt of the United States and Japan with the aggregated debt of all members

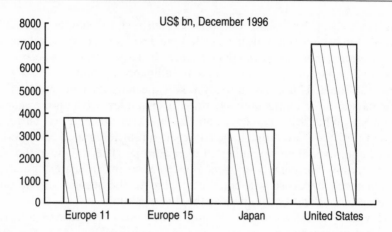

**Figure 5.3**   Public sector debt
*Source:* BIS

of the European Union (Europe 15) and of the most likely initial members (Europe 11), that is, all members except Denmark, Greece, Sweden and the United Kingdom.

There will thus be two to three benchmark yield curves for different risk classes, starting from a common short-term rate with futures contracts along each curve. This is a major development where the total of future trading can safely be expected to be much larger than today's sum of parts. Hedging costs could fall as basis risk is being diminished (a hedge of an AA-exposure with an AAA-instrument is imperfect if the yield spread is volatile). Recent innovatory products allowing the hedge of basis risk would suffer, but the overall gain due to more reliable benchmarking is certain. Whereas Europe's futures on non-government securities are much less significant than the United States', the combined volume of futures trading in European government securities already exceeds US volumes.

In addition to these benchmark issues there will be contracts for different financial instruments as securitisation will catch up in the integrated European market with the United States and institutional investors will play a similar role (see Chapter 10).

The three largest derivative exchanges in Europe are LIFFE, MATIF and DTB. They have done extremely well in recent years, as illustrated in Figure 5.4, although MATIF has lost steam. Together MATIF and DTB have about the same trading volume of LIFFE. Each of these exchanges derives most of its business from a very narrow range of contracts. Half of LIFFE's trading depends on three products: the German government bond contract, the German money-market contract and the British money-market contract. If MATIF were to lose its French government contract, its trading volume

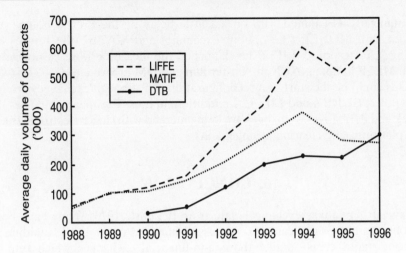

**Figure 5.4** The three largest derivatives exchanges in Europe
*Note*: 1996 to August only; DTB figures for 1996 to July only
*Source*: DTB, LIFFE, MATIF

would halve. DTB is slightly better diversified and relies more heavily on German equity contracts which are less challenged.

Because MATIF is so dependent on its French government contracts, it has made great efforts to position itself favourably for the Euro-bond contract. Its hopes stem from France's central role in the EMU process, whereas Britain is on stand-by. The French Treasury has helped by declaring that it will convert all of its existing debt into Euro bonds from the first day of monetary union. LIFFE relies on the importance of London as a global financial centre and on its establishment of intercontinental trading links with exchanges in Chicago and Tokyo. The DTB banks on the benchmark quality of German government debt and its status as the biggest electronic trading exchange in Europe. It is merging its trading and clearing facilities with SOFFEX, Switzerland's derivatives exchange, to create a new system called Eurex. A trading agreement with SIMEX is planned.

All three major European exchanges create new contracts along the DM yield curve to gain market share before European Monetary Union. LIFFE and DTB have launched a one-month future contract and DTB a contract based on 30-year German government bonds. DTB in 1997 intensified the battle for market share by launching a series of equity options and stock market index products based on Europe's leading company stocks; a contract based on a basket of other European government bonds and one based on the volatility levels on the Frankfurt stock exchange. LIFFE is expected to offer similar products.

The major event in transnational co-operation so far has been the formation of EUREX as a result of a merger between Switzerland's SOFFEX and

Germany's DTB, joined with only a little delay by the French bourse, together with MONEP (the options exchange) and MATIF (the futures exchange). In response, LIFFE has launched the idea of a loose co-operation with MEFF in Spain, AEX in Amsterdam and OM in Sweden.

This could be the start of a reconfiguration of European exchanges around two poles, EUREX and LIFFE. In addition, in most European countries the stock and derivatives exchanges are being merged with single electronic tracking platforms and clearing arrangements.

# 6. CONCLUSION

Financial derivatives exchanges date from the early 1970s. They have been among the most significant and successful financial innovations, avoiding so far any major crisis—unlike those non-financial exchanges which rely on physical delivery. This chapter has described in some length the organisation of the exchange-cum-clearing-house structure. Whilst in some respects improvements are possible on many exchanges, the overall picture is one of exceptional efficiency and reliability. The exchanges are administratively lean institutions, confronted with relentless worldwide competition as their products cannot be patented or otherwise protected. Customers are protected by a system of mutualisation of risk which leaves their counter-party—the clearing-house—always fully covered by being party to both sides of any trade, with an additional safety cushion of margin payments.

Competition has forced exchanges to innovate continuously, often only held back by regulators. The three major early innovations have been cash settlement, index trading and electronic trading.

Exchanges replicate successful contracts on other exchanges and create new contracts, mostly based on slight differentiations whenever there is enough perceived demand. In recent years they have not kept up with the pace of growth of OTC markets for a variety of reasons. The exchanges fought back by offering 24-hour electronic trading (a prerequisite in forex markets, for example); by introducing flexibility into contract specification (a major advantage of OTC products); by offering clearing-house facilities to OTC traders, such as global netting and market pricing; and by competing with the spot market leg of swaps by offering rolling spot. In addition exchanges have promoted development of totally new products, such as insurance derivatives.

The clearing-house/exchange institution's remarkably reliable risk-management and efficiency is, in this author's view, a central model for regulatory reforms, to be discussed in Chapter 9.

Over the coming years, three factors will have profound effects on the exchanges. One is the spread of derivatives exchanges to emerging markets, offering the leading exchanges potential for joint ventures and the creation of a global network. This trend is further enhanced by a second factor, the decreasing cost of electronic trading. Finally, an integrated financial market is developing in Europe with a degree of completeness, size and liquidity comparable to the US markets.

# ENDNOTES

1 Much inspiration for this section was gained from Miller (1991).
2 The Chicago Board of Trade (CBoT), had actually proposed exchange trading of options on common stocks as early as 1969. Such options, however, fell under the jurisdiction of the US Securities and Exchange Commission, which, at that time, was reluctant to grant approval. Setting to rest the SEC's professed concerns about speculation and insider trading in options delayed the opening of the Chicago Board Options Exchange for more than five years. In fact, already in the 1920s there was trading of options at the CBoT. They were options on commodity futures, however, not stocks, and they were banned by Congress in the late 1930s.
3 Asquith and Meulbroek (1995) show that the costs imposed by regulators on short-selling stock (prohibitions for some investors such as public pension funds, margin requirements and the "plus tick" rule, allowing investors to sell a share short only at a price above the last sale price) prevent the market functioning efficiently. They found that large short positions are good predictors of future underperformance.
4 The initial impetus was provided by some special features of US tax law that gave substantial unintended tax benefits (since removed) to futures trading in T-bills.
5 But some physical delivery does take place, creating problems. Not only must the physical costs of supporting the delivery system be incurred, but the right to demand delivery at contract expiration can confront unwary traders with delivery squeezes when the time for contract close-out comes. Maintaining a regulatory apparatus to deal with such close-out problems is one of the costs of futures trading (see Miller 1991, p. 14).
6 Although the original authorisation of the CFTC in 1974 had the unintended side-effect of displacing state restrictions on cash settlement of futures contracts, the legal steps that positively affirmed cash settlement were not fully in place until 1981.
7 The first of these, based on the Valueline Average, was introduced by the Kansas City Board of Trade in February 1982. It was quickly followed in April of the same year by a CME contract based on the S&P 500 stock index and in May by a New York Futures Exchange contract based on the New York Stock Exchange index. By June 1983 the volume in these three futures contracts on a share equivalent basis exceeded that on the New York Stock Exchange, and this has been a regular occurrence since then.
8 Strictly speaking, an option is not a security, but a contract based on, among other things, securities. The success of the CBOE led a number of other US and international exchanges to introduce options markets. These included the American Stock Exchange, the Philadelphia Stock Exchange, the European Options Exchange in Amsterdam and the London Stock Exchange. Today options are traded on all major exchanges around the world.
9 This section follows closely Moody's (1995). BIS (1997) offers a detailed and critical analysis.

10 There are exceptions to this general rule. Some clearing-houses function only as regulators and administrators of trades and not as counter-parties to transactions.

11 Examples of defaults (or near-defaults) of clearing members and/or crisis situation related to exchange-listed contracts include: default of the YMEX potato contract (1970s), the wool options contract (Sydney Futures Exchange, 1970s), the Bourse de Commerce de Paris (1974), the Kuala Lumpur Commodity Exchange crisis (1984), default of Volume Investors Corp. (New York Commodity Exchange, March 1985), the International Tin Council crisis (London Metal Exchange, October 1985), the crash of the Hang Seng Index futures contract (Hong Kong Futures Exchange, 1987), default of First Options of Chicago, Inc. (Chicago Board Options Exchange, October 1987), Fossett Corp. (Chicago Board Options Exchange, October 1989), Jordan Sandman Futures Ltd. (New Zealand Futures Exchange, November 1989), Drexel Burnham Lambert Ltd. (London Clearing House, February 1990), default on a margin call of a major participant at the Kobe Raw Silk Exchange, (February 1990), suspension of trading of US. dollar futures on the Moscow Futures Exchange (October 1994) (source: Moody 1995).

12 Links between clearing-houses have taken two forms: clearing links and mutual offset systems. Clearing links involve a "home" exchange and an "away" exchange whose members may also trade the contract. The "away" clearing-house assumes counter-party risk until positions are transferred to the home clearing-house (generally at the end of each trading day). For example, for the Euroyen futures contract, the London Clearing House has established a clearing link with the Tokyo International Futures Exchange. A mutual offset system (the first one was established in 1984 between CME and SIMEX) allows participants to choose the clearing-house with which the position will be held. Both clearing-houses involved are exposed to risks *vis-à-vis* each other as positions can be transferred from one exchange to the other.

13 However, not all clearing-houses function as principals to cleared trades. Some Japanese clearing-houses do not become counter-parties to the traded contracts. Their function is limited to regulation of members and administering of contract performance. Although they can take a wide range of measures in unusual market conditions—e.g., they would substitute and assume the contracts of a failed member—these clearing-houses do not have contractual relationships with either members or customers. The absence of a contractual relationship may have unanticipated credit implications in severe market conditions.

14 Clearing members usually require a larger margin from their individual customers than the margin required by the clearing-house and use the surplus funds as a revenue source. This also allows them to discriminate in favour of their own OTC products.

15 For example, the new rules require futures brokers and traders registered with the CFTC to disclose financial information in regard to the futures and cash market risk exposure of their parent and affiliated companies and to supply the CFTC with organisational charts detailing various businesses that could affect their ability to honour exchange-traded derivatives contracts. How this reporting will help prevent problems at related entities from harming the creditworthiness of the clearing member is not apparent.

16 Moody's report (1995) argued that some clearing-houses (without naming them) may not be equipped in terms of internal controls and membership requirements to cope with incidents such as the Barings problem.

17 Financial regulation in the United States is complex, with many regulators at both the state and federal levels. Broadly speaking, the CFTC regulates "commodity contracts", such as futures and options on futures, whereas the SEC regulates "securities" such as options on indices of securities and on individual stocks.

18 In arriving at the total daily margin requirement SPAN also takes into account inter-commodity and inter-month spread positions, which usually reduce the total margin requirement.

19 There are also differences among clearing-houses with respect to the kinds of assets that can be used by clearing members to satisfy margin requirements. Margins can be deposited as cash, highly rated debt securities, equities, bank guarantees, and letters of credit. These assets can have widely varying risk characteristics themselves (e.g., credit and market risks) and can diminish the value of margin as a risk-absorbing tool.

20 The transfer of the non-defaulting customer accounts to another clearing member may be problematic if members are reluctant to accept them. For example, after Barings' failure, clearing members were unwilling to take on the positions of Barings' customers without large collateral payments. This situation presented a considerable problem for some customers, who struggled to raise additional funds because Barings failed to return their initial margins.

21 Three large floor traders who were customers of Volume Investors, had a large number of "naked" short-call positions on gold when prices suddenly shot up. These three traders were unable to meet the margin call generated by the rise in gold prices, and thus they failed. In turn, this resulted in Volume Investors being unable to meet US$26 million in margin calls to the clearing-house because of the traders' shortfall. The clearing-house seized the entire accumulated margin posted by Volume Investors on behalf of all its customers in order to pay the other member firms. This left the non-defaulting customers of Volume Investors with no margin at the clearing-house.

22 This is the case at the Osaka Securities Exchange and posed a problem for Barings' customers.

23 Financial exchanges are, however, not entirely free of problems. One, amounting to an argument in favour of screen-based trading is that pit-trading, in theory a very efficient way of matching sellers and buyers, can be manipulated in many subtle ways. In early 1997 a quarrel over floor practices on the CME led to the dismissal of several board members. Independent traders complained that floor brokers formed "associations" to share profits and dominate the market. Associations are permitted, and the CME even allows, 25% of trade to be transacted within an association—hence by-passing the floor. There are also complaints that associations have too much control over the flow of customers' orders into the pit. Rules influenced by the broker associations even determine who stands where in the pit. In 1995 this allowed a trader on the CME to sell his spot for US$1 million.

24 In 1993 a ring dealing member (Crédit Lyonnais Rouse) apologised for its part in a market "squeeze" and paid a fine of £100 000.

25 A homogenous good need not mean that all units of the good are identical, but that, if not identical, they can be made equivalent. Thus, many agricultural commodities have grading guidelines or general criteria which permit delivery of slightly different units. For financial instruments the equivalence may be based on certain maturities being considered deliverable supply and on properly arranged conversion factors.

26 In addition to the effect on price volatility, the existence of monopolistic control of the underlying commodity can have an impact on the deliverable supply. A squeeze, in which one or a few suppliers take control of the deliverable supply, typically reduces the volume of trade as other market participants become wary of manipulated prices. In 1979–80, an unsuccessful attempt was made to corner the silver market, reducing volume in silver futures contracts on the Commodity Exchange Inc. (COMEX) and the CBoT by 74% and 83% respectively. Governments

which stockpile commodities may also affect the perceived supply and thus affect prices. Thus, a successful futures contract is often accompanied by a *broad ownership for the deliverable supply* (see also Technical Insight 5.3).

27 Until expiration September 1997. Starting with the December 1997 contract, the bond is defined with a maturity between 8½ and 10½ years, and a coupon of 5.5%.

28 The set of conversion factors does not quite make all bonds equivalent due to "convexity", a non-linear relation between price and yield of fixed income instruments, thereby giving rise to a "cheapest-to-deliver" bond.

29 Inclusion of an additional contract at any rate benefits from cost-savings in margining cross-product positions.

30 One reason the 90-day Commercial Paper (CP) contract never gained acceptance among potential hedgers is that the US Treasury Bill futures contract provided highly liquid, short-term interest rate hedging at low cost relative to the new, illiquid CP contract.

31 A well-known failure is the replication on LIFFE in 1991 of the successful ten-year ECU contract on MATIF, launched in 1990. In 1991, 54 000 contracts were traded on LIFFE and 7000 in 1992 (the contract was suspended in 1993), compared to 546 000 in 1991 and 1 354 000 in 1992 on MATIF.

32 The most important elements are demonstrating the hedging use and making sure prices cannot be manipulated. Despite the requirement for CFTC approval, in recent history CFTC has not rejected contracts based on their own (private) opinion as to potential success or failure of a contract. As long as the exchange can successfully argue that the contract will not be used for primarily speculative purposes and that there are no obvious ways in which the price can be manipulated, the CFTC's stance has been to let the exchange take the risk of failure. However, the CFTC does not approve duplicate contracts. Contract specifications must differ in at least one dimension before approval is granted.

33 In 1995 the House of Representatives' Banking Committee held a hearing into whether the CFTC should be absorbed by the larger Securities and Exchange Commission (SEC) which regulates the securities markets. The Committee's chairman, Rep. Jim Leach, said that he had an impression of an agency "on the brink of default on its responsibilities".

34 On 17 October 1995 the CBoT opened the first electronic market in used plastic milk containers, old newspapers and glass bottles. If the CBoT Recyclables Exchange blossoms, it might eventually list rubbish futures.

   The CBoT thinks that the greater transparency of its market will make buying and selling rubbish easier and cheaper, especially for small companies. The exchange will also establish some much-needed standards for commodities traded on it. Used paper, for example, whose price has increased from US$2 per ton in 1993 to US$58 per ton in 1995, comes in versions as varied as newspapers and corrugated cardboard, all with differing degrees of contamination.

   Although it is an oddity, the new market for recyclable material may well fly. Waste Management Inc., America's largest rubbish collector, says that it will use the exchange; big buyers of waste materials, such as International Paper and Johnson Controls, which processes plastics, are also interested.

   The recycling market is not the CBoT's first attempt to hop onto the environmental bandwagon. In 1993 it began holding the first ever public auctions for pollution permits. Issued by America's Environmental Protection Agency (EPA) as a way of controlling acid rain (the EPA will gradually reduce the number of permits that it sells), these allow purchasers—which are usually power plants—to churn out sulphur dioxide.

35 On the same day as the launch of BTF, LIFFE also introduced Flex options on the FT-SE 100 stock index. This, too, was designed to meet the requirements of the more demanding institutional investors.

36 A major incentive in this initiative is the Federal Crop Insurance Act, which proposes radical reform of the US crop insurance programme. It would mean the end of most ad hoc relief payments to farmers after droughts, floods and other disasters. The government would provide insurance cover for 50% of a farmer's expected production, but extra cover would have to be bought from private insurance companies.

37 A welcome feature of the proposed contracts is the government support they have attracted. The CBoT and USDA gave a joint presentation to the CFTC and the regulator's response was positive.

38 To date, the United States has dominated developments in insurance derivatives, but Bermuda-based insurers active in the OTC business are now targeting Europe. As yet, Europe has no exchange-traded insurance derivatives, but the groundwork is being done. The LIFFE is monitoring developments closely but has no plans to launch its own insurance derivatives contracts at present.

39 The decision to develop Globex was taken in 1987. Efforts to convince the CBoT to drop a rival project, Aurora, delayed opening to 25 June 1992. In 1994 CBoT left after governance issues with the CME.

40 As well as its link with the CBoT and TIFFE, LIFFE also has links with SIMEX, the Singapore exchange, which is already tied to CME in one of the most successful exchange link-ups.

41 The New York Mercantile Exchange's tie-up with the Sydney Futures Exchange will allow Sydney brokers to trade electronically Nymex's oil and natural gas contracts during the Australian day, whilst the Philadelphia Stock Exchange has a link with the Hong Kong Futures Exchange.

42 Here is a problem of terminology. What used to be called the Eurodollar market is now called the Euromarket. This needs to be renamed (suggestion: Xenomarket) to distinguish it from the market of instruments in Euro.

# 6

# Customised Risk Management in OTC Markets

*How to lose money on a long put when markets crash*

Kenzo Takahashi is a successful, hardworking factory manager in Tokyo. His earnings and lifestyle have allowed him regularly to save sizeable amounts which he has put into his bank account and, during the second half of the 1980s, also in Japanese stocks. This was an obvious choice since Japanese stocks had been increasing year after year, generating very attractive price increases, while the whole world applauded Japanese efficiency and admired the unstoppable ascent of the Japanese economy. When the first signs of overvaluation of Japanese stocks hit the headlines in 1989, Kenzo was not overly concerned—a reaction he was to regret after 1991 when the Tokyo market collapsed and his book gains evaporated.

Kenzo then faced a serious dilemma. After 1991 monetary policy in Japan had been formulated to keep interest rates low to ease the absorption of the financial collapse and facilitate investment. Bank accounts and bonds, therefore, did not appear as attractive investment opportunities. Kenzo had lost his confidence in the Japanese stock market and, moreover, he regularly read reports about the risk of Japanese banks unloading stockholdings acquired a long time ago with book values still at low acquisition prices.

He then made an extraordinary decision. He opened an account at the Tokyo office of Merrill Lynch with the intention of diversifying his portfolio and, for the first time, investing abroad. He still believed, generally, in the Asian miracle, but, also, after many discussions with Hitoshi Nakayama, a friend working as a broker, in the financial know-how of the Americans. The Merrill Lynch broker recommended a mutual fund (managed by Merrill Lynch) investing in Hong Kong shares. Kenzo bought shares in the fund when the Hong Kong Stock Exchange index (the "Hang Seng") stood at 7800.

His timing was extremely fortuitous. The day after his purchase the Hang Seng started on a steep ascent that brought the index close to 12 000 in early 1994.

Kenzo was rubbing his hands with satisfaction. Presumably his fund was doing even better as fund managers were highly experienced (and remunerated) specialists in stock picking. He, therefore, called his Merrill Lynch broker to check his gains, but to his surprise the price of his fund's shares had increased by only 30%, compared to the 50% of the Hang Seng index. Subtracting 6% for up-front purchase commissions from the 30% price increase, he began to wonder whether the fund managers were really worth their fees.

In addition, he became concerned about securing his gain (which, after all, was a nice return due to his lucky timing), as he had already once experienced the loss of large book gains.

Selling and realising a net 24% gain did not appeal to him because he saw no other interesting investment opportunities and, after all, the Hang Seng could increase even further—an opinion held by many professionals.

A friend teaching finance at university, Masaichi Yoshino, advised him to keep his fund and purchase put options on the Hang Seng to hedge his downside risk whilst preserving the fund's upward potential. He consulted his Merrill Lynch broker who told him that there were no exchange-traded options available on the Hang Seng, but that Bear Stearns, a New York investment bank, had issued options (HXP) that could suit him particularly since their exercise date was 6 October 1996, providing coverage for 2½ years. These were options on the AMEX Hong Kong 30 index, traded OTC and exercised in New York. This index was a good substitute for the Hang Seng, with a correlation between the two close to one. But, of course, it was not highly correlated with his fund underperforming the Hang Seng.

On 28 February 1994 Kenzo bought 1000 of these put options at US$6.125 a piece. The Hang Seng had already declined to 10 410 on 28 February 1994 and the AMEX Hong Kong 30 was at 520. The actual exercise formula was:

$$\text{Cash settlement (in US dollars)} = \frac{\text{Strike price} - \text{Spot price}}{3 \times \text{Fixed exchange rate}}$$

Kenzo felt at ease, although his friend told him that 1000 put options were not enough for full protection. Nevertheless, whichever way the market went he would either gain something from his fund investment or from his put options.

Nearly a year later, in early February 1995, he called Merrill Lynch to check on his situation. The Hang Seng had fallen dramatically and moved in January between a low of 6968 on 23 January and 7918 on 5 January. Since he expected his put options now to be worth a fortune, he eagerly enquired about their value. To his amazement his puts had risen from a low of US$5 at the beginning of January to US$6.81 on 23 January. He really failed to grasp, given his recently acquired knowledge about put options, how the index could decline by 25–30% and the price of the put *fall*.

Since his Merrill Lynch broker was unable to give an explanation (other than guess that volatility may have fallen), he returned again to Masaichi.

Because the HXP is, in fact, an American option (meaning that it can be exercised before expiration), Masaichi had to consult the specialised literature. After eventually tracking down the relevant data, he succeeded in understanding what appeared at first sight difficult to believe.

He first computed historic and implied volatilities and noticed that the latter were, at times, nearly double the former. That suggested to him either serious mispricing or expectations difficult to extract from historic data. At any rate, volatility had declined by at least 30% from February 1994 to January 1995. Using historic volatilities he computed the theoretic price of the put options. He obtained US$4.43 for 16 February 1994, as compared to the market price of US$6.125 so that on purchase Kenzo had paid too much. Computing the prices for January 1995, he noticed that the market price was frequently *below* the theoretical price, exactly the opposite to the situation in February 1994. For example, on 23 January, when the market price was US$6.81, the theoretical value was US$8.10. Even more surprising was the result he got by decomposing the theoretical value into its intrinsic value (if exercised today) and its time value (the value due to the fact that the intrinsic value can still increase until expiration day). The time value was over US$3.50 in early 1994, but now with reduced volatility and a shortened time residual to expiration (but still 504 days to maturity), the time value on 23 January was only US$1.03. The intrinsic value was, therefore, US$7.07 (US$8.10 −1.03). Given that the market price was US$6.81 the time value was therefore negative. The inconsistency was not only observed for one day, but for 15 out of 20 days in January. (The time value can never be negative as it is always preferable to have an option than not and the implicit time value of a US option would entail arbitrage through exercising the option.)

Kenzo was forced to learn several lessons. First, a passive strategy, as he had adopted is only a very rough protection. When he placed his put, it was out-of-the-money as the AMEX Hong Kong 30 stood at 520, above the exercise price of 514. He therefore only obtained a (partial) hedge for a decline below 514. Moreover, the correlation between the value of the put and the index (the "delta") is not a constant; it was about −0.5 at levels of the index close to 500 and rose to nearly −1 in January 1995. To be fully hedged he should have bought a number of options corresponding to the initial delta of −0.5. Over time he should have sold options as the delta was rising to −1.

Second, although Kenzo felt comfortable with a very long maturity put option, he had underestimated the effect of the variation of all the factors included in the price of options. The theta (derivative of the price of the put with respect to the time to maturity) ranged from 0.002 to 0.001 during the period from February 1994 to January 1995. As the passage of time reduced time to maturity, it also reduced the price of the put. Furthermore, as the interest rates passed from a level of 5% in February 1994 to 8% in January 1995, the price of the put was pushed down again. From February 1994 to January 1995, the combined effect of the passage of time and of rising interest rates produced a decay of 30% in the price of the put. Finally, with an epsilon (the reaction of the put price to changes in volatility) of 10, a drop in volatility from 0.5 to 0.25 implied a fall in the price of the put by US$2.5.

Finally, the price of his put option differed significantly from its theoretical value, violating basic arbitrage principles. The only (unsatisfactory) explanation he was offered was lack of liquidity in that market. The option was seriously overvalued when he purchased and undervalued when he wanted to sell. This kind of surprise has kept Kenzo away from OTC products with scarce liquidity ever since.

———•———

> "You can call it [the use of
> derivatives] whatever you want,
> but in my book it's gambling."
>
> *Representative Henry Gonzalez,*
> *Chairman, House Banking Committee*


K ENZO's experience highlights several problems of OTC products: lack of transparency, of liquidity and of competitive pricing.

To gain perspective, Section 1 provides an overview of the growth and proliferation of over-the-counter (OTC) products in comparison to exchange-traded derivatives.

OTC markets (the markets for custom made derivative products including swaps, forwards, caps, floors, collars, swaptions, etc.) have revolutionised the risk management and financing practices of corporations, banks, securities houses, governments and retail investors. The new products and services they provide have brought about significant efficiency gains to the economy as they allow users to alter cheaply and speedily the payment and risk characteristics of their assets and liabilities whenever desired. They also allow users to arbitrage away excessive rate differentials across countries, credit classes and maturities to reduce funding cost. Accompanying the explosive growth of the OTC derivative markets, some unique market characteristics have, however, developed. These have caught the attention of regulators, in particular the view that significant systemic risk might have built up.

Their concern was also heightened by the recent incidents of big losses by some corporate users of derivatives, as described in Chapter 3. In the United States, there is a debate that the banks highly involved in OTC derivative trading might be imposing a negative externality, like pollution, on the public by shifting part of the cost of bearing risk to the public through the Federal Depository Insurance System and that deposit insurance premiums could be lower if banks did not participate in OTC derivative activities.

During the last decade financial intermediaries in the major developed economies have focused increasingly on risk management, particularly market risk and, as a consequence, have become intensive users of derivatives. In addition, steadily rising customer sophistication has created opportunities for funding activities to include options to pay-back early, to tie interest rates to some activity index such as a stock exchange index, or to offer warrants for debt-equity conversion. Similarly, for any asset-manager derivatives have become a daily tool. Banks, even those who are not major dealers, have therefore become active participants in the derivatives market.

A number of important structural consequences follow from this evolution. For a start, banks have become aware of the need reliably to evaluate their risk exposure and be ready to invest in risk-management technology. They also see mergers or acquisitions as a way to acquire the skills or to amortise these costs more easily and achieve a greater netting of exposures inside the firm. On both accounts—greater risk-management ability and more comprehensive internal netting—the costs of OTC products have declined in relation to exchange-traded products.

However, there is still counter-party risk in the netted OTC positions to which the capital adequacy rules need to be applied, so that, once more, credit risk is moved to the forefront. During recent years, intermediaries have pursued various strategies to lower OTC-related credit risk. One is through collateralisation (or cash settlement) of swaps according to contractually defined conditions. This, in a way, resembles variation margin payments for a futures contract. Another, more radical, approach tries to embrace more fully the advantages of the clearing-house approach. Typically, a number of banks get together to create an organisation that copies several features of the clearing-house structure, but limits direct access to founding members. Several such projects are discussed in Chapter 9. The special characteristics of OTC markets that particularly worry regulators fall into three classes: heavy bank involvement (Section 2); heightened risk of contagion (Section 3), and inadequacy of the existing regulatory framework (Section 4). Section 5 is focused on a new instrument that facilitates counter-party risk management and, in all likelihood, will have a great future: credit derivatives. Instead of listing myriads of recent slightly differentiated new products, I analyse the potential of credit derivatives in more detail.

# 1. MARKET DEVELOPMENTS

In its configuration, the OTC market has little in common with an exchange-centred market. It has no location (contractual parties can be anywhere in the world) and, therefore, no address; it has no defined membership and, therefore, no rules; it has no defined products for trade and no boundaries (an OTC derivative may be traded as such or embedded in a security). It is, therefore, difficult to define the OTC market precisely; difficult to obtain meaningful statistics; and difficult to regulate either by market participants or external regulators. The only way to impose some rules is to aim at market participants in each jurisdiction. This is inefficient as the potential market is the world and market participants can come from different regulatory domains within each jurisdiction. It is, therefore, not surprising that OTC markets are much less regulated (arguably too little) than the exchanges (arguably too much). This is a clear advantage of OTC markets and at least one reason for their phenomenal success.

The OTC derivative markets have been the fastest growing markets for financial products in recent history. Subject to the proviso about reliable statistics, Table 6.1 provides data for exchange-traded and OTC derivatives

**Table 6.1** Markets for Selected Financial Derivative Instruments (US$ billion)

| | Notional Amounts Outstanding | | | | | | | |
|---|---|---|---|---|---|---|---|---|
| | 1990 | 1991 | 1992 | 1993 | 1994 | 1995 | 1996 | % Increase 1990–1996 |
| Exchange-traded instruments | 2 290.4 | 3 519.3 | 4 634.4 | 7 771.1 | 8 862.5 | 9 185.3 | 9 884.7 | 331 |
| Interest rate futures | 1 454.5 | 2 156.7 | 2 913.0 | 4 958.7 | 5 777.6 | 5 863.4 | 5 931.1 | 308 |
| Interest rate options[1] | 599.5 | 1 072.6 | 1 385.4 | 2 362.4 | 2 623.6 | 2 741.7 | 3 277.3 | 447 |
| Currency futures | 17.0 | 18.3 | 26.5 | 34.7 | 40.1 | 37.9 | 50.3 | |
| Currency options[1] | 56.5 | 62.9 | 71.1 | 75.6 | 55.6 | 43.2 | 46.5 | |
| Stock market index futures | 69.1 | 76.0 | 79.8 | 110.0 | 127.3 | 172.2 | 198.6 | |
| Stock market index options[1] | 93.7 | 132.8 | 158.6 | 229.7 | 238.3 | 326.9 | 380.2 | |
| Over-the-counter instruments[2] | 3 450.3 | 4 449.4 | 5 345.7 | 8 474.6 | 11 303.2 | 17 712.6 | 25 453.1 | 638 |
| Interest rate swaps | 2 311.5 | 3 065.1 | 3 850.8 | 6 177.3 | 8 815.6 | 12 810.7 | 19 170.9 | 729 |
| Currency swaps[3] | 577.5 | 807.2 | 860.4 | 899.6 | 914.8 | 1 197.4 | 1 560.0 | 170 |
| Other swap-related derivatives[4] | 566.3 | 577.2 | 634.5 | 1 397.6 | 1 572.8 | 3 704.5 | 4 722.0 | 734 |

*Notes*:
1 Calls and puts.
2 Data collected by the International Swaps and Derivatives Association (ISDA) only; the two sides of contracts between ISDA members are reported once only.
3 Adjusted for reporting of both currencies; including cross-currency interest rate swaps.
4 Caps, collars, floors and swaptions.
*Source*: BIS (August 1997)

world-wide to gain an order of magnitude of the tempo with which derivatives have developed. The total of notional outstanding in 1995 amounted to US$27 trillion or 370% more than in 1990. Of that total, the OTC products represented roughly two-thirds.[1]

Interest rate instruments (interest rate futures, interest rate options, interest rate swaps) accounted for more than half of the total of both exchange traded and OTC products, relegating currency instruments to second, and equity-based instruments to third rank. Exchange-traded currency futures and options have been declining in recent years. One possible explanation is that screen-based OTC trading is particularly well suited for that market.[2]

In addition to standardised options, a number of option-related instruments have also been developed in recent years some of which are captured in Table 6.1 under the heading "other swap-related derivatives". These include caps, collars, floors and swaptions which are privately negotiated options on interest rates or interest rate indices. It is this category which has achieved the highest growth since 1990 with some 560%. Other securities with embedded options, such as callable bonds (holders of these bonds have the right to repayment before maturity at pre-specified conditions), have also become popular. Finally, warrants on bonds have come to be fairly widely used.

Table 6.2 provides a regional distribution of outstanding OTC contracts at the end of March 1995, including forwards and cross-border double-counting. Notional values of outstanding interest rate contracts amount to over US$35

**Table 6.2** Notional Amounts Outstanding and Market Value of OTC Derivatives (US$ billion)

| | World | US | UK | France | Germany | Japan |
|---|---|---|---|---|---|---|
| OTC interest rate derivatives[1] | 35 621 | 8146 | 10 382 | 4122 | 1964 | 5100 |
| Market value[2] | 982 | 179 | 342 | 109 | 41 | 185 |
| OTC foreign exchange derivatives[3] | 17 700 | 2644 | 1428 | 1595 | 1255 | 3211 |
| Market value[4] | 1624 | 183 | 236 | 98 | 116 | 561 |
| OTC equity and stock index derivatives | 630 | 123 | Europe 278 | | | 100 |

*Notes*:
1 Forward rate agreements, swaps, OTC options and other OTC products, net of local double-counting but without adjustments for cross-border double-counting.
2 Sum of positive and negative market (replacement) values.
3 Forwards, foreign exchange swaps, currency swaps, OTC options and other OTC products, net of local inter-dealer transactions.
4 Sum of gross positive and negative market (replacement) values.

*Source*: BIS (May 1996)

trillion or twice the outstanding notional value of foreign exchange derivatives. These figures may appear inflated as, say, a swap between a US and a UK institution enters both into the US and UK statistics. This is, however, not an artificial increase, as both parties are exposed to potential future counterpart risk. The largest amount of notional OTC interest rate derivatives are located in the United Kingdom; the largest amount of OTC foreign exchange derivatives in Japan.

Market values reflect counter-party risk. Despite outstandings of foreign exchange derivatives of only half outstandings of interest rate derivatives, replacement values are nearly double as risk in foreign exchange contracts is a multiple of interest rate contracts (in foreign exchange contracts, by necessity, there is an exchange of principals).

The geographic attribution of notional amounts and replacement values is based on book location and not headquarters. The role of US institutions is more important than is suggested by data in Table 6.2, given the prominent role played by US institutions in foreign financial centres.

Table 6.3 gives the average daily foreign exchange turnover for both spot and OTC derivatives transactions, net of local and cross-border inter-dealer transactions. This is the famous "US$1 trillion a day" amount frequently quoted in the press. Gross amounts (not shown) reached US$1864 billion in April 1995, of which the United Kingdom accounted for US$571 billion, the United States US$294 billion, Japan US$196 billion, Singapore US$125 billion and Hong Kong US$104 billion.

**Table 6.3**  Foreign Exchange Turnover in April 1995 (Daily Average, in Millions of US$)

|                       | Total     | US$     | DM      | Yen     | GBP     | FF     |
|-----------------------|-----------|---------|---------|---------|---------|--------|
| Spot                  | 494 190   | 351 439 | 268 340 | 109 039 | 46 322  | 40 379 |
| Outright forwards     | 96 860    | 76 915  | 30 195  | 28 353  | 9 760   | 7 195  |
| Foreign exchange swaps| 545 862   | 518 317 | 112 111 | 136 696 | 50 450  | 42 642 |
| Total                 | 1 136 912 | 946 671 | 410 646 | 274 088 | 106 532 | 90 216 |

*Note*: Every transaction is counted twice, that is, once in each currency involved.
*Source*: BIS (May 1996)

Spot transactions account for some 45% of total. In the spot market the US dollar enters into 70% of transactions (out of 200%, since there are always two currencies involved in each trade), the DM into more than 50%. The preeminence of the US dollar is even more pronounced in forwards (nearly 80%) and swaps (over 90%).

In the currency swap sector end-users account for more than half of total, whereas for interest rate swaps interbank business dominates. For the latter the US currency only accounted for one-third of new business in 1995 against three-quarters in 1987.

With all derivatives markets being influenced by similar financial environments, the more rapid *recent* growth of OTC products compared to exchange-traded products begs an explanation. There is the fact that exchange-traded instruments are reaching the mature stage of their life cycle, that regulations have stifled innovation, that (so far) they have failed to become global operators and that margin requirements exceed the capital and liquidity costs of OTC positions. Structural factors, such as the growth of large derivatives portfolios held by major intermediaries with offsetting exposures—enhanced by the recent wave of mergers and acquisitions—and cash-based hedging strategies using repos have pushed exchange-traded products to a marginal role of hedging the net overall residual position.

OTC deals have also benefited from increased collateralisation mechanisms and the significant improvement of the credit rating of major US dealers. The innovatory dynamism has remained untamed and bid/ask spreads on plain vanilla instruments have become unattractive. Nevertheless, major dealers feel compelled to maintain a strong presence in plain vanilla instruments because of the opportunities to add more rewarding business.

## 2. SIGNIFICANT BANK INVOLVEMENT

The involvement of banks in OTC derivative activities has increased significantly over the years. In June 1992, the total volume (in notional value) of financial derivatives (including interest rate swaps, futures, forwards, options and currency swaps and options) held by US bank holding companies was US$5.23 trillion. By end-1995, this amount had increased to US$16.5 trillion.

Many regional banks in the US have also started to sell derivatives products to clients in addition to using derivatives as a financing and risk-management tool for themselves. This trend of growing involvement of small/regional banks which might not have the advanced computer systems and expertise needed to manage risk related to their derivative activities has added to the concern by the regulators. Given the close interrelation between banks in many derivatives deals and the role of banks in the payment system and in financial intermediation, the failure of banks can have major effects on the entire economy.

Some of the reasons for the growing involvement of banks in OTC derivative activities are discussed in Goldstein *et al.* (1993). Competition from the financial markets and non-bank financial institutions has depressed lending margins. OTC derivative activity is a new profitable business which is being seized by banks to substitute for their less profitable traditional lending.[3]

There is also a second explanation which treats OTC derivative activity more like a complement to banks' traditional lending business. As shown in Chapter 4, OTC derivatives can be used in banks' asset-liability management (ALM) to reduce funding cost and smooth maturities mismatch. This can reduce risk exposure to changing market conditions and improve a bank's competitiveness in its traditional lending business. This view is strongly supported by the share of interbank business in interest rate swaps. Accounting for only 32% in 1987, it represented 57% in 1995.

Traditionally banks have to face a maturity mismatch between assets and liabilities and therefore have a need to hedge interest rate risks. However, since loans are basically streams of payments, the use of forward or futures contracts might not be the most direct or cost efficient way to hedge such risks for banks. OTC derivatives like swaps which involve the exchange of two streams of payments are ideal for the situation. For example, faced with the risk of an increase in interest rate, a bank holding a pool of fixed-rate loans can transform the payments into a variable rate loan by using a fixed-for-floating rate swap. As another example, in anticipation of a rate decline, a bank holding a pool of variable rate loans can transform the payment into a fixed rate loan by entering into a floating-for-fixed rate swap. Academic research supports the view that banks that use OTC interest-rate swaps have experienced greater growth in their commercial and industrial loan portfolios relative to banks which do not use interest rate swaps. This empirical evidence supports the view that banks' OTC derivative activities are complementary to their traditional business.

**1988 Basle Accord**

There are also other factors that explain why banks' involvement in OTC derivative activities has grown so fast. One of these is that there was no capital requirement for these transactions prior to the Basle Accord (1988), to be implemented by end-1992, as OTC derivative products are off-balance sheet contractual arrangements. OTC derivatives are traditionally treated as off-balance sheet items because they are contracts rather than securities and they tend to have zero replacement cost at initialisation. As such, banks are not required to report these transactions on the balance sheet (there are exceptions, such as foreign exchange swaps according to International Accounting Standards). The transactions are reported in footnotes to the financial statements and only limited details are traditionally reported. Since prior to the 1988 Basle Accord, bank capital requirements were based solely on balance sheet figures, no explicit capital charge was needed for OTC derivative transactions. Compared to "on-balance sheet" products, OTC derivatives benefited from a regulatory loophole until the implementation of the 1988 Basle Accord.

Whilst exchange traded products are also off-balance sheet in nature, many OTC products, such as forwards and swaps, have a cash flow advantage over the exchange traded products. Essentially, no cash outflow is needed for OTC derivative transactions as the contracts are designed to have zero initial replacement cost and no margin deposit is required. Banks can therefore improve their return on capital by engaging in OTC derivatives transactions. This is essential for banks in a highly competitive environment.

In 1988, in the light of the inappropriateness of traditional balance sheet based capital standard, the Basle Committee issued capital standards to deal with the *credit risk* of both on- and off-balance sheet activities. Special treatment was given to off-balance sheet interest rate and currency contracts. Specifically, the capital charge for a contract is computed as 8% of the risk-adjusted exposure of the contract which is found by multiplying the credit equivalent of the contract to a risk weight appropriate for the counter-party involved. Corporate counter-parties carry a risk weight of 1 and banks in OECD countries carry a risk weight of 0.2. (Banks, therefore, have a competitive advantage over corporations in swap contracts.) The credit equivalent of the contract can be computed from one of two methods: the so called "current exposure method" (which is the method predominantly used) and the "original exposure method".[4] The add-on factors and the conversion factors for interest rate and currency contracts are given in Table 6.4.

While the 1988 Basle Accord imposes capital charges on bank OTC derivative positions, they tend to be lower than the margin requirements for comparable exchange traded products. For instance, the amount of capital charge for a swap is generally lower than the margin requirements of a portfolio of

**Table 6.4**   Add-On Factors Under the Current Exposure Method and Conversion Factors Under the Original Exposure Method (Basis Points)

|  | Interest rate Contracts | Currency Contracts |
|---|---|---|
| Current exposure method: | | |
| Less than one year to maturity | nil | 100 |
| One year and over to maturity | 50 | 500 |
| Original exposure method: | | |
| Original maturity of: | | |
| – less than one year | 50 | 200 |
| – one year and less than two years | 100 | 500 |
| – For each additional year | 100 | 300 |

*Source*: Basle Committee on Banking Regulations and Supervisory Practices, International Convergence of Capital Measurement and Capital Standards, July 1988.

futures contracts that can closely match the payment patterns of the swap. As such, OTC derivative products still have an advantage over exchange traded products after the adoption of the 1988 Basle Accord. Technical Insight 6.1 provides a concrete example.

Finally, the fact that the 1988 Basle Accord focuses only on credit risk might have also induced banks to substitute other risk factors. For example, banks have increased their interest rate and exchange rate risks, and reduced their credit risk by engaging more in those trading activities for which price risks are more important than credit risk. These trading activities might include short term proprietary trading, trading for hedging purposes, etc. Furthermore, since OTC derivative products can be used to repackage risk and can therefore allow users to substitute interest rate and exchange rate risks (with no capital charge) for credit risk (with capital charge), the concentration of the 1988 Basle Accord on credit risk might also have led to the popularity of some OTC derivative products which bear more price risk than credit risk.

Whilst it is hard to explicitly measure the effect of the 1988 Basle Accord in this regard, some rough indications can be obtained by looking at the trading account profits of some banks actively involved in the OTC derivative markets, before and after the implementation of the Basle Accord.[5]

## Dominance by a Small Number of Large Players

Accompanying the rapid growth of bank OTC derivative activities is the concentration in just a few major banks/securities houses. At year-end 1992, the total volume (in notional principal) of interest rate and currency swaps was US$5.5 trillion. The 10 biggest participants in the markets accounted for

**Technical Insight 6.1**   Capital charges vs. margin payments

Consider a five-year swap contract with a notional principal of US$10 million where the party pays a fixed 7% and receives LIBOR semi-annually. Under the so-called "original exposure method" of the 1988 Basle Accord, the credit equivalent of this contract is US$10 million (the notional principle) times a conversion factor of 5% (for interest rate contract with five years to maturity). That is, the credit equivalent for this contract is US$500 000. The capital requirement is 8% of this credit equivalent which is equal to US$40 000. Alternatively, the credit equivalent of the contract can also be computed according to the so-called "current exposure method" of the 1988 Basle Accord. Under this method, the credit equivalent is computed as the sum of the replacement cost and an add-on factor which is 0.5% of the notional principal (for an interest rate contract which is more than one year to maturity). At year-end 1992, according to "Swap Monitor", the average replacement cost for all major US dealers is 2.3% of the notional principal. Assuming that our swap has a replacement cost equal to the industry average, then its credit equivalent is US$230 000 plus an add-on of US$50 000 which is equal to US$280 000. The capital requirement is 8% of this amount and is therefore equal to US$22 400. This is smaller than the amount computed using the "original exposure method".

The payment pattern provided by the swap can also be closely approximated by a portfolio of Eurodollar futures contracts. The 90-days Eurodollar futures contract traded on the CME has a contract size of US$1 million. It is basically a contract that delivers a 90-days Eurodollar CD rate on the expiration date of the contract. Maturity ranges from three months to seven years (at three months' time intervals) are available. To cover a five years' long payment stream which spans 20 three-month periods, a total of 20 90-days Eurodollar contracts of different maturities are needed for every US$1 million notional principal. With a notional principal of US$10 million, a total of 200 Eurodollar futures contracts are needed to deliver a payment pattern that can approximate the payment stream of the five-year swap. Since the initial margin is US$400 per contract for hedgers and US$540 per contract for speculators, the total initial margin requirement is US$80 000 for hedgers and US$108 000 for speculators. These are substantially higher than the capital charge required under the 1988 Basle Accord (computed according to either the "original exposure method" or the "current exposure method"), let alone the fact that the margin requirement has to be satisfied with highly liquid assets.

There is, thus, a fundamental difference in the risk treatment in both market segments. If the regulatory objective is to reduce systemic risk further, then the capital requirements on OTC positions is insufficient. Exchange-based contracts are essentially risk-free: their cost could be a useful benchmark.

more than US$3.1 trillion or 60% and the 20 biggest participating banks and securities houses accounted for more than US$4 trillion of all outstanding interest rate and currency swaps.

Table 6.5 summarises the concentration in OTC derivatives with data for 1995. Compared to 1992, concentration has become even more marked. The top 10 US banks accounted for close to 90% of the notional value outstanding of all US banks, equal to US$16.5 trillion. The replacement value represented US$191 billion, or about one-half of the total trading portfolio.

Table 6.6 lists the ten US banks with the greatest credit exposure from derivatives, together with the notional amounts held. For example, counter-party risk in J.P. Morgan's derivatives portfolio is US$33.6 billion, an amount far in excess of its tier-1 capital. Chase Manhattan Corporation holds a notional amount that is close to one-third of amounts held by all US banks. Concentration, already high in previous years, is steadily increasing.

**Table 6.5** Derivatives Position and Trading Activity of the Top 10 Banks and all US banks in 1995 (US$ Billions)

| Item | Top 10 Banks | All Banks |
|------|--------------|-----------|
| Type of Derivative Instrument | Notional amount of derivatives outstanding as of year-end | |
| Interest rate contracts | 10 231 | 10 800 |
| Foreign exchange contracts | 5 286 | 5 366 |
| Equity, commodity, or other contracts | 361 | 361 |
| Total | 15 878 | 16 527 |
| Positions in Trading Portfolio | Fair value as of year-end | |
| Trading assets | 255 | 275 |
| –Derivatives | 95 | 100 |
| Trading liabilities | 159 | 169 |
| – Derivatives | 97 | 102 |
| Total trading positions (absolute value) | 414 | 444 |
| – Derivatives | 191 | 202 |
| Type of Risk Assumed to Earn Profit | Trading profit from all sources for year | |
| Interest rate | 2.9 | 3.3 |
| Foreign exchange | 2.0 | 2.4 |
| Equity, commodity, or other | 0.8 | 0.8 |
| Total | 5.7 | 6.5 |

*Source*: Federal Reserve Bulletin (1996)

*Derivatives and Their Markets*

**Table 6.6**  Ten US Commercial Banks with the Greatest Exposure to Credit Risk from Derivatives on 31 December 1995 (US$ billions)

| Institution | Credit Risk Exposure[1] | Total Notional Amount of Derivatives Outstanding |
| --- | --- | --- |
| J.P. Morgan | 33.6 | 3403 |
| Chase Manhattan[2] | 28.0 | 4728 |
| Citicorp | 19.4 | 2301 |
| Bankers Trust New York | 12.1 | 1742 |
| BankAmerica | 8.3 | 1515 |
| First Chicago | 7.3 | 801 |
| NationsBank | 3.3 | 1006 |
| Republic New York | 3.0 | 268 |
| State Street Boston | 0.6 | 58 |
| Bank of New York | 0.6 | 56 |

*Notes*:
1 Exposure taking into account the effects of legally enforceable bilateral netting agreements.
2 Pro forma combination for Chemical Banking Corporation and Chase Manhattan Corporation.

*Source*: Federal Reserve Bulletin (1996)

The most cited reason for such dominance by the big banks is that the market participants have a strong preference for trading with highly rated counter-parties in the OTC derivative markets because of the concern about counter-party risk and the lack of disclosure. This preference has also stimulated a movement towards the establishment of AAA Special Purpose Derivatives Vehicles (SPDVs) by large securities houses which do not have AAA rated status to improve their competitiveness.[6] In May 1966, the US authorities allowed commercial banks to create a derivatives product subsidiary. The market's verdict on SPDVs in general has been mixed. Full immunisation in case of bankruptcy of the parent company has not been tested. Acquisition of AAA rating is costly and this cost must be justified, but given the recent significant improvement in the creditworthiness of US banks, after the downgradings of the early 1990s, the regulatory approval may have been granted too late to have a major impact.

There are also other factors that contributed to this concentration, such as the existence of economies of scale in hedging. Usually, a dealer in the OTC derivative markets cannot find two matched counter-parties instantly when a derivative product is customised for one party. Initially, the dealer will take the other side of the position until a counter-party is found. In the meantime, the dealer will manage to hedge these open OTC derivative positions using exchange-traded products. Since dealers have many OTC derivative positions in their books, some of these positions might offset each other, so that they only need to hedge the overall net exposure. Scale economies in hedging exist because the larger the dealer, the higher the probability of finding offsetting positions in his book. This reduces the hedging cost in terms of margin requirements and transaction costs and suggests that it might be less efficient for end-users to hedge interest rate or exchange rate risk themselves by using exchange traded products even when these provide similar protection.

There are additional scale economies in the OTC derivatives markets that lead to high concentration. In particular, there are scale economies in technological development, information acquisition and learning. Given the complexity of some of these products, the dealers who construct the tailor-made products, also perform an economic function of lowering the aggregate learning cost. As the design of customised derivative products is complicated and the learning process costly, it is not economically efficient for every dealer to learn how to design structured products.

However, while it might be efficient for a few agents (the major dealers) to learn and then provide the service to the others (the users), the resulting information asymmetry can create problems of its own, especially since OTC products are not being traded in the open market and price information (except for the plain vanilla products) is generally not available. As revealed by recent events (commented on in Chapter 3), the problem is that the user might not fully understand whether the product so designed by the dealer is really appropriate for him. The user also might not be able to understand fully the amount of risk involved by taking a particular OTC derivative position. The asymmetry in information and the absence of price transparency increases the potential that dealers exploit the less well-informed end-users.[7]

High concentration in the OTC market is the result of economies of scale. It would, therefore, not be economically efficient to attempt a reduction in concentration. But, if one of the major institutions were to default, the systemic spillover could be potentially disastrous. It is not clear why society should bear such a risk. Therefore, Chapter 9 makes proposals to reduce the social risk without touching concentration.

# 3. CONTAGION RISK

In OTC derivatives markets two features suggest increased contagion risk. A large amount of inter-dealer positions and a high replacement cost to total asset ratio expose the major OTC derivatives dealers to a domino effect in the case of failure of a large dealer. The increased linkages between financial markets, in each economy and across borders, brought about by OTC derivatives activities speed up the transmission of turbulence from one market to another.

**Large Amounts of Inter-dealer Positions**

A salient feature of the OTC derivatives markets is the existence of very large inter-dealer derivative transactions for reasons explained in the previous section. Table 6.7 breaks down the worldwide outstanding notional OTC derivatives contracts and their market value by main counter-party categories. Only some 12% of notional interest rate derivatives has as counter-party non-financial customers and some 18% of foreign exchange derivatives.

**Inter-market Linkages**

The concern over systemic risk is redoubled by the tightening of the linkages between markets brought about by the development of the OTC derivative markets. Increased linkages imply an augmented potential for a turmoil in one market to be transmitted to other markets.

The tightened relationship between markets is the result of a widespread ausage of OTC derivative products for cross-market arbitrage. For instance, a foreign bond issue together with a currency swap is frequently used to lower funding cost by exploiting different spreads to interest rate benchmarks in two currencies, thereby facilitating the transmission of interest rate shocks from one country to another. The interest rate policies of the Federal Reserve, the Bundesbank or the Bank of Japan are observed intensively all over the world, and not only in domestic markets. When US interest rates move the rest of the world follows closely. As another example, a fixed-for-floating interest rate swap can be used together with the issuance of a floating rate note to reduce funding cost for an institution with relatively low credit rating by exploiting the differential credit spread between short-term and long-term instruments. This can increase the linkage between the high rated and the low rated bond markets.

The strengthening of cross-market linkage can also be driven by the joint use of OTC derivative products and exchange-traded products to create specific return/risk profile or cash flow pattern.

**Table 6.7** Notional Principal and Market Values (March 1995) (US$ billion)

|                                  | Total  | Other Dealers* | Financial Institutions* | Non-financial Customers* |
|----------------------------------|--------|----------------|-------------------------|--------------------------|
| OTC interest rate derivatives    | 35 621 | 24 708         | 6566                    | 4347                     |
| Market value                     | 982    | 684            | 157                     | 139                      |
| OTC foreign exchange derivatives | 17 700 | 11 703         | 2817                    | 3157                     |
| Market value                     | 1 624  | 1 109          | 180                     | 335                      |

*Note*: * net of local inter-dealer double-counting

*Source*: BIS (1996)

A further increase in cross-market linkages is the use of exchange-traded instruments to hedge open OTC derivative positions. Dealers in the OTC derivative markets generally do not have a book in which all long positions are exactly offset by corresponding short positions. While some of the risk exposure can be reduced by the arrangement of inter-dealer positions, the remaining net open positions are usually hedged with exchange traded assets. The consequence is that a link between the OTC derivative markets and the exchange traded markets is established. The existence of such a linkage can facilitate the transmission of problems in the OTC derivative markets into the exchange traded markets.

# 4. REGULATORY INADEQUACIES FOR THE SPECIFICITIES OF OTC MARKETS

Several characteristics of the OTC derivatives markets pose serious problems for the existing regulatory framework, despite significant recent adaptations. I note here the sources of concern and pursue the analysis in Chapters 7 to 9.

Among these characteristics the most significant are:

- the off-balance-sheet nature of OTC derivatives transactions which has rendered the traditional regulatory tool of balance-sheet-based bank capital requirements ineffective;
- a growing complexity of products and the lack of a generally agreed pricing approach which can significantly complicate the measurement and control of risk;
- the flexibility and tailor-made nature of the products which have virtually paralysed the traditional instrument-based approach to asset market regulation;
- the wide range of users which has further incapacitated the institution-based approach to financial market regulation;
- the global nature of the markets which makes the co-ordination of regulatory policy difficult, due to the lack of co-ordinated and timely information collection which makes the evaluation of the probability and impact of a system-wide problem and the design of a contingency plan almost impossible.

These characteristics are discussed in turn.

### Off-balance sheet Nature of OTC Derivative Transactions

Traditionally, bank regulators have used capital requirement as a tool to ensure that banks have the capital to absorb potential losses so as to safeguard against potential systemic disturbances to the financial system, and to create a fair competitive environment for banks. The capital requirement is usually specified as a minimum required level for a balance-sheet ratio such as equity/total assets.

The significant involvement of banks in OTC derivatives transactions which are off-balance sheet in nature has essentially rendered the use of balance sheet ratio-based capital requirement ineffective. The seriousness of this problem can be seen by comparing the balance sheet assets of the money-centre banks to their off-balance sheet derivative holdings. For example, for J.P. Morgan, Chase Manhattan or Bankers Trust, the notional principal of outstanding interest rate and currency contracts represents more than ten times the value of their balance sheet assets.

The problem is further complicated by the fact that a swap, unlike a loan, normally does not involve up-front cash payments. In general, OTC derivative products are merely contracts to exchange payments in the future with the rates chosen to make the initial value of the product equal to zero. As such, at initialisation, there is really no exposure to credit risk. The risk of an OTC derivative position is a potential future exposure resulting from a changed mark-to-market value of the contract as the market rates (the yield curve or the exchange rate) or the credit rating of the counter-parties change. Naturally, the potential exposure is higher, the longer the maturity of the product. For swaps, the contract life can be as long as 15 years, and therefore the potential exposure can be substantial. For foreign exchange swaps, in particular, the accumulated exchange rate changes can be very large and much larger than for interest rate swaps. Just consider a US dollar/Korean won swap concluded before the free fall of the won at end-1997. Recently, the downgrading of Japanese or Korean banks (among others) have enhanced awareness of the counter-party risk of such long-dated contracts.

## Growing Complexity of Products

The growth of the OTC derivative markets is marked by the increasing complexity of products. The notional value of more sophisticated outstanding OTC derivatives products, such as caps, collars, floors and swaptions, has increased from US$566 billion at year-end 1990 to US$4722 billion at year-end 1996 (Table 6.1). Other sophisticated derivative products like "structured notes", "knock-outs", and many other exotic options are also growing at rates above market average. Chapter 3 gave concrete examples of the problems even very sophisticated end-users have experienced.

There are various reasons for the popularity of more and more complicated products. On the demand side, as the market environment becomes more volatile and the number of inter-yield curve arbitrage opportunities has declined, the demand for more complex hedging instruments and the demand for more complicated ways to reduce funding cost have increased, although spectacular losses made by inexperienced end-users, discussed in Chapter 3, may have chilled the fervour of some.

There is also a supply-side reason to this growing complexity of products in the markets. More complicated products are more profitable and therefore more attractive to dealers. Given the intense competition in the OTC derivatives markets, the spread that a dealer can charge for plain vanilla products has become very low. For example, the bid-ask spread of a 10-year swap rate has fallen in 1995 to about only four basis points from over 10 basis points in the mid-1980s.[8]

However, there is also a counteracting force. Even if a dealer is not taking any proprietary position, he is still facing some risk as the hedges he uses are rarely perfect. Hence, the dealer might not want to offer some products which cannot be hedged satisfactorily unless an appropriate spread can be charged.

**Tailor-made and Flexible Nature of OTC Derivative Products**

A salient feature of the OTC derivative markets is that the largely custom-made products are privately negotiated between the user and the dealer. Furthermore, the products can be rather different and can have many components like bonds, forwards and options. For example, a plain vanilla swap paying fixed interest rates, receiving floating interest rates, can be viewed as the combination of a long position in a floating rate note and a short position in a fixed rate bond. Alternatively, a plain vanilla swap also has a payment pattern similar to that of a series of forward contracts. As another example, a swaption can be viewed as a portfolio of options on futures/forward contracts. This flexible nature of OTC derivative products allows the OTC derivative markets to cut across many jurisdictions and basically incapacitated the existing instrument-based regulatory framework of asset market which defines the jurisdiction boundary of a regulator by the product type (see Technical Insight 6.2).

The only influence that the SEC and the CFTC have on the OTC derivative markets is through their power over the registered dealers and brokers in the securities and futures markets who also participate in the OTC derivative markets. They regulate these dealers and brokers by imposing reporting requirements and net capital requirements. Furthermore, they can also indirectly affect the functioning of the OTC derivative markets by their regulation of the exchange-traded derivative markets as many exchange traded products are being used by market participants to hedge OTC derivative risk.

**Wide Range of Market Participants**

In addition to banks, OTC derivatives are used by saving associations, corporations, and even governments and international organisations. The use of

**Technical Insight 6.2**    Regulatory no-man's land

For example, the OTC derivative markets in the United States are not regulated directly by the Securities and Exchange Commission (SEC) as OTC products are contracts rather than securities. The SEC registers and regulates the initial offerings of securities and securities options (but not securities futures) under the Securities Act of 1933. It also regulates the secondary securities market based on the anti-fraud provision of the Securities Exchange Act of 1934. However, while a plain vanilla swap can be viewed as a bond portfolio, it is not publicly offered. Non-public offerings are exempted from the registration requirement with the SEC under Section 4(2) of the Securities Act of 1933. Furthermore, since swaps are legally not securities according to US Federal Law, the Securities Exchange Act of 1934 and the Investment Company Act of 1940 are not applicable. As such, swaps are not regulated by the SEC and market participants are not required to be registered dealers.

The OTC derivative markets in the United States are also not directly regulated by the CFTC as OTC products are privately negotiated and were formally exempted from the Commodity Exchange Act (CEA) of 1974. The CFTC is responsible for supervising and regulating all futures contracts traded on a regulated exchange. The CEA embraced two principles: one was reliance on the exchanges themselves, as the primary regulators were subject to federal oversight, and the second functional regulation, the principle that all regulation of a given type of economic activity (here, risk shifting) should be done by one agency. The CFTC has the important prerogative of approving any new futures contract.

Transactions in foreign currency, security rights and warrants, mortgage instruments, repurchase options and government securities are defined as non-commodities by the Treasury Amendment, Section 2(a)(1)(A)(ii), of the CEA and are, therefore, exempted from CFTC jurisdiction. Furthermore, privately negotiated forward contracts, which are individually tailored in maturity terms, terminable (absent default) only with the consent of the counter-party without an exchange offset, and unsupported by a clearing organisation or margin system, are not covered by the CEA. As such, while swaps are similar to a portfolio of forward contracts, they are usually interpreted by the market participants to be outside the jurisdiction of the CFTC. The legal uncertainty was finally cleared in January 1993, when the CFTC formally exempted swaps from all provisions of the CEA. This is three months after the CFTC was granted the exemptive power by the Futures Trading Act which was signed into law in October 1992. Hence, swaps are neither regulated by the SEC nor by the CFTC.

interest rate swaps and currency swaps by non-financial institutions has grown substantially. The amount of interest rate swaps used by governments and international institutions has increased from just US$47.6 billion at year-end 1987 to more than US$242 billion at year-end 1992. The use of interest rate swaps by corporations has also increased significantly, from about US$128 billion at year-end 1987 to about US$666 billion at year-end 1992. Currency swaps used by governments have increased from US$33.9 billion to US$110.6 billion in the same five-year period. For corporations they have increased from US$51.6 billion to US$282.2 billion.

The main reason why so many different kinds of institutions participate in the OTC derivative markets is that OTC derivatives, due to their custom-made nature, can provide a wide range of services which are useful for the financing and risk-management practices of many different types of agents. Technical Insight 6.3 illustrates.

**Technical Insight 6.3**    Examples of OTC Uses

*Example 1*: OTC derivatives can be used by a corporation to alter the risk and payment characteristics of its existing debt. Anticipating an increase in the interest rate, a corporation can transform its existing floating rate debt into a fixed rate debt by using a plain vanilla swap paying fixed and receiving floating. The corporation can also transform its floating rate debt into a putable fixed rate debt by using a putable swap paying fixed and receiving floating. The "put" characteristic allows the investors to demand earlier repayment.

To partially hedge the risk that the anticipated rate increase might not occur, the corporation can transform its existing floating rate debt into a callable fixed rate debt by using a swap paying fixed and receiving floating together with a swaption paying floating. The swaption gives the corporation the right but not the obligation to enter into the swap. Alternatively, the corporation can buy a cap so that the issuer of the cap will pay the difference between the floating rate index (e.g., LIBOR) and the capped rate. It could also buy a swaption paying fixed and receiving floating, or it could enter into a forward swap paying fixed and receiving floating if it expects the interest rate increase will not come immediately. If the corporation currently has a callable fixed rate debt, then anticipating an increase in interest rate and a decline in the value of the call feature, the corporation can save interest expense by eliminating the call feature by using a swaption with the same call day, paying fixed and receiving floating.

*Example 2*: A corporation having a fixed rate debt can alter its liability by using OTC derivatives to benefit from an interest rate fall. In the simplest case, the corporation can transform its fixed rate debt into a floating rate debt by entering into a plain vanilla swap paying floating and receiving fixed.

It can add a call feature to its existing fixed rate debt by entering into a swaption paying floating and receiving fixed. The corporation can also benefit from the expected decline in interest rate by buying a floor for which the issuer pays the excess of a floor rate over a floating rate. The following table summarises various possibilities to change the liability structure of a borrower.

Using OTC Derivatives to Change Liability Structure

| Original position + | OTC derivative = | Transformed position |
|---|---|---|
| Floating rate debt | Swap (pay fixed) | Fixed rate debt |
| Floating rate debt | Putable swap (pay fixed) | Putable fixed rate debt |
| Floating rate debt | Swap (pay fixed) swaption (pay floating) | Callable fixed rate debt |
| Floating rate debt | Cap | Capped flexible rate debt |
| Floating rate debt | Forward swap | Lock-in fixed rate |
| Callable fixed rate debt | Swaption (pay fixed) | Fixed rate debt |
| Fixed rate debt | Swap (pay floating) | Floating rate debt |
| Fixed rate debt | Swaption (pay floating) | Callable fixed rate debt |

In addition to transforming the risk and payment characteristics of existing liabilities, OTC derivatives are an attractive means of reducing funding cost by taking advantage of the differential between long and short-term quality spreads or of the differential between the domestic yield curve and a foreign yield curve. Typically, a borrower with a low credit rating needs to pay a higher rate than a higher rated borrower. This quality spread is usually lower for floating rate debt than for long-term fixed rate debt so that corporations with low credit ratings have a comparative advantage in the floating rate market and corporations with high credit ratings have a comparative advantage in the fixed rate market.[9] The low credit rating corporation can therefore lower its fixed rate funding cost by borrowing in the floating rate market and then enter into a plain vanilla swap paying fixed and receiving floating. Similarly, the high credit rating corporation can obtain a lower floating rate funding cost by borrowing in the fixed rate market and entering into a plain vanilla swap paying floating and receiving fixed. A similar argument also hold for agents in different countries. A corporation usually pays a lower quality spread in its own country than abroad. As such, a corporation needing funding in a different currency can save money by borrowing in the domestic market and then swap the amount into the desired foreign currency.

Another reason why OTC derivatives are so popular is that OTC derivatives allow risk to be managed timely and cheaply. For instance, if a corporation, given its view on the evolution of interest rates, desires to replace callable fixed rate debt with a floating rate debt, it can always call back the fixed rate debt and then issue a new floating rate note. However, both the calling back of the existing debt and the issuance of the new debt involves significant time and cost. Entering into a callable swap (which can effectively be done in a day or so) is much faster and cheaper in terms of transaction costs. In a volatile environment speed is key.

While many corporations could use exchange-traded derivatives for their hedging requirements, there are at least two advantages in using OTC derivatives. One advantage of OTC derivatives is that they can be fitted to the specific need of a user. While some OTC derivatives (like the plain vanilla swaps) can be mimicked by a portfolio of futures contracts, the replication of more complicated OTC derivatives might be difficult if not impossible. Another important factor is that OTC derivatives and exchange-traded derivatives have very different cash flow implications as no margin payments are required for the former. Furthermore, unlike banks and securities houses, non-financial corporations are not subjected to capital requirements, so for them an OTC product is definitely more advantageous.

**Globalisation of the OTC Derivative Markets**

The OTC derivative markets have become increasingly global in nature. At the end of 1987, the notional value of all outstanding US dollar interest rate swaps represented about 79% of all outstanding interest rate swaps in the world. However, by end-1992, the share of the US dollar fell to 46% and by end-1995 to one-third. Similarly, the amount of non-US dollar currency swaps has also increased substantially relative to US dollar currency swaps.

The globalisation of the OTC derivative markets is natural as the use of many OTC derivative products, for example currency swaps, is basically for arbitraging yield differentials across countries. Over time, more and more users around the world have recognised the usefulness of OTC derivative products for cost reduction in funding and risk management.

It took financial intermediaries in developed countries time to set up the organisational structures for OTC derivative business—often entailing a transfer of their marketing and risk-management activities to London—and thereby to catch up with US institutions. In the meantime, the US institutions had already globalised their operations and established subsidiaries in the major economic centres in the world for marketing of US and local products for re-exportation. European and Asian institutions are eagerly catching up.

## 5. NEW DEVELOPMENTS

Innovative product design is essentially demand-driven. There is hardly a day in the market without a deal that, in some detail, is different from others. Recently, the markets have favoured dual-currency bonds, binary currency options (paying a fixed amount if the underlying reaches a predetermined level or remains within a defined range, and nothing otherwise) and other barrier options. Convergence in European interest rates in preparation for European Monetary Union stepped up demand for products hedging yield spreads.

End-users favour stock index linked investments with a guaranteed flow value (usually equal to the issuing price) at the price of less than 100% of the index-linked gain. The wholesale market is successfully refining equity and currency warrants, including standard call and put options, complex range and barrier structures as well as exotica, such as "quanto" (an instrument denominated in a currency other than that in which it is traded) or instruments in which the payout is based on the performance of several underlying assets. Technical Insight 6.4 describes a few recent option developments.

The most significant and innovatory product development is, in my view, the development of *credit derivatives*.

Credit derivatives share several characteristics with other more traditional derivative products, enabling users to single out the (credit) risk of any given assets and transfer it to another party while retaining ownership of the underlying. In unbundling risks, derivatives enable users to tailor their risk exposures more closely to their preferences or constraints.[10]

As is the case with any derivative instrument, credit derivatives can be divided into forward (including swaps) and option-type contracts. Technical Insight 6.5 explains the logic of the main contract types available.

### Economic Benefits from Credit Derivatives

To the extent that they provide a more systematic way of evaluating and transferring credit risk, credit derivatives offer financial institutions a flexible tool for the management of risk.[11]

**Technical Insight 6.4**    Options: recent innovations

One drawback of hedging strategies relying on options is the high cost. A number of recent innovations have reduced the cost by targeting the gains more narrowly.

A *contingent premium option* has the particular feature that the option premium is paid when the option expires and not at the time of purchase. Moreover, the premium is only payable if the option expires in-the-money (has value). In fact, it is like buying insurance now and paying only if needed.

What is the downside? First, the premium of the contingent option is higher than that of a standard option. Second, a loss can still be made when the option closes just barely in-the-money. Thus, contingent premium options are ideal for low probability events of large price swings (typically catastrophic events).

*Knock-out options* (a particular type of barrier options) were heavily used in the yen-dollar market in 1995, as discussed in Chapter 3. The specific feature of these options is that the option vanishes when a second strike price, the knock-out level, is reached. This limits the potential gain and, for that reason, the premium is lower. It is a low-cost product to hedge normal price movements.

*Spread options* serve to protect the value-added of a firm or a particular activity. The spread between the price of gasoline and the price of crude oil provides a hedge for an oil refinery. Typically, one side of the spread is a raw material and the other side an industrial output. Spread deals were done for a soya bean crusher (soya beans—soya oil), for a baking firm (wheat—bread) and for a smelter (electricity—aluminium). The costs of spreads are considerably lower than the cost of separate options on both of the underlying.

*Basket options* are based on an index of industrial or primary commodities. They may serve a diversified purchaser and are cheaper than individually purchased commodity options because the volatility of a basket is always less than the sum of the component volatilities.

The creation of an active market for credit derivatives will allow users to dynamically manage credit risk exposure to specific counter-parties or groups of counter-parties in targeted economic sectors depending on their expectations of economic and financial developments. Credit derivatives can be used to reduce excessive concentration in particular credits or to diversify exposure into sectors with promising risk/return profiles. By easing credit constraints through the reduction of overly concentrated exposures, they can enable

**Technical Insight 6.5**   Credit derivatives

A credit derivative is a financial instrument whose value is derived from an underlying market variable reflecting the credit risk of a public or private entity. The underlying market variables are predominantly bonds and loans while the vehicles used to achieve credit protection are provided by the swaps and options markets.

The objective of credit derivatives is to isolate and price the credit risk from an underlying instrument. Specific products can then be tailored for individual investors requiring credit protection in the same way they require interest rate or currency risk protection. Payouts can be triggered by a number of events, including a default, insolvency, a rating downgrade or a stipulated change in the credit spread of the reference asset.

Currently the market divides roughly into two strands: one offering plays on credit spreads (credit spread forwards/options), the other protection from default risk (credit event/default swaps). The credit spread is calculated as the difference in yield between a credit-sensitive name and a risk-free benchmark bond.

While a credit spread forward curve has by nature a positive slope, forward credit spreads are not good indicators of future spot spreads. Thus investors can monetise their view on credit spreads by betting against the implied forward spread, typically by selling out-of-the-money put options or buying spread-linked notes, hence without the credit risk.

In a *total return swap*, the arranging bank would position the target loan or bond on its books and transfer to the investor all the economic aspects of the asset, including price changes, coupon payments, fees, prepayment and amortisation charges. In return, the investor pays the bank a benchmark rate, such as LIBOR plus a spread, or the funding rate for holding the asset. The swap would be settled at predetermined intervals on the basis of the market value of the swap, with any positive change being paid by the banks to the counter-party and any negative change being paid to the bank. Variations on the theme have included swaps where investors exchange the flows of one credit-sensitive name against another, or arbitrage the spread between the loan of a borrower against the same entity's bonds or equity.

But where the real growth is expected to come from is the second category, the credit default family of products, the only true credit derivatives.

A typical case is where an investor is prepared to take the default risk on an underlying bond or loan, by selling a put option on the notional value of the asset, thus earning premium up-front. In swap arrangements the protection buyer pays the counter-party a periodic fee (as a percentage of the notional amount). If default occurs, the option seller/swap counter-party pays the full notional amount to the protection buyer.

For investors who cannot or prefer not to engage in swaps or other derivatives transaction, intermediaries offer *credit-linked notes* as an alternative means of achieving the risk profile created by credit derivatives. Typical instruments combine the features of a standard fixed income security with a credit option. Interest and principal are paid, as is the case with regular fixed income securities, but the credit option allows the issuer to reduce interest payments if a key financial variable specified by the note's documentation deteriorates. Such instruments provide the issuer with the opportunity to purchase credit insurance from investors. Many structures are based on pools of assets and give investors returns that are equivalent to purchasing a diversified portfolio of loans.

Protection against default is far more complex to price, and the market is still at a very early stage of development in terms of modelling the risk. The difficulty is that credit events, such as default, are rare events (discontinuous stochastic processes or "jumps"). More statistical material is available for bond or loan portfolios and pooled credit risk is therefore much easier to price.

Pricing default risk is based on the correlation between the interest rate risk, default risk and recovery rate of the underlying instrument—a tricky task, given that default is a one-off, often unanticipated event, for which there is no correlated, offsetting position with which to hedge.

financial institutions to free up credit lines or utilise them more fully, thus enabling them to make more efficient use of their capital. For example, a credit portfolio manager identifies a need to reduce exposure to a specific credit to free up lines for another profit opportunity or portfolio diversification opportunity by replacing exposure to credit A by exposure to credit B. A possible solution would be to sell the undesired credit exposure. But this may be difficult to do, (e.g., when there is no market) or the client relationship may suffer. By purchasing a default swap, or by entering into a credit switch, these drawbacks are avoided.[12]

Credit derivatives can increase the ability of market participants to arbitrage differences in the pricing of credit risk between various underlying asset classes (such as loans and bonds) and investment horizons (which can vary significantly from one credit instrument to another). They can also enable financial institutions of different credit quality to engage in mutually beneficial transactions, therefore helping reduce sectoral and maturity gaps in the availability of credit. This is a potentially very important contribution of credit derivatives, as the market for risk is far from the competitive ideal. There are structural reasons, notably asymmetric information, but also regulatory reasons; for example, the price for a credit guarantee provided by a bank that could have taken the risk through making the loan itself must reflect the fact that the same own funds are required to back up the guarantee as are required for the loan.

Credit derivatives are of very recent vintage and the market is, therefore, still modest in size, concentrated in a small group of primarily North American commercial and investment banks. The size of transactions varies between US\$30 and 50 million and the total of outstanding contracts is estimated close to US\$40 billion (1996). Credit default swaps (or default puts) and total return swaps are the most actively used structures followed by credit spread options.

As always in the early product cycle of derivatives, the customised nature of transactions and the resultant lack of standardisation mean that the initial arrangement of contracts remains complex. Secondary market trading is still lacking and premiums for settling contracts prior to expiration can be high. This lack of liquidity is explained by a number of factors, including the lack of liquidity of some underlying assets (loans in particular), the limited transferability of most structures, the heterogeneity of the instruments offered, and the small number of market participants possessing the expertise and technology required for the dynamic management and pricing of credit risk.[13]

Thus, in spite of efforts made towards more standardised documentation, the number of variables that are open for negotiation makes such transactions substantially more complex than for standard derivatives. Credit derivatives also raise new regulatory issues, including whether the shift of economic exposure results in a corresponding transfer for legal and regulatory purposes. Such a transfer gives rise to a counter-party credit risk that is akin to replacement risk in the more traditional financial derivatives. Another important issue is whether some of these instruments should be treated as derivatives or credit instruments for capital adequacy purposes, as no formal guidelines have yet been published.

It is difficult to make definite statements about the potential for growth of credit derivatives. Several elements point to further expansion. With the greater sophistication of interest rate and currency risk-management techniques, their application to credit risk is likely to spread further. Market segmentation (resulting from regulatory, structural, institutional or credit factors), by giving rise to mispricing between instruments, should provide numerous arbitrage opportunities. Failures of large financial institutions and the growing popularity of asset-backed securities are creating greater interest in the broad issue of active credit risk management. Success in reducing inflation in OECD countries and therefore in maintaining interest rates at low levels is likely to heighten the search for yield, and consequently give greater importance to credit risk trading. However, much will depend on the extent to which products, pricing and documentation can be standardised and regulatory issues resolved.

Credit risk markets are among the last strongholds of non-competitive markets, be it only for asymmetric information. Credit derivatives will, without a doubt, improve credit risk markets. In this sense their economic value cannot be overestimated.

# 6. CONCLUSION

OTC derivative products provide essential tools for risk-management of financial institutions and corporations. The market has maintained its innovatory dynamism and has kept up its vigorous growth. Compared to exchange-traded products, OTC products during recent years have been the winners.

There are several reasons for this. One is the customised design of OTC derivatives to fit the precise needs of the user. A related advantage is the innovative potential as demand and standardisation is typically limited during the early phase of the product cycle. In this chapter an important example, credit derivatives, illustrated this point. But even for plain vanilla products, for which exchange-traded equivalent instruments exist, growth of the OTC market has been higher. The major dealers with heavy investment in know-how and technology have a clear competitive advantage in the OTC markets, whereas institutions with lower credit rating or know-how would operate on the same footing in exchange-traded products. Even if margins on plain vanilla products are unattractive, the major dealers still maintain their market share as much customised business is complementary to plain vanilla business. In addition, screen-based trading is the appropriate technology for plain vanilla products.

In recent years, US money-centre banks have also benefited from improved performance and hence improved credit ratings, and several mergers have increased the average size and hence the internal exposure netting of the top banks. With the geographical spread of derivative users, major non-US institutions are slowly catching up (the major British, German, French, Swiss and Japanese banks), adding both demand and supply to OTC markets. And, finally, perhaps the most important explanation is that the playing field is tilted by much less regulation of OTC markets in comparison to the exchanges. One important reason is that exchanges are much more easily regulated than the elusive OTC market.

There are, however, also new and important problems. One is the counter-party risk of the major dealers in the off-balance sheet derivatives book. Banks are actively engaged in managing that risk ever more efficiently. Risk-reducing collateral agreements have seen considerable success in recent years and banks are also busily developing various ways of greater mutualisation of risks—an important topic for the future, discussed in Chapter 9.

The concentration of OTC derivatives on a dozen or so major dealers is a source of concern. This and other structural elements of the market—large amounts of inter-dealer positions, growing linkages between different financial markets—and an improving but still unsatisfactory worldwide system of supervision, are sources of deep concern. This concern is the starting point for the next chapter, to be followed by a search for a regulatory framework that reduces systemic risk without hurting market developments.

# ENDNOTES

1 According to BIS (August 1996), the global amount outstanding of OTC derivatives contracts at end-March 1996 is estimated at US$47.5 trillion. The data shown in Table 6.1 are much lower because only one side of a contract is retained, effectively halving the total. In addition, forward agreements are excluded because they are structurally similar to spot transactions and half of the deals in foreign exchange forwards have a maturity of less than one week.

2 An important development in recent years has been the greater use of electronic dealing or broking systems. In a "dealing" system, the counter-party is known to both transactors before the trade is executed, whilst in a "broking" system the transactors know their counter-party only after execution. According to a BIS survey, in April 1995 about one in every seven spot forex transactions was executed through an electronic system. At present, they only handle spot transactions.

3 OTC derivatives trading is a natural area as the evaluation of credit risk is essential in the OTC derivative markets and banks are experienced in dealing with such risk. The logical force of this argument may, however, not find its counterpart in practice. This argument takes OTC derivative activity as more or less a substitute for some of the traditional businesses of banks.

4 Under the "current exposure method", the credit equivalent is computed as the sum of the replacement cost of the contract and an add-on factor which is a fixed percentage of the notional principal of the contract. Under the original exposure method, the credit equivalent is computed as a percentage (given by a conversion factor) of the notional principal of the contract.

5 The Basle Accord was progressively implemented and took full effect by the end of 1992. There are quite a few cases in which the amount of trading profit has jumped substantially after the implementation of the Accord. For example, J.P. Morgan's trading profit was US$0.9 billion in 1990, US$1.3 billion in 1991, and US$1.4 billion in 1992. The amount then jumped to a high of US$2.6 billion in 1993. As another example, the trading account profit of Citicorp was US$1.0 billion in 1990, US$1.5 billion in 1991, and US$1.3 billion in 1992. Then it jumped to US$3.1 billion in 1993. Whilst a change in market conditions can explain part of the increase in trading

account profit, the increased involvement in short-term proprietary trading, which is more sensitive to market risk, is also likely to be a factor.

6  For example, Merrill Lynch, Salomon Brothers, Goldman Sachs, Lehman Brothers, Paribas, among others have set up their AAA SPDVs subsidiary units. While there are large variations in the legal construction of these SPDVs, the major reason for their establishment is that, in the absence of a dynamic management of credit exposure, many high-rated end-users restrict their OTC derivatives trade to counterparts rated AA or above.

7  In May 1996, a US federal court set a legal precedent by ruling that a US corporation involved in swap transactions could not require any special duties of care on the part of its counter-party since both were acting as sophisticated participants in the transaction. This decision potentially reduces the threat of litigation against intermediaries in comparable deals.

8  Whenever new products are launched the returns to dealers are, of course, much higher. For example, for the first inverse floaters or bond issues with a collar swap, dealers could get 60 basis points risk-free!

9  In a risk-neutral world this argument is only valid if bond or swap markets misprice credit risk.

10  Already in Chapter 1, it has been seen that this is not a new idea. Traditional banking and securities market instruments involving contingent third-party default payments, such as standby letters of credit, revolving credits, bond insurance and financial guarantees, have existed for many years. What is new perhaps is the systematic attempt to quantify such risk and break it down into fundamental building blocks.

11  BIS (August 1996).

12  Credit derivatives, like derivatives in other markets, can be used to avoid some of the disadvantages of cash market transactions, such as transaction costs, unfavourable tax treatment or the costly unwinding of associated market risk exposure (such as that on interest rates or foreign currency), or illiquidity. This ability to modify exposures without engaging in potentially unfavourable transactions in the underlying market should therefore prove useful to any financial institution holding illiquid assets, such as commercial banks, investment banks, mutual funds and insurance companies. The adjustment of credit risk profiles without the need to transfer the ownership of underlying assets is particularly valuable for commercial banks, whose exposure to particular borrowers or counter-parties can be reduced without endangering business relationships. As another example, an investor may prefer to invest in government bonds for liquidity reasons, although he may be happy to accept more risk and obtain a higher return. Adding a credit derivative to his portfolio allows him to retain his liquidity advantage in government paper and to engineer his investment risk exactly according to his preferences.

13  Since payments are contingent upon the occurrence of defaults or other credit events, the drafting of sound legal language defining precisely the type of event and the subsequent contingent payment is crucial. The documentation must also clearly specify how the protection buyer will be compensated upon the occurrence of a credit event; and how claims are settled.

# PART III

# PUBLIC POLICY OPTIONS

«HOW DO YOU MANAGE TO REGULATE THE PREDATORS ?»

# 7

# Are Derivatives a Threat to Global Financial Stability?

## The global financial crash of October 2001

The years 1999 to 2001 were exceptional years in financial history. In the United States the stock market boom that had started in 1993 went through a serious downward correction and banks, which had become major traders on their own accounts, saw their profits squeezed dangerously. Weaker institutions were absorbed by the largest domestic and foreign banks and waves of concentration spilled over the country, eased by the repeal of Glass–Steagall.

European banks felt the brunt of global competition and domestic deregulation in a period of tight monetary conditions, following the start of European Monetary Union and introduction of the Euro. Fiscal sobriety (a requirement for admission to the EMU) and the Community's inability to lower its social safety costs did not help to stimulate sagging growth. Banks experienced difficulties with their loan books—especially their real estate lending and their equity holdings—and earned meagre returns from what was left of their intermediation activity. Disintermediation started late in Europe, but with a vengeance.

Japanese banks, which were still suffering from absorbing the costs of the real estate and stock exchange bubble bursts of the early 1990s, had for too long fudged their accounts by not providing fully for their bad loans. They also suffered from having to pay back the large government loans received during the 1990s to avoid bankruptcies.

But there were also bright spots, the brightest of all being China. After the successful integration of Hong Kong, China's growth rate continued unabated at around 10% per annum, although bad loans (already equal to US$600 billion or 70% of GDP in 1995) mainly to loss-making state-owned enterprises pervaded the balance sheets of China's large, state-controlled banks. The yuan had become convertible and Hong Kong's financial expertise had proved most helpful in reforming and reshaping China's financial sector. Only regulatory supervision was still a far cry from international standards and accounts not so transparent, but, according to most financial experts, convergence to western standards was simply a matter of time. As a result of these extremely positive developments, the stock markets in Hong Kong and Shanghai soared. From the end of 1998 to the end of 2000, Shanghai's index had increased by 110% and the Hang Seng by even more. Global investors poured funds into China to benefit from the big China push, also propelled by dire market conditions at home. Markets had calmed during 2001, but it was clear to everybody that the bulls were just taking a rest before launching the next stampede. It was the best of times for those long in Chinese stocks.

Prudent investors bought index call options, those more gambling-prone bought futures; few felt the need to hedge in view of the clear positive trend in stock prices. Put options on the index were, however, traded on both exchanges and also over-the-counter, but with little liquidity. Some western gurus predicted that before the moon festival of the year 2002 stocks would surge through their so far unsuccessfully assailed resistance levels.

The yuan had substantially benefited from the massive capital inflows and a healthy current account surplus since 1 July 1997, the day Hong Kong returned. Not too long ago the US dollar was worth 15 yuan. In early October 2001 it had fallen to 9 yuan. Most currency dealers expected the yuan to gain further in value. It was truly the best of times.

One of the many people who became rich, in fact very rich, during those years was Wang Pei, a 27 year-old chief trader of South China Bank Corporation (SCB) with headquarters in Guangdong. However, for tax and regulatory reasons, most of the trading was carried out in Macau and Wang Pei was the star of the Macau team. By early October 2000 it became known that he, alone, had made profits of US$6 billion for his bank during the last 12 months. These were the best of times, but still it took exceptional know-how and skills to make that amount of money. Wang Pei was proud to tell anybody willing to listen—and there were plenty in the bars and clubs of Macau, Hong Kong and Guangdong—that he had made several hundred million dollars for himself (the exact amount varied from one bar to another!). Wang Pei was highly educated and his MBA degree from Harvard, duly enlarged, covered one wall of his office. He had only a tired smile for those who compared him to a certain young Singapore trader who also had quite a reputation back in 1994. Being Chinese he did not appreciate comparisons with a British citizen and, at any rate, he possessed an intimate knowledge of how China "worked", a deep conviction about the potential of Grand China, and a gambler's instinct that he shared with many of his compatriots and that he considered distinctly Chinese.

SCB held a sizeable portfolio of Chinese stocks and a large loan portfolio with heavy exposure to the booming real estate sector. On the liabilities side, deposits were important but during recent years the bank had borrowed massively in dollars from US and Japanese banks. This turned out to be an extremely profitable strategy as US and Japanese interest rates were much lower than in China and the yuan had been appreciating. Short-term interest rates in China moved between 11 and 13% (as compared to 3–5% in Japan and the United States), mainly due to the high (over 20%) and accelerating inflation rate.

Wang Pei had long futures positions on both the Hong Kong and Shanghai indexes, and had massively issued long-term put options (up to three years) on individual stocks and the indexes, which were traded over the counter. In addition, being convinced that the yuan would appreciate further, he had accumulated a huge amount of long forward contracts on the yuan, mainly against yen, but also against US dollars.

Wang Pei's strategy was nothing exceptional. His views were shared by most traders and also by his top management. In fact, his derivatives positions reflected the same strategic views as the overall balance sheet structure of his bank: long in Chinese stocks and loans, short in US and Yen funds. What was special about Wang Pei was the courage and ruthless logic with which he translated his views into positions of mind-boggling size.

SCB was one of the very large semi-privatised banks, ranking twenty-first in the world, for which the state still held 51% of capital. The Basle Regulatory Recommendations were generally respected, although adapted to "Chinese conditions" as was only normal. Top management was informed about the derivatives positions and the bank operated a sophisticated, multi-layered value-at-risk model. But being long on everything Chinese and short on foreign currencies did not show up as being risky in the bank's model. This was not the case in the models of the US or Japanese banks and their Chinese exposure was important. Moreover, before October 2001 the relative calm in the markets during 2001 and hence low volatilities had significantly reduced value-at-risk as compared to the previous year.

Then, on 18 October 2001, a decision was taken that turned the best of times into the worst of times. For some time the accommodating policy of the People's Bank had been criticised by the conservative members of the Central Committee and by a large part of the population. Inflation was rising rapidly and visibly getting out of control. Labour shortages in the major coastal production centres became serious and wages there reached levels that were 10–15 times those of the poorer inner provinces. A great many people had become outrageously rich through speculation and their ostentatious behaviour shocked the general public and the still widely held egalitarian values of China's society. Those members of the Central Committee in favour of a more vigorous anti-inflationary policy finally won the upper hand and it was decided to jack-up interest rates sufficiently to cool the overheated economy. The People's Bank's intervention rate was abruptly increased from 10% to 20% and, on Friday, 19 October—entering Chinese history books as "White Friday"—stocks in Hong Kong and Shanghai tumbled by more than 10%, on 22 October by another 9% and the bears gathered momentum. By the end of October the stock markets in China had declined by over 40%.

Foreign investors scrambled to pull out their funds and the yuan crashed. The exchanges day and night resembled Chinese New Year to make their margin calls and close out positions for investors unable to cover margins. Losses were colossal, but at least the exchanges did their job. Investors in the OTC market were not as lucky, as many counter-parties simply evaporated. Borrowers had difficulties in rolling-over their credits and one bank after another experienced serious liquidity shortages—not to speak of catastrophic balance sheets. The payments system came to a complete halt as major banks were unable to cover their short positions and the People's Bank was unwilling to intervene on a large scale, for both the state-owned and private banks, given the Central Committee's decision to curb credits in order to control inflation better.

SCB was particularly hard hit. Its foreign lenders called back their funds, but SCB was unable to comply. Margin payments on its futures positions were made initially, but by 23 October their positions were closed out—at losses already exceeding SCB's capital. The put options it had issued started to be exercised, but the bank, after an initial effort, was unable to pay up. Counterparts that had bought these options for hedge purposes suddenly had no hedge at all—except for a legal claim of dubious value. The same was true for its dollar and yen forward contracts. SCB tried to call back its loans, but borrowers were equally hard hit and unable to respect maturity deadlines or advance payment schedules. Savers panicked and withdrew—or tried to withdraw—their deposits.

All in all, Wang Pei's position reached a loss of US$10 billion, mainly with foreign counterparts. As he argued later, had SCB not experienced difficulties across its entire balance sheet, the derivatives book by itself might not have broken the bank (a claim later refuted by a study carried out by a special commission appointed by the government).

The Chinese banking system was devastated, with virtually all banks, even the most conservative ones, falling prey to the bankruptcy virus. Counterparts abroad which were dragged into difficulties or bankruptcy (fund managers, security houses, banks) caused a snowball effect in several Asian countries, including Japan, and in the United States. The direct effect of the Chinese crisis on Europe was less serious as Europe had less exposure to China. But when Japanese and US banks were dragged into difficulties, European banks started to suffer seriously. What had started as a local event in distant China caused ripples throughout the world. Many US politicians blamed the global nature of financial markets and the high leverage provided by derivatives for the disaster and urged steps to uncouple US markets and seriously curtail derivative products.

Strong pressure from the Federal Reserve and the Bank of Japan brought the Chinese authorities to launch a major "revitalisation campaign" for China's financial sector. However, the Chinese authorities made it clear that foreign counterparts should have known what they were doing, that previously they had largely benefited from the boom in China and that they had had, or should have factored in, a risk-premium for dealing with counterparts in China.

The Chinese authorities were also deeply disappointed by the refusal of Japan and the United States to provide emergency loans and to waive any claims on Chinese counter-parties resulting from the crash. They interpreted this refusal as an unfriendly attempt to harm China and slow down its long march to world supremacy. (After Hong Kong's return and a revision of the national accounts in the year 2000, China's economy was second only to the US economy and expected to overtake the US within the next ten years.) After the crash China-bashing was, indeed, a buzzword in Washington, but it is fair to say that US and Japanese tax payers were already heavily plucked after saving their own financial systems—for the second time in just one generation!

In retaliation China would not recognise any claims due to loans or derivatives contracts which were unfulfilled. To circumvent any stepped-up international pressure, Chinese banks were declared bankrupt and revamped under new ownerships with capital provided by government agencies. Although the exact budgetary costs of the "revitalisation campaign" is unknown, estimates range between US$200–300 billion. The costs to US, European and Japanese taxpayers of saving their banks substantially exceeded these estimates. Even more dramatic was the non-budgetary cost: a shattered financial system, widespread bankruptcies and job losses, and a recession lasting several years. Wang Pei, like other traders, lost part, but not all, of his quickly amassed fortune. Most savers were less lucky.

On 28 December 2001, the leading financial newspaper in Beijing summed up this period and the deception with imported financial technology with another import:

"It was the best of times, it was the worst of times, it was the age of wisdom, it was the age of foolishness, it was the epoch of belief, it was the epoch of incredulity . . ."

and urged the Chinese to return to traditional values. Indeed, ancient Chinese forecasting techniques, tried and tested for four millenia, had predicted the crash and therefore those who had lost their fortunes had to blame their own blind adulation of Western values. The year 2000 was the year of the Dragon and, as every Chinese child knows, the Dragon provokes and foreshadows big events. The last year of the Dragon, 1988, was also an excellent year for the stock exchange but foreshadowed 1989's Tian An Men Square events. The most dramatic year of The Dragon was 1976 when stocks in China did not exist yet, but three great leaders passed away, millions died in earthquakes and the profound regime change was announced. As if these historic events were not proof enough, the 28 December 2001 newspaper edition reproduced a perfectly "neutral sample": the Nikkei 225 Average for the years 1949–96 (thus independent of the present events in space and time), during which the average price increase of Dragon years was 43% and the average price of Horse years was −4.7% (the year 2002 was a Horse year).

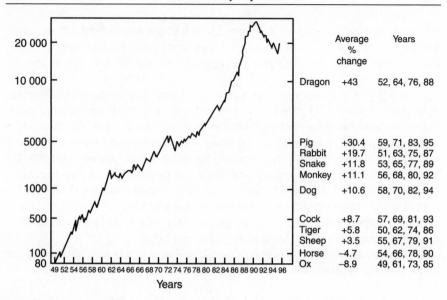

**Figure 7.1**   Nikkei 225 average (semi-log scale)
*Source: Beijing Financial Times*, 28 December 2001

> ". . . there are fears that derivatives fuel
> financial-market uncertainty by
> multiplying the leveraged, or debt based
> buying power, of hedge funds and other
> speculators—an uncertainty that could,
> if the things went wrong, threaten
> the whole of the world financial system."
>
> "Your Financial Future", *The Economist*, 14 May 1994

WHEN I wrote this story about a world financial crisis in the year 2001, my friends thought that it was too far-fetched. After the Asian crisis of 1997 they reconsidered. Of course, derivatives are only an instrument that makes hedging and speculating easier. They were neither the cause nor the main agents in the Asian crisis of 1997. It is the combination of reckless borrowing, bad investments, weak regulation tolerating financial follies far too long, that caused the problem. And whenever such problems emerge in a global economy, they infect the rest of the world. The first victims are those with a weakened immunisation system, those countries with large exposures and weak financial systems. The lenders, investors and writers of derivatives are typically institutions in the leading financial centres, so they are affected as well.

What, then, could be the potential danger posed by the ever-growing use of derivatives?

Derivatives have made major contributions to the efficiency of the global financial system through improved pricing and allocation of risk, and the use of derivatives has made it possible to redistribute, configurate or contain financial risks in ways that are not easily made possible in cash markets. At the same time, however, recent financial history has provided ample evidence, illustrated in Chapter 3, that the growth of derivative markets has made financial crises considerably more virulent, and the fast growth and widespread use of derivatives has increased the risk of financial disturbances. As in earlier instances of successful product innovation, rapidly growing demand for the new products has stimulated the development of a new industry with new markets and new participants. Furthermore, unlike many industrial innovations, the growing use of derivatives has complemented, rather than displaced, an existing industry.

At present the financial system is in a decisive transition period: market developments have run ahead of the ability of regulators to respond to the new challenges (this is discussed in Chapter 8) and the increasingly ineffective regulatory and supervisory infrastructure in the major markets will have to be redesigned on an international basis to cope with the new environment (Chapter 9). Until this is done there will be significant risks associated with the growth of derivatives markets. Many market participants tend to play down the risk of a major financial crisis with systemic effects. But, according to a survey conducted by the Group of 30 in 1997, leading global institutions put the likelihood of a serious disruption of the international financial system at *one in five* over the next five years. Would you travel by air if you were told that the chances of a crash were one in five?

In this chapter, Section 1 discusses systemic risk, the principal regulatory concern, taking up the challenge thrown down in the last chapter. Section 2 then shows how derivatives have worsened the dynamics of financial crises and Section 3 their increased contagiousness. Except for operational risk, surveyed in Section 4, this chapter does not discuss risks—business risks, learning risks—that have raised the potential of a financial disturbance within the industry itself. These issues were analysed as part of the OTC industry in Chapter 6.

# 1. SYSTEMIC RISK

Systemic risk is the risk of a financial disturbance that causes widespread disruptions elsewhere in the financial system which then fails to perform one or more of its functions, such as the allocation of funds/resources, the provision of liquidity, the pricing of assets, and the transmission of monetary policy. Such disruptions can lead to untimely liquidation of positions of firms and possibly liquidation of firms.

The probability of a system failure is dependent on a chain of events:

- The probability of turbulence in one or more of the financial markets (including the foreign exchange, bond, equity and derivatives markets).
- The probability that a problem in one market or institution spills over to the other markets or institutions.
- The probability of a banking system failure. The financial systems can fail without involvement of derivatives. But derivatives raise the risks for three reasons: they represent a truly global market; they provide high leverage; and they escape financial supervision more easily than other products.

This framework is well illustrated by the Asian financial crisis of 1997. Thailand, Malaysia, Indonesia and the Philippines are, to varying degrees, highly indebted to foreign lenders and have weakly regulated domestic financial systems. High foreign debt by itself is not a problem if borrowed money is well invested. But this was not the case. When Thailand abandoned its fixed exchange rate, the baht value of foreign debt increased proportionally. This and the crash of the stock market exposed the fragility of the Thai financial system.

Within one week the Thai crisis had turned into a regional crisis, with the Philippines, Malaysia and Indonesia experiencing the same problems. Of course, speculators reversing their initial Asia-euphoria started to speculate against Asian currency, mainly using derivatives. Combined with stock sales and a lending stop, the initial crisis blew up out of proportion. Even countries with sounder fundamentals—Sinagapore, Hong Kong, Taiwan—became targets of speculation, leading to a collapse of Hong Kong stocks. Derivatives did not play a major role at the beginning of the crisis. Foreign lenders in domestic currency had swapped their exposure to hedge currency risks. But borrowers, generally, had not hedged in order to benefit from lower interest rates of dollar, yen and European currency loans. Thus, it was rather the *lack of hedging* that created the vulnerability. The Asian crisis of 1997 thus serves as a prime example of the potential benefits of hedging. The very steep fall of the currencies—totally unrelated to basic considerations of competitivity—was initially furthered by speculation relying on derivatives for greater leverage. But, as currencies pursued their free fall, the momentum was sustained by forward hedges of borrowers. So, derivatives, as everywhere else, were in no sense a cause of the crisis. Lack of hedging was a cause and late hedging a destabilising factor.

The Prime Minister of Malaysia, Mr. Mahatir attacked speculators, notably George Soros, as the real culprits. In this he was quite wrong. But speculators did show considerable irrationality by negatively reassessing all emerging markets. Latin America and, to a lesser extent, Eastern Europe saw their stocks crumbling and within days the risk premium on their foreign bonds rocketed sky-high. Western counterparts with exposure to these regions obviously made losses and, on 27 October, the New York Stock Exchange experienced a drop of over 500 points, the largest one-day loss ever in absolute terms.

The IMF, World Bank, Asian Development Bank and national governments provided emergency assistance to the main countries concerned. Subject to economic adjustment, Thailand can count on US$17 billion and Indonesia on US$40 billion.

If the crisis had stopped there, the damage would have been limited. But then two heavyweights, Korea and Japan, were drawn into the problem arena. Both have banking systems that are virtually bankrupt as a result of weak regulation, problematic government meddling, previous real estate and stock collapses, and an unwillingness to clean up the banks' balance sheets. The crisis in Asian emerging markets—large clients for exports and receivers of loans—tipped the balance. The international community is assisting Korea with a US$57 billion package and Japan should have the means to bail out its banks. Just how rotten the situation is, is difficult to say, in part because the obligations in derivatives markets are not known. At any rate, Korea's external debt was first estimated in November 1997 at US$120 billion and then revised to US$200 billion in early January 1998. So much for reliable information. Thus, after having disrupted emerging markets around the world, the main industrial nations are likely to be spared from a big spillover. But their growth prospects have already been revised downwards and banks with heavy exposure to Asia will suffer. What started as a problem in Thailand has destroyed a generation's effort to create wealth in South-East Asia, has upset the political equilibrium and has spread its ripples very rapidly over several continents. What a measure for the social gains from risk-management!

I now look more closely at the role of derivatives in the three components of systemic risk.

**Probability of Extreme Financial Market Turbulence**

The probability of extreme financial market turbulence as in the foreign exchange markets in 1992 or in bond markets in 1994 is the result of various factors. The most common one is excessive speculation, amplifying market developments justified by economic fundamentals. Derivatives are speculators' main instruments because transaction costs are low, leverage is high and they totally escape traditional regulation.

The amount of leverage available to the speculator is an important practical factor, as it can magnify the impact of speculation. But, the increased use of high leverage products can increase the risk of failure of the users as was illustrated in Chapter 3. A sudden loss of liquidity can produce substantial problems for market participants and can increase the probability of big price swings which can adversely affect the ability of the markets to perform their allocation and their pricing functions. Recent examples include the collapse of CMOs in 1994 and of collared-floaters in 1994.

**Inter-market Spillover**

As already discussed in Chapter 6, even without a change in the probability of turbulence for the markets individually, an increase in the spillover of turbulence from one market to another market can imply an increase in systemic risk. Essentially, linkage or spillover can amplify the turmoil in a market by broadening the number of affected market participants. Increased linkage can make it more difficult to contain a problem to one market, as was illustrated by the Mexican crisis discussed in Chapter 3 and the Asian crisis of 1997, thus making it hard for individual governments to design specific actions to maintain the smooth functioning of the markets.

Several developments can be identified which have enhanced spillover risks. One is the increased market interdependence resulting from liberalisation and globalisation of financial markets. Derivatives have made an important contribution to globalisation. Typically, in every currency swap, the counter-parties span more than one country. More generally, derivatives serve to unbundle risk and to reallocate them to different markets so that problems in one necessarily spill over to others. The tightened linkages between markets have systemic implications because a shock or a major default in, say, the OTC derivative markets can spill over into the exchange-traded futures or options markets, which, through arbitraging or rebalancing behaviour, can in turn have an impact on the underlying asset markets. These linkages can transform a single market turbulence into a multi-market turbulence and hence can substantially increase the number of affected market participants. For example, a turmoil in the OTC derivatives markets might actually perturb the primary securities markets.

The presence of inter-market linkages can also make the isolation of the problem in a certain market difficult, if not impossible. The 1994 turbulence in the bond and foreign exchange markets gave a good indication of volatility spillovers from one market to another and that such spillovers are caused or enhanced by the intermarket linkages.

In 1997, the banking system was shaky, with large parts of the books in risky real estate loans, and a large part of the liability side in foreign exchange in several Asian countries (Thailand, Indonesia, Philippines, Malaysia), South Africa's rand only supported by massive outstanding central bank forward operations, Latin America again geared up and the Japanese banking system in reanimation. What would happen if several countries in Asia defaulted simultaneously?

## The Probability of a Banking System Failure

The soundness of the banking system is crucial to the smooth functioning of the financial system, given that the banking system plays a key role in the payment system, and provides liquidity to financial markets. As such, a failure of the banking system could have significant implications on the financial system as a whole. The probability of a banking system failure is determined by the probability of individual bank failure, the impact of individual bank failure on the banking system, and the correlation of bank failures.

It is important to note that the failure of an individual bank or a small number of not very large banks will not cause a banking system failure. An individual bank failure will have a systemic effect only if the bank is very large and plays a key role in the banking system, or if the bank failure can cause spillover effects.

Several factors can contribute to a higher probability of individual bank failure: lack of diversification, difficulties measuring and controlling risk especially in extreme market conditions, insufficient capital reserves, heavy involvement in highly leveraged proprietary trading and higher impact of some risk factors. The speed of intervention by regulators is also of key importance.

In the United States regulators intervene early and may require actions or may even close a bank before it is insolvent. In other countries regulators tend to act *ex post*. A good illustration is provided by the Asian crisis of 1997.

Essentially, these contributing factors can also feed on each other. For example, lack of diversification—an essential cause of the S&L crisis in the United States—and the involvement in speculative trading in volatile markets can lead to the insufficiency of capital reserves. There is an important moral hazard problem in that banks, facing severe competition, might not have the incentive to cover higher risks with more capital. Moreover, the amount of prudential capital reserves, computed by banks on the assumption that the financial system is in sound condition, may not be sufficient when some extreme events occur.

Are general banking crises a thing of the past? Not at all. In OECD countries as recently as 1991–93, Scandinavian governments bailed out their banks at the cost of 8% of GDP in Finland and 5% of GDP in Sweden. This is only the fiscal cost, neglecting the macroeconomic cost of adjusting the economy to these realities. In developing countries banking crises are quite frequent with fiscal costs often in excess of 10% of GDP (50% of GDP in Kuwait 1990–91, 41% of GDP in Chile 1981–83, 18% of GDP in Venezuela 1994–95, 12–15% in Mexico 1995–97). In most cases the national crisis did not contaminate other countries due to a combination of factors: the economy being too small and relatively closed to the outside world, or, in the case of Scandinavia, the government guaranteeing bank liabilities. Mexico's crisis was more complex and spilled over into Argentina whose macroeconomy and banking sector were in comparable frail conditions. In 1995 panicky Argentines withdrew 40% of their deposits, speeding up the banking crisis. The US$38 billion international support provided to Mexico was partly motivated by the fear of spillover effects. Again, the same can be observed in the Asian crisis of 1997.

## 2. DERIVATIVES: THE DYNAMITE FOR FINANCIAL CRISES

Although the industry has rapidly moved up the risk-management learning curve, the explosive growth has increased the risk of operational problems as relatively inexperienced newcomers crowd into the field. In recent years, financial disturbances, therefore, have, on several occasions, turned into full-blown crises that became magnified in derivatives-connected domestic and international markets and spread around the globe with more violence and force than had been imaginable before the 1990s. In fact, whilst a global disaster has not yet occurred, international and national financial crises have broken out with alarming regularity in the last few years and are likely to continue to reappear with regularity in the future. Crises seem to have become part and parcel of the international financial environment.

The key feature of recent market stress situations has been a sudden sharp, often short-lived downward movement in some major asset prices, such as equity values, bond prices or exchange rates. Prominent examples are the worldwide collapse of equity prices in October 1987, the turbulence in European currency markets in 1992 and 1993, the decline in global bond prices and the disaster of mortgage-backed securities in 1994, the collapse in emerging markets in 1995 and 1997. Episodes of precipitous declines in asset prices are frequently preceded by a period in which market prices of the assets concerned surpass levels justified by fundamentals. A sudden revision in the expectations and views of market participants, perhaps due to an unexpected event, then leads to an equally sudden reassessment of current price levels, triggering large and often disorderly movements in prices with considerable overshooting. On occasion, rapid movement in asset prices expose weaknesses in the risk positions of some market participants, leading to losses on a massive scale and occasionally major failures.

The most outstanding examples are the losses of Metallgesellschaft, Barings and Orange County, discussed in Chapter 3. On other occasions, a revision of expectations will produce adjustments in portfolios that force the abandonment of a system of fixed parities, such as during the ERM crisis or in the Asian crisis of 1997. In each of these cases the severity, contagious nature, and the sheer size of the financing flows involved were heavily influenced by the use of derivatives. Derivatives contributed to the boom during the build-up phase preceding the asset price decline and also accentuated the price adjustments during the crisis. This is not to say that derivatives by themselves cause sharp asset price movements, but in times of stress they amplify short run price volatility and price movements. These mechanisms reinforce each other.

There are four specific features of derivatives markets that have made financial crises more virulent and contagious and policies to deal with crises less effective: lack of market transparency; dynamic hedging of options exposure and concentration of options strike prices; the high and erratic liquidity dependence; and the large potential size through leverage of speculative positions.

**Lack of Market Transparency**

One of the most important factors generating instability during periods of financial stress is the lack of "macro-transparency", that is, the lack of knowledge on the part of market participants about the depth of demand and supply at various price levels. Derivative positions, whether OTC or exchange-generated, obscure the underlying structure of financial positions in various markets and make it harder to estimate aggregate positions. Derivative-based buy and sell orders explode onto markets as prices in the cash markets move beyond threshold values, and they thereby push prices further into one direction. The buy/sell orders that can be potentially triggered by portfolio insurance and dynamic hedging are not known to market participants. The effective demand and supply schedules in various markets are obscured, so that market dynamics remain hidden. Stabilising speculation is largely absent until prices have fallen well outside the normal trading range. The lack of transparency of the macro financial environment is, of course, nothing but a reflection of the lack of transparency of the financial activities of the individual global financial institutions highlighted in the previous chapter. Relevant examples (discussed in Chapter 3) are the dynamic hedging during the 1987 equity crash; the impact of the derivative activities by Mexican financial institutions on the dollar/peso market during the peso crisis; the impact of knock-out and other barrier options on yen/dollar exchange rate volatility; the impact of leveraged derivative position taking—misjudged by the major central banks—during the ERM crisis.

### Dynamic Hedging of Options Exposures

Dynamic hedging involves heavier trading in the underlying assets in periods of rapid price movements than during periods of relative stability: sharper price movements translate into larger modifications of the various sensitivity measures of derivatives (the "Greek alphabet" of options) and therefore heavier purchases (if prices rise) or sales (if prices fall). If many market participants rely on dynamic hedging of their derivative exposures, adversely affecting the price of the underlying cash instrument, they could even exhaust cash market liquidity, thereby seriously exacerbating price movements. Traditional stop-loss orders and portfolio insurance programme have the same effect on underlying prices as dynamic hedging. Technical Insight 7.1 explains how it works and how even monetary policy can be affected.

Concentration of options strike prices at market prices perceived as critical barriers by market participants can elicit significant selling pressures when prices approach such levels. The rapid decline of the yen *vis-à-vis* the dollar in February 1995, discussed in Chapter 4, was in large part due to the heavy use of barrier options by Japanese corporations.

### Destabilising Liquidity Dependency

In normal circumstances derivatives contribute to greater liquidity in the markets for the underlying instrument. In times of stress, the opposite may happen. With greater uncertainty, bid–ask spreads widen, some market participants may withdraw altogether, and concerns about credit risk or liquidity of the underlying asset may stifle new transactions. Illiquidity in derivatives markets will disrupt the trading of risk, and therefore risk management, so

**Technical Insight 7.1**  Market destabilisation produced by dynamic hedging

Two concrete examples illustrate the potential problems caused by dynamic hedging.

*Delta hedging*: Delta measures the sensitivity of the value of the call option (the delta of a put is equal to the delta of a call −1) to small changes in the price of the underlying asset. *Delta hedging* means balancing a portfolio so that its delta is zero. As a result, the portfolio value will be insensitive to small changes of the underlying asset value. A delta neutral portfolio behaves like a riskless asset.

Consider, for example, the Japanese holder of a cash position of US\$40 000. If he wishes to delta hedge his position, he will sell a US\$/yen call option on US\$100 000 with a delta of 0.4. He may not find a strike price that delivers a delta of exactly 0.4, but can always get close. Strike prices at the money have a delta of 0.5; as strike prices move out of the money, delta goes to zero and, as strikes go in the money, delta moves to 1.

However, a delta hedge rigorously holds only for an instant because the delta fluctuates with the price changes of the underlying asset, except for options out of the money. Therefore, the seller of options has to hedge dynamically, that is, constantly adjust his position. This leads to selling the underlying asset when its price moves down and buying it when the price moves up. It is by design market-destabilising.

Similar destabilising effects result from other dynamic hedging techniques, such as the creation of synthetic options (i.e., replicating an option with a combination of the underlying asset and treasury bills). In all those cases purchases are required when the price of the underlying asset increases and sales when the price decreases.

*Hedging mortgage-backed securities*: As already shown in Chapter 3, mortgage-backed securities (MBS) represent one of the three largest markets for debt instruments in the United States. They have an uncertain final maturity because of embedded options in the form of early repayment, which are also present in derivative products, such as certain structured notes or amortising rate swaps. The inherent risks cannot be statically (i.e., once and for all) hedged and require continuous adjustment. As with portfolio insurance, such dynamic hedging may produce positive feedback on already declining prices, particularly during periods of financial stress. A study by the Federal Reserve Bank of New York shows that such hedging in early 1994 had amplified the repercussions of monetary policy tightening on long maturities in the US

Treasury market. As such hedging has become a standard feature in US financial markets, the study concludes that short-run dynamics of the US yield curve may have permanently altered.

How do MBS hedging activities affect the Treasury yield curve? When interest rates rise, homeowners prepay their home mortgages more slowly, causing the expected maturity of MBS to increase. (In fact, homeowners enjoy an option to prepay their mortgages with little or no penalty.) Extended maturities (and durations) imply higher risks. Prices of MBS fall, therefore, for two reasons: higher market rates and increased risk. To hedge (partially) against this risk, dealers and portfolio managers take short positions in similar duration Treasury securities. As MBS durations increase, hedgers reshuffle their short positions in favour of longer maturity treasuries. The resulting steepening of the yield curve could reduce prepayment even further and reinforce yield curve steepening.

It is estimated that from October 1993 to April 1994, dynamic hedging of MBS risk resulted in Treasury market sales of over US$300 billion in ten-year Treasury equivalents. This helps to explain the 40 bp flattening of the US Treasury yield curve between ten and 30 years.

*Source:* BIS (1994, Annexes 2 and 5)

that hedging strategies result in involuntary risk exposure. Investors are induced to liquidate positions in cash markets and thereby amplify price movements and transmit the shock across markets. For example, difficulty in hedging exchange rate exposures may induce foreign investors to liquidate their underlying positions in a country's equity or bond markets. Market illiquidity, in general, makes market participants more vulnerable to adverse shocks and may cause liquidity problems if firms cannot close out their in-the-money positions.[1]

Margin and collateral calls on derivative positions increase in times of heightened volatility, and the increased need to finance such calls in a short period of time, frequently intraday, greatly aggravates the impact of a price decline and spreads the decline to other markets. Such calls have to be met, without exception, or the investor risks having his position closed out. As a first line of defence, the investor will draw on standby lines of credit with the money-centre bank—the risk-management institutions. These banks, in turn, will access the interbank market to mobilise intraday or next-day good funds. An increase in the interbank or overnight rate is inevitable, and unless such an increase in the short-term rates is dampened by central bank open-market intervention, funding costs of institutions relying on short-term funding, such as broker/dealers, will increase. In extreme cases, and without central bank intervention, institutions relying on short-term finance may be forced to liquidate part of their asset positions, thereby putting further downward pressure on asset prices. It is not hard to see that this situation could easily get out of hand as the ever-more pressing search for liquidity imparts downward pressure on a whole array of asset prices. Only forceful and speedy central bank intervention will forestall a meltdown, as was the case with the Fed's intervention in the 1987 stock market crash.[2]

In addition, operational difficulties can surface. First, it may be difficult for the banking system to get the good funds to where they are needed.[3] In essence the problem here is that the good funds that are due to the gainers on the derivative contract cannot be recycled fast enough back to the losers, when temporary excess demand for liquidity develops. Similarly, when the money-centre banks make margin calls to cover their exposure to the counter-parties of their OTC derivative contracts they will not be prepared to extend their exposure by granting the investor further short-term lines of credit. Hence the investor will have to find the liquidity somewhere else, most likely through the sale of assets. Furthermore, in the face of possible doubts about the solvency of borrowers with large derivative positions, banks may not be willing to extend further credit, thus forcing liquidation of these positions, further depressing prices.

Second, the spread of trading of derivative contracts outside the currency of denomination has raised questions of how to finance large-scale margin calls during times when the relevant banking system and central bank are closed. For example, the trading of US dollar futures in Singapore or London may precipitate margin calls when the US banking system is closed. Since local banks cannot generate good dollar funds it will not be able to meet the margin call intraday.

This problem is especially acute in foreign exchange markets, easily the market with the largest daily turnover, and counter-parties from all over the world. There are an estimated 150 000 transactions every day, necessitating twice as many currency flows. The New York based Clearing House Interbank Payments System (CHIPS), through which most dollar forex transactions are settled, routes US$600 billion in forex transactions on average each day. Settlement is final when unconditional and irrevocable. Funds that are received and deemed "final" through a central bank settlement system are also called "good" funds. Only central banks can provide settlement finality since their capacity to create money permits to compensate for any failures to deliver funds into the payments system by a participant. In all private bilateral or multilateral settlement systems failures can occur. The failure of Bankhaus Herstatt in 1974 with US$620 million of uncompleted trades is the most famous case. It was shut down after it had received deutschemarks for these trades during German payment hours, but before the New York payments system was open for it to pay over the corresponding dollars.

At the same time as the exchanges start calling for increased margins on the exchange-traded products, the major OTC institutions will also be pressuring their counter-parties to put up collateral or margin money, thereby exerting further pressure on the system.

In short the need to settle losses on derivative positions, intraday or over-night, which is in and by itself a very commendable risk-management require-ment, can create a demand for vast amounts of liquidity. Failure by the banking system to provide such liquidity can lead to a major financial crisis.

**Leveraged Speculative Position-taking**

Given the potential leverage offered by derivatives at low transactions costs, derivatives facilitate the taking of speculative positions. Derivatives have made it easier for the relatively uninformed investor to aggressively establish speculative market positions, for example through institutional retail invest-ment vehicles. Such investors will tend to reinforce a bullish market and they will support the overshooting of asset prices. During a crisis these investors will also be the ones who lose their cool, and they will liquidate their positions into the declining market. The less informed the investor, the more likely he is to undertake imitative trading. This is not to say that the herd effect is limited to novice investors, as institutions also tend to seek safety in numbers. Deriva-tives markets tend to be significantly more liquid than cash markets, and hence derivative markets allow investors to exit or enter into spot market-equivalent positions quickly and cheaply. Hence a precautionary exit from markets becomes cheaper and easier.

The leverage made possible through the use of derivatives can lead to very large losses that affect other markets. For example, the losses of Orange County reported in Chapter 3 were due to leverage and the episode had a major impact on the municipal bond market in the United States.

Potential speculative financial positions have become much larger with the leverage generated through the use of derivatives. The activities of the macro hedge funds are entirely directed at taking derivative-leveraged positions in the world's major markets in order to benefit from market moves. Together, such funds can easily account for positions in excess of half a trillion dollars in global money, capital, exchange, or equity markets. Thus, the potential for market destabilising moves has become much greater, as was illustrated in Chapter 3 with the examples of the ERM and Mexico crises and the 1994 bond market turbulence. Correspondingly, any attempt by central banks to support a desired market outcome has to be backed by much larger resources than ever before.

The leveraging made possible through the use of derivative transactions has also vastly increased the volume of private cross-border gross financial flows.

The information required by central banks to make appropriate crisis management decisions is frequently missing and the reaction time has shortened.

Whilst speculation, in principle, is stabilising, it can, in specific circumstances, destabilise the market. The same is true for hedging. For example, in October 1987 heavy selling in the futures market pushed futures prices to a discount to stocks. Index arbitrageurs responded by buying futures and selling the underlying stock. Thereby downward pressure on stocks prices was created—exactly the feature anticipated by sellers of futures. Having been proved right, selling pressures on futures increased further. A *hedging overhang* developed as portfolio insurers were unable to keep pace with the level of selling dictated by their hedging models and as liquidity (i.e., buyers) disappeared. By the market's opening on 19 October, portfolio insurers had sold less than a third of the US$12 billion stock-equivalent amount of futures to be sold on the basis of their model hedge strategies. This created a hedging overhang of US$8 billion on the next day, and futures went to a discount to stocks as stock trading was stalled and hampered by several factors. Futures sales became an expensive way of delta-hedging and many portfolio insurers either made heavy losses or remained unhedged (see BIS 1994, Compendium of annexes).

A hedging overhang occurs when prices move so fast that risk-management programmes fail to re-establish the hedge in time. Some hedging products may be highly effective in normal two-way markets, but they become ineffective when there is a large price break, turning a hedged into an unhedged position. In addition, the combined effort of market participants to re-establish the hedge frequently adds to market pressure in terms of amplified price declines and vanishing liquidity because, in a market where the price declines, the hedge programme will sell the underlying asset.

## 3. GLOBAL DERIVATIVE FINANCE: THE FUSE FOR CONTAGION

With market and product segmentation largely gone from globally integrated markets so that financial products have become more substitutable and with institutional portfolios becoming more internationalised, financial crises tend to spread more rapidly across domestic and international markets. The growth of derivative finance has contributed to the risk of crisis-contagion in several ways, already touched upon in Chapter 6. Foremost among these are the undefinable and unlocalisable nature of the OTC market, the derivative-induced lack of transparency, the breakdown of hedging and valuation of derivative positions in the face of major breaks in asset prices, the growing concentration of the derivatives industry and the operational risks of the large players.

**Lack of Micro Transparency**

The lack of transparency of the financial activities and risk positions of financial intermediaries has added to the risk of major financial crises. Financial markets function most efficiently when market participants have access to information that facilitates the prompt and accurate pricing of assets, and when market participants dispose of enough information to be confident about their risk assessment of individual firms. Currently, management of the major derivative dealers is becoming increasingly precise in assessing the firm's own risk exposure, but such information is not available to outsiders. In addition, financial intermediaries' risk-management systems and risk control systems are not transparent. Such opaqueness can amplify market disturbances. During episodes of market stress a lack of information about a firm's market and credit risk exposures, and a lack of confidence in its risk-management abilities, can create an environment in which rumours alone can cause a firm's creditors to lower their exposures, thus impairing access to funding at the very time when it is needed most.

The lack of transparency leads to defensive position-taking, precautionary runs, testing of institutions, all of which spreads the disturbance from a single institution to other parts of the financial system that are not directly involved in the crisis. A lack of detailed knowledge of similar institutions will push liability holders into a precautionary reduction of exposure to all institutions that appear similar to the troubled institution. Derivatives make it cheaper and faster for market participants to "run" from suspected institutions, making the system more fragile, and putting a premium on financial disclosure.[4]

This phenomenon of "precautionary running" or "testing the institution" is, of course, nothing new in the market for bank liabilities, but it now also occurs in non-bank markets that are perceived to be subject to liquidity problems, including many of the OTC derivative markets. Through the use of derivatives market participants can run from a market at low cost and with great speed, facilitating a "run from a market" for precautionary reasons. Recent examples of runs are investors' exit from the mortgage-backed securities markets (analysed in Chapter 3), the perpetual floaters market, and the commercial paper market during the Penn Central failure.

Spillovers across markets can be caused by the hedging behaviour of market participants who frequently hedge or build up speculative positions in nearby markets. Although it generates basis risk, such an approach is often the cheapest way to hedge a position in the market where the corresponding derivative instrument is not sufficiently liquid to accommodate large-scale transactions, or where for some reason hedging possibilities do not exist in the first market. As a result of such hedging in nearby markets, price breaks in one market will spread via the hedging positions to these nearby markets.

An inability of investors to assess their exposure due to a lack of legal certainty will contribute to precautionary runs from institutions and markets. Perhaps the best-known cases of temporarily upsetting swap markets were the Hammersmith and Fulham rulings, making swaps agreements by British local government bodies unlawful and void; the CFTC decision that swaps are not futures; and the failure of the Osaka Exchange to separate customer margin accounts from those for proprietary trading.

**Valuation Uncertainty**

Large and rapid price movements will increase uncertainty about the value of derivative positions during times of stress. Pricing of derivatives requires smooth and continuous price movements, as breaks in price movements introduce *valuation uncertainty*. There are significant difficulties in understanding, pricing and managing inherently complex derivative instruments, particularly longer-dated instruments, for example currency options. The statistical and mathematical techniques which underlie pricing and trading strategies are based on the assumption that historical distributions of price changes are good guides to future volatility. Uncertainty about the value of derivative positions may lead to liquidation sales into declining markets, aggravating the price decline, and it may also lead to hedging in parallel markets, thus spreading pressure to these markets.

**Concentration**

The risk-management business is increasingly *concentrated in a handful of global dealers*, as was seen in Chapter 6 and these have large inter-dealer positions. Thus disturbance in one derivatives house are very likely to spill over into the others. Individual institutional crises become industry crises. The perception of these problems may also lead investors to run from all derivative firms when one of the major houses is experiencing problems.

# 4. THE RISK-MANAGEMENT INDUSTRY: IS THE TRIGGER UNDER CONTROL?

**Operational Risk: Payments and Settlements Risks**

The greatly increased transactions volume in a diverse set of derivative instruments and the growth of dynamic hedging of options exposures has significantly increased the risk of payments and settlements problems, particularly when involving cross-border trades. Intraday settlement credit has grown exponentially, largely due to increased trades involving derivatives. For example, derivatives are the fastest growing segment of the global forex markets. In the United States intraday credit extended by the Federal Reserve has grown to exceed US$150 billion on an average day.

Since 1989 the turnover of forex derivatives has more than tripled, compared to a 50% increase of spot market operations. The global foreign exchange market is the largest market with daily transactions on average of US$1200 billion, followed by the market for US government securities with an average daily turnover of US$175 billion (April 1995) and a much lower growth rate.

The foreign exchange market is exposed to settlement risk caused by a participant in this global market. Large settlement sizes pose at least two problems. The first is called Herstatt risk, named after the failure of Bankhaus Herstatt in 1974. Banks are exposed to large amounts of cross-border settlement risk because irrevocable settlement of the separate legs of a foreign exchange transaction may be made at different times. For example, delivery of yen to the Tokyo correspondent bank of a New York bank occurs during Tokyo business hours. The corresponding delivery of dollars by a New York bank to the US correspondent bank of a Japanese counterparty would occur during New York business hours. Since the two national payments systems are never open at the same time, this gives rise to the risk that, after the first counter-party has already delivered one side of the transaction, the other counter-party may go bankrupt and fail to deliver the offsetting currency.

The second problem is a liquidity issue. Failures to pay could arise from operational or systems problems, as well as a counter-party bankruptcy. In most cases, operational failures can be resolved within a 24- to 48-hour period and overnight funding can be obtained to cover the failed delivery. It is not uncommon, however, to have more than US$2 billion outstanding between banks overnight. A large operational failure could surpass the ability of even some of the best-capitalised institutions to access money markets, especially when notice of the failure is received during off-hours in the institution's domestic market or when the undelivered currency is not one in which the exposed institution customarily borrows. This is an especially salient issue in emerging markets where transaction sizes are growing, but the physical infrastructure for payment and settlement systems may not yet be adequate to accommodate transactions in large numbers or sizes.

Either of these problems can lead to a situation in which a delivery failure causes a systemic problem. The most commonly articulated scenario is a "domino effect", in which the failure of one large bank causes a second bank to fail, which causes a third, and so on. Another situation might arise in which, independently, a small number of institutions fail to deliver, causing other institutions to fail or to encounter liquidity problems.[5]

Additional risks inherent in the risk-management industry—the infant industry risks, the concentration risk and the growing complexity of products— were already discussed in Chapter 6.

# 5. CONCLUSION

The potential for debilitating disturbances that may not be containable to the institution or market of initial impact and, indeed, may spread like bush-fire across tightly linked global markets, makes clear that the restructuring of financial policy in response to the evolution of the financial environment has become the major public policy challenge as this century comes to a close. In the global environment, the epoch of discretionary national monetary policy is over, and the epoch of financial policy has arrived. Achieving financial stability in this new environment will remain the major policy challenge well into the next century.

This chapter proposes a framework for assessing systemic risk. It starts with the likelihood of individual banking failure, to which the leverage of derivatives and connected problems, such as risk control, contribute significantly. As long as the problems, or even bankruptcy, of an individual institution do not cause problems for other institutions, there is no systemic problem. However, with high exposures in OTC derivatives markets such a scenario is unlikely. Derivatives, indeed, contribute to connecting various market segments and their institutions.

During recent years financial crises of concern to the international community have become increasingly frequent. Individual institutions, or even countries, have suffered colossal losses. But, in most cases, emergency interventions, such as international support to Mexico in 1994 or to Thailand, Indonesia and Korea in 1997, have been able to contain the impact of the crisis. This should not be taken as proof that everything is under control. A worldwide crash of the financial system is a remote possibility, but one that should be avoided nevertheless. This is the sense of Pascal's wager, not to accept the infinitely small probability of an infinitely large loss.

This chapter takes the view that derivatives are dynamite for financial crises and the fuse-wire for international transmission at the same time. Unfortunately, the ignition trigger does not seem to be under control.

Chapter 8 explains why the present regulatory ammunition is insufficient to guarantee systemic stability. Chapter 9 then proposes a novel regulatory framework for the problems identified in this chapter.

# ENDNOTES

1 Illiquidity in any particular market may be overcome by using highly correlated other market segments. But often illiquidity spreads across connected markets precisely because investors use arbitrage opportunities.

2 During the Barings crisis, failure of Japanese firms to separate customer from proprietary margin money at the Osaka futures exchange led some players to withhold margin money due, thus producing a liquidity crisis which was resolved only through the forceful intervention of the US CFTC.

3 Chapter 3 gave the details of the famous incident of intra-day margin calls from the Chicago futures exchanges on 19 and 20 October 1987, deliverable to the clearing banks in Chicago, which ran into difficulties because problems arose in the transfer from New York to Chicago.

4 Before the crash of the Tokyo stock market investors had closed their eyes to the lack of transparency of accounts presented by Japanese corporations. Since the crash investors factor into their evaluation of Japanese stocks the uncertainty about information provided.

5 Using actual gross settlement numbers from a specific day in 1994 when the yen appreciated against the dollar by 5%, MULTINET, a proposed multilateral netting facility, was able to show that the failure of the participant with the largest position within their system could have caused the failure of a number of other participants. This example, constructed with a simulation comprising only a few institutions, shows how a large settlement failure can be potentially disruptive to the smooth functioning of the international financial system.

# 8

# Challenges for the Established Financial Order

---

## *The Butterflies of Finance*

Life in the Amazon is at times generous and heavenly, but gruesome at other times. It is a delicate equilibrium conditioned by rainfall and heat and Nature's response. In some areas there has been no rain for about a hundred years, followed by a hundred years of continuous deluges. Entire species disappeared during the long cycles of drought alternating with deluvial rains, whilst others adapted.

Many miles away from Manaus there is an area—largely unknown to the outside world as it is uninhabited by the human race and therefore ignored in Claude Levi-Strauss' *Tropics*—split into two parts by a huge ravine. In that area the natural cycle had recently changed dramatically. Periods of relentless heat and devastating rains alternated more rapidly, making it even more difficult for both plants and animals to adapt. None of the inhabitants in the area understood why Nature had become less stable (or more "volatile" as fashion-prone parrots preferred to squawk) or how to cope with the additional risks and threats to life.

The left bank of the ravine was especially hard hit. During the drought/deluge cycle, a couple of years without rain had had catastrophic effects on the animal population. Entire valleys were filled with flattened animal corpses, offering a horrible sight: their skins resembling weather-worn, ragged cotton sheets, tongues hanging out of distorted faces and skinny claws clutching useless, burnt-out plants.

On the other side of the ravine conditions were generally—but not always—better. The dry years had less effect there, thanks to the affluents of certain rivers bringing water from far away. Heat and ground water combined to maintain lush vegetation and plenty of food for all. The jungle population made the most of this plenitude and engaged in constant merrymaking with the result that the population expanded rapidly. There were more and more of every sort of species and whilst the heads of certain fish began to take the form of an ape's, the backs of some apes started to resemble tails of certain fish. Similar strange shapes and resemblances developed among the other merry animals.

There were, however, signs of a more general decline in discipline and moral standards. Overcrowding led to territorial disputes and fighting. Many locals fell prey to the omnipresent vicious cobras; black panthers grew dangerously in numbers and, worryingly, became fatter and fatter, whereas the otherwise wily and wise macacos—generally accepted as the arbiters in local disputes and leaders in emergency situations—started to fight among themselves. Only the pitiless rain years calmed the animal spirits, but also washed away large parts of the crops, plants and population into the ravine.

The starving animals of the left bank registered with envy the reports of the travelling parrots about the opulent times on the right bank and wagged their heads disapprovingly about the ensuing fights and killings.

Paulo V, the tallest, wisest and most respected macaco on the left bank, had for a long time scratched his virtually bald head, reflecting on the sad state of affairs brought about by Nature's incomprehensibly increased volatility.* If only a way could be found to cross the ravine! This would bring greater wealth to everybody: during times of famine on the left bank, animals would be able to migrate to the right bank or bring back juicy fruits to ease local conditions. In exchange, during times of hardship on the right bank, animals in search of greater safety and peace could migrate to the left bank and be happy there.

One burning hot day, resting in his hammock and sucking a banana wrapped in large maté leaves, Paulo V had an inspiration. A new species had developed since climatic volatility had increased: an amazingly huge butterfly (the "mega lepidoptero"), which inspired the other animals with awe and apprehension. Its wings spread so wide that the sun became invisible to the animals on the ground and when several of these butterflies glided overhead in close formation the whole left bank was cooled by their shade. Paulo V again thought over something his favourite female companion had whispered in his ear during yesterday's prolonged, tender scratching session. She had observed the difficulties these big clumsy things experienced in sucking from the flower buds which were crushed under the giant butterflies' landing.

Paulo V saw a possible deal for the benefit of everybody. What if the macacos with the help of others—possibly the industrious ants—were to collect the flower seeds, store them in a safe place and offer them to the butterflies in exchange for shade from the sun during the dry season? Even better, after the rain had returned and had enlivened the worn-out soil, but before the continuous rainfall turned into a deluge, the butterflies could form a giant umbrella by spanning their wings across the sky and protect the land below. And would such a deal not help in multiplying the number of giant butterflies so that the whole of the left bank could be protected day and night by alternating time shifts? More butterflies would need more food and hence improve the macacos' negotiation potential and their terms of trade.

Paulo V encountered stubborn resistance in the council of elders. His proposal appeared to most of them to be far-fetched and Paulo's enthusiasm ill-placed. But Paulo knew the weaknesses of his kin and, in particular, their abhorrence of any

---

* This anthropomorphism is for the sake of clarity and ease of understanding.

physical effort. Only when the ants' delegates made formal promises to take care of the work, and after recalling the threats of famine, did the council consent to a trial.

It turned out to be a great success. Soon every adult male macaco was negotiating privately with the butterflies, on terms not known to others, to protect his own plot of land or to journey to the right bank and back, laden with delicious exotic fruits, sweet-looking female macacos with a fairer complexion, and other precious goods.

The whole land prospered as never before. The butterflies prospered as well, swelling their numbers and growing in size with each generation. Plants, which had been forever fighting desperately for survival, strengthened under the protective butterfly umbrella and gave forth abundantly delicious, sweet, juicy fruits, both during the dry and the rainy years.

All the animals were deeply grateful to the wily and enterprising macacos—the only animals able to negotiate with the butterflies—and brought them beautiful presents and offered their services. The most active dealers in the shade and trade business were among the young macacos—not the brightest, but not the most stupid either. Some of the most aggressive and successful ones were seen in the heat of the night riding on fierce black panthers, in their arms beautiful young female macacos, stressing their natural beauty with banana skins wrapped around their waists, their heads crowned with pineapples and small, beautiful oranges dangling from their ears.

Over time, however, some problems emerged. One windy day, a butterfly was sent off to the right bank from the last, distant agglomeration in the south-east of the left bank by a certain Filho do Li, a young, ambitious and widely admired macaco. The butterfly, too heavily loaded with precious fruit, was sent off to the south, as Filho do Li expected the wind to blow northwards. But his expectation turned out to be wrong, as an earthquake turned the winds and the strong north wind pushed the butterfly far off course to finally perish in the ravine. Filho do Li now doubled his bet to offset his loss and sent off several butterflies, again southward. Their wings became entangled in the stormy currents over the ravine and they crashed as well. However, their last desperate flutterings for survival accelerated the storm into a violent tornado, uprooting the trees on the right bank, hurling entire villages into the ravine and devastating large parts of what had been a paradise before.

The surviving butterflies demanded compensation for the death of their relatives from Filho do Li's clan. The Li clan lost every grain in its possession. Those who had entrusted goods to Filho do Li for transportation also demanded compensation, but most remained empty-handed as the Li clan was bankrupt. The surviving animals on the right bank also presented claims for compensation as they blamed the stupidity of Filho do Li (who, in the meantime, had been placed behind bamboo bars) and the butterfly activity in general for their sufferings. A big dispute developed between the animals of the two banks; claims were made on one day and doubled the next; acceptance of responsibility was totally rejected at first and some compromise offered next. But who should pay? All the left bank animals? After all it was the macacos' idea. All the macacos? Surely not. It was only too visible that the young macaco traders had benefited outrageously all along. Unfortunately, they had spent their riches as quickly as they had got them.

Even worse, an old macaco saying is that bad events seldom travel alone and, indeed, whilst the dispute raged and no settlement was in sight, the sky opened up and the long awaited rains, which were expected to last only a few days, followed the storms. But, to the disbelief of the onlookers, the butterfly squadrons still covered the sky as no macaco was ready to take the responsibility and order retreat. Not a single drop of rain reached the ground, so that the delicately elaborated butterfly strategy failed miserably. (Remember that the sky cover was to be lifted for temporary rainfalls to allow the soil to soak up sufficient water and the umbrella was to be reopened for protection against never-ending diluvial rains or the parasol extended for the alternative of scorching heat.)

Many animals, mostly the older ones who had grown up in the old times when butterflies were tiny and unimportant, had been openly critical of the butterfly strategy for a long time. Although they readily admitted the advantages, they always felt uncomfortable and nagging doubts plagued them. Now they raised their voices a pitch higher and some went as far as to request replacement of Paulo V as their leader. Some urged immediate action to eliminate or lock up the butterflies. The risk of a hysterical butterfly hunt grew by the day. Other apes pleaded for greater selection of admissible butterfly traders and establishment of approved butterfly types, vigilantly controlled and supervised by a group of selected, experienced macacos.

Paulo V carefully spat out a used maté-wrapped banana and nervously selected another to soothe the strain and distress. He knew the first step was to consult with Losco, the wise ape from the right bank, and exchange information with him before preparing a plan of action. He already had some fuzzy ideas about how to proceed in order to preserve the advantages of the butterfly strategy and avoid catastrophes in the future.** For that he needed an experienced second opinion.

Here is what he came up with: instead of allowing all macacos to deal on their own terms directly with the butterflies, he wanted to centralise deals for approval by a board of wealthy and experienced kinsmen who had to guarantee the deals with their own flower seed supplies and who had the right to check each macaco's resources and request safety deposits before allowing them to trade. He expected the board to establish proper rules of behaviour and to weed out uncommon deals or deals creating danger for the community in the interest of their own respectability and survival of their wealth. He saw a good chance of winning Losco for his plan and hoped, thereby, to save the butterfly strategy and stop the cacophony of the short-sighted and belligerent macacos, demanding a terminal butterfly hunt from the top of their trees.

———•———

** Although sly, old Paulo V made everybody believe that the rescue plan was his idea, the truth is, as always, more complex. Luis-Paulo, one of his mischievous grandsons who had sought his fortune in Manaus City, had one night infiltrated the American Express office and carpetbagged some "souvenirs". Among them was a stack of papers, one hundred copies of an essay written by two economists, unknown to even the best connected macacos, with the grandiose title "The Wild Beast of Derivatives: To Be Chained Up, Fenced In or Tamed?". Paulo V alone among his macaco colleagues, took the time to listen to a translation provided by a learned parrot.

"In the 1980s, the only banks
to fail will be those involving
fraud or gross negligence."

*Samuelson 1980, p. 282*

A s many institutions, which thought they were hedged or had a well-managed risk exposure, found out, hedges may evaporate in situtations of severe market disruptions. Financial markets are closer to the Amazonian jungle than we would like to think. Is there nothing to be done?

The growth of the financial risk-management industry is profoundly challenging financial policy—the supervision and regulation of financial institutions and markets. The growing use of derivatives is lessening the restraint on the global risk-management institutions exercised by the existing regulatory and supervisory structure, and it has shifted the balance of power in favour of these institutions and away from regulators and the rest of the financial sector. This development has supported the expansion of the OTC derivatives markets discussed in Chapter 6, which in turn has had the effect of increasing the severity and virulence of financial disturbances around the globe (Chapter 7), of undermining market integrity and of making the job of effective supervision of financial institutions and markets much more difficult.

Section 1 of this chapter recalls the basic rationale of the classical framework for financial policy, which gave Paul Samuelson the confidence expressed in the quote above. Section 2 then acknowledges that this framework is totally inappropriate for modern global financial markets extensively using OTC derivatives. Section 3 notes the consequences of lost supervisory effectiveness, thereby establishing the need for a fundamental revision of the financial policy approaches. Section 4 discusses accounting standards and disclosure requirements as the basis for greater supervisory effectiveness. Section 5 evaluates the Basle capital standards elaborated with the aim of reducing the probability of individual bank failures. Section 6 reviews other current proposals for reducing systemic risk.

A pure market-based financial system, without any supervisory involvements is a very tempting and attractive notion, but too romantic for real world solutions. What is difficult to achieve, however, is the delicate balance between unhampered market dynamism and supervisory effectiveness in preventing systemic crises and promoting market efficiency. Despite all the recent progress achieved in improving supervisory standards, this balance is still not within reach.

# 1. THE CLASSICAL PARADIGM OF FINANCIAL POLICY

The rationale for the establishment of many of today's major central banks was to ensure an elastic supply of currency to avoid the recurrent liquidity crises caused by bank panics. The responsibility for financial stability is explicitly incorporated in the G10 central bank statutes. The experience of banking panics in the 1930s, particularly in the United States, served to strengthen the view that central banks should be the lender of last resort whose purpose it was to prevent bank panics.

By the mid-1970s Bagehot's dogma, that central banks should lend generously into the market to solvent institutions (perhaps at a penalty rate) during periods when bank depositors run for cash, had been extended to include support for all failing institutions—even insolvent ones—as long as their failure were thought to infect other institutions, i.e., the central bank extended its support to all those institutions that were viewed as too large to fail. Central banks in most of the major industrial countries stood ready to underpin key financial institutions in their jurisdictions and they also stood ready to supply liquidity in the traditional sense (during the 1987 stock market crash the Federal Reserve temporarily increased the money supply by one-third during a 48-hour period). By the beginning of the 1980s, the notion of a more finely woven financial safety net—one that now included an explicit recognition that some institutions are too large to fail, in the sense that their failure was judged to put the entire banking system at risk—had taken root.

This development was most readily apparent in the United States, where it was publicly acknowledged by central bank officials that deposit liabilities (including those due to non-resident creditors) of financial institutions would be guaranteed even if such liabilities were not formally covered by the existing insurance scheme. In other words, whether the inability of a bank to meet its payments obligations was due to temporary illiquidity or insolvency, important institutions threatened with failure could expect direct financial support.[1] In fact, if the institution is sufficiently important, it does not even have to be a bank: witness the central role of the Federal Reserve Bank of New York in the orderly demise of Drexell Burnham Lambert—a brokerage firm.

Similar policies emerged in other industrialised countries. Recent examples include the banking crises in Japan and in Scandinavian countries; Johnson Matthey Bankers (UK), Credit Lyonnais (France), Banco di Napoli (Italy), to name only a few. In other words, central banks no longer just supply liquidity to the money markets during periods of liquidity crises, but they put their capital—or that of the Treasuries—at risk by lending directly to failing individual institutions, preferable against collateral, but, if necessary, also without. Furthermore, central banks assume responsibility for preventing payments system illiquidities. This expanded role of the modern central bank has over the past two decades become a part of the institutional landscape, and by now has become a political imperative in most G10 countries.

As a *quid pro quo* central banks acquired the power to regulate and supervise the activity of banks in order to limit the risk in the banking system that they were underwriting. In some countries these powers were legally anchored, in others they were acquired through moral persuasion or through the leverage that privileged access to their borrowing windows gave to central banks. As extensively discussed in Chapter 2, US banking became one of the most regulated, controlled, and "guided" industries.

The United States was not unique in this regard. In other countries the set of banking activities remained likewise restricted. Few countries, other than the United States, had liquid capital markets and so the securities activities of banks in these countries also remained limited. In some countries, e.g., France, sectoral credit allocation schemes ensured that major lending decisions themselves remained under the control of the state. The fraction of banking systems outside the United States and the United Kingdom that was state-owned was large and in many countries, until recently, even predominant (Germany, Italy, Spain, Latin America). Of course, that meant that the public sector had completely assumed the guaranty of bank liabilities, and also controlled the asset side. Although some countries (e.g., Germany) did not have an extensive set of restrictions on the activities of banks, in the absence of competition "conventions of prudent banking" proved just as restrictive. In many instances, capital account restrictions prevented banks from participating fully in international markets.[2]

*Ratio-based capital requirements* were the most important and the most effective tools for controlling risk in the balance sheet of financial institutions. Although disintermediation into the direct debt markets was a way to avoid the cost of capital requirements, only the best credits had the opportunity to by-pass the banking system. By and large, until the 1980s there were only limited substitutes for bank credit. Without the use of derivatives the possibility of reducing the impact of capital requirements through off-balance sheet transactions remained limited.

Similarly, *reserve requirements* on certain classes of deposit liabilities served as an effective check on the size of the banking system. The lack of well-developed overnight repo markets in government securities meant that banks could not turn their reservable deposit liabilities into non-reservable repo obligations to achieve equality between the level of required reserves and desired reserves. Hence minimum reserve requirements were binding and limited the expansion of the banking sector. Furthermore, as part of the *quid pro quo*, central banks in many of the major industrial countries also taxed banks by imposing an unremunerated reserve requirement.

Regulations were enforced through *compliance-based supervision,* i.e., bank examiners or external auditors made sure that the financial activities of the bank, as recorded in the balance sheet and profit-and-loss statement, were in accordance with the regulations promulgated by the central banks, and they were largely successful. Although in some countries there was a gradual process of disintermediation from the banking system, this did not lessen the effectiveness of bank regulation. There was little off-balance sheet business and foreign exchange trading was the only significant OTC activity. All in all, the accounting standards and financial disclosure rules were sufficient to produce a reliable picture of the banking firm. Balance sheets were slow to change: what you saw was what you got. Technological limitations in the field of information and communication limited the ability of banks to innovate to escape regulatory restrictions. The fact that during this period there were some major bank crises (caused in the United States by the less-developed countries' debt crisis in the early 1980s and the regional real estate busts in the mid and late 1980s) has to do with a misreading of broad trends by financial institutions and regulators alike (both thought that sovereign countries do not go broke and that real estate assets were undergoing a permanent revaluation).

Hence, the post-1930s paradigm of financial policy had evolved into *a fairly stable balance of countervailing forces between regulators and banks*; a regulatory equilibrium in which the cost of the safety net was at least partially internalised by the banking sector. The safety net was sufficiently well-knit to prevent systemic financial crises, central banks had learnt the technique of injecting liquidity into threatened institutions, if and when necessary, while restrictions on the activities of banks and the compliance-based, institution-by-institution supervision and inspection went a long way toward keeping the cost of safety in line with the benefits flowing from the stability of the financial system. This happy state of affairs was not to survive the derivatives-driven financial revolution of the 1980s and the 1990s.

## 2. PARADISE LOST

The balance between regulators and banks was upset by two developments. First, a more active day-to-day liquidity support (driven to some extent by monetary policy considerations) in the 1980s created a more hospitable environment for the rapid expansion of derivative markets and institutions. Second, the existing regulatory methods and compliance-based supervision were severely compromised in the late 1980s by the very nature of the derivative industry: its ability to engineer non-regulated products, its lack of transparency, the speed and size of derivative transactions, the lack of international harmonisation. In other words, financial authorities—particularly in the United States—inadvertently tended to support the growth of the finance industry, while at the same time their ability to control risk in this industry was waning. Thus the widespread use of derivative transactions, broadly defined, by global financial intermediaries and investment institutions (institutional investors, hedge funds) inexorably has been altering the balance between regulators and financial institutions in favour of the latter.

## The Need to Manage Day-to-day Liquidity in Money Markets

The growth of liquid money, derivative and capital markets drew central banks deeply into the task of managing day-to-day liquidity in the financial system through active intervention in the money markets, rather than confining such intervention to extreme crisis situations. Involvement in the day-to-day management of money-market liquidity has been a key structural change in the support provided by central banks to financial markets. The risk-management business proved to be liquidity-hungry and only central banks can credibly backstop liquidity. The growth of organised exchanges requires that the banking system be able to marshal liquidity to customers to meet frequently massive intraday margin calls. Such margin calls put stress on the interbank market and force increases in the overnight money rates.

Similarly, temporarily illiquid OTC positions need to be financed. Without intraday management of liquidity, overnight money rates would be significantly more volatile. The involvement of central banks in the smoothing of overnight rates grew out of a desire to give a clear monetary policy signal. For example, it was thought for a long time that a sudden increase in the overnight rate could be interpreted as a tightening of monetary policy, but now the signal extraction problem has become much harder. Although this development advanced furthest in the United States—including the stabilisation of the Fed Funds rate—it also took hold in the other leading industrial countries.

By stabilising the Fed funds rate the central bank has had a profound impact on the financial system. Many of the important players—broker/dealers, banks—can now be more thinly capitalised since they do not have to absorb the losses that would come with large swings in the overnight interest rates. Hence it became cheaper to support a large derivatives book. This policy to backstop liquidity has provided very fertile ground for the growth of liquidity-hungry risk-management finance. Indeed, as argued in Chapter 2, much of the extraordinary development of international risk-management finance is due to the generous support of the Federal Reserve in managing liquidity in the money markets.

Simultaneously, the growth of derivative finance has greatly increased the transactions volume in financial markets (both of the underlying securities and of derivatives themselves) and with it the payments volume. As a result, intraday payments-related credit has grown exponentially. Any disruption to the payments flow, originating with a failing institution or an operational disturbance, will cascade across the system, and hence central banks always stand ready to provide payments finality in net-settlement payments systems. *Central banks took the liquidity risk out of derivative finance and thereby provided a significant subsidy to the risk-management industry.*

The importance of risk-management finance in financial markets has become such that financial authorities, even more than before, do not dare to let a global banking institution fail for fear that such a failure could precipitate other failures and perhaps bring about a general financial crisis. The concentration of derivative activities (as shown in Chapter 6) and the role of the lending institutions in the wholesale payments system and in the interbank markets are of such importance that a failure could produce a chain reaction (as explained in Chapter 7). These institutions (a dozen US banks plus leading banks in the G10 countries) are the foundation on which the rest of the financial system rests. Hence the degrees of freedom the central banks have in their decision to refuse liquidity support to money and derivative markets, and, if need be, directly to global banking institutions, are quite limited. Again, such potential support has become an important element in the liquidity risk calculus.

**Derivatives as the Nemesis of Compliance-based Supervision**

Derivative products allow financial institutions to engineer any regulated position into a less regulated one or to transfer the claim/obligation into a foreign jurisdiction. This has considerably blunted the regulating sword and by itself questions traditional regulatory means. Identical activities carried out by a bank or a non-bank dealer are regulated differently and to some extent not at all. All together derivatives transform the meaning of a balance sheet and, although banks' balance sheets have never been very transparent, they have become even less so. Traditionally, a bank's loan book evolved slowly so that periodic controls were sufficient. A derivatives book can dramatically gain or lose value in seconds. No periodic inspection will do. This pessimistic picture becomes still bleaker, as the derivatives market is global whereas supervisory jurisdiction is national and international co-operation is still in its infancy. I look at these arguments one by one.

*(a) The breakdown of financial regulation based on institutions and balance sheets*

Financial institutions have during the last ten years perfected their ability to shift products and activities outside the jurisdiction of the regulator. Derivatives have made it possible to create synthetic financial instruments with the same properties as those that are regulated. For example, in order to acquire a desired interest rate exposure, a bank traditionally had to raise short deposits and make long loans—subjecting itself to reserve requirements and capital charges. The bank can now obtain the same exposure with an interest rate swap, avoiding reserve and capital requirements. Indeed, it now needs to raise reservable deposit money only to finance straight on-balance sheet credit risk positions.

Through the use of *various types of swaps* the financial institution can significantly alter its risk positions without changing its on-balance sheet positions. For example, a bank may be a supreme performer in the corporate debt market because of its ability to evaluate corporate credit risk. Assume that it earns on average 100 basis points above the corporate bond index and that it enters into a swap contract that requires paying the total rate of return on the corporate bond index in return for receiving the total return on the S&P 500 index (by arbitrage the swap price should be zero). It could now pay a customer who would like to invest in equity up to 100 basis points above the S&P 500 index at no added risk. Thus its expertise in the corporate bond market allows the bank also to sell itself as a superior performer in any other market, in this case the equity markets, by virtue of the swap markets. In this sense, firms with specialised skills can nevertheless market a broad range of products. Since a fixed income manager can convert himself into an equity manager, does it still make sense to classify financial institutions according to their specialisation?[3]

Another illustrative example: a UK investment company buys a 20% stake in a manufacturing company in India. This would be classified as foreign direct investment in the balance of payments of the United Kingdom and of India. Assume now that the UK company swaps the return on the equity investment against Libor plus 250 basis points with a financial institution based in India that is not allowed to hold an outright equity position. Hence the balance-of-payment data has become meaningless, since there has not been an increase in direct foreign investment.[4]

Other examples of transforming on-balance sheet positions into different risk positions involve the conversion of debt into equity and vice versa. For example, if holders of equity sell forward the return on the equity through a swap transaction, then surely they have turned the equity position into a debt position.[5]

These examples illustrate that current accounting standards are based on on-balance sheet *value allocations* and do not look at *risk allocations*. Exposure risk accounting will need to be adopted if there is to be effective external financial accounting and regulation. Some firms are already quite advanced in developing such risk accounting systems as part of their managerial accounting systems, based on their internal risk-management system.[6]

From these examples, one can formulate the following fundamental proposition:

"risk-weighted capital requirements placed on financial institutions cannot be binding for long, because financial institutions can use an assortment of derivative transactions to establish a risk profile such that the amount of capital it is forced to hold will, in fact, be the equilibrium amount of capital it desires to hold. Derivatives allow financial institutions to change the shape of financial instruments in such a way as to circumvent financial regulations in a fully legal way."

Furthermore, global financial institutions are now able to locate financial transactions and positions outside geographic regulatory borders.[7] For example, the foreign exchange derivative and spot market is a global electronic market where the transactions can be booked in any number of locations. Financial institutions have a long history of avoiding financial and fiscal requirements, as argued in Chapter 1. But now they also have the perfect set of tools to do so.

Several large securities firms and insurance companies have created affiliates dealing in derivatives. In the United States these affiliates are subject to Securities and Exchange Commission (SEC) or state reporting requirements, but are not subject to federally imposed capital standards or on-site inspection by federal regulators, unlike bank derivative dealers. The unregulated (or nonbank) dealers account for about 30% of total US outstanding positions of OTC derivatives dealers (General Accounting Office 1994). Thus a significant proportion of OTC derivative activities are escaping the usual regulatory supervision because institutions, rather than functions (activities) are regulated[8]

## (b) The opaqueness of banking institutions

The information content of the financial data that is routinely available to supervisors and to the public at large is considerably more limited now than in the past. The widespread use of derivatives has virtually eliminated any meaningful information from the currently available financial data and it has made the financial system far less transparent than it used to be when institutions were primarily in the on-balance sheet business. In particular, the concentration of risk-management/derivative activity in the global money centre banks has made banks—who, traditionally, have not been subject to strict disclosure and mark-to-market requirements—even more opaque.

An immediate consequence of the lack of transparency regarding the activities and market positions of financial institutions is that financial markets themselves have become more opaque. Aggregate statistics on exposures and market activities of global financial institutions are generally lacking. Hence market participants have greater difficulty in assessing the depth of the market at various price levels, i.e., the demand and supply schedules are much more difficult to estimate, and the assessment of the market's liquidity characteristics has also been made more difficult. The impact on prices of bunching of certain buy and sell orders which trigger features embedded in some derivatives (e.g., forex knock-out options) cannot be off-set by speculators since such information is not readily available.

In simplest terms, current financial accounting and disclosure practices in global markets are still geared towards measuring on-balance sheet exposure of financial firms. Hence the aggregate risk positions of financial firms with an extensive derivative book are not readily available to outside observers and, unless the firm has a sophisticated risk-management system, its aggregated risk positions may not even be available to its management on a timely basis. In any event, disclosure of certain derivative positions alone does not help in evaluating the risk of the institution. To arrive at a complete description of the firms' overall risk positions the off-balance sheet derivative positions and on-balance sheet cash-market positions have to be integrated.[9]

The assessment of the *credit risk of the firm's derivative book* is made difficult because there is no standardised way to measure such exposure. Even if firms disclose their *current credit risk exposure* to counter-parties, i.e., the cost of replacing the cash flow of contracts with positive mark-to-market value (replacement cost), few firms provide analyses (or the data to facilitate such analyses) of *potential credit risk exposures*, i.e., exposures that may be realised over the life time of the contract as a result of a movement in the price underlying the contract. The current credit exposure—the replacement value—tends to look modest given the size of the underlying notional amounts, usually less than 5% when fully netted, but it is the potential exposure that is relevant for assessing the firms' risk. Consider, for example, a 15-year dollar/DM currency swap. At initiation credit risk is zero since the value of the swap is zero. But the potential credit risk is enormous: the mid-1980s was a period during which the dollar reached a low of 40% of its high against the DM. Two specific features of the swap market are, first, that firms do not make available the breakdown of current risk exposures according to the creditworthiness of their counter-parties; and, second, that it is difficult for market participants to ascertain the rate of non-performing derivative contracts and the level of provisions for such contracts. By contrast a non-performing item in the loan book generally has to be provisioned according to a well-defined set of rules related to the extent of arrears, and the level of existing loan loss provisions should be a good reflection of the expected losses on the loan book—at least in the short run.

The *market risk of derivative portfolios*—the impact of changes in underlying prices on the value of the portfolio—is also inadequately disclosed. Although the more sophisticated institutions are capable, and some do, provide information on market risk in the form of value-at-risk (VAR) calculations (see Chapter 4), such information does not allow an assessment of market risk by major risk categories—interest rates, foreign exchange rates, equity and commodity prices—for the institution as a whole. Value-at-risk models are themselves not easy to assess because they rely on correlations estimated on historical data. But correlations among market variables are unstable in times of market stress, so that evaluation of VAR models would require an understanding of how correlations affect VAR estimates.

The most difficult risk to estimate with any precision is *market liquidity risk*, the risk that a position cannot be eliminated quickly either by liquidating the position or by establishing an offsetting position. The reason for this shortcoming is that a good assessment of liquidity risk requires information regarding the aggregate size and structure of markets that is not easily available (price elasticities for transactions of different sizes, trading volumes in connected markets, market concentration). What would be most needed are indicators of liquidity in times of financial stress, but this information is difficult to extract from past data as the basic infrastructure changes from crisis to crisis. Market liquidity is likely to be less resilient to shocks in markets where the market-making function is highly concentrated. Credit exposures among dealers are also high when market-making is concentrated. Contagion risk is therefore increased and the market's ability to absorb large price shocks impaired. Market participants know as much about liquidity risk as about earthquakes: they exist, will happen and are bad. But they cannot forecast when, where and how bad.

*(c) Speed and size of financial transactions*

The speed with which on- and off-balance sheet risk positions can be changed by financial institutions makes it impossible for bank supervisors to follow in continuous real time the financial picture of the bank. In addition, the periodicity of even the most ambitious supervisory regime, compared to the speed with which positions are changed, is too long to obtain an effective picture of the financial activities of banks. The problem is all the more acute since the size of positions that can be taken has increased radically with the ability of market participants to use the leverage available through derivatives. Thus, an institution that intended to compensate a deterioration of profits with a double-or-nothing gamble, can place a very large bet on short notice, without being hampered by the relevant supervisor.

A bank balance sheet in the 1970s was not going to change much from one bank examination until the next one six months later and the product line of a bank was not going to change either. Indeed, institutions did not change much. A bank, was a bank, was a bank. To run a bank into the ground took time and a good examiner would have caught a fatally mismanaged balance sheet. (This is not to say that in the aggregate the examiners got it right. Undue concentration of assets, such as in real estate or lending to developing countries was not generally viewed as objectionable.) Today, if the management of a bank is inclined to place a highly leveraged bet with the banks' capital three times before lunch it can do so without revealing its activities to the supervisors, that is, the rules of the game have changed. Thus on-site inspection has lost its usefulness, as could be seen clearly in the examples of Chapter 3.

The logical conclusion is that only on-line position information on the banks market activity is useful for the supervisory purposes. However, this approach would require the central bank to sort through the wealth of on-line information, requiring a massive infusion of technology and manpower. Given that a regulatory approach based on quantitative restrictions on the risk positions of banks is likely to be matched by the ability of banks to circumvent such restrictions through financial engineering and the shifting of activities to unregulated products and locations, one is left with the possibility of more subjective interpretation of the activity of banks. In this case the feeding and analysis of on-line information on the risk positions of a bank still leave open a question: what should a central bank do with such information? In the absence of clear quantitative rules (these can always be circumvented), would supervisors pass subjective judgements about what types of risk positions held by different reporting institutions are acceptable, and which are not acceptable? It is doubtful that any central bank would want to find itself in such a position. In the end one is inexorably driven to the conclusion that the current approach to the regulation and supervision of banks is rapidly becoming ineffective for the most important part of the financial system, namely the global risk-managing banking institutions.

## (d) Lack of international harmonisation of supervision and regulation

There remain vast differences in the national financial reporting and disclosures rules and practices. For example, much of the Metallgesellschaft problem was the accounting treatment of the gains on forward delivery contracts. In effect, this produced a US$2 billion difference between German and US accounting data relating to the valuation of the firm. Hence a supervisory assessment of the risk of the firm's derivative positions would have arrived at radically different conclusions depending on which set of financial accounting standards were used.

The lack of stringent consolidated supervision is also a major source of problems. For example, Daiwa in New York was able to hide significant losses for over a decade because of the failure of Japanese supervisors to examine Daiwa's accounts on a consolidated basis.

The lack of co-ordination among futures regulators led to different sets of rules regarding risk management at the organised futures exchanges, a problem that became clearly visible in the Barings case, discussed in Chapter 3.

We are now in a world where very low transaction and marketing costs make it profitable to introduce new intermediation products and, indeed, to change the institutional form of intermediaries (AAA-rated derivatives vehicles) in response to small changes in consumer tastes, operating costs, or regulatory taxes; hence the regulatory framework is quickly outdated. All these argue for functional regulation, rather than product-by-product or institutional regulation.

Despite some convergence of supervisory and regulatory practices among the G10 countries, regulations are still so different as to lead to regulatory arbitrage. Indeed, institutions can now more easily than ever before shift activities from location to location to minimise regulatory taxes.

Following the Windsor Accord (1995) issued by securities and futures exchange authorities after the Barings' bankruptcy, financial market supervisors have begun to execute broad information-sharing and co-operation agreements in an effort to increase the effectiveness of their market surveillance activities. Heads of state and governments for the G7 countries have placed financial market globalisation and systemic risk on the agenda of the summits at Halifax in 1995, Lyons in 1996 and Denver in 1997. Responses by the Basle Committee and IOSCO described means to improve collection and exchange of information between banking and securities regulators across borders and new standards for supervision of cross-border banking (Basle Committee and IOSCO 1996, Basle Committee 1996, IOSCO 1996). So the problems and risks have been recognised up to the highest political level. Efforts to deal with a global market are building up. At this time, it is too early to form a judgement on the chances of success.

# 3. THE CONSEQUENCES OF AN INEFFECTIVE GLOBAL FINANCIAL POLICY

Two consequences are readily visible: over-expansion of the OTC markets and loss of market integrity, both contributing, to an unknown extent, to potential disaster.

## Over-expansion of the OTC Markets

The problem with current arrangements in global financial markets is that the cost of the implicit or explicit liquidity support extended by the central banks to financial institutions is largely borne by the public sector, while the benefits of the growth of global risk-management finance are largely accruing to private market participants. In more technical language, the cost of the public sector support for the global financial industry is not properly internalised by the industry. Thus, as is to be expected, the current rules of the game are introducing major distortions in the business decisions of global financial institutions, in addition to being fraught with moral hazard (i.e., to take risks for which the public purse will help out in the advent of financial difficulties).

The current rules of the game between the regulators and the regulated financial institutions dictate that banks enjoy the full benefits of an extensive safety net, for instance, lender-of-last resort protection, liquidity support in money markets, payments system support, without having their on and off-balance sheet activities and financial positions sufficiently restricted through capital requirements, reserve requirements, or through other restrictions on their activities designed to reduce the risk of failure. The inevitable distortions in the pricing and allocations of risk have had a profound impact on the architecture and the stability of the financial system.

As should be expected, the safety net has directly supported the rapid development and growth of derivative finance, which is the most liquidity dependent of all financial activities and thus the greatest beneficiary of current policy. It has also fundamentally influenced who-does-what in this industry as the protected sector has been able to expand into new areas of business that benefit considerably from the central bank guarantees. The most notable example is the explosive growth of the bank-dominated OTC derivative market and the OTC spot and forward forex market. This development raises the question whether global banking institutions would be the main participants in the OTC derivative business, or more generally whether these banks would be the driving force in the risk-management business in the absence of the liquidity safety net provided by the central bank?

By supporting the liquidity of money and derivative markets through their smoothing of the Fed funds rate and their implicit support of the dealing banks, central banks—particularly the Fed—have supplied an important subsidy to this industry. As a result, the capital cushions held by broker/dealers and banks are much less than what would be the case in the absence of such guarantees. The example of Hong Kong is instructive in this regard. The Hong Kong Monetary Authority (HKMA) has made it very clear that it is prepared to let institutions fail. As a result, Hong Kong institutions find it necessary to hold a capital cushion of about 20% of assets (see Garber 1996).

In addition to distorting the who-does-what decisions, the extensive implicit or explicit liquidity support of global financial institutions and markets also creates significant moral hazard. That financial institutions should want to assume additional risk in certain circumstances is easily understood: the additional risk is partially borne by the central bank, while the financial institution appropriates the remuneration for carrying the additional risk. During times when the banking sector is performing well, banks will have sufficient franchise value to provide incentives for management to preserve the value of the bank. But during times of stress, institutions on the verge of insolvency may engage in "double or nothing plays": banks hold other people's money. As long as the franchise value of banks is high, as it is in the mid-1990s, the latter consideration is not very important, i.e., there is enough franchise value left in the major financial institutions to prevent them from playing double or nothing.

**Loss of Market Integrity**

International derivative transactions make it easy to hide market manipulation, so that it has become more difficult to ensure market integrity, i.e., the detection and prosecution of insider trading. The growing acceptance of the Memoranda of Understanding ("Windsor Declaration") among securities regulators has been helpful for the exchange of market information among supervisors and it has made cross-border market manipulation more difficult. Once market irregularities are discovered, it is necessary to examine the trading accounts of the suspects and this frequently conflicts with bank secrecy law. But a number of countries have recently enacted insider trading laws that facilitate investigation.

# 4. IMPROVED ACCOUNTING AND DISCLOSURE STANDARDS[10]

The problems generated by a market that has become a main stage for international finance, but on which information is difficult to interpret or is not even available, have not escaped notice. In each crisis, such as in Mexico 1994/95, central banks or international agencies have realised that the information available was incomplete and misleading because off-balance sheet obligations were absent from the official statistics.

### Accounting Standards

Myron Scholes, a leading expert on risk-management, describes the accounting treatment of derivatives as "full information, no knowledge: not even basic information is published about risk".

Once accountants argued about how to account for goodwill. Derivatives make that debate look deceptively simple (*Financial Times*, 27 June 1997, Survey, p. 111). Accounting for derivatives is the new Holy Grail of financial reporting, because if the search for a way of accounting for derivatives fails, then the whole purpose of annually published accounts will be called into question in the age of real-time data. Can annual accounts serve to illustrate future risks rather than simply give details of the past?

The International Accounting Standards Committee (IASC) has been entrusted with the task of forging a global financial reporting code. The IASC, however, has not been able in 1997 to agree on a US proposal that all financial instruments, derivatives or not, should be marked-to-market, including, controversially, investments held and long-term bonds. Variations in market values would then affect reported profits and key market indicators, such as earnings per share. One recognised exception would be hedging transactions. The practical difficulty is, of course, to identify complex, global hedges. One can also count on the markets' ingenuity to find instruments that have less or no impact on profit and loss accounts. At any rate, the present accounting reforms under discussion, to be endorsed by IOSCO and accepted at national levels, would revolutionise the accounts of the world's big companies.

## Disclosure Standards

During recent years regulators have spent much time on improving disclosure rules. This is to be achieved by more detailed reporting requirements and more comprehensive and appropriate accounting standards. Better co-ordination of disclosure requirements and data collection across borders are also viewed as much needed given the international nature of the OTC deriv-ative markets. The basis for meaningful reporting requirements are improved accounting standards that reflect the specificities of derivatives.

Disclosure of credit and market risk has become a major task for regulators. There are still important challenges, however, that the industry and regulators are likely to face in the future. All of these challenges point out the difficulties involved in defining a single measure of risk that captures comprehensively all of the risks inherent in the financial activities of a financial institution. They pose major challenges for banks' internal risk management and for super-visors in assessing safety and soundness.

Quantitative disclosure requirements have focused mainly on the trading book of an institution. A case has been made by some market participants for not treating the trading book separately, however. One reason is that a more comprehensive picture of the risk exposure of a financial institution is necess-ary to assess the safety and soundness of the institution. An additional prob-lem is that because credit and market risk are not independent, they cannot be measured separately and then simply added together. In general, how to aggregate market and credit risk in order to obtain a comprehensive picture of a firm's risk exposure is a question that still needs to be answered.

In 1997 an important breakthrough was achieved by J.P. Morgan, sup-ported by five other major banks, launching "CreditMetrics". As with "RiskMetrics", the objective is to generate a more comprehensive approach to risk by taking into account diversification through cross-correlations and assess each exposure on its own merit rather than through undifferentiated broad categories of risk classes. The ultimate aim is both better measurement of credit risk and lower capital requirements for well-diversified banks with a high credit quality.

CreditMetrics is for credit risk what RiskMetrics is for market risk so that aggregation into a single value-at-risk is within reach. It assesses individual and portfolio VAR due to credit exposure and facilitates aggregation of all credit exposure, for example, in loans, swaps or forwards. The model starts with measurement of the probability that a particular credit will default. This probability is basically derived from credit ratings. (The database is, therefore, only useful for large counter-parties.) It then plots the probability that over time a loan or portfolio of loans will default (using Markov chains). The hope is that the Basle Committee will accept this approach now that it has accepted the principle of bank-internal modelling.

This is, however, far from certain. Credit risk models are relatively untested, although some banks have been using them with names such as risk-adjusted return on capital (Raroc) or return on economic capital (Roec). Little is known about the stability of credit-risk evaluations over time (the stability of Markov chains), the importance of geographic coverage is still to be established, and there are a host of other problems. A major worry is that, unlike traded securities, there is no continuous update on the riskiness of a loan. Rating agencies update their evaluations on an annual, or at most quarterly, basis and often discover problems after they have occurred.[11] Credit risk evaluation and correlations projected for the maturity of a long-dated loan are extremely difficult and, in practice, arbitrary. The past is a good guide for tomorrow (as in RiskMetrics), but not for the next ten years.

Market and credit risk received privileged attention in regulatory proposals, but liquidity, legal and operational risks can be equally significant. The failure of Barings can be attributed to operational risk, the risk of losses due to mismanagement, human error, and lack of control. Legal risk, or the uncertainty about the validity and enforceability of contracts, is a permanent problem. For example, there is considerable uncertainty about whether some netting arrangements are enforceable, especially when they involve institutions from more than one country, and there is also uncertainty about the validity of the transaction itself. After suffering large losses from derivatives trading, various end-users have sued or accused dealers of unauthorised trading, misrepresentations of risks inherent in instruments, and not disclosing valuable information on pricing and risk. Liquidity risk, uncertainty about whether a position can be liquidated rapidly at current prices, has also increased in importance, as was illustrated by the Askin case in Chapter 3. Although there are indicators of market liquidity, such as bid–ask spreads and market-trading volume, they tend not to be accurate measures of risk in times of market distress. Moreover, it is difficult to estimate how quickly liquidity can change under extreme market conditions.

Because of the dearth of good measures of these kinds of risk, it is difficult for financial institutions to provide senior management, shareholders, and counter-parties with accurate assessments of the riskiness of their portfolios. In addition, these non-quantifiable risks are not independent of the market and credit risk. Legal disputes often arise after a significant increase in market risk or a major adverse event. Moreover, an increase in credit risk may be associated with an increase in liquidity risk. When the market has information (or hears a rumour) that a major counter-party might default on its obligations, the counter-party may lose its access to existing credit lines and credit markets in general.

## 5. REDUCING SYSTEMIC RISK: THE BASLE APPROACH

Reducing systemic risk by reducing the probability of bank failure is the approach that regulators have focused on. To achieve this the Basle Committee on Banking Supervision has worked on improved capital structure since the mid-1980s. The first major achievement was the 1988 Capital Accord, implemented by late 1992. As was shown in Chapter 6, the 1988 Basle Accord has various shortcomings. Specifically, it is too narrow as it focuses almost exclusively on credit risk. By ignoring other risk factors like interest rate risk and exchange rate risk ("market risk"), which are especially important for a bank's trading book, but also non-negligible for the "banking" book, it can lead to a miscalculation of the amount of capital needed to absorb potential loss. It also creates distortions by inducing banks to use their capital to back up high-risk exposure since all commercial loans, independently of their rating, fall into the 100% risk category or to substitute interest rate and exchange rate risk for credit risk by modifying their portfolios accordingly.[12]

### The 1995 Basle Accord

The Basle Committee has released in April 1993 a set of proposals to revise the 1988 capital standards. The 1993 proposals consider:[13] the capital requirements for market and credit risk exposures of the banks' trading book positions (speculative or hedging positions), and the recognition of netting for capital adequacy purposes.

The 1993 Basle proposals were heavily criticised especially by larger banks. The main critique was that banks have very different kinds of risk structure, netting, and risk-management capacity. Hence, whilst rules for credit risk pose lesser problems, the rules for market risk had to be re-thought—a rather hopeless task. The Basle Committee then accepted the proposal that banks use their internal risk-management system to calculate capital requirements, subject to certain standards in model specification. The required output is value-at-risk. For banks not using a risk-management model of acceptable standards, the "standard approach" of the 1995 Accord applies. The Accord also accepts modelling for certain positions (e.g., options) in combination with the "standard approach".

The 1993 Basle proposals were revised in 1994 and approved in 1995, as an Amendment to the Capital Accord (the "1995 Accord") to be implemented by the G10 supervisory authorities by year-end 1997 at the latest. The general approach is to split the assets of a bank into a loan and a trading book. Credit risk is the source of concern for the loan book and the 1988 Basle Accord deals with that. The greatest worry concerning the trading book is market risk and only to a lesser degree credit risk.

---

**Technical Insight 8.1**   Credit risk for derivatives default

The capital standard for swaps, forwards, purchased options and similar contracts are computed as follows. First, the credit exposure is computed. Second, this credit exposure is multiplied by a risk-weight of 50% rather than 100%, as most counter-parties tend to be first-class names.
  Computation of the credit exposure includes the following steps. A bank sums:

- the total replacement cost (obtained by marking-to-market) of all its contracts with positive value (RC); and
- an amount for potential future credit exposure ("add-on") calculated on the basis of the total notional principle amount of its book, split by residual maturity, as follows:

Capital Ratios for Potential Credit Exposure (% of Notional)

| | Contract | | | | |
|---|---|---|---|---|---|
| *Residual maturity* | *Interest rate* | *Exchange rate, gold* | *Equity* | *Precious metals, except gold* | *Other commodities* |
| <1 year | 0.0% | 1.0% | 6.0% | 7.0% | 12.0% |
| 1–5 years | 0.5% | 5.0% | 8.0% | 7.0% | 12.0% |
| >5 years | 1.5% | 7.5% | 10.0% | 8.0% | 15.0% |

Netting is admitted for transactions subject to novation or subject to any other legally valid form of bilateral netting. To take into account netting, there is an add-on for netted transactions equal to

$$(0.4 + 0.6 \, \text{NGR}) \, A_{\text{gross}}$$

where

NGR = level of net replacement cost/level of gross replacement cost for transactions netted

and

$A_{gross}$ = sum of individual add-on amounts of transactions netted
= notional * capital ratio

Credit exposure is then equal to:
$$RC + (0.4 + 0.6\,NGR)\,A_{gross}$$

Example: A currency swap book with one counter-party and with remaining maturities between one and five years has a replacement value (of those in-the-money only) of US$10 million for a notional value of US$1 billion and a NGR of 0.3. Then:

Credit exposure = $10 + [1000 \cdot 0.05\,(0.4 + 0.6 \cdot 0.3)]$ = US$39 million

In this computation US$10 million are for a current credit risk. An additional US$29 million accounts for future potential increases in credit exposure reflecting (through the capital ratio) the type of contract (or historical volatility) and maturity, and the extent of netting. Netting, in this example, reduces the add-on from US$50 million to US$29 million.

## The Standardised Method

Under the new Basle framework, trading book positions (including derivatives) are classified into debt and equity instruments, to which are added the bank's total foreign exchange and commodities positions. A market risk exposure (based on net positions) and a specific risk exposure (based on gross positions), specific to a particular security, is computed for each group. The total capital requirement is the sum of the capital charges for the four groups of market instruments and the capital charge for the bank's loan book which is computed according to the 1988 Basle Accord but with more general recognition of bilateral netting.[14] A tier-3 capital category is introduced for the capital charge for market risk, representing short-term subordinated debt. Tier-3 capital is limited to 250% of tier-1 capital. This means that a minimum of 28.5% of market risks needs to be supported by tier-1 capital that is not required to support risks in the remainder of the book. The Capital Adequacy Directive issued by the EC Commission shares the same structure.

In order to ensure consistency in the calculation of capital requirements for credit and market risk, the measure of market risk is multiplied by 12.5 (i.e., the reciprocal of the minimum capital ratio of 8%) and added to the sum of risk-weighted assets compiled for credit risk purposes. In the calculation of market risks for derivatives, they need to be converted into positions of the relevant underlying which become subject to specific and general market risk charges.

The standardised method proceeds by "building blocks" for groups of instruments. Capital factors are specified by maturity tranches for both market and specific risks.[15] Both the 1995 Basle Accord and the European Capital Adequacy Directive allow the sophisticated market participants to use more accurate duration measures for interest rate risk exposure and a simulation approach for estimating foreign exchange risk exposure. However, such alternatives are subject to a strong requirement that the results be in line with that from the "standard" methods proposed.

For options, a simplified approach with standardised factors is offered to banks handling a limited range of purchased options. Banks which write options or handle large positions of purchased options must use the delta-plus method, that is, they must report option positions equal to the market value of the underlying multiplied by the delta. In addition, banks are required to measure gamma and vega for the calculation of the total capital charge. More sophisticated banks have the right to base the market risk capital charge for options portfolios and associated hedging positions on a prescribed scenario approach.

### Can the New Capital Standard Reduce Systemic Risk?

The capital standards of the 1995 Accord can potentially contribute to a decline in systemic risk by reducing the probability of bank failure. However, the exact amount of risk reduction is unclear. By recognising interest rate risk, exchange rate risk, and the price risk of equities and commodities, the new capital standard can, to some extent, correct for the banks' bias toward non-credit risk in position taking. In addition, given the broader coverage, the trading book exposure will be more appropriately measured. This will yield a more appropriate level of capital reserve for banks and can better capture the positive externality that bank safety has on the entire financial system.

By recognising the reduction of market risk brought about by entering into opposite positions, the new Accord essentially increases the relative cost of taking an unhedged speculative position and decreases the relative cost of providing an intermediary function. This will discourage banks' speculative/proprietary activities and encourage banks' hedging or intermediary behaviour and thereby reduce systemic risk.

However, the effectiveness of this approach of reducing systemic risk can be weakened by various factors. First, the flexibility of OTC derivative products virtually allows the banks to transform risk from one kind to another. Even though the 1995 capital standard is much more comprehensive than the 1988 standard, it necessarily considers only a limited number of risk factors. It is practically impossible to have a simple and applicable standard that can cover all risk. As such, there is always room for the banks to tilt their activities towards the kind of risk that requires little or no capital reserve.

Second, in a more and more complex market environment, there are fundamental difficulties in using capital standards as a regulatory tool. With sophisticated instruments and an ever changing market environment, a relatively strict and easy to understand capital rule like the 1988 Basle Accord is likely to yield a capital charge which is either too high or too low. In fact, any simple and easy-to-implement capital standard will have that problem. The 1995 standard is already quite complicated and risks becoming obsolete as participants can alter their behaviour to benefit from the necessarily rigid design of the standard. Such reactions could impose even more risk on the system.[16]

Finally, it is important to note that the Basle Accord is just for banks. The playing field can easily be unlevelled as banks are competing with the securities houses which are in some countries subjected to different capital requirements by the securities and exchange regulators.[17] In order to have an effective capital requirement which does not favour some market participants over others, it is important to harmonise the capital standards for banks and securities houses internationally. While the International Organisation of Securities Commission (IOSCO) has been working on this issue for some time, disagreement within the IOSCO Technical Committee has delayed the proposal of an action plan. Without proper harmonisation, the effect of unilaterally improved capital standard on reducing systemic risk will be weak.

# 6. REDUCING SYSTEMIC RISK: ALTERNATIVE APPROACHES

In this section a number of alternative approaches are discussed. The first represents the most significant breakthrough by market participants: acceptance in the 1995 Basle Accord of internal risk-management models to assess capital needs. No political agreement on any of the other alternatives discussed in this Section has been reached, but all are on the agenda of international regulatory working parties. The second approach still deals with individual bank failure, but aims at reducing regulatory micro-involvement. This is the "pre-commitment approach". The other approaches deal with the interphase of bank failure and systemic risk; namely, reducing the systemic repercussions of individual bank failure.

## (a) Value-at-Risk

The acceptance of in-house risk-management models by the 1995 Basle Accord is attractive from several viewpoints.[18] First, it does not require detailed supervision nor proprietary information. Second, this approach aggregates the market risks of any complex portfolio of various positions. It comes out with one number, yet is as comprehensive as necessary. Third, firms should be best at assessing their own exposure risk. This knowledge is fully used in the internal model approach. It can also be hoped that the demonstration of superior risk management by some firms would induce others to catch up. For example, J.P. Morgan was quick to make its RiskMetrics (the analytical model, the historical database with regular up-dates, and software) available to all market participants and thereby demonstrated its leadership quality.

A survey conducted by the Basle Committee and IOSCO in 1995 and repeated in 1996 reveals substantial but uneven progress in disclosure performance. Table 8.1 summarises the results of the second survey with respect to quantitative information about market risk. The top German, Japanese and Swiss banks are all reporting value-at-risk (VAR) data. The US institutions apparently have the best disclosure record in terms of the type and the extent of information disclosed. Whilst this may reflect confidence in their risk-management systems, it is also the case that the Federal Reserve Bank of New York has taken a more active role than other central banks in promoting the disclosure models—partly as a way of forestalling new regulatory initiatives.

The 1995 Accord specifies a number of quantitative and qualitative criteria for the use of in-house models to ensure a minimum degree of prudence, transparency and consistency. The technical aspects of compiling VAR were presented in Chapter 4. VAR has to be computed daily, using a 99% one-tailed confidence interval; a minimum price shock equivalent to 10 trading days (holding period) has to be used;[19] and the model must incorporate data for at least one year. The capital charge will be the higher of:

- the previous day's VAR;
- three times the average of the daily VAR of the preceding 60 business days.

The multiplication factor of three was heavily criticised by banks. However, several reasons plead for this additional security cushion:

- the need to provide for adverse market conditions over an extended period of time;
- market price movements often display patterns, such as "fat tails" that differ from the statistical simplifications used in modelling;
- the past is not always a good approximation of the future;
- models cannot adequately capture event risk arising from exceptional market circumstances;

**Table 8.1** Banks Disclosing VAR Data in Their 1995 Annual Reports (by Country)

| | Banks Surveyed | Banks Reporting VAR Data | % |
|---|---|---|---|
| Germany | 7 | 7 | 100 |
| Japan | 7 | 7 | 100 |
| Switzerland | 3 | 3 | 100 |
| United States | 10 | 7 | 70 |
| France | 8 | 5 | 63 |
| United Kingdom | 8 | 3 | 38 |
| Canada | 6 | 2 | 33 |
| Italy | 8 | 2 | 25 |
| Belgium | 3 | 0 | 0 |
| Netherlands | 3 | 0 | 0 |
| Sweden | 4 | 0 | 0 |
| Total | 67 | 36 | 54 |

*Source*: Basle Committee/IOSCO Technical Committee.
Survey of derivatives disclosure, November 1966 and Taylor (1996).

- many models rely on simplifying assumptions to value complex instruments, such as options.

Banks are allowed to recognise empirical correlations not only within broad risk factor categories, but also across risk factor categories, provided the supervisory authority is satisfied by the bank's system to measure correlations.

Models deal more extensively with general market risk than with specific risk factors. Banks whose models take little account of specific risk will be subject to the full specific risk charges of the standardised approach. This can be reduced to 50% if specific risk is modelled.

Whilst regulators abstain from evaluating internal risk-management models, there is an *ex-post* evaluation procedure ("backtesting"). Backtesting requires that the bank records the number of times its one-day 99% VAR estimate is violated during the preceding 250 trading days (roughly a year).

The Accord defines three zones for the results obtained: green, yellow and red. For 250 observations, a binomial distribution gives a probability of 95.88% that five or fewer exceptions occur when the true level of coverage is 99%. This is the green zone. The test results are consistent with an accurate model, and the possibility of erroneously accepting an inaccurate model is low.

The yellow zone begins with five exceptions, and the red zone with 10 exceptions. The probability of obtaining 10 or fewer exceptions is 99.99% if the true coverage level is 99%. Hence, test results are extremely unlikely to have resulted from an accurate model, and the probability of erroneously rejecting an accurate model on this basis is remote. In between the green and the red zones, in the yellow zone, results could be consistent with either accurate or inaccurate models. In this case, it is recommended that the supervisor obtains additional information before taking action.

If a bank's model falls into the red zone, the supervisor should automatically increase the multiplication factor from 3 to 4, and investigate the reasons for such a large number of misses.

Banks using the internal models approach must have in place a comprehensive stress testing programme. Supervisors will provide specific scenarios for stress testing, but each bank is expected to develop its own stress tests based on the characteristics of its portfolio. Banks should provide supervisory authorities with a description of the methodology used to identify and carry out the scenarios as well as a description of the results.

The 1995 Accord sets minimum standards and provides ample discretion for supervisory authorities to go further. For methodology, parameter values, coverage and data, users have choices as long as national supervisors agree. The cost of this flexibility is lack of uniformity.

Some regulators argue that it is important to evaluate and regulate the risk-management *system* of individual banks to ensure that banks participating in the OTC derivative markets have an adequate system. The argument is that since the first line of defence against excessive bank risk is the risk-management system used by the banks, a sound bank supervisory approach should include the evaluation of such systems. Furthermore, given the changes in the nature of banking, a supervisory approach that focuses on the evaluation of the risk-management system of individual banks might be more efficient and effective than writing more complex capital standards for "all" banks. The 1995 Accord goes a long way to meeting this view, short of stopping at a model tested and approved by regulators.

A fundamental dilemma is generated by the difference between a model optimal for risk management, on the one hand, and optimal for regulatory purposes, on the other. Banks have an incentive to adapt the model in such a way as to reduce required capital—even when, from a risk-management point of view, a different choice would have been made. The problem is that banks either operate two systems, thus foregoing the benefit of basing regulation on existing management tools, or they operate a biased system.

Another difficulty is that a generally agreed approach to measure and control risk is lacking. This is especially true for the more complex products, for which there are often great discrepancies across banks on the model or the parameter values used for pricing and risk calculation. In fact, a key element of competition among the banks is their pricing and risk-management techniques. Without knowing precisely the right approach for the measurement and control of risk, it is impossible for the regulators to evaluate the risk-management system of individual banks.

Given the necessarily complex nature of each banks' risk-management system and that very extensive simulation runs are required to evaluate the effectiveness of a risk-management system, it is very doubtful that the regulators would have the manpower and expertise to fully understand the risk-management system of every bank and be able to evaluate them.[20] Furthermore, changes in parameter values and models in the risk-management system are often needed when the market environment (product availability, risk factors, and market volatility) changes. This would require a frequent re-evaluation of the risk-management system of the banks which is practically impossible. There is no alternative to creating incentives for major banks (small banks pose less systemic risk) to act responsibly. A precondition for more self-regulation is, as argued in the next chapter, a firm no bail-out commitment by the central bank.

More generally, the need for regulation is justified only when there is market failure or externality. There is no evidence or reason why the market participants would not have the right incentive to better measure and control their own risk as these are crucial to their successes in the business. In fact, all major market participants have already invested heavily in powerful risk-management systems. It is also likely that many market participants are already much more advanced in terms of risk-management skills than the regulators. As such there is no reason why the evaluation of individual bank risk-management systems by the regulators would reduce systemic risk.

Regarding the concern that some smaller banks without a sophisticated risk-management system might be engaging in excessive OTC derivative activities, it is important to note that the failure of one or two small banks without a good risk-management system will not have enough impact to cause a systemic problem. In fact, as part of the market mechanism, poorly managed banks should be allowed to fail. The bank regulators' job is not to eliminate bank failure altogether by performing the risk-management function for all banks, but to reduce systemic risk and to maintain the smooth functioning of the banking system.

### (b) The Pre-commitment Approach

A further innovation has been proposed by the Federal Reserve Board and is being tested in New York: the *pre-commitment approach* (PCA). Under the PCA a bank is required to specify the maximum loss it could potentially suffer on its trading activities over a designated horizon. This maximum loss estimate becomes the bank's market risk capital requirement. With the bank's maximum loss estimate comes a commitment to manage its trading exposures so that losses are contained within the pre-committed amount. If cumulative trading losses exceed the capital commitment at any time during the designated period, the bank would be subjected to some form of corrective action or penalty. Public disclosure of the pre-commitment is recommended to enhance the incentives of the scheme and to strengthen the credibility of the policy.

The advantage of this approach is that it focuses on *outcomes* instead of risk management *tools*. It thereby encompasses the quality of risk management as well as the accuracy of the risk-measurement process, whilst avoiding the verification of the quality of proprietary risk measurement models.

There are, however, drawbacks. One is that the PCA may not deter undercapitalised institutions from attempting a "go-for-broke" strategy. Bank regulators, therefore, need to identify in advance banks for whom the penalties would not act as a deterrent to taking excessive risks. These banks require closer supervision of a more traditional type. The PCA would thus minimise supervisory micro-management which would become complementary.

A second potential problem could arise in adverse market conditions forcing banks to close out their positions and thereby add to market destabilisation. Regulators would then need to suspend penalties during times of unusual financial market distress. Whilst no regulatory regime is foolproof against a bank gambling for resurrection, the issue is problematic. Regulators would have to judge when market distress is sufficiently exceptional. Such a decision and its financing is quite difficult. Moreover, credibility of the approach is at stake. Finally, whereas the first problem is likely to concern an individual bank, the second problem is systemic and, if regulatory action is not taken immediately, both types of problems could arise simultaneously.

### (c) Reducing the Impact of Individual Bank Failure?

The concentration of OTC derivatives in a few large money-centre banks adds to systemic risk by increasing the impact of some market participants on the system. That is, the dominance by a few large players can increase systemic risk by the transformation of some idiosyncratic shocks into system-wide shocks.

In order to reduce systemic risk, one possibility is therefore to weaken the dominance situation. That is, some kind of decentralisation is sought. However, this might cause efficiency losses as the concentration of derivative activities is due to the strong preference for highly rated counter-parties, the existence of scale economies in hedging costs, technological development, information acquisition, and learning. Given the significant scale economies, decentralisation is likely to introduce substantial inefficiency. Furthermore, smaller dealers generally do not have the capital and the expertise to maintain a comprehensive risk-management system. As such, it is in fact possible that risk might be increased by favouring entry of less qualified players into the market.

Some regulators have argued that banks should be barred from speculative activity in derivative markets. They have emphasised the importance of identifying the source of revenue for the market participants; to differentiate, especially for the dealers, profits from proprietary trading/speculation and profits from intermediation. While appealing, it is indeed unlikely that a line can be drawn between speculation, hedging and general intermediary-based involvement in the OTC derivative markets. The reason is that an open position that looks like a speculative move might offer a partial hedge for a more complicated aggregate position. It might also be the result of a temporary imbalance in the process of searching for another matching counterparty. Whilst, in theory, there are solid grounds for denying banks with large speculative OTC positions access to the Federal Deposit Insurance,[21] implementation would be problematic.

### (d)  Reducing Interbank Spillover?

There are two possible ways to reduce the amount of interbank linkage or spillover: reduce the amount of inter-dealer/interbank positions, or reduce the impact of a default by a bank on other banks through a buffer or insurance arrangement. The first approach is unattractive as interbank trade is an efficient and relatively inexpensive way for the banks/dealers to reduce their risk exposure by matching up their opposite open positions. The second approach is more plausible. It can take several forms. The simplest one is to use some kind of collateral arrangement between the dealers (but not necessarily between a dealer and a customer). By requiring a collateral, the spillover of a default is reduced.

The problem with collateral arrangements is that they are necessarily bilateral in nature and hence forego the benefit of multiparty offset. Furthermore, the quality of collateral can vary and hence the amount of protection to the system is less clear.

OTC derivative products can increase cross-market spillover because one of their essential uses is for cross-markets arbitrage. OTC derivatives can also increase market linkage as they are often used jointly with other exchange traded instruments to achieve certain risk/return or payment profiles. While linkages can be reduced by restricting the use of OTC derivatives for these purposes, the restriction will also eliminate most of the benefits from OTC derivatives. As such, this is not a very promising approach.

### (e)  Devoted Regulator for the OTC Derivative Markets?

Another policy proposal is to establish a regulator/supervisor for the OTC derivative markets. The OCC has suggested the formation of an interagency task force to study issues in the OTC derivative markets and the Federal

Deposit Insurance Corporation (FDIC) has recommended joint examination of the derivatives dealers by the bank regulators.[22]

Whilst it might be true that having a devoted regulator for the OTC derivative markets can facilitate the collection of information and improve the efficiency and effectiveness of the regulation of the OTC derivative markets, there is however a broader and more fundamental issue regarding regulation. Specifically, the growth of the OTC derivative markets has challenged the appropriateness of both the instrument and institution based approach to regulation. The problem is how to set-up a regulatory structure that can handle a "market" with no borderlines, no location and very flexible products, close links to other asset markets in which bank and non-bank intermediaries around the world operate.

Many, including the author, are convinced that the entire regulatory framework should be modified for effective bank and asset market supervision and regulation. Suggestions are made in Chapter 9. Otherwise, just creating another regulator might only make the regulatory structure more complicated. Bank regulators and the securities and futures market regulators would still have influence on the OTC derivative markets as they regulate a significant portion of the participants in the OTC derivative markets. In a regulatory structure with overlapping boundaries of jurisdiction, participants can potentially benefit from grey zones in the regulatory structure. Furthermore, more confusion might be introduced. As with the lack of disclosure, the lack of a devoted regulator for the OTC derivative markets does not, on its own, cause or contribute to the build-up of systemic risk. As such, it cannot be a direct medicine for the reduction of systemic risk.

# 7. CONCLUSION

The rapid growth of derivative markets has propelled them to the main stage of global finance. Unfortunately, this revolution in the financial markets has upset the traditional regulatory balance. Existing regulations are inappropriate for dealing with derivative finance; they distort the incentive structure and leave major risk areas unattended.

The question is not whether regulation is necessary. Appropriate regulation is necessary and, unfortunately, needs to be of an entirely new type, as proposed in Chapter 9, compared to existing balance sheet controls. The financial industry's claim that less or no regulation would be best is unconvincing given the risks identified in this and preceding chapters.

So far the major international regulatory effort has focused on reducing the risk of individual bank failure by imposing risk-adjusted minimum capital standards. This approach has ended in a cul-de-sac.

Better suited for the problem of derivatives books is the acceptance of a bank-internal risk-management model for setting capital requirements against market risks. Whilst better, it also suffers from many defects and practical problems.

Another area in which regulators in recent years have made progress is disclosure rules and exchange of information. Both suffer, however, from the still very unsatisfactory accounting rules for derivatives.

All these innovations are positive contributions, but fail to fully address the problem, namely, the subsistence of considerable systemic risk. The next chapter proposes a novel approach to grasping the problem of systemic risk.

# ENDNOTES

1 "Too big to fail" was officially adopted in the United States with the insolvency of the Continental Illinois National Bank (Chicago) in 1984. At the time of its failure, the Continental Bank was the seventh largest bank in the country. The FDIC did not fail the bank legally and provided assistance to protect the par value of all uninsured, as well as insured, deposits of the bank and of the creditors of the parent holding company.

2 Full capital account convertibility only applies to a small number of OECD countries and is a recent fact even for countries such as the United Kingdom, France or Italy.

3 Another question raised by this example, is how the bank who accepted funds for investment in equity, but who invested the funds in corporate debt and swapped the debt index against the S&P index, would classify the activity. Is it fixed income or is it equity? Furthermore, assume the counter-party is a European bank, is it fixed income in Europe or fixed income in the United States?

4 Garber (1996) concludes: ". . . though derivative products . . . forwards and swaps . . . do not affect measured net capital inflows or outflows, they blur the information in sub-categories of the capital accounts. Specifically, they make a mockery of the use of capital account categories to attempt to measure the aggregate short foreign currency position of an economy."

5 Similarly, leverage ratios become increasingly meaningless for financial firms. A firm with 100 in equity buys a bond A for 1000 through a repo contract of 900, and borrows bond B and sells it short in the market for 1000. If it short sells bond B through a reverse repo, it invests the 1000 generated form the sale of the bond in cash which is used to collateralise the transaction then it has assets of 1000 in bond A, plus 1000 of cash totalling 2000 implying a leverage ratio of 20:1. If instead it had undertaken a "borrow-vs.-pledge" form of financing, it would use the proceeds from the sale of bond B to pay for bond A and then pledge bond A as collateral for the short position. In this case equity capital of 100 is invested in cash and total assets are only 1100 implying a 11:1 leverage ratio. But the economic position of the firm and the exposure of its creditors is identical under either financing (Merton 1994).

6 This situation cannot be redressed by putting restrictions on derivatives without also covering other functionally equivalent alternatives. There are many ways of taking a levered position on the S&P 500 all of which are economically equivalent positions.

7 "The increased flexibility and global mobility of institutions, together with derivatives technology for creating *custom* financial services at low costs, have far-

reaching implications not only for custom financial services but also for national stabilisation policies as well." "Policy makers are speculating against the long-run trend of declining transactions costs if they assume that the traditional frictions within their individual financial system will allow nation-states to continue to pursue monetary and related policies with the same degree of control as in the past" (Merton 1994).

8 The differences between an institutional and functional approach to the regulation of financial activity can be seen from the example of insurance. Insurance contracts guarantee the value of an asset under specific circumstances but so does a put option. These two contracts serve the same function: they protect the asset value against loss. But the issuing institutions—an insurance company and an options exchange—are radically different institutions, subject to different regulatory regimes. Functionally, however, they provide the same value (Merton 1992).

9 "To develop useful information the financial industry needs to develop a new balance sheet format to capture the current mixture of risks assigned to either on- or off-balance sheet status based on outmoded concepts of what qualifies as an asset or a liability" Heisler (1995).

10 Based on IMF (1996).

11 One potential problem with this approach is that the rating might not reflect the financial condition of an institution during a period of market distress. For example, Orange County, California, went from a rating of AA to a rating of junk in one day. Or, more generally, rating agencies, like regulators, are typically one step behind the facts.

12 Under the 1988 Basle Accord, only netting by novation is recognised for the purpose of calculating capital requirement. Netting by novation refers to a process where initial contractual arrangements are replaced by new ones. The 1991 Lamfalussy Report suggested that bilateral netting, to the extent that it is legally enforceable, should be allowed as it can improve the efficiency and the stability of the banking system by reducing credit exposure, liquidity risk and transaction costs. The 1995 Accord incorporates these suggestions.

13 For greater detail, see, for example, IMF (1995).

14 The rationales behind this structure are: (1) Interest rate, foreign exchange and equity price risks are different in nature and require different measurements, (2) market risk is common across trading positions and hence should be computed on a net basis, (3) specific risk is idiosyncratic in nature and hence should be computed on a gross basis, and (4) credit risk is the most important risk element for items in the loan book which are to be held for long horizons.

15 Although this building-block approach is somewhat arbitrary and invariant to specific risk situations as they evolve over time, much greater harmonisation was achieved.

16 There are also other practical issues which can hinder the effectiveness of capital standards as a regulatory tool. In particular, there is always some limit as to how often regulators do check the capital reserve of the banks to ensure that the capital requirement is met without being too bothersome to the banks. Regulators lack the army of skilled analysts necessary to do frequent (in fact, on time) check-ups, given the short-term and complicated nature of trading book positions. The international scope of the markets make this problem even worse, as highly co-ordinated efforts of regulators in many different countries would be needed.

17 For example, in the United States, securities houses are subjected to the capital requirement of the SEC which utilises a different approach than that of the Basle Committee. Under the so called "Net Capital Rule" of the SEC, a minimum level of liquid net worth is required after some deductions, the so called "haircuts", to

account for market and credit risk. The haircut for unrealised profit associated with OTC derivatives positions is 100%. The SEC is considering modifying the Net Capital Rule to better capture the credit and market risk of derivative products.

18 Already in a report issued in July 1993, the *Group of Thirty* recommended that the management of each market participant should determine clearly the policies on the uses of derivatives instruments and the management of accompanying risk.

19 This is usually done by multiplying the one-day VAR by the square root of 10. This is a non-linear approximation and a ten-day modelling also serves to incorporate non-linearities in the ten-day revaluation of option positions.

20 This is a general problem with more detailed regulatory involvement: the experience and expertise required is such that regulatory agencies have little chance of attracting that kind of staff, generously paid by finance houses.

21 See, for example, Hönig (1996). The President of the Federal Reserve Bank of Kansas City argues: "In light of the costs and difficulties of implementing prudential supervision for larger institutions who are increasingly involved in new activities and industries, the time may have come to sever the links between these institutions and the safety nets."

22 In a report issued in October 1993 the CFTC recommended, the establishment of an interagency council to promote co-ordination among the involved regulators in the US. House Rep. Leach has introduced, in January 1994, a bill on a "Derivatives Supervision Act of 1994" to form a joint regulatory agent specifically for the OTC derivatives markets. The General Accounting Office, in a report issued in May 1994, has recommended that the SEC should take on the responsibility to supervise and regulate the OTC derivative markets.

# 9

# A Financial Policy Model for the Next Century

## *The Challenge of Global Money*

National finance has national rules; global finance will have global rules. But "rules" is a term that means different things to different people. Its meaning needs to be clarified before a global umbrella can be unfurled over tomorrow's financial system. Hence the first thing on the checklist: regulation or supervision?

Regulation or supervision?
The biggest danger to 21st century world finance may well be an excess of official zeal. In their search for tidiness and comprehensiveness, governments may lay down rules for financial institutions that are far too restrictive for economic health. Economic growth requires finance. Both involve risk. Any plan to create a risk-free financial system would stifle growth. Financial institutions should be in the business of understanding risk, managing it, spreading it; they cannot be in the business of avoiding it.

One test of whether people appreciate this distinction is the vocabulary they use. Particularly when it is applied to banks, "supervision" is the appropriate word, not "regulation". Of course, a supervisory approach has a core of rules, to do with capital ratios, the avoidance of over-concentrated lending, etc. But it is based on a recognition that financial firms differ. Each has its specialities, its particular style, its regional or local bias, and periodically it may want to change its priorities and the way it runs its businesses. Provided it sticks to the core rules, no supervisor should want to stop it being flexible and imaginative.

"Regulation", on the other hand, is inclined to start from the premise of homogeneity: a bank, is a bank, is a bank. It sets out detailed rules, believing they will cover a wide range of circumstances. That approach may work in the case of, e.g., fire regulations in factories: so many extinguishers and fire escapes per thousand square feet, certain building materials banned, and so on. In finance, however, the regulatory attitude is not just unsuitable; it can also be dangerous. It carries with it the sense that financial safety is simply a matter of setting the rules and getting them obeyed. It thinks it is dealing with the details when in fact it seldom gets near them.

Supervision is better on the details, because it is less mechanical and more judgemental. It is, therefore, incidentally hard to do well. But unless the supervisory approach prevails in the 21st century, the chances are that the financial system will be overseen by a politician's caution and a lawyer's pen. Commerce will hardly get a look in.

Even with the supervisory approach, it will not be easy to get the next century's system right. The checklist has to include this awkward issue.

### The principle of global supervision

To some, the phrase itself implies a global supervisor. Fortunately, that temptation has already been resisted. Any truly global system will build on the framework already adopted in the main OECD countries. It will certainly cover banks; it may also (see below) include various non-bank institutions.

The essentials of a cross-border supervisory system are not hard to define, but much harder to introduce and then keep in good working order. For example, the principle of home-country responsibility sounds sensible and practicable: country A's supervisor monitors the worldwide operations of all banks from A, and central bank A has lender-of-last-resort power for all A banks. But the value of that principle gets fuzzier as more countries join the global system. If country X's banks decide to spread abroad, would other supervisors take the word of their counterpart in X, and would they be sure that central bank X would mount a bail-out if one were justified?

These questions will have to be answered. If they are not, the supervisory system may become excessively complicated. Responsibilities will not be clearly defined. Gaps will emerge. Supervisors will be expected to do too much. Their likeliest response would be to limit the number of countries whose supervisory credentials they respect, perhaps on a regional basis, which would produce the opposite of an open global market.

If that possibility exists for banking, it is more likely for financial institutions as a whole. What started in the past twenty-five years as cheeky competition for banks could become a central supervisory conundrum next century. It goes by an ugly word: disintermediation.

### Disintermediation

The process is familiar: instead of depositing with banks and borrowing from them, certain big companies lend and borrow directly with one another. Or they borrow direct from investors, or what are known as "non-bank banks". Whatever form it takes, disintermediation cuts out the banks. On the face of it, there may be nothing wrong with that. Disintermediation may be cheaper, quicker, more convenient. However, it poses two potential threats that grow as it does:

- When banks lose business they may be tempted to take bigger risks with what they still have, or in seeking new customers. It is right that banks take risks; that is what they are there for. But they must know how to price risk correctly, and they should have a balanced portfolio of risk. In seeking new business to replace the disinter-mediators, a banker is likely to be less good at pricing its risk (at least initially). And his portfolio, shorn of some big customer, loses some of its balance.

• For supervisors, disintermediation can be tricky. If they are expected to extend their knowledge and power to non-bank institutions that are assuming some form of banking risk, that could overstretch them. They would be right to wonder where the process would stop, because experience so far has shown that inventive minds can push disintermediation a long way.

Could supervisors and central bankers draw a line around banks, and in effect say that all other types of lending and borrowing are not their concern? This is hard to imagine. Certainly, disintermediated lending that is foolish will cause economic damage, because resources are wasted. It may cause financial damage as well, if the disintermediators have built up such an interwoven system that a loss anywhere damages confidence everywhere. This is the "systemic threat" that central bankers aim to avoid in banking. It currently does not exist to the same degree in the commercial-paper market, for example, partly because the participants are better than normal bank depositors at discriminating between one borrower and the next. But, taking an extreme case to make the point, suppose that disintermediation grew so much that it did away with banks altogether. In those circumstances, supervisors and lenders of last resort would still have the worries about the liquidity, capital adequacy and riskiness of the whole system that they do today. Over time, it seems, they will have to turn their attention to at least some of "non-bank banking".

### Payment and settlement

This is the dull end of finance—dull, but crucial. By definition, markets of any sort involve transactions, right through to the point when the seller has been paid by the buyer. Until that point, the whole transaction remains uncertain. The financial system is often compared to an inverted pyramid: it is seldom appreciated that every stone of that pyramid involves uncertainty. The more primitive the system, i.e., the longer the delay between undertaking to pay and actual payment, the greater the uncertainty.

This is unsatisfactory for all concerned. "The cheque is in the post" is only slightly worse than knowing that the cheque is in the system, still undebited and uncredited. For buyer, seller and all financial intermediaries, it would be far better to know that accounts were being settled in "real-time"—instantaneously, or at least during a working day, rather than being left with those awkward pauses.

Supervisors, too, would rest easier if real-time settlement were a reality. Their nightmare is that of any individual seller writ large: that a financial institution will go under, leaving huge bills unpaid. Since other institutions would have been proceeding on the assumption that the bills were going to be paid, they would be damaged, not just by the direct loss of the unpaid bills, but also through the extra business they had already written for the nest layer of the pyramid. Without real-time settlement, any financial system is vulnerable to what may start out as only a little local difficulty.

It therefore makes excellent sense for every national system to hasten to real-time settlement. But that is not enough, because many payments in a domestic currency are, in fact, just one end of a foreign-exchange transaction. In Switzerland today, the proportion is already 90%. As finance goes truly global, the proportion will rise everywhere. The security promised by real-time settlement is not complete until national settlement systems are linked together. Imagine a large payment of yen by an Indonesian trading house for an Australian delivery of wheat: when that can be instantly credited to the Australian account in New York which is even then moving temporarily into zloty futures, the financial system will be much more efficient, and much safer, than it is today. That is a back-office task for back-office working groups, but the worldwide benefits would be immense.

Derivatives

This is the snazzy side of finance, the world of futures and options and swaps. Derivatives are derived from cash markets in currencies, equities, interest rates and so on, which confirms the image of the inverted pyramid. An outsider's unease grows when he learns that many derivatives are concocted by "rocket scientists"—bright young mathematicians—who are employed by people who do not really understand what the wizards are up to. So the outsider was hardly surprised when, in January 1992, the president of the New York Federal Reserve, Gerald Corrigan, said that "high-tech banking and finance has its place, but it's not all it's cracked up to be. I hope this sounds like a warning, because it is."

A portent of disaster ahead? Perhaps, but so far derivatives have a reassuring record. That is partly because they are designed to reduce risk: when an institution buys a currency and sells the future, it protects itself against a sudden lurch in exchange rates.

The other reason why derivatives have so far been a benign addition to the financial chemistry-set is that they are dominated by big firms. In America, on one estimate, just seven banks do 90% of the business in interest-rate and currency swaps. Such banks are easily supervised, familiar with each other, and good at their job. If and when derivatives become an arena for thousands of institutions from dozens of countries, they may pose greater risks for the system as a whole.

The best protection against that possibility is information. Banks will need to know more about the counter-parties on the other end of a derivatives deal, and more about their own portfolios. Supervisors will need more information on cross-border derivative business, and a clearer sense of where risks are real rather than imagined. Thus far, information has been patchy. In tomorrow's world, it must be thorough.

*Source*: Adapted from Rupert Pennant-Rea, *The Economist*, September 1993

> "Florence cathedral clock has hands that
> move 'counter clockwise' around its 24-hour dial.
> When Paulo Uccello designed the clock in 1443,
> a convention for clockfaces had not emerged.
> Competing designs were subject to increasing returns:
> the more clockfaces of one kind were built, the more
> people became used to reading them. After 1550,
> 'clockwise' designs displaying only 12 hours had
> crowded out other designs . . .

*Arthur 1989, p. 82*

> Under increasing returns,
> competition takes on an evolutionary character, with
> a 'founder effect' mechanism akin to that in genetics.
> 'History' becomes important . . . This suggests that there
> may be theoretical limits, as well as practical ones, to the
> predictability of the economic future."

*Arthur 1990*

THE discussion in Chapter 8 suggests that the various approaches focusing on the reduction of the probability of bank failure as the means to reducing systemic risk might not be very effective. For example, the use of more complicated capital standards to reduce the probability of a banking system failure is difficult because inherently no capital standard can cover all risk factors, and hence, market participants will always have the flexibility to shift their trading towards those risks that carry little or no capital charge. This type of behaviour on the part of the market participants might increase overall systemic risk.

The regulation of banks' risk-management system also might not have a substantial effect on reducing the probability of a banking system failure. Shortcomings are: the lack of a generally agreed effective approach for risk management and control (i.e., the lack of a benchmark); the amount of manpower and expertise needed to fully understand and test the risk-management system of all major banks; and the lack of incentives for market participants to conform their risk-management system to regulatory standards.

The much-discussed strengthening of the regulatory structure through the establishment of a new, dedicated OTC derivative market regulator, the improvement of disclosure and reporting requirement, and better adapted accounting methods are all very useful, but might fail to contain systemic risk, as the set of regulatory tools has not really changed. Without any new tools to regulate the market, it is unclear how the recent regulatory advances in better information collection and how the new capital guidelines can be used effectively.

A complete rethink is therefore required. Section 1 proposes a general framework facilitating organisation of the main ideas in the following sections. Sections 2 and 3 deal with the financial infrastructure and argue that a more modern infrastructure can dramatically reduce overall risk and alleviate the regulatory burden on market participants. Section 2 discusses a very important infrastructural change for the derivatives business, namely the migration of OTC contracts to a clearing-house environment or even to organised exchanges. Section 3 proposes to expand the regulatory span from banks (only accounting for 20% of financial intermediation in the United States) to the entire financial industry. This would allow a shift in the regulatory focus from institutions to functions. In exchange, however, the heavy regulatory artillery applied to banks could be sunk and regulators could adopt a much more hands-off approach. This then leaves the redefinition of the role of regulation to Section 4.

# 1. THE ARCHITECTURE FOR REGULATORY RETHINKING

Previous chapters have demonstrated that derivatives have profoundly changed the nature of financial intermediation and that, whilst regulations have evolved, they have always remained a step behind market developments. One remarkable dissonance between market developments and regulatory adaptation is that markets and the leading institutions have bounced forward onto new territory, whilst regulators have tip-toed on traditional turf. As a result regulations are, despite improvements, out of tilt, distorting the playing field and unable to cope with the risks of a global market. What is necessary is more than changes at the margin, it is a complete rethinking of the regulatory approach.

Regulation of the financial industry in the next century has to cope with the difficulty that financial intermediation is not what it used to be. An increasing share is being originated by non-banks, and even institutions with the name of banks are increasingly doing business outside of traditional banking. The leading international banks are financial conglomerates generating more revenues from trading on own account, securities intermediation, derivatives dealing, advisory services, fund management and insurance products than from deposit-financed lending. They are global players, whereas regulators are national institutions, raising questions both about the desirability of national financial policy support and the capacity of national regulators to effectively supervise global institutions. The flexibility of derivative products have repeatedly been shown in previous chapters to allow institutions to locate their risks at very low cost anywhere they like along the product, cost centre, location or time axis. In this four-dimensional space regulators lack the physics to do their job.

As there is little hope that this kind of physics will be available one day, rethinking of the regulatory problem would best start from a recognition of new realities and from a definition of what is desirable and feasible. Regulations should deal with market imperfections; their concerns should be restrained to systemic risk, protection of small savers and the achievement of an unhampered and levelled playing field. Their concern should not be the protection of individual institutions, or the favouring (intentionally or unintentionally) of specific activities. In pragmatic terms, day-to-day supervision should seek to achieve less and instead encourage market participants to use fully their risk-management capacity and to behave responsibly. The superior risk-management capacity of market participants has been demonstrated most conclusively by their recent successful initiatives to use sophisticated internal risk-evaluation models (e.g., RiskMetrics and Credit-Metrics) instead of the Basle capital rules whose risk weighting is closer to the paper than the electronic era.

Rethinking the regulatory framework could most usefully start from the basic fact that any market activity takes place within a particular *infrastructure*. Merton (1990) uses the comparison of transport. Infrastructure results from society's basic choices about rail, road or air transport for the development of economic activities within a given space. Once the physical infrastructure is in place, a basic legal infrastructure needs to be added to avoid, for example, continuous inefficient bargaining over who should drive on the left or the right. For efficiency and safety reasons it is useful to agree on *codes of conduct*, such as speed limits, parking rules and so on. Unfortunately, these rules are not self-enforceable and violations can create substantial social damage. They need, therefore, to be *monitored* and *sanctioned* by external agents.

The role of an external agent is least questioned for infrastructure, given the economies of scale involved, making, at times, a unique (hence monopolistic) road, track or pipeline connecting two points optimal for society. Beyond the national border there is an imperative need for co-ordination (e.g., to link rail systems) or for an international agreement (e.g., airspace control).

Comparing finance with transport is useful because a few key facts emerge intuitively. Product innovation is conditioned by the available or expected infrastructure. Therefore, whatever infrastructure public policy makes or does not make available is decisive for the extent and nature of innovation. Public policy cannot be neutral. Causality also runs the other way: infrastructure responds to product innovation and then sets the stage for further product developments. From this viewpoint, the current lag of regulations behind market practices is a very typical phenomenon. Motorways were not built to make motorcar travelling possible, nor were they built after fast-driving cars first became available. For some time dirt roads were adequate, but at some point a new type of infrastructure became necessary. Infrastructure can stifle, mislead or unchain the potential of product innovation. Not building airports limits the expansion of air traffic and of aircraft technology; fostering road and air traffic infrastructure provides no incentives for developing fast trains.

In finance, the issues are very similar.

1. At the most basic level, *infrastructure* is provided by the organisation and legal support of markets. Whether trade can take place anywhere, or only

on organised exchanges; whether the central bank supports market liquidity; whether the financial industry is segmented or not, such are the basic choices about financial infrastructure, conditioning the superstructure that will evolve. Today's OTC markets have developed with very little infrastructure and resemble air traffic in unregulated sky. Hence the concern about accidents.

2. Within a given infrastructure, *supervision* constitutes the second level of regulatory actions. Prudential regulation has been a main focus of past regulatory efforts to ensure prudent attitudes (rules on exposure to individual clients, minimum capital standards) and codes of conduct (e.g., illegality of insider trading) ensure that clients are treated fairly even in cases of strong informational asymmetries in favour of the intermediary. Whereas decisions about the infrastructure are one-off, supervision is carried out on a daily basis—either well or not depending on a host of circumstances. The problem with supervising market participants is that they are unlikely to be equal and that not all may be caught in the regulatory net. As long as banks were the only or main financial intermediaries and changes in a bank's balance sheet took time to materialise this problem could be neglected. Now it can no longer be ignored. Functional regulation must succeed institutional regulation. And supervision must, as much as possible, be replaced with better designed incentives that encourage self-regulation.

3. The third level concerns the *regulators* themselves. Their basic philosophy (Should some risks be socialised? Can banks fail? Can the largest banks fail?), their weighting of various objectives (safety of depositors, undistorted markets, stability), their approach (anticipatory or post-factum intervention, hands-off or hands-on) are all key to the ultimate safety and performance of the financial system.

The interactions of the three levels are intense and complex. Safer infrastructure requires less severe rules of conduct (speed limits are usually higher on motorways than on country roads). Separation of motorists from pedestrians (walking along a motorway is forbidden, as is driving a car on a pavement) dramatically lowers the risks for pedestrians and the need to monitor driving behaviour for their safety. Regulators are not insensitive to market participants' needs, wishes or problems. There is, therefore, a choice to be made. This author is in favour of a better adapted infrastructure.

## 2. RISK-MANAGEMENT THROUGH CLEARING-HOUSES

A major infrastructural innovation would be development of clearing-houses as central risk-management institutions. Two basic approaches are possible.

One is to manage OTC positions with a clearing-house structure without trading these products on an exchange. This is the much simpler alternative. It has the disadvantage of making daily valuation model-dependent, although a clearing-house valuation model would reflect generally accepted state-of-the-art and would be publicly known. The full benefit of market pricing, including the benefit of liquidity, would require making plain vanilla OTC products tradeable on the exchanges. Not an impossible step, but a big and difficult one. In this section, I mainly discuss the clearing-house solution, but refer to the additional steps necessary for a clearing-house/exchange solution.

As discussed in Chapter 5, a clearing-house offers the following advantages: (1) it typically increases the liquidity of the market as finding a counter-party with the right demand and credit worthiness is no longer an issue, given that the clearing-house is basically the counter-party to every trade; (2) it substantially reduces the amount of credit risk as payment is guaranteed by the clearing-house; (3) it promotes more general participation and increases the level of competition in the market; (4) it facilitates payment and settlement; and (5) it improves data collection and transparency.

Clearing-house risk management significantly improves price information which is essential for determining risk exposure. Currently, while the price information for standard products like plain vanilla swaps is easily available, the market prices for more complicated OTC derivative products are hard to get. In fact, since many OTC derivative products are tailor-made for end-users and can be rather complex in nature, their prices are derived with the help of (proprietary) models of the institution supplying the product. It is therefore possible that another institution using a different model and a different set of assumptions might price the product very differently.

This price discrepancy problem is severe for the more complicated products. Worst of all, since the price is known just between the dealer and the end-user, price information for comparable products from comparable institutions cannot be obtained. Such information is, however, very important for the end-users as Proctor & Gamble, Gibson Greetings (see Chapter 3) and others have found out. It is likely that, if prices are computed with a well-known and agreed valuation model by a clearing-house and regularly published, then the problem of unavailability of reliable market prices can be greatly reduced.

In terms of systemic risk, the use of a clearing-house structure reduces the impact of interbank spillover as the deposit of clearing margins makes the default of one dealer immaterial to other dealers. Essentially, through marking-to-market and a proper setting of the margin level, the incentive to default and the impact of a default can be substantially reduced as the mechanism does not allow the accumulation of a huge negative marked-to-market value.

Could it not be that the use of a clearing-house might increase rather than decrease systemic risk as it will subject all market participants to the risk of a clearing-house failure? This concern might be appropriate for weakly organised clearing-houses, but virtually all the financial clearing-houses are safely structured. In the OTC derivative markets dealers have strong incentives to arrange inter-dealer positions as an effective and low cost way to hedge some of their market risk, essentially by offsetting long and short positions across dealers. The consequence is that there is a large amount of inter-dealer positions which could generate a domino effect should a big dealer fail. In other words, the linkage is there already even without the existence of a clearing-house. The clearing-house merely replaces bilateral offsets from inter-dealer trades by a more formalised and efficient way of multilateral netting. With explicit margin requirements, loss sharing rules, a centralised credit line, and a more formal structure which can be regulated and closely monitored, the impact of the failure of a dealer can be strictly confined. Over time, clearing-houses have adjusted their intraday risk management to evolving needs (intraday settlement of margin deficits) and this appears as the most promising way to enhance further clearing-house safety. *Clearing-houses are a demonstration of the effectiveness of self-regulation.*

### (a) Expanded Scope of Clearing-houses: Specific Issues

To achieve a migration from OTC markets to clearing-houses, several specific issues (standardisation, netting, margin requirements, membership) need to be resolved.

*Standardisation*

It is often thought that setting up a clearing-house necessarily means the setting up of an exchange and that for this, product standardisation is needed. This would then basically eliminate most of the benefits derived from the product customisation ability of the OTC derivative markets.

While most clearing-houses are associated with an exchange, an exchange is not necessary for the functioning of a clearing-house. Essentially, a relatively loose form of clearing-house is no more than just a multilateral netting scheme.

The standardisation of products can facilitate trade and improve liquidity, but it is not necessary for the functioning of either an exchange or a clearing-house. In fact, it is indeed possible that custom-made products can be provided in a clearing-house/exchange environment. All that is needed to manage OTC contracts by a clearing-house is a certain volume (i.e., some standardisation) and an approved valuation model.

What is true is that plain vanilla products are among the most popular OTC derivatives products and their terms are quite standard. Hence, if it is more convenient to clear more standardised products, it is also possible to have a clearing-house for the more standardised swaps and leave the more complicated but less important (in terms of transaction volume) customised derivatives products in the OTC markets. Indeed, as the bulk of OTC derivative trading is in plain vanilla products, the protection derived from setting up a clearing-house for these products might be sufficient to reduce significantly the amount of systemic risk without incurring very high cost and complicated clearing techniques.

Plain vanilla products could already be traded on the exchanges without any difficulties. Even rather complex OTC derivative products can indeed be decomposed into several basic components, some of which are standard plain vanilla components while others are more sophisticated option components. Hence, on product customisation, a dealer would only need to design and service the more complex components which are to be added to the standard components to produce the final product. The standardised components can then be traded on an exchange, as Technical Insight 9.1 illustrates.

Decompositions as illustrated in Technical Insight 9.1 provide a method to identify the more standard products to be routed through a clearing-house or even an exchange. For instance, the decomposition of a swap with a not so common maturity structure into a swap with a more standard maturity structure and one or more forward swaps allows the clearing of the more standard component to be done in a clearing-house while the dealer will customise the forward swap portion for the user.

Should the trading of such products on an exchange be desirable, the decomposition example also offers some hints on a more standardised contract line-up. For instance, since almost all swaps can be decomposed into a series of forward contracts or forward swaps, the problem of standardisation can be formulated as one that searches for a forward swaps maturity structure that can accommodate the popular interest rate swap products at a particular time. Alternatively, swaps can be decomposed into caps and floors which are more like securities than forward contracts as they have non-zero market values at initialisation. Caps and floors can be traded on an options exchange. Indeed, "flex" caps and floors, analogous to the flex options being traded on the exchanges, can also serve as the basic building blocks for many OTC derivative positions. Essentially, the user can set the cap and floor rates and maturities to match that of a swap desired. In other words, flex caps and floors can be a way to securitise swaps if so desired.

*Across-product netting*

The decomposition of swaps into more basic components also has implications on the clearing or netting of positions on different products. A usually

**Technical Insight 9.1** Decomposition of customised derivatives into standardised components

Consider an 11-year swap with a notional principle of US$100 million for which a party X will pay fixed (7%) and receive floating (LIBOR) from a dealer on a semi-annual basis. The deal will have the following cash-flow pattern:

$$\text{(Net cash inflow)}_t = (0.5 * (\text{LIBOR}_{t-1} - 7)/100) * (100m); \quad t = 1, 2, \ldots, 22$$

where $\text{LIBOR}_{t-1}$ is the six-month LIBOR rate at time $_{t-1}$. There are various ways under which this swap can be decomposed into more basic components.

In the simplest case, the swap can be decomposed into a long position in an 11-year floating rate note and a short position in an 11-year fixed rate bond. The cash flows decomposition is as follow:

*Long floating rate note position:*
$$\begin{aligned}
\text{Cash flow}_t &= (0.5 * \text{LIBOR}_{t-1}/100) * 100m; & t &= 1, 2, \ldots, 21 \\
&\quad (0.5 * \text{LIBOR}_{t-1}/100) * 100m + 100m; & t &= 22
\end{aligned}$$

*Short fixed rate note position:*
$$\begin{aligned}
\text{Cash flow}_t &= -(0.5 * 7/100) * 100m; & t &= 1, 2, \ldots, 21 \\
&\quad -(0.5 * 7/100) * 100m - 100m; & t &= 22
\end{aligned}$$

*Combined position:*
$$\text{Net cash flow}_t = (0.5 * (\text{LIBOR}_{t-1} - 7)/100) * (100m); \quad t = 1, 2, \ldots, 22$$

In fact, this is the decomposition on which the marked-to-market value of a swap is usually calculated. The value of the swap is simply computed as the difference between the value of the floating rate note and the value of the fixed rate note. The market value of these two bond components can be obtained from standard discounting methods.

The swap can also be decomposed into a series of forward interest rate contracts with expiration dates matching the 22 payment dates. The cash flow of a contract expiring at time s is:

$$\text{Cash flow}_s = (0.5 * (\text{LIBOR}_{s-1} - x_s)/100) * 100m$$

where $x_s$ is the forward rate for the fixed-term contract expiring at time s. This is slightly different from a usual forward contract as the LIBOR rate used is the one at time s–1 instead of the one at time s. It is important to note that the forward rate will differ from contract to contract and will generally not equal 7%. Hence, the payments derived from the series of forward contracts will differ from the payments derived from the swap on every payment date. However, this payment difference is fixed and is known at the initialisation of the series of contracts. As such, the discrepancies can be settled by an up-front payment between the two parties which is equal to the present value of the series of fixed cash-flow discrepancies.

The swap can also be decomposed into a more standard 10-year swap and a one-year forward swap with an expiration date 10 years from now. The cash-flow patterns of the two components are as follow:

*Cash flow of a 10-year swap paying fixed (fixed rate = $F_{10}$):*
Cash flow$_t$ = (0.5 * (LIBOR$_{t-1}$ −$F_{10}$)/100) * (100m);     t = 1,2, ..., 20

*Cash flow of a one-year forward swap paying fixed (forward fixed rate = $f_{10,1}$):*
Cash flow$_t$ = (0.5 * (LIBOR$_{t-1}$ −$f_{10,1}$)/100) * (100m);     t = 21,22

Again, given that a ten-year swap rate will in general not be equal to a 11-year swap rate, $F_{10}$ is generally not equal to 7. Similarly, the forward swap rate, $f_{10,1}$, will also not be equal to 7. Hence, there will be a minor discrepancy between the combined cash flows of the 10-year swap and the forward swap to that of the 11-year swap. However, the series of discrepancies is fixed and is known at the initialisation of the positions. Hence, it can also be settled by an up-front payment between the two parties which is equal to the present value of the series of discrepancies.

As another possibility, the 11-year swap can also be decomposed into a floor and a cap. A cap will pay the holder the difference between a floating rate and a fixed rate should the floating rate be higher than the fixed rate. A floor will pay the holder the difference between a fixed rate and a floating rate should the floating rate be below the fixed rate. Caps and floors are essentially portfolios of interest rate options.

Suppose the cap and floor have a 11-year life span, then the cash flow pattern is as follows:

*Cash flow of a 11-year cap (at 7%):*
Cash flow$_t$ = Max[0, (0.5 * (LIBOR$_{t-1}$ −7)/100) * (100m)]; t = 1,2, ..., 22

*Cash flow of a 11-year floor (at 7%):*
Cash flow$_t$ = Max[0, (0.5 * (7 −LIBOR$_{t-1}$)/100) * (100m)];

*Combined cash flow:*
(Net cash flow)$_t$ = (0.5 * (LIBOR$_{t-1}$ −7)/100) * (100m);

cited technical difficulty regarding the use of a clearing-house mechanism for OTC derivatives is cross-products netting. In general, the clearing member only needs to post a margin on its net open position which he could eliminate by trading with another dealer having an opposite position.

When calculating this net open position, there are two approaches. One possibility is to net positions in the same product. In this case, there will be an entire schedule of open positions one for each product or product category. For example, there will be an overall net position for five-year swaps, an overall net position for ten-year swaps, an overall net position for 12-year swaps, etc. This is the easiest approach in terms of netting and clearing. However, this approach cannot incorporate all the advantages of position netting.

Another possibility is to net across different product groups. In order to achieve this, one needs to convert various derivative products into basic elements. The netting can then be done by netting positions for each basic element. As long as there are fewer basic elements than the number of types of OTC derivative products, a more general clearing will be achieved.

*The margin cost*

Margin requirements are frequently seen as an obstacle for the feasibility of a clearing-house arrangement. As argued in Chapter 5, many end-users prefer to use OTC derivatives instead of the exchange-traded products because OTC products do not require any margin payments and because positions are not marked-to-market on a daily basis. As such, there is really no cash outflow, other than the payments specified in the contract. The worry is that if a clearing-house arrangement were established and margin requirements imposed, then this cost advantage of the OTC derivative markets would be gone.

This concern is relevant. However, since the margin requirement charged by the dealer to end-users can be different from what the clearing-house charges the dealers, the ratio of these two margins can be adjusted to produce a reduction in systemic risk at only a moderate increase in the cost of using OTC derivatives. For instance, one can charge a higher clearing margin to the dealers (on a netted basis) than the variation margin to the end-users[1] (usually on a gross basis). At present, rather the opposite happens as dealers are more eager to sell OTC products than exchange-products with very low spreads. Moreover, the users' cost is, to some extent, offset by the reduction in credit risk.

It is also important to note that the clearing margin is more for the protection of the system while the variation margin charged by the dealers is for the protection of the dealer. The objective is to reduce systemic risk by reducing the impact of a failure of a dealer on other dealers in the markets. The objective is not to guarantee that no dealer will fail. Furthermore, since the clearing margin is charged only on the dealer's net overall position while the variation market charged by the dealer to the end-users is basically on a customer-by-customer basis, it is not necessarily the case that the dealer has to back up a clearing margin/variation margin ratio above one with own funds.

## General or restricted membership?

A practical question about a clearing-house arrangement is whether it is a feasible approach. The argument is that the current market structure, however inefficient, does allow the big dealers with high credit rating to dominate the market and to charge a credit premium for their service. This will not be the case under a clearing-house structure as the clearing-house itself will actually serve as a counter-party to every trade and therefore the credit-worthiness of the counter-party is no longer a major concern. As such, the currently dominating players in the markets have no incentive to support a clearing-house arrangement. Without their support, the clearing system simply cannot work.

The underlying presumption is that a clearing-house structure necessarily implies a much broader membership than the current informal group of dominating dealers. It is also presumed that the currently dominating dealers necessarily have to face a reduction in their advantages over their lower rated and less capitalised competitors. These presumptions are probably too strong as a clearing-house can indeed be designed to exclude dealers with low credit ratings and to retain a reasonable amount of the benefit enjoyed by the currently dominating dealers. For example, capital and credit rating requirements can be placed on clearing-house membership.[2] The clearing margin and the loss sharing rule can also be set to be dependent on the relative credit quality of the members. Furthermore, clearing members can also charge a fee for clearing for the non-member dealers. These arrangements can give some incentive for the currently dominating dealers to join a clearing-house system.[3]

## (b) Clearing-house Technology for OTC Products: Recent Initiatives

A clearing-house has several attractive features which can be offered as separate services. It performs, first, the function of a back-office, recording each trade, pricing each position and monitoring the position on the basis of a risk evaluation model. Once the amounts due to counter-parties are established, these amounts are settled through cash payments. These payments are made on a netted basis on all contracts between the clearing-house and its members.

It is easy to see that each service is valuable by itself and could be offered independently of others. For example, pricing by the clearing-house has the advantage of independence and eliminates the dependence of the final user on his dealer. It ensures pricing transparency, regularity and objectivity.

The same can be said of risk-evaluation models. Each dealer may have its own model, unknown to the end user, and not comparable among dealers. Whatever a clearing-house uses must be approved by the profession and will always be the same independently of the dealer used. Monitoring is therefore carried out on a uniform standard, and certainly at a much lower cost than would be the case for bilateral contracts.[4] In general, all the clearing-house functions enjoy strong economies of scale, whether it is back-office operations, risk evaluation, monitoring or pricing.

It could thus be argued that even for OTC contracts which are customised and therefore illiquid, so that no trading takes place on the exchange, there are advantages to transfer OTC contracts from the dealer's back-office to the clearing-house. The next, but separate, step would be to add to the back-office function the risk-management function and subject these contracts to unilateral clearing and margining.

Is this theory? Not at all. Exchanges are keen to offer market participants the flexibility of OTC products with the security of the exchange environment and clearing-house mechanism. They are also keen to take advantage of the knock-on business from OTC transactions which are at the margin hedged on exchanges. In recent years, the CBoT and the CBOE have launched some new products called "flex options". Unlike the usual standardised products, flex options can be customised by the traders according to the need of the big institutional users. Basically an investor can set his own exercise price and the expiration date. The flex options being traded on the CBOE are linked to the S&P 100, the S&P 500 and the Russell 2000 index (see Technical Insight 9.2.) The flex options being traded on the CBoT are linked to Treasury bond futures and are closer to OTC products like interest rate swaps. In March 1994, the European Options Exchange launched "flex" options on Dutch government bonds. Like their US counterparts, the expiration date, strike price, and option type, are set by the investors. All these market developments are evidence that standardisation is not absolutely necessary for an exchange/clearing-house to function. The issue is one of relative costs.[5]

But it is not only in the product development that exchanges are able to service the derivatives industry. As concerns mount over counter-party risk in derivatives, exchanges are also looking at how they may lend their experience in that area to the OTC sector. Already the Swedish-based OM exchange offers a tailor-made clearing service for swaps and other OTC trades in Stockholm and at its London subsidiary OMLX, while in Spain Meff is prepared to provide clearing for the Spanish swap market.

**Technical Insight 9.2**   New exchange traded products: flex options and rolling spot

In February 1993 the CBOE launched Flexible Exchange (Flex) Options on the S&P 500 and S&P 100 stock indexes. For the first time, users of exchange-traded contracts were able to negotiate expiry date, strike price and exercise style—making these new contracts direct competitors with similar OTC products.

The first CBOE contracts have been a roaring success. What users most appreciate are the traditional advantages of an exchange-traded contract (a counter-party, liquidity and daily mark-to-market valuation) over an OTC product, combined with the traditional advantage of OTC products, namely customisation.

The contracts were such a success that other exchanges (American Stock Exchange and CBoT) have launched their own flex options. The CBoT's flexible contracts are based on two-, five-, 10- and 30-year US Treasuries.

While competitors to OTC products, flex options are perfect hedge instruments for OTC traders and help in reducing the cost or increasing the competitiveness of OTC products.

In June 1993 the CME launched a *Rolling Spot* sterling/dollar future. This contract is similar to a spot transaction, but is not automatically settled after two days. The initial price of a deal is the same as in the spot market, but positions are rolled forward every day unless closed out. In the cash market, deals must be settled within two days.

The advantage of the rolling spot is increased flexibility and lower cash commitment. Instead of paying-up the contract sum only margin payments must be made. Hence traders of smaller and poorer credits have access to this market.

Nevertheless, the sterling/dollar contract was a flop. Apart from a few contacts traded after the launch, there was no demand. Success only came with the introduction in September 1993 of a DM/dollar contract.

Exchanges outside the US have also caught up and created rolling spot contracts, sometimes called Deferred Spot contracts (on the SIMEX).

With the growth in the amount of swaps now supported by collateral, the industry is looking to the expertise from exchanges/clearing-houses in the management of that collateral.[6] It is with this in mind that Chicago's futures exchanges, CME and CBoT, have planned their services for the OTC sector. CME has developed the Swaps Depository Trust, while the Board of Trade

Clearing Corporation (BOTCC) offers its Hybrid Instruments Transaction Service (Hits).[7]

A further indication of the convergence of OTC and exchange-traded derivatives is provided by the efforts of banks to set up clearing systems. The Bank for International Settlements in 1996 expressed concern about intraday and overnight risks in the foreign exchange markets. The BIS threw its weight behind netting and invited banks (the Group of Twenty—G20—a consortium of 80 leading banks from Europe, North America and Japan) to come up with an industry answer to the problem of foreign exchange settlement risk ("Herstatt risk"). FXNet, set up in 1984, provides an automated system for netting *bilaterally* between its member banks. It handles over 10% of the world's foreign exchange flows. Echo, which started in 1995, goes further by offering *multilateral* netting: members transfer their trades to the Echo clearing-house and settle up with a single payment at the end of the day. A North American rival, Multinet, also offers multilateral netting. All other operations in this huge market are cleared bilaterally on a back-to-back basis with correspondingly higher risks.

The G20 picked up the BIS gauntlet and created CLS Services in London. In 1997 CLS took over Echo and Multimet to offer real-time settling of foreign exchange transactions. It thus goes beyond multilateral netting which certainly reduces risk by as much as 80% but does not eliminate it altogether. Its objective is multi-currency netting with finality before settlement. To achieve this, the creation of a global foreign exchange settlement bank is planned, ensuring that both sides of a trade are completed in real-time by simultaneously crediting and debiting each of the two banks' accounts (as each bank delivers one currency and receives another, the situation is fully balanced). This is called "continuous-linked settlement". As virtually all forex transactions will be handled by CLS, this industry solution effectively eliminates settlement risk and offers a safe infrastructure for global forex markets.

Whilst the exchanges prepare to attract OTC products and OTC dealers increasingly adopt clearing-house structures (netting, collateralisation, standardisation), non-exchange based securities clearers are also offering clearing-house technology for OTC business.[8]

**(c) Policy Implications**

Clearing-houses have been in use since the 18th century to facilitate clearing and settling of domestic payments. It is therefore surprising that the clearing-house construction for derivatives has not advanced farther, particularly in the light of the liquidity-enhancing and risk reducing features. Recent BIS reports support various forms of multilateral clearing for the purpose of risk reduction.

By contrasting the organisational structure of the OTC market with that of the exchanges, it has become apparent that the exchanges have the edge in providing liquidity, a transparent market environment and in reducing, as well as managing, credit risk, whilst the OTC market has the edge in providing a greater choice of customised products. The key question, therefore, is whether the increased risk generated by OTC markets is offset by the gains from customisation. There is good reason to believe that this is not the case. As already stated, an examination of the OTC books of several major dealers suggests that the bulk (about 75%) of the OTC market is made of up plain vanilla items.[9] Indeed, such a conclusion is also supported by common sense, as the existing number of dealers simply could not have the capacity to customise every one of several trillion dollars worth of contracts. In addition, a large part of the remaining non-standard contracts can be partially standardised.

The choice of contracts to be traded on the exchange would depend on which would have the largest trading volume, and which are easiest to standardise and to value. Obvious candidates for being traded on an exchange are the interest and foreign exchange swaps, forwards, and options of frequently encountered maturity, strike price, and face value. The residual contracts, or parts of contracts, would remain with the dealers so that the credit evaluation and pricing expertise of dealers would continue to be needed. In addition, banks would garner the business of funding the margin requirements of exchange.

For the clearing-house-only solution, a clearing-house will have to agree on rules for valuing listed contracts, which will be easier the more standardised the contract. If, say, two thirds of the OTC transactions currently outstanding were routed through a clearing-house (some traded on an exchange, most non-traded), then a maximum of about US$80 billion of margin requirements (two thirds of replacement value, not taking account of netting) would need to be financed (GAO, 1994) and paid to holders of contracts that are in-the-money. Most of this credit would end up on the balance sheets of the clearing banks so that off-balance sheet credit positions would become on-balance sheet credits (Phillips, 1993). Banks would have to set aside 8% capital against the US$80 billion similar to the capital to be held against the replacement value of their off-balance sheet derivative books.

Importantly, the risk management and the multilateral netting features of a clearing-house would mean that its credit rating could readily become AAA even when its members are rated lower. Thus, the establishment of, say, a swap exchange/clearing-house would give counter-parties, currently excluded from the OTC markets for lack of sufficient credit quality or of risk-management capacity, access to swap exchange since marking-to-market will reduce or eliminate the credit risk. Participants in swap markets currently worried about adding to their exposure to individual dealers would then have the AAA clearing-house as counter-party.

Moving some OTC derivative trading to an exchange and most of the remainder to a clearing-house would thus greatly improve market transparency and solve some of the financial disclosure issues vexing regulators. In addition, a clearing-house structure has a built-in incentive structure—mutual responsibility—that would make it largely self-regulatory; it will therefore shift the burden of supervision and regulation back to market participants. Members would have an incentive to police each other in order to limit clearing-house losses. Supervisors and regulators, in turn would concentrate on the clearing-houses. With one or several OTC clearing-houses in place there would be less need to be concerned about achieving legal certainty on all kinds of bilateral and multilateral netting arrangements. Instead it would suffice to have legal certainty for multilateral netting done by the clearing-house and for the priority claim of the clearing-house to the margin money and guarantee fund, which already exists in all major financial centres.

At present, the playing field remains tilted in favour of the OTC markets, since the capital requirement for OTC positions translates into a cost to the dealer's counter-party of less than the counter-party's cost of having to finance the margin payments needed over the life of the contract. Indeed, *regulatory neutrality* would be achieved only if capital requirements for OTC contracts were raised sufficiently so that counter-parties' cost of obtaining an OTC contract (without margin requirement) from a dealer is approximately equal to the cost of funding margins for the identical contract traded on an exchange. This would provide the necessary incentive for high-volume OTC activity to migrate to an exchange/clearing-house structure. Overall there would be an economic gain: lower transaction costs and less systemic risk. The operating cost of an exchange tends to be less than that of a dealer system because of economies of scale generated by the high fixed cost of any trading and monitoring infrastructure and thanks to multilateral netting.

The cost of exchange-traded contracts is a relevant benchmark for the cost of achieving (virtually) zero systemic risk. Regulators concerned with systemic risk should take this benchmark to set the capital requirements of OTC products at the same level. Not doing so distorts markets and, in the end, raises questions about the credibility of regulatory concern about systemic risk.[10]

Even in the absence of increased capital requirements, pressure is already building up for a move towards a clearing-house structure of some key OTC derivative contracts. Such pressure comes from lower rated banks determined to increase their access to OTC types of derivatives, from counter-parties who want to reduce their exposure to individual dealers, and from the futures exchanges, who are introducing OTC-type products (e.g., flex options) which allow for some customisation with regard to expiry date, strike price and exercise style on expiration date. Most progress is being made in multilateral clearing[11] and settling of foreign exchange transactions to overcome the time-zone problem.

The key position of derivative markets in the financial system as a whole implies that their transparency, integrity and liquidity are an important public good. Hence the apparent tilting of the playing field in favour of the OTC markets, implied in the current regulatory structure, should be re-examined. By increasing capital requirements for OTC derivative positions and thereby making them at least as costly as exchange/clearing-house positions, it is possible to induce a shift towards the exchange/clearing-house market structure. In terms of the various risks generated by OTC derivative activity, credit risk would be reduced by marking-to-market with margining, transparency of price discovery would increase, liquidity risk would be reduced by the fungibility of contracts, legal risks would be eliminated under existing laws, and operation risk would be reduced. In sum, systemic risk would be substantially reduced without increased regulation. Quite to the contrary, regulation could be focused on the clearing-house. All the difficulties of effective supervision of dealers in a global market would be overcome with one sweep of the brush.

Such an approach would also be broadly consistent with ongoing efforts to reduce systemic risk in the financial system and to increase transparency through the shift towards real-time gross settlement for wholesale payments.

## 3. PHASING OUT THE BANKING FRANCHISE AND INSTITUTIONAL REGULATION

The traditional bank, transforming deposits into loans, is becoming a marginal segment of the financial sector, but regulatory tools and goals have retained their traditional focus. It does not make sense to supervise J.P. Morgan in the same way as a "Mum and Dad" bank that collects deposits to make loans and to guarantee the deposits of both. Deposit insurance creates moral hazard problems and has been identified as a major factor in the S&L crisis costing US taxpayers up to 4% of one year's GDP.

How can the desire to protect savers be reconciled with the equally important requirement not to put taxpayers' money at risk and thereby increase moral hazard, and the need to treat J.P. Morgan differently from any small bank? Differently, here, means two things: less hampered by general regulatory rules fitting the average bank, but neither J.P. Morgan nor the small traditional bank, because J.P. Morgan knows more about risk management than any regulator and the small bank has difficulties with complicated regulations, such as value-at-risk models, _and_ less implicit regulatory support.[12]

At present, if any of the world's major banks failed, central banking (and ultimately tax money) support would protect depositors' insured deposits and, most likely, uninsured deposits as well. Because banks are considered special, particularly special when big, a rescue operation would be organised with public money and by regulators twisting the arms of healthy banks to take over the failed bank. And, typically, regulators will delay surgery for fear of the pain. In recent years this has been happening in Japan on a large scale, in Scandinavian countries, in France, in Italy, and in many emerging countries. The costs can be amazingly high, higher than those of any other natural or man-made disaster as shown in Chapter 7. Society has a clear interest to induce banks to act responsibly and, in case of failure, not to socialise private costs. The latter may well be regarded as a necessary condition to achieve the former.

The implicit guarantee of intervention to provide liquidity in crisis situations, provided, for example, by the Federal Reserve, may be justified as long as interbank and repo markets are not sufficiently developed.[13] But, because market participants adjust their strategies to this implicit guarantee, this commitment may well have to be reviewed when well-developed money markets exist.

The views of academics and practitioners converge more and more to a workable approach based on two key components. The first consists in *isolating* deposit protection. The model for all such infrastructural renovations are money market funds. The most extreme proposal comes from Bryan (1988): to create "narrow" banks whose only purpose is to accept deposits and invest them in liquid short-term securities, very much like a money market fund, but with equity as an additional risk cushion. Depending on the restrictions imposed on admissible securities in terms of credit standing, maturity and liquidity, all risks (credit, market and liquidity risks) can be reduced as much as judged desirable and, except for outright fraud, deposit insurance would become redundant. As observed by Bisignano (1997), the narrow depository bank is in a sense a natural evolutionary outcome of the "unbundling" of financial services.

A more pragmatic and workable proposal is due to Pierce (1991). He proposes to isolate the *monetary functions* of banking in what he calls monetary service companies (MSCs). They can be legally independent parts of a financial conglomerate, but only MSCs can offer checking accounts and only MSCs can be part of the central bank-backed payments system. They do not need a separate physical location and customers might even be unaware of the legal separation of MSCs from the other divisions of a finance group. Keeping the MSCs within a financial conglomerate has the advantage of not foregoing economies of scope among different financial activities and of lowering the cost of MSCs. The full range of financial services could still be offered by a single supplier in a single location.

MSCs' assets are restricted to cash and marketable short-term securities—MSCs cannot make loans, nor even grant daylight overdrafts. The main task of MSCs would be to invest safely and to manage payments—no more maturity transformation, no risk on counter-parties, or only on a very limited scale. Checking accounts may still be insured—privately or otherwise—but such insurance would be much less costly than at present, given the high quality and liquidity of the MSC's assets. The rest of the financial conglomerate, which Pierce calls financial service company (FSC), can be fairly unrestricted or unregulated. In fact the name "bank" has disappeared from Pierce's terminology and FSCs would be regulated like any other industry.

As participation in the payments system is restricted to MSCs, systemic risk is very low. Funds must be deposited before a MSC can make a payment because overdrafts are ruled out. Credit lines must, therefore, be arranged among FSCs before the payment order. Problems could, therefore still arise and, if an FSC cannot make payments because it fails to arrange credit lines, other FSCs may experience difficulties. But this is no different from company A failing because it cannot recuperate IOUs from company B. Depositors are outside this circuit and so, in principle, is the central bank.

More generally, with the advent of collateralised settlement systems, institutions have to put up collateral to back payments. Then they no longer put the system at risk, so the need to restrict access to only those who are supervised (banks) diminishes. This last bastion of bank privilege is, therefore, likely to be eliminated. The logical consequence is to restrict access even further to MSCs or to open access to any financial intermediary, subject to credit standing, management record and minimum transaction volume.

The present focus of prudential *regulation* on institutions could then be replaced by regulation of certain *functions* (credit exposure, market risk, etc.). Regulation would, in principle, span all financial institutions thus ending regulatory distortions across institutions and effectively deal only with some financial functions, those that are exposed to market failure. Codes of conduct would still aim at market participants (only institutions and not functions "behave") so that institution-based rules would survive but against the background of servicing a specific function.

Functional regulation is the only practicable way to avoid regulatory discrimination. Merton (1994) gives a good example. In the United States, if a bank holds a mortgage on its balance sheet, it would have to maintain a 4% capital requirement. A non-bank holding the mortgage would not face the same constraint. This is the typical problem of institutional regulation. If, instead, the bank continues to originate and service mortgages, but sells the mortgages and uses the proceeds to buy US government bonds, then no capital requirement is necessary. If it wished, the bank could still receive the full economic equivalent of holding mortgages by entering into an amortisation swap in which it receives the return on mortgages and pays the returns on US government bonds. The bank would then have a position as if it were actually holding the mortgages, but its balance sheet would only show US government bonds and its capital requirements would have been reduced from 4% to 0.5%. Such examples can be generated *en masse*, and they all point to the dead-end of regulating the specific activities of banks. The only way out is to give up detailed institutional regulation and subject financial groups to functional guidelines.

It may be useful to describe the motivations and goals of functional regulations in more detail. First, the motivations. As was argued in Chapter 1, financial functions have been remarkably stable in history. What has changed is technology which has generated new techniques and products to carry out the functions and, as a result, institutions have changed. At any time one can observe the same phenomenon across borders: in all countries the basic financial functions (clearing and settling of payments, pooling of resources, transferring of resources across time and space, managing risk, providing price information, creating incentives to fulfil contracts) are the same, but the way they are executed depends on the institutional framework that varies greatly from country to country. Not only are functional uses of products more stable than the institutional forms of their vendors, they are also more uniform across national borders. They thereby constitute a better basis for international regulatory co-operation.

The main gain from a functional regulatory focus is to establish a level playing field by bringing all providers of a function under the same regulatory rule. Several examples were given in this book, demonstrating the equivalence between totally different products serving exactly the same function, such as an insurance guaranteeing interest and principal payment of a bond which is equivalent to a portfolio of the bond and a put option. Treating both operations from a functional point of view, rather than from an institutional one, reduces the opportunities for institutions to engage in "regulatory arbitrage", which wastes resources and undermines regulatory goals, and reduces the opportunities for rent-seeking and regulatory capture. The regulatory capture that exists at present is, however, one major reason for doubting that the economic logic of a functional approach will easily succeed.

A concrete functional regulatory proposal is due to Sandner and is quoted in Miller (1994). Figure 9.1 describes the basic idea of a Department of Financial Regulatory Service with eight separate commissioners each covering one clearly specified functional area, and all serve together, along with an additional chairman, on a governing board.

One can quibble with the details, but certainly the overall structure is much simpler and more rational than the existing regulatory structure in the United States. My own functional framework would include:

1. lending;
2. investment (savings products, such as money market funds, speculative products (below investment grade bonds) guaranteed investment products, such as pension plans);
3. risk management (fiduciary services, hedge structuring, financial engineering such as creation of structured notes);
4. insurance underwriting, distribution and guarantees;
5. processing and safekeeping (including payment services);

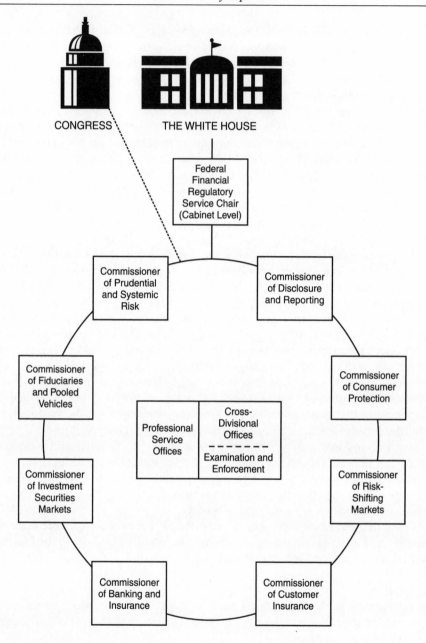

**Figure 9.1**   Proposed federal financial regulatory service
*Source*: Chicago Mercantile Exchange, Model for Financial Regulation, quoted from Miller (1994) © 1994 Elsevier Science, Amsterdam
Reprinted with kind permission

6. transaction intermediation (checking services, debit and credit card processing, brokering);
7. underwriting, market making and distribution.

In the light of this discussion the proposals in this chapter are clearly functional. Instead of regulating OTC products and exchange-traded products differently and by different regulators, this chapter argued that they serve the same function and should be regulated identically. The other basic proposals, creation of MSCs, recognises the specific deposit and payment functions. For the remainder of the financial service company, the recent initiatives of market participants are the right pointers: internal risk models generate estimates of market and credit risk (whether from lending or from OTC derivative positions) which have to be backed up by appropriate capital. The two categories, market and credit risk, are wide enough to minimise regulatory arbitrage and, if applied to any financial service company (rather than only to banks, as is the case at present), institutional arbitrage would be reduced as well.

## 4. REDEFINING THE RELATIONSHIP BETWEEN CENTRAL BANKS AND FINANCIAL INTERMEDIARIES

To discuss the future role of central banks, one must make some assumptions about the future financial infrastructure. It seems reasonable, in the light of the discussion in this chapter, to expect evolutionary paths along the following infrastructural avenues:

1. Clearing-houses will play an increasing role in view of their scale economies in mutualising risk management.
2. Isolation of deposit risk by creating monetary services companies within financial conglomerates, forced by law to invest deposits in liquid, low risk securities, effectively taking away the special banking franchise from financial conglomerates.
3. Alternatively, acceptance of banking systems, such as the German or Swiss systems based on universal banking, which have had to forego central bank support and state-backed deposit insurance and rely on mutual insurance. More diversified asset structures provide a slightly better hedge for deposits than loans alone—but not as much as a MSC.
4. Fully collateralised payments systems, such as TARGET, the future payments system operated by the European Central Bank.

Any of these avenues diminishes the need for direct involvement by the central bank. Once financial intermediation can be treated like any other industry, there is no longer any reason to entrust regulatory supervision to the central bank. In the United States the Federal Reserve only supervises a fraction of the banking system, in Germany the Bundesbank is not in charge of regulating banks, and in the United Kingdom the new 1997 Labour government has transferred the regulatory task from the Bank of England to the Securities and Investment Board. This creates the opportunity to regulate the entire British financial industry with common, undiscriminatory approaches along functional lines—something the Central Bank at the apex of the banking system, but not of the financial system, could never have done. This does not imply that there has to be one super-regulator, although this is an option. Several regulators could co-exist, each one responsible for a particular type of function and not for a particular type of institution.

The roles of monetary policy and of regulators would be neatly separated, with the additional advantage that the central bank would be under less pressure to act as lender-of-last-resort to an institution with solvency or liquidity problems. That this separation works has been demonstrated in countries such as Germany or Switzerland where separation has been a fact of life for a long time.

Separate, independent regulators can then limit their supervisory function to monitoring the financial intermediaries' risk-management systems, their respect of traditional codes of conduct and basic prudential regulations, and their disclosure of information to other market participants. In principle, little direct supervision would be necessary. Financial firms would pursue their business like any other firm: a long, but not complete way to "free banking" or, better, "free financial intermediation". This leaves unanswered one crucial question: *quid* "too big to fail"? Whilst any firm should know that there is no safety net, it is difficult to make this credible to the most important institutions. The difficulty is not unique to banking (after the Chrysler rescue, should one believe that the US government would let Boeing, GM or IBM go under?), but more pronounced. Failure of a major bank would not only affect its employees and shareholders (important stakeholders), but many lenders as well (CD and bond holders)—as with any other corporation. The only difference is the existence of a special class of lenders, namely depositors. If they are taken care of through a MSC or any other ring-fencing arrangement, then it should become possible to let even the largest banks fail.

The Central Bank's role of lender-of-last-resort was never intended, but nevertheless regularly practised, for cases of insolvency. It was intended for situations of illiquidity which, with developed money markets, have become a remote possibility, except during periods of exceptional stress. Bail-outs of financial institutions would, of course, still be possible if the government so decided, but it would be much more difficult to justify a bail-out to taxpayers if deposits are not at risk.

This no bail-out policy is already a powerful signal for self-regulation, but may lack credibility, especially for large banks, until a real test case occurs.

One possibility is to require large banks to issue credit derivatives regularly (explained in Chapter 6) and use the price of derivatives to judge what the market thinks of the bank.

What then are central banks supposed to do once they have withdrawn from bank supervision? The obvious answer seems to be that central banks should focus on monetary policy. This is certainly what the Bundesbank does and what the Bank of England will do. But, as argued in more detail in the next chapter, this job is not likely to last for long as electronic money will soon make cash and checking accounts superfluous and money-market fund-like investment vehicles allow a flexible management of near-money securities. The money base has already been shrinking and, with a disappearing money base, the monetary control of the central bank in five to 20 years will disappear. What will remain is the important role of the central bank in providing liquidity when exceptional circumstances temporarily perturb money markets. Its objective should not be to stabilise rates, but rather to cap rates potentially reaching for the sky. Nor should the central bank fund those borrowers whose illiquidity and/or deteriorating solvability requires an increased risk premium. The most effective and neutral instruments for rate capping are repos and futures markets, not the discount window or unsecured, direct lending.

Is this not a risky strategy? After all, in the October 1987 crash, when dealers' credit lines evaporated, it was only thanks to the Fed's rapid liquidity injection and arm-twisting of banks that a liquidity crisis among banks and dealers was avoided and the bourses' landslide stopped. This may be true, but the other side of the coin, developed in Chapter 2, is that knowing that the Fed will be there to help out encourages banks and other intermediaries to hold less capital and less liquidity. This is what I called the unintended subsidy to derivatives dealing. In order to avoid such unintended effects, rather than the trivial cost of the Fed assuming a high credit risk for a few days (but only because all is well that ends well!), is it not high time to make market participants assume fully the risks they take? In countries where the monetary authorities have made it clear that they will not intervene, such as Hong Kong, Germany and Switzerland, intermediaries hold much more capital and liquidity and, indeed, have avoided crashes without central bank help. Even on a day-to-day basis, the volatility of overnight rates in the United States and Germany are very close (Kasman 1992).

Many such proposals have failed, or could fail, to gain political acceptance if there is no wide international acceptance. A good example is provided by Folkerts-Landau *et al.* (1996) who argue that the US financial system and the US dollar are benefiting from the more generous support of Fedwire by the Federal Reserve in comparison to the (future) European real-time gross settlement (RTGS) system. It is, therefore, difficult to establish fair competition among financial systems based on different infrastructures.

In addition, there remains the problem posed by the rapidly evolving internationalisation of finance. Lesser regulatory direct interventions reduce the problem somewhat, but more international co-operation in building infrastructures is certainly desirable.[14] An important proposal along the lines suggested above was made in 1997 by the Group of 30. The proposal consists in the creation of a steering committee to set standards for the way global institutions run themselves. The committee would represent the leading global financial groups, but work closely with national supervisors, and would set out standards of best practice in areas such as credit assessment and provisioning, disclosure and operational controls. The effort is targeted at the wholesale end of the financial industry as national supervisors would be reluctant to leave areas, such as the treatment of retail investors, to self-regulation.

Another private sector proposal was published by the Institute of International Finance in 1997. This report suggests that financial supervisors should create a special supervisory arrangement for globally active financial institutions (less than a hundred institutions in 1997) whose key goal is to foster the safety and soundness of the global financial system.[15] This arrangement should initially focus on collecting information on common risk types (credit risk, contingent credit risk, market risks) to establish a "risk-based supervisory framework". (This is clearly a functional regulatory approach.) The home country supervisor for each globally active group should receive information on common risk types and should use it to generate an assessment of the group's global risk profile. This assessment should be communicated to supervisors for individual entities in the group. This implies that supervisors accept other supervisors' judgements—a process already well established in Europe with the single passport approach.

Beyond that co-operation there is a need to deal with inter-country spillovers. Surveillance of less mature financial markets is a new responsibility of the IMF (including supervision of supervisors) that is certain to gain in importance.[16] The Bank for International Settlement acts as a co-ordination forum for developed financial markets to which graduated emerging markets have been admitted in 1996.

# 5. CONCLUSION

Regulators have to do less and return their risk-management responsibilities to market participants. They also have to do a better job, ending present competitive discriminations due to the fact that institutions and not financial functions are being regulated. Most of these implicit penalties or subsidies are unintended. As argued repeatedly in this book, the Federal Reserve's role in ensuring liquidity even for the most pronounced stress situations has subsidised the most liquidity intensive activities, in particular OTC dealing.

Regulators must simultaneously extend their coverage from banks (a species threatened by extinction) to all financial intermediaries and reduce the risk for taxpayers' money.

All this is achievable if the basic infrastructure of the financial industry is renovated. This chapter has made two important proposals. The first consists in stopping the subsidisation of OTC activities and facilitating migration to clearing-house arrangements. The second is a redefinition of the banking franchise by isolating the deposit and payment functions within financial conglomerates in legally separate companies, secured by liquid, safe securities and strict prohibition of lending activities. The small sub-set of financial intermediation providing monetary services would still be "special"—a small price to pay for "normality" of all other financial services.

There are thus practical ways of lowering systemic risk whilst reducing the supervisory pressure on the financial industry. But will they be adopted? Even if all parties concerned agreed to the proposals made in this chapter, the answer is far from certain for two reasons. The first is that regulators tend to become captive of the regulatees and derive benefits from the established equilibrium. The second reason is that, as for clocks in the 15th century, financial evolution generates economies of scale and is, therefore, path-dependent. That is, at some point an institutional arrangement is adopted even if it is not optimal. Once established it is very difficult to reverse the trend and opt for another solution (see Miller 1994 and Bisignano 1997).

# ENDNOTES

1 In comparison, in an equivalent OTC deal there are no margin payments at all.
2 Most clearing-houses are owned by small groups of large banks.
3 Given that the use of a clearing-house structure can reduce the impact of inter-bank spillover and hence the amount of systemic risk, less stringent capital requirements are needed. This reduction in capital requirement can be used to give the currently dominating dealer banks the incentive to join a clearing-house structure.
4 If there is no agreement on the standards of a valuation model, then a great advantage of the clearing-house approach will be lost. This has been a feature marring Hits.
5 The Philadelphia Stock Exchange has taken the notion a step further with its *United Currency Options Market* (Ucom). Ucom allows trading in up to 110 currency pairs in a more flexible structure than previously existed. These include the usual dollar, yen and large European currencies, as well as some smaller ones, such as the Italian lira and Spanish peseta. In the future more currencies will be added to reflect the growing interest in such areas as Eastern Europe and China. Already PHLX is setting up a relationship with the Hong Kong Futures Exchange to trade Ucom products. HKFE, meanwhile, launched its own currency products, Rolling Forex, futures contracts on the deutschemark and the yen.
6 Available figures from the International Swaps and Derivatives Association (ISDA) suggest that in 1995 up to 10% of the replacement value of the swaps (totalling US$78 billion) are collateralised. ISDA expects that level to grow.

7 There are four key parts to the project, or four services separated out of the traditional clearing-house exchange-service package. The first involves on-line evaluation, either on the basis of market prices or, when not available, on theoretical values. In addition to pricing availability, this service has the advantage of being provided by an independent and credible party. Second, collateral management and administration with regular revaluation of market positions and collateral requirements. Third, an electronic bulletin board for listing customised OTC transactions—without revealing the identity of counter-parties. Fourth, and perhaps most important, a standardised cash-swap facility, offering exchange-traded, plain vanilla swaps.

8 CEDEL, a Luxembourg-based clearing organisation, has developed its Global Credit Support Service (GCSS). Designed to cover all credit exposures, GCSS is particularly attractive for swap counter-parties who want full collateralisation on a regular mark-to-market basis. CEDEL takes advantage of a Luxembourg legal concept, the _fiduciary_, which has legal title to the collateral it holds, thereby eliminating legal uncertainty on a contract between parties of different jurisdictions. Strictly speaking, CEDEL does not offer itself as a clearing-house for swaps, but as an agent for holding and managing swaps collateral.

9 Folkerts-Landau and Steinherr (1994).

10 The advantage of dealers in customising risk-management products will remain important. But the increased capital requirement will imply that the price of the customised products will rise _vis-à-vis_ the standardised exchange-traded product. Thus their cost will be more reflective of their risk.

11 A path-breaking innovation for a robust legal framework for a multilateral payments system is the "single obligation structure". Developed by the Ecu Banking Association, the Single Obligation Structure is a legal concept of payments obligations defined from the outset on a net basis. The balance established for each participant in the payments system every time a payment order is transmitted constitutes the valid and enforceable payment obligation or claim of each participant towards the community of all other participants.

12 Already in 1986 Chase Manhattan undertook a study of the value of its banking charter and discovered that its business, which depended on a banking charter, had lost money, while its more profitable half dozen businesses could be conducted without a charter. The major competition in these areas came from non-banks. Quoted from Bisignano (1997).

13 In 1996, the global size of the repo market is estimated at US$3000 billion, with the United States accounting for US$1500 billion, France US$220 billion and Germany US$110 billion.

14 The Basle Committee and IOSCO produced a joint statement for the Lyon Summit in 1995 formulating eight basic principles for fostering co-operation between banking and securities regulators. An informal tripartite group of G10 supervisors from the three main financial sectors (banks, securities, insurance firms) embarked in 1993 on a study of supervising financial conglomerates.

15 Supervisors have also turned to the thorny problem of financial conglomerates spanning more than one industry segment, without much success so far. The international banking, securities and insurance supervisors (the Tripartite Group) looked at the issues in their 1995 report.

16 Goldstein (1997) proposes a voluntary international Banking Standard—a set of minimum standards in eight key areas of banking supervision—for developing countries. Compliance is proposed to be monitored by the World Bank and the IMF.

# PART IV

# A LOOK INTO THE FUTURE

*«IF ONLY THERE WERE A FUTURES MARKET FOR DOCTORS' EARNINGS ?»*

# 10

# Derivatives: the Future of Finance

---

## *Antofagasta (Chile), Summer of 2020*

Carlos Salas is a 60 year-old physicist living in a comfortable home on the outskirts of Antofagasta. In his younger days he had the impression of living at the end of the world and had felt cut-off from the mainstream of new developments in his field of study and everything else. But he remained in his native town because he loved the Pacific coast and the beauty of the nearby Andean mountains.

All this had changed in the second half of his life. His computer connected him to the rest of the world as well as those living in Santiago, or New York for that matter.

Since his retirement ten years ago, he has had ample time to take care of his personal finances and to think about how financial markets work. It's now already many years since he last visited his bank or that he had a peso in his pocket. A chip card takes care of all his payments and every day he receives a detailed statement of all his expenditures and his net worth. He stopped his newspaper subscription some fifteen years ago, when he started to have all real-time information on screen. For a modest payment he also has access to specialised providers of news, economic and financial data world-wide, analyses of companies, securities and derivatives market performance, optimal portfolio management results, and much more. His father Julio still invested exclusively in Chilean securities, because Chile was the frame of reference that he thought he understood best. Carlos seizes an opportunity whenever he can find one—and anywhere in the world. Information and transaction costs are the same everywhere, so there is no reason to constrain himself to Chilean investments. His investments are well diversified and he carries little risk that cannot be diversified.

In fact, his account is with a bank in Dacca, Bangladesh for convenience and cost. It is a very convenient account called "global account". It is global in the sense that his pension rights, all his properties (his house, car, securities), his hedges (such as his real estate futures hedge) and liabilities are contained in this account. Computers continuously keep track of his account and constantly mark both assets and liabilities to market, making them effectively liquid.

The global account greatly facilitates financial processing and reporting. His overall "net worth" is computed daily and, should he so desire, he could instantly draw on the value of his pension rights, or of his house, to buy a new fishing boat.

Automated analytics provide him with customised investment management, making his accounts far superior to mutual funds in the old days. In effect, he manages his own mutual fund. For his investments he still occasionally uses a broker. But most of the time he just consults his global electronic bulletin board and enters his offer directly to the seller without passing through an intermediary. He sometimes feels like his own banker in this global market and actually enjoys his video-chats with counter-parties all over the world.

Probably because of his training in theoretical physics, he enjoys even more following research in finance, all available on his screen. He compares the evolution in finance to the much older change from Newtonian physics to quantum physics and Einstein's theory of gravitation. In their continued efforts to isolate risks that can be priced separately, to simulate and forecast events that are non-linear and often chaotic, researchers in finance have taken inspiration from thermodynamics, quantum physics, neural systems, chaos theory and molecular biology.

One area of physics that had turned out to be particularly useful in finance has been the gauge theory. Carlos had done research work at the Institute of Spectroscopy in Moscow with Kirill Ilinski, after having read his paper "Gauge Theory of Arbitrage" (1997). Treating net present value and exchange rates as a parallel transport in some fibre bundle makes it possible to map capital market structures onto quantised gauge fields (representing interest rates and prices), interacted with a money flow field. The gauge transformations of the matter field (cash flows) correspond to a dilatation of security units which can be eliminated by a proper tune of the gauge connection. The curvature tensor for the connection consists of the excess returns over the risk-free interest rate for the local arbitrage operation. Free quantum gauge theory is equivalent to log-normal walks of asset prices. In the general case, capital markets can be mapped onto the quantum system of particles with positive ("securities") and negative ("debts") charges which interact with each other through electromagnetic fields.

This modelling can easily handle deviations of the distribution functions from the log-normal framework. Effects, such as changes in the shape of the distribution function, "screening" of its tails for large price movements and non-Markovian memory of price random walks are well explained by dampening of the arbitrage and directed price movements of speculators. The derived dynamic portfolio theory has as static limit the standard portfolio theory of the 1990s. The dynamic version, in which time-dependent correlation functions play a role of response functions of the market to external perturbations, is much more powerful and comprehensive and tracks markets much better.

These advances in finance have substantially reduced the amount of unwanted risk borne by individuals, firms or government agencies. Risks are better quantified, priced and, hence, managed. Reflecting on the gains to society of these scientific advances, he is impressed by a local example: two years ago two tunnels through the Andes were completed for better communications with neighbouring Argentina. A single Chilean entrepreneur masterminded the financing of US$27 billion.

> "Banks are dinosaurs. Give
> me a piece of the transaction
> business—and they are history."
>
> *Bill Gates*

D URING the next twenty-five years one should not expect a repeat of the innovatory transfiguration of financial products that occurred over the last twenty-five years. This judgement is based on two touchstones. The first is that all those "seeds lying under the snow" have come to the surface as significant innovations. Second, if the view is correct that innovations were mainly driven by the desire to circumvent regulations and taxes, then in a more de-regulated world where financial products are no longer taxed in a discriminatory fashion (at least in some countries), the past innovatory thrust is on the ebb, except in countries where regulations and inefficient tax structures are still in place and there is a need to catch up.

In this author's view, financial systems will primarily create hedge vehicles against types of risk for which instruments are not available at present; create new opportunities for risk sharing, risk policy and inter-temporal or spatial transfers of resources ("completing the markets"); create higher liquidity for traded assets and render currently non-tradeable assets tradeable. Higher liquidity and competitive pressure in a global market with a larger number of suppliers and cross-product substitutes will lower transaction costs and bring about reductions in "agency" costs caused by either asymmetric information between two parties or the principal's incomplete monitoring capacity of the agent's performance. To see what is at stake, it is useful to recall that even in the United States, where markets are the most developed, only some 13% of total household wealth is in assets for which liquid markets exist (*The Economist*, 14 May 1994). The remainder is in illiquid assets, such as human capital (72%), real estate (8%), equity in unincorporated business (3%) and other.

Although one cannot predict with precision entirely new kinds of financial innovations, the application of existing techniques to so far uncovered or new problems will have a major impact—even more fundamental and pervasive than the innovations of the past twenty-five years.

This optimism is based on available economic insights. This book has demonstrated the substantial gains for individuals and society as a whole of efficient instruments for trading off unwanted risks. A huge potential gain is there to be harvested. But will it? My answer is yes, because the basic knowledge is available and the incentives to satisfy potential demand are provided by huge remunerations to innovators as in the past. And the continued process of innovation is fuelled by substantial synergies: each new product increases demand and facilitates growth, which in turn increases demand for the derivative product, lowering its transaction costs, and relaunches the synergetic process.

Today, futures or options exist for a variety of financial assets: foreign exchange, debt instruments, individual stocks or stock indexes. They are available in standardised products, traded on exchanges, or on a custom-built basis supplied by financial intermediaries. They are available as such or embedded in a structured deal, decomposable into the basic financial transaction and the derivative (e.g., swaps, bonds with warrants, bond issues with a DRS). Two trends can be expected. First, the sustained growth of structured assets and liabilities with embedded options as financial intermediaries are compelled to achieve product differentiation for income generation. At least one thing is sure: competition shaves off spreads on plain vanilla products. Banks will become more and more suppliers of securities or contracts incorporating derivatives structures related to ever more numerous performance indexes, and trade these products on their own account. Second, as argued in preceding chapters, standardised derivatives will increasingly migrate to a clearing-house structure, precisely because the income they generate will be insufficient for tying up banks' capital.

I expect that over the next twenty-five years markets will develop that allow the hedging of "macro risks", to an extent comparable to today's exchange rate and interest rate risk, with major consequences for the behaviour of the economy. One consequence will be that governments' policies (regulation, taxation) will be blunted and thereby inefficiencies reduced. I discuss these macro risks, not so much with the aim of a complete analysis of what is to come, but rather as examples for the pervasive consequences of some foreseeable innovations.

Section 1 demonstrates that institutional investors—the prime movers of the US financial evolution during the last twenty-five years—will become equally important players in Europe and Japan, with similar needs for risk-management finance, and similar positive feed-backs for capital market development.

The following sections look at specific issues where derivatives will play a major role. Section 2 gives a particularly important example of equity swaps that result in efficiency gains and make controls of domestic capital markets ineffective.

Section 3 turns to corporate ownership rights and traces possible changes derived from the decomposition of current ownership rights into separate risk categories, priced and traded separately as derivatives.

Although financial transactions in stocks, debt and foreign exchange entail major risks, there are macro risks which affect every man and woman and for which derivatives do not yet exist. The three major macro risks that spring to mind are: inflation (Section 4), variations in personal income or economic activity (sectoral or geographic) (Section 5) and in real estate (Section 6).[1] Very appropriately, Section 7 raises the question of whether all these dramatic changes together imply the end of banking.

# 1. THE ASCENT OF INSTITUTIONAL INVESTORS

The management of securities portfolios has become one of the world's fastest growing industries. Fuelled in part by the global bull markets in the 1990s, the worldwide stock market capitalisation is approaching US$20 trillion in 1997. The value of the world's fixed income markets adds up to a similar figure. It is estimated that the assets of the global asset management industry exceeded US$22 trillion at end-1995. This included US$8.2 trillion of pension funds assets, US$5.3 trillion in mutual funds assets and US$6.4 trillion in assets held by insurance companies. Market liberalisation, privatisation of government-controlled assets, pension reforms and demographic trends all point to continued strong growth of institutional investments, sustaining the global bull market further.

Chapter 2 made the point that a very important ingredient of the American model of finance has been the importance of institutional investors. They played the key role in promoting shareholder value and thereby strongly influenced the evolution of corporate governance; they contributed and sustained disintermediation; they applied professional asset and risk management and have become by far the most important end-users of derivatives.

It is to be expected that institutional investors will rise to similar importance in other developed economies with comparable repercussions on the financial industry. For one, taking advantage of the opportunities offered by a global market and by science-supported portfolio and risk-management techniques is beyond the means of most individual investors. But, perhaps more importantly, in many developed countries the demographic evolution and public budget constraints make it mandatory to replace non-funded pension schemes by funded pension schemes.

**Pension Funds**

Table 10.1 shows that public sector pension expenditure in 1995 represented only 4.1% of GDP in the United States as compared to over 10% in most European countries. By 2040 these costs will reach 20% of GDP in some European countries and 15% in Japan. In any pay-as-you-go system the cost of employer and employee contributions is directly reflected in companies' gross labour costs, so that countries with rising costs for pensions face a competitive disadvantage in international competition.

The discrepancy between funding and costs are such that reforms are unavoidable. For example, in Italy the stock of financial assets held by pension funds and life insurance companies represented 11.4% of GDP in 1995 (Table 10.2), whereas pension expenditures were 13.3% in the same year. In contrast, financial assets of pension funds in the same year were 130.3% of GDP in the

**Table 10.1** OECD Projected Pension Expenditures as Percentage of GDP (Under Existing Programmes)

| Country | 1995 | 2000 | 2010 | 2020 | 2040 |
|---|---|---|---|---|---|
| United States | 4.1 | 4.2 | 4.5 | 5.2 | 7.1 |
| Japan | 6.6 | 7.5 | 9.6 | 12.4 | 14.9 |
| Germany | 11.1 | 11.5 | 11.8 | 12.3 | 18.4 |
| France | 10.6 | 9.8 | 9.7 | 11.6 | 14.3 |
| Italy | 13.3 | 12.6 | 13.2 | 15.3 | 21.4 |
| United Kingdom | 4.5 | 4.5 | 5.2 | 5.1 | 5.0 |
| Canada | 5.2 | 5.0 | 5.3 | 6.9 | 9.1 |
| Australia | 2.6 | 2.3 | 2.3 | 2.9 | 4.3 |
| Spain | 10.0 | 9.8 | 10.0 | 11.3 | 16.8 |
| Netherlands | 6.0 | 5.7 | 6.1 | 8.4 | 12.1 |
| Belgium | 10.4 | 9.7 | 8.7 | 10.7 | 15.0 |

*Source*: Roseveare et al. (1996)

United Kingdom or 86.1% in the United States, with respective pension expenditures of 4.5% and 4.1% of GDP in 1995.

The successful shift to funded pension programmes with the need to produce sizeable returns on pension assets will, among others, require greater amounts invested in equity than hitherto, a more international asset base and more intensive use of risk-management techniques (derivatives). Derivatives are important for efficient day-to-day management and, perhaps more importantly, to hedge in a declining market. The importance of portfolio insurance (explained in Chapter 4) becomes tangibly clear when remembering that the US stock market reached its level of 1972 in real terms only in 1987—15 years later (see Chapter 3). In Japan, the stock market in 1997 was at half the maximum level of 1989. It is painful to imagine what contribution-based pensions would be for unhedged pension funds moving into the market just before a very long decline.

To get a feel for the changes to come, it is instructive to compare the United Kingdom with Germany. The United Kingdom has a stock market capitalisation of US$1396 billion (end-1995), as compared to US$575 billion in Germany. UK pension funds held more than half of their assets of US$814 billion (1995) in domestic equity and one-quarter in international equities. German pension funds with US$70 billion in 1995 held less than 10% in equity.

**Mutual Funds**

As for mutual funds, they have grown in the United States at a compound rate of 26% from 1978 to 1996, or from US$56 billion in 1978 to US$3540 billion in 1996 with 9% invested abroad (exceeding in that year for the first time deposits in banks). This is expected to double by 2001 and a lot of catching-up can be expected outside the United States. On a per capita basis, in 1996 Americans held mutual funds worth US$14 000 as compared to US$2300 for Germans or Italians, US$3500 for the British, but US$9500 for the French.

Mutual funds have been phenomenally successful despite obvious shortcomings. They are very much like the equally successful tour operators. Both benefit from asymmetric information and the reasonable assumption that professionals have better information and management tools. Nevertheless most mutual funds available to retail investors under-perform relevant market benchmarks, like tour operators for similar reasons: high operational costs, trying to be smart by half in stock-picking, misjudging market trends.[2] Clients buy on the basis of a lavish prospectus that invites dreaming and they pay up-front. Although all the photographs shown in the prospectus were taken on sunny days, it may, of course, rain. And the hotel may possibly not be as luxurious and its staff not as helpful as the pictures suggested. Competition is useful, but if most tour operators disappoint, one may spend many miserable vacations before the search is successful. Regulation can help in making sure that clients are not misled. But index funds are more encouraging: funds that take as a benchmark, say, the S&P 500 and either replicate it or, more cost effectively, invest in S&P 500 futures are a sure way of tracking the benchmark at minimal cost.[3] As more and more futures instruments become available, this technology can be used for an increasing number of markets, thereby mounting the competition needed for non-index funds.

A systemic bias viciously affects mutual funds. When the stock market falls, mutual fund investors sell, forcing the fund to sell shares in a declining market. Given the importance of the industry, selling can accentuate the stock market's decline, accelerating mutual fund liquidation, and so on. Only funds operating hedge strategies, or locking in investors for extended periods, such as hedge funds, would escape this destabilising dynamics.

Table 10.2 depicts the growth of institutional investors in major countries. If the United States is taken as a benchmark then the scope for increased financial investments by pension funds and other institutional investors in Japan and European countries is truly gigantic. The potential demand of financial assets promises well for the success of privatisation of state-owned companies, or the stock market introduction of non-public companies and a sustained bull market for the next generation. Against this background, the single European currency, completing the integration of the European capital market, should also benefit from this trend of a greater role for institutional investors and support this trend.

**Table 10.2** The Growth of Institutional Investors—Financial Assets as a Percentage of GDP

| | Pension Funds and Life Insurance Companies | | | | | Collective Investment Institutions | | | | | Total | | | | |
|---|---|---|---|---|---|---|---|---|---|---|---|---|---|---|---|
| | 1980 | 1985 | 1990 | 1995 | 1996* | 1980 | 1985 | 1990 | 1995 | 1996** | 1980 | 1985 | 1990 | 1995 | 1996* |
| United States | 41.8 | 58.1 | 67.9 | 86.1 | 92.5 | 5.0 | 11.7 | 19.2 | 35.8 | 42.8 | 46.8 | 69.7 | 87.1 | 121.9 | 135.2 |
| Japan | 18.9 | 27.7 | 45.2 | 62.0 | 59.9 | 2.4 | 6.0 | 12.2 | 10.7 | 9.0 | 21.3 | 33.7 | 57.4 | 72.7 | 69.0 |
| Germany | 19.3 | 27.5 | 31.4 | 39.2 | 42.5 | 3.2 | 5.8 | 9.8 | 15.3 | 18.1 | 22.5 | 33.3 | 41.2 | 54.5 | 60.6 |
| France* | 9.1 | 14.0 | 20.6 | 39.6 | 45.2 | 2.8 | 14.5 | 31.1 | 35.7 | 37.6 | 11.9 | 28.5 | 51.7 | 75.4 | 82.8 |
| Italy*** | 1.4 | 1.7 | 7.0 | 11.4 | 12.2 | | 2.3 | 3.4 | 6.6 | 9.6 | | 4.0 | 10.4 | 18.0 | 21.8 |
| UK | 28.2 | 43.2 | 82.8 | 130.3 | 134.4 | 2.1 | 5.7 | 8.4 | 16.1 | 17.7 | 30.3 | 48.9 | 91.2 | 146.4 | 152.1 |
| Canada | 30.4 | 38.1 | 47.7 | 62.5 | 65.7 | 1.5 | 2.5 | 5.3 | 18.8 | 24.7 | 31.9 | 40.6 | 53.0 | 81.3 | 90.4 |

*Notes*: * For German, France and Italy, all insurances.
    ** For Japan, March; for Italy and the UK, September.
    *** Total assets; at book value.

*Sources*: National data

## 2. THE END OF CAPITAL CONTROLS

As illustrated by the turmoil in European exchange markets during 1992–93, central banks are powerless to maintain fixed exchange rates in which market operators have stopped believing. Some economists have proposed to re-introduce capital controls in Europe (e.g., Eichengreen and Wyplosz 1993) or, worldwide, a tax ("Tobin tax") to blunt the knives of speculators. These proposals neglect, however, the fact that, with well-established derivatives markets, speculators need not transfer currencies in the spot market. A spec-ulator expecting a fall in value of, say, the British pound can sell pounds forward in the futures market, buy a put option or enter into a currency swap. He can do so with a domestic or a foreign counter-party. For some of those operations no initial cash outlays are necessary, for others (options) only a small amount is required. Capital controls, in the presence of established derivatives markets, are ineffective.

Capital controls are justified by their proponents on the basis of the social cost of "excessive speculation" and the instability and increased uncertainty caused thereby. In emerging or developing countries capital controls are maintained to prevent flight of domestic capital. These are valid points. All capital controls, however, also cause social costs because they help to sustain domestic policies that induce the capital flight in the first place. As a conse-quence domestic asset holders are prevented from a desirable diversification and foreign inflows are discouraged by the increased transaction costs. The social costs of capital controls are particularly high on a per capita basis for small countries since the potential gains from international diversification are largest for the small countries whose domestic economy is by necessity less diversified.

Of course, capital controls cannot easily prevent residents from diversifying. For example, they could buy futures or options on stocks abroad. But such a diversification strategy is difficult to manage. It would be easier and more advantageous to swap domestic returns for foreign returns, as proposed by Merton (1990) and others (see Technical Insight 10.1). This author does expect that such swap markets will develop for very much the same reasons the swap market initially developed to get round UK capital controls.

Note that this swap innovation is not designed to circumvent the stated objective of the capital-control regulation, to prevent domestic capital flight. Instead, it is designed to eliminate (or at least reduce) the unintended and undesirable "side effects" of this policy on efficient risk-bearing and diversification. There are pension funds in Canada and other smaller countries that carry out such swaps to improve diversification. Whether or not stock index swaps turn out to be a major real-world innovation is to be seen. This author believes it will. It also demonstrates how a simple but finely tuned financial innovation of trivial intrinsic cost could help reduce the social cost of "blunt" policy tools that affect many countries around the world.

---

**Technical Insight 10.1**   Stock index swaps

Suppose that small-country domestic investors (perhaps through domestic mutual funds or financial intermediaries) who already own the domestic equity were to enter into swap agreements with large foreign investors. In the swap the total return per dollar on the small country's domestic stock market is exchanged annually for the total return per dollar on a market-value-weighted average of the world stock markets (or of a sub-set, say, the US stock market). This exchange of returns could be in a common currency, dollars, or adjusted to different currencies along similar lines to currency swap agreements. The magnitudes of the dollar exchanges are determined by the notional or principal amount of the swap to which per dollar return differences apply. As is the usual case with swaps, there is no initial payment by either party to the other for entering the agreement.

Such a swap agreement effectively transfers the risk of the small country stock market to foreign investors and provides the domestic investors with the risk-return pattern of a well-diversified international portfolio. Since there are no initial payments between parties, there are no initial capital flows in or out of the country. Subsequent payments which may be either inflows or outflows involve only the difference between the returns on the two stock market indices and no principal amounts flow. For example, on a notional or principal amount of

US$100 million, if, *ex post*, the world stock market earns 12% a year and the small country market earns 15%, there is only a flow of US$3 million in that year out of the country. The small country investors make net payments precisely when they can "best" afford it: namely, when their local market has outperformed the world markets. In those years in which the domestic market underperforms the world stock markets, the swap generates net cash flows into the country to its domestic investors.

Foreign investors also benefit from the swap by avoiding the costs of trading in individual securities in the local markets and by not having the problems of corporate control issues that arise when foreigners acquire large ownership positions in domestic companies of small (developing) countries. Unlike standard cash investments in equities or debt, the default or expropriation exposure of foreign investors is limited to the difference in returns instead of the total gross return plus principal (in the example, US$3 million vs. US$115 million).

The potential exposure of foreign investors to manipulation by local investors is probably less for the swap than for direct transactions in individual stocks. It is more difficult to manipulate a broad market index than the price of a single stock. Even if settlement intervals for swaps are standardised at six months or one year, the calendar settlement dates will differ for each swap, depending on the date of its initiation. Hence, with some swaps being settled every day, manipulators would have to keep the prices of shares permanently low to succeed. Furthermore, with the settlement terms of swaps based on the per period rate of return, an artificially low price (and low rate of return) for settlement this year will induce an artificially high rate of return for settlement next year. Thus, gains from manipulation in the first period are given back in the second, unless the price can be kept low over the entire life of the swap. Since typical swap contract maturities might range from two to 10 years (with semi-annual or annual settlements), this would be difficult to achieve.

*Source:* Merton (1990)

# 3. OWNERSHIP AND CORPORATE GOVERNANCE

As argued in Chapter 1, the move from unlimited liability to limited liability was a major innovation that facilitated the collection of large sums of public savings, allowed savers to invest in small amounts in a given enterprise and spread the risk over a portfolio of shares. Without limited liability the modern corporation would not exist and, presumably, neither would large-scale industrial production. Privately owned firms or partnerships have virtually disappeared from Fortune's 500 largest firms in industry, though they were more successful in banking. Goldman-Sachs, the British merchant banks and Geneva's private banks are, or were, held in partnerships. This can be a major disadvantage, particularly in an expanding market where new capital is required to maintain market shares.

A good example is provided by the fate of the glorious British merchant banks, five of which (Morgan Grenfell, Hoare Govett, Barings, Warburg and Kleinwort Benson) were recently absorbed by continental European universal banks, and other financial institutions were absorbed by large city or US institutions (Smith New Court) able to provide the necessary capital and distribution outlets. What put the merchant banks in a difficult position was the globalisation of financial markets, making it necessary to have a presence in the United States, in Asia and in Continental European markets. Merchant banks have the expertise, but lack the capital. The time for partnerships appears to be definitely past its high noon, except for smaller undertakings. At least, so it seems.

Ronald Coase (1988) asked the Nobel-prize worthy question: "Why do firms exist?" The reason is embarrassingly simple, but important: transaction costs. The costs of co-ordinating diverse activities that contribute to a final product and of making contracts with managers and workers, of transacting with lenders and owners can be very substantial, but if the firm has a *raison d'être* this co-ordination cost must be lower than buying all inputs from independent suppliers. The biggest problem is that not all possible contingencies can be specified in a contract and that conflicts over "implicit contractual terms" are cheaper to resolve within the firm than through the courts. But if transaction costs explain the firm—as friction explains why cars need an engine—then any technological change that reduces transaction costs has an implication for the optimal configuration of the firm. For example, lower costs of data transmission have made it possible to contract out back-office work to distant places. Therefore, lower costs in managing risk should affect the firm, in particular its financial and ownership structure.

Chapters 1 and 3 made the point that shares (and bonds) are options on the value of a firm that serve as general hedges (buffers) against adverse events. If identified risks are hedged or sold off, then the need for own funds is reduced: the optimum amount of equity varies inversely with the development of markets of risk. Even the desirability of a stock-exchange listing is strongly influenced by the extent and sophistication of derivatives markets. A stock listing traditionally provides two advantages: risk diversification and capital for expansion, but also two disadvantages which have held back the majority of firms from going public: the loss of private information and the increase in "agency" costs (owners are self-motivated, managers require monitoring and incentives, such as a share in profits). As financial markets become more complete and increasingly derivatives allow the handling of risks in a more focused way, capital, as a primitive and costly safety net, becomes less essential. This then is the time when knowledge, focus and very precise incentives for stakeholders become cardinal, and new forms of partnerships evolve.

Incorporation also raises problems. The most visible problem is "corporate governance" as shareholders have lost control of management.[4] Examples are management failures unchecked by company boards, management appropriation of profit shares (often in the form of free options) that seem uncorrelated to managerial performance, or at least that are difficult to justify with measurable value-added by management. By itself, a profit share—as provided by option schemes—is an efficient way of remunerating management on a performance basis and thus provides the right incentives. The difficulty with today's technology is that company results cannot easily be disentangled into the various sources of company success (inherited product structure, favourable external environment, managerial strategy).

Equity-owners unwillingly took a sort of revenge when take-over specialists started to identify firms that can do better under a new management or whose value is inferior to the sum of its parts (negative synergies), in which case it is more profitable to buy the firm with debt leveraged buyout—(LBO) and sell off its parts individually. Shareholders and the corporate raider split the profits of this positive-sum game, often even paying off incumbent management. In other cases companies under-perform not for lack of managerial strategy, but for lack of vision by the owners. In such cases management (and workers) organise management buyouts (MBO), replacing own funds with debt and restructuring the company unhampered by previous owners. At times, such firms return to private ownership—at least for a transition period.

The joint-stock ownership has solved some problems (the appeal to a broad supply of capital), but in what appears today as a rather inefficient way. If stock markets were efficient allocators of capital, then there would not have been scope for the massive waves of LBOs and MBOs since the 1980s. This wave was carried by a number of financial innovations making it possible to assemble huge amounts of money (the biggest take-over required US$30 billion), at times by an individual investor. Junk bonds (where the option characteristics of bonds are especially transparent) provided a large part of the take-over-funding and investors reduced the high risk inherent in each individual take-over by spreading them across a portfolio of take-over operations. Derivatives also play a cardinal role: typically, loans are structured with embedded options; the risk of rising share prices following the launch of a take-over is usually hedged with early acquisitions of call options; the risk of rolling over short-term funding is hedged with treasury futures; and so on. Without the vast array of derivatives that are usually part of complex take-over financing, risks for raiders would be even higher and less focused, and take-overs would be more restrained.

## The Role of Equity

The question that concerns us is whether the institution of share capital in its present form, with all its limitations, will survive unchanged. If not then corporate raids for value creation would continue—which, by itself, is an inefficient way of reallocating resources. Over the last 200 years there have been limited modifications and experimentation with share capital, such as the creation of preferential shares. They—like convertible bonds—are assets that combine debt and equity features. Is there scope for more substantial innovation?[5]

Advances in financial theory have, to date, done relatively little to improve our understanding of how assets acquire value. Thus, while it is possible to be certain about the present value of an equity derivative contract, it is not yet possible to describe the value of the asset underlying the derivative in other than traditional terms. However, it is to be expected that as mathematical modelling improves, and as more inquiry is focused on financial theory, new and more sophisticated ways of thinking about value will emerge. These will inevitably challenge the principles of corporate capitalism and ask, *inter alia*, three questions:

1. Whether in the long run traditional financial securities (i.e., stocks and bonds) which agglomerate separate risks are compatible with financial techniques which seek to atomise risks in order to price them separately?
2. Whether it is rational in a world where risks can be more accurately described to support the continuation of the rival constituencies of owners and managers in the joint-stock corporation?
3. Whether joint-stock corporates are therefore inefficient creators and conduits of value and might in future be replaced by an alternative institutional structure?[6]

Enterprise profits are the result of both exogenous events (inflation, GNP growth, evolution of sectoral demand, the exchange rate for export markets and imported inputs, the evolution of interest rates) and of decisions within the firm. Some outside risks can now already be hedged (exchange and interest rates, commodity prices) and those that cannot will one day become hedgeable (inflation, GDP and sectoral risks). The firm's result can then be more closely identified with managerial decisions and remuneration of managers can then be more solidly based on the firm's results.[7]

### Firms without Share Capital?

It is thus even imaginable that firms without share capital will evolve. Firms themselves can issue options for which they cash in the premium. Debt can be assorted with warrants that shift control over the firm to debt-holders when debt service falls below pre-set standards. Control over the firm would then not be fixed once and for all, but would depend on the firm's performance: as long as debt is serviced, managers remain in control and share profits among themselves, and with holders of call options issued by the firm. If performance slacks, control is shifted to debt-holders who will replace the incumbent management.[8] At any rate, in the absence of differential taxation and bankruptcy risk, the Miller–Modigliani theorem makes the point that there is no optimal ratio of debt to equity financing. Would lenders be reluctant to lend to a firm without equity? Probably not if they obtain control when critical performance criteria are reached. Moreover, the absence of traded equity does not mean that the firm does not have any own funds.

As argued in this book, financial theory and accounting standards are moving inexorably towards more precise descriptions of different risks. Once this is possible, it will open the way for firms to issue securities which make traditional shares and bonds redundant, or at least replaceable. New types of securities, called "risk participations" by Freeman (1994), will allow firms to describe themselves in new ways and allow investors to select only those aspects of a firm's risk profile that appeal. Some firms may choose to issue only a few broad-based participations. Others, including those whose stock-in-trade is in the various risks they manage as intermediaries, may issue a hundred or more, each class of participation defining a discrete element or category of risk. Among the risks which might be separated, described and packaged are fluctuations in the value of: long-term assets such as property; volatile short-term trading risks; counter-party risks, economic and country risks; specific operational risks; and legal risks. But the exact applications are difficult to predict, for they will depend on what finance theory discovers about the attributes of different assets.

Clearly, the sum of a firm's participations will represent something comparable to today's equity risk, but, crucially, without the ownership rights.[9] Investors wanting exposure to all of a firm's risks will be able to bundle participations into portfolios with specific characteristics. Moreover, it will be a straightforward matter to create derivative products based on the participations, or combinations thereof. Arguably, such contracts will have an economic advantage over today's contracts, for the price of the underlying participation will be more transparent than is the price of an equity today.

These speculations, at first glance futuristic, are in fact based partly on failed recent experiments. The so-called Unbundled Stock Unit (USU) was invented by Shearson Lehman, an investment bank, as a solution to a perceived problem—that direct equity investment implies an exposure to at least three significant risks (namely, capital growth, current income, and future dividend flows) not all of which may be desired by an individual investor. By buying back a chunk of a firm's common equity and unbundling it into three classes of security, each reflecting one of the risks, Shearson hoped to attract investors. The USU failed after objections from regulators about its tax implications. However, an additional reason for the negative reception by some pension fund investors was that the creation of the USU involved the disappearance and probable under-pricing of ownership rights. This point is explored below.

In some respects, the USU was an idea far ahead of its time. Its inventors saw that the bundling of several risks into a common share was unhelpful. However, they viewed the risks in narrow, traditional terms, as those embedded within the claims just described. In future, participations will define actual risks run by the corporation in its routine course of business, and will allow investors to participate directly in those risks. In other words, the idea of unbundling will be supported by a far more powerful methodology than was available to investment bankers in the past.

The advent of risk participations will obviously have profound implications, not least for the firms that issue them. The traditional equity has been convenient in one sense. By its inclusion of residual risks, it created an obligation of ownership and set up a tension between owners and managers which has for decades driven the firm's quest for value. However, as today's heated battles over corporate governance have made clear, it is far from certain that ownership has any quantifiable economic merits.[10] The successful owner-managed firm is an uncomfortable juxtaposition for the troubled public company riven by dispute between shareholders and managers.

It may be that investment without ownership rights will prove a more efficient proposition for most investors. After all, the only costs of expressing dissatisfaction with a firm's performance would be the transaction costs of selling an investment, and in future such costs will be minimal. It should be borne in mind that the debt/equity model of corporate finance was developed in an era when there were huge transaction costs associated with company formation and investment. Again, a more finely tuned model seems appropriate in a future where, for instance, the information gap between companies and investors will be significantly lower.

The greatest obstacle to such innovations is the risk of bankruptcy—the main reason for holding own funds which typically are more expensive than borrowed funds because of higher risk. A market pricing bankruptcy risk is, however, already developing. See the example of "credit derivatives" in Chapter 6.

**Changing Roles of Stakeholders**

Even if it is unlikely that in a generation's time all firms will be financed in this way, it is safe to expect the proliferation of different organisational and financial models. Traditional equity as such is likely to lose in importance and so is the formal control by shareholders. In firms where shareholders remain, incentives for both managers and lenders will be structured differently and the influence of each group over the decisions of the firm will be structured in a variety of ways with greater flexibility.

So far I have not discussed the role of workers. Workers take considerable non-diversifiable risk: independently of personal performance, each individual worker may lose his job or suffer a loss of income if the firm underperforms. And there is the problem of creating the right incentives for workers' performance. Distribution of shares to workers is one way in which some firms try to provide incentives and foster identification with the company. But such a scheme is not optimal from a risk diversification point of view.

A large part of the firm's risk that is also borne by workers can, of course, be hedged through purchase of puts on the firm's stock,[11] once a market for options on the firm's stock has developed. Traded options are, of course, different from the option rights now awarded in many firms to top managers. With a market for options, employees have a tradeable instrument so that they can get in or out whenever they so desire. Even with fixed wage contracts employees can then structure their income from the firm in any way they like; by buying options to obtain performance-related income for any share of their income.

To make these things happen, accounting standards will need to be refined to become an acceptable measure for distribution of the unlisted firm's results. And, as few workers will be inclined to undertake that kind of financial engineering for themselves, they will rely on intermediaries (insurance companies, pension funds, new "income protection managers") to do it for them.

In recent privatisations of large state-owned firms, derivatives have played a key role in sweetening the deal for employees. For Deutsche Telekom's privatisation, signalling the loss of more than 40 000 jobs, an employee stock ownership programme was arranged, using derivatives to allow employees to benefit from five times any gains in the share price, while protecting them from any decline, during the six-year scheme.

This arrangement also helped increase demand for the deal (the second largest ever) and compensate for the lack of a domestic investor base. Similar arrangements were used in the privatisation of the French firm Rhône-Poulenc and, for the protection of retail investors, in the Spanish oil company, Repsol. Privatisation of many state-owned companies in Europe, usually facing fierce resistance from workers, will be eased by such programmes, and motivation and corporate identification will be enhanced.

# 4. A CPI FUTURES

Inflation risk is an important example of macro risk for which a futures contract was already in existence. Inflation is a major concern for policymakers in every country because it creates personal and social inconveniences and losses. Although by the mid-1990s inflation in industrialised countries is at a remarkably low level by historic standards, this is not the case in other parts of the world. Nor is there a guarantee for maintained price stability in advanced countries in the future. For long-term decisions in particular, it would therefore be convenient to be able to hedge the inflation risk.

Consumers are concerned with maintaining the purchasing power of their income. The proper measure for purchasing power is the consumer price index (CPI). Producers may be more interested in indexes which are better correlated with the prices of their output, such as the wholesale price index or sub-indexes of the producer price index. I concentrate on the CPI for its wide appeal. It is, however, clear that if a CPI contract were to become successful, more specialised indexes would follow.[12]

Economic rationality would require the writing of all inter-temporal contracts in terms of *real* rather than nominal quantities, that is the contracts should be indexed to inflation. However, this is not the case and in some countries indexing is even forbidden by law (e.g., in Germany). Typically, debtors benefit from unexpected inflation as the real value of their debt declines. As most government bonds are denominated in nominal rather than real terms, governments are the main beneficiaries of inflation (the "inflation tax"). At times, long-term increases in the rate of inflation have virtually wiped out the savings of people who have put their retirement savings in long-term bonds. (US bondholders will painfully remember the early 1980s, whilst Germans have still not forgotten the hyperinflation of the 1920s.) There is no compelling advantage in tying the real value of, say, retirement income to the price level by buying nominal bonds.[13]

As suggested by Shiller (1993), in addition to short-dated CPI futures, it would be interesting to establish a perpetual claim or a perpetual futures market or other long-horizon futures markets. Since there is (at least at present and only in industrialised countries) little uncertainty about inflation in the near future, most uncertainty about inflation is of the far-horizon variety. A single perpetual futures market in the CPI could be used in conjunction with any other perpetual futures market to convert, in effect, the alternative asset from being a nominal rate to an indexed rate.

As was shown in Chapter 5, there are good reasons for futures markets to be most liquid in near-by maturities (one, two or three months). Is it not pointless to propose a futures contract based on a perpetual index? Not at all, once we distinguish between the maturity of the underlying asset (which can be a three-month Treasury bill or a ten-year Treasury bond) and the maturity of the futures contract. A perpetual does not pose any particular problem—it is in a sense the cleanest type of contract because it has no specific maturity— and offers the advantage of perfect fungibility. This implies that a futures contract can be created without a final maturity. Hedgers acquire contracts and hold them as long as they wish to hedge. Daily price determination will reflect the long-run views of inflation, properly discounted.

In the 1970s, Milton Friedman and others, such as Lovell and Vogel (1973), proposed the creation of a CPI futures contract. Due to delays in regulatory approval a CPI contract started trading only in 1985. This was extremely unfortunate timing as by 1985 inflation in the US had fallen to below 4% after having reached 14% in 1980. As shown in Figure 10.1, the long-run volatility of the CPI, however, has fully justified the attempt. Given the lack of familiarity of end-users and of traders with this product and the fact that the inflation risk was much lower than during previous years, the contract was traded in very low volumes. To cut losses the contract was suspended in 1988.[14]

In the mid-1990s inflation in the OECD countries has reached historically low levels and there is no perceived need for such a contract. But this is not the case in most emerging countries (e.g., Mexico and China, to name only two major countries) and there a CPI contract would offer major potential benefits.[15]

How would such a contract work? Let us suppose that the CPI today is at 100 and for the next year the price of the CPI futures is at 105 as a result of expectations that lead people to buy or sell the CPI futures. If in a year's time the actual CPI is 108, the buyer of a futures contract receives three and the seller pays up three. If the actual CPI is 102, the buyer has to pay three and the seller receives three. In either case the buyer and seller are protected from unexpected outcomes of the CPI.

What makes the creation of a CPI contract particularly easy is that it is cash-settled and there is no delivery option. There is not even an underlying asset for delivery. All that is needed is a well-constructed and accepted CPI. This is probably the most abstract and fool-proof type of futures contract. Whenever there is an underlying asset (say, pork bellies), there is a problem of contract specification (no two pork bellies are identical) and of delivery squeezes. In large liquid spot markets (say, foreign exchange or T-bills) these

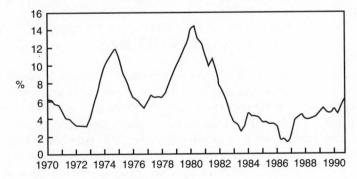

**Figure 10.1**   US inflation rate, 1970–90

problems do not usually exist (but see Chapter 4). Cash settlement without delivery constraint represented a progress. Cash settlement without delivery possibility because no underlying asset exists is a further step forward.

Availability of a CPI contract would have far-reaching economic consequences. Cyclical economic activity is, among others, induced by "unexpected" or "surprise" inflation (Lucas 1978, Gordon 1992). But a producer who has a CPI hedge is unaffected (or less affected) by surprise inflation than an unhedged producer. Hence cyclical variations in economic activity will be attenuated.

Inflation itself will have less hysteresis (will be less dependent on the past inflation record), or less in-built, historically inherited, inflation momentum. As shown by Fischer (1977), Taylor (1980) and others, inflation is shifted forward by wage contracts over longer periods (from one to several years) into which are built inflationary expectations. If workers can hedge the inflation risk and thereby protect the purchasing power of their nominal wage, there is no need to incorporate a risk premium (for underestimating future inflation) into longer term contracts. The built-in momentum in the inflation process would be reduced and inflation would be determined more by current factors than by expectations inspired by the past.

Buyers could be workers (or their unions acting on their behalf, insurance companies acting as intermediaries) who entered into a wage contract for a year or longer and who had negotiated the wage on the basis of an expected change in the CPI. They could no longer be fooled and would effectively transform their nominal wage contract into a real wage contract. Suppliers could be firms whose output prices track the general CPI closely and who would suffer from an actual consumer price inflation smaller than the one incorporated in the nominal wage contracts. In countries where the difference between expected and eventually realised inflation can be high (in China a 5–10% difference is not uncommon and in hyper-inflation countries even much more), the gains from the availability of such a contract can be several percentage points of GNP, particularly when the reduction of output to surprise inflation is taken into account.

## 5. A GNP FUTURES

Most economic activities are correlated with GNP, some strongly, others weakly and a few even negatively ("inferior goods"). The revenue of most suppliers of goods and services is negatively affected by lower than expected GNP growth and their investment outlays partly depreciated. In situations like this both capital owners and workers suffer, the latter being forced to cut back their current consumption or accept a higher debt burden to sustain their income. As with any risk, small unexpected changes for short periods of time are of less concern than more pronounced and longer-lasting declines in GNP.

Consider, for example, a Japanese entrepreneur or worker who in the late 1980s could look back to more than 30 years of extremely high growth, on average close to 10% per annum. He would have expected a slowdown in growth as the Japanese economy matured, but might have been worried about a "harsh landing" induced by political reaction to Japan's sustained current account surplus, increased demands on Japan for international peace and development commitments, and so on. The possibility of hedging by buying future GNP would certainly have been attractive. Unfortunately, it was not available and the growth of Japan's economy since 1990 has been dismal.

The Japanese example is not unique. If Eastern Europeans could have traded future GNP since the opening of their economies, they could have hedged against the substantial uncertainties associated with the transition of their economies. German unification was also confronted with a highly uncertain outlook: a "new frontier" view of a Germany growing rapidly into a rich European powerhouse, its growth propelled by the increased demand generated by reconstruction of former East Germany; and a more pessimist "Mezzogiorno" view according to which Germany's growth would suffer from fiscal overburdening, waste of resources by dumping subsidies into the new Länder which might serve more local interest groups than the growth process. If investors could hedge the risk of low growth, much more investment would be committed to East Germany, as is currently the case.

A GNP futures contract on China's (or India's, Mexico's, Brazil's) GNP?[16] What an extraordinary instrument for investors: instead of buying a portfolio of inefficiently priced and traded shares, one can bet at low cost on GDP growth. Investors who see opportunities in profitable projects in these countries can hedge unwanted non-project related risks, such as macroeconomic imbalances, reforms that may be blocked, or political turmoil. It would even be a solution for interested investors to gamble on future growth of countries like Cuba or Vietnam where shares do not exist yet.

How would such a contract work? In fact there are several interesting choices. All would have in common, however, that market values would be based on observations of incomes themselves, not on observations of prices of claims to these incomes. One possibility is a contract based on future GNP (next year, next three years, next ten years) with technicalities similar to those of the CPI contract. Another choice is a contract based on the present value of the perpetual stream of future GNP discounted by the appropriate interest rates (Shiller 1993). The advantage of this contract would again be its "fungibility", that is, there is only one such contract at any time. It would be an ideal instrument for hedging against all future variations in GNP, whereas short-dated contracts would allow hedging against risk during specific time intervals. As for the CPI contract, it can be expected that markets will develop for both the present value and the specifically dated GNP contracts. Technical Insight 10.2 provides details.

**Technical Insight 10.2**   GNP contracts based on perpetual claims

Shiller (1993) proposes two kinds of markets for claims on a series of aggregate income index values: perpetual claims and perpetual futures markets. The perpetual claims are like stock exchange traded securities and perpetual futures are like contracts traded at futures exchanges.

To investors, that is, longs, a perpetual claim on an index is merely a security that pays a dividend proportional to the index value forever. For example, the index value might be national income scaled to US$1000 in some fixed base year, so that the dividend on the claim would always be proportional to the announced national income. The dividend is paid on every date that a new value of the index is announced, so that quarterly indices would pay quarterly dividends, and annual indices would pay annual dividends. As with any other security, the investor can buy and sell this security at any time and receives both dividend income and capital gains and losses.

What is needed to create liquid markets for perpetual claims on income indices is an exchange with a clearing-house to facilitate the flow of perpetual claims from suppliers to investors. Moreover, exchanges can effectively guarantee creditworthiness of claims and payment of dividends and capital gains using the methods of daily marking to market and margin requirements, as explained in Chapter 5.

With exchange-guaranteed perpetual claims, dividends would be paid by those people who freely take the other sides of the perpetual claims contracts (the shorts). Only shorts pay dividends and so for every long position there is an equal short position. The shorts are not required to hold a claim on an income flow equal to the dividend they must pay (which, at any rate, do not exist). The purpose of the perpetual claims market is to create such assets.

By carefully monitoring margin accounts, the securities exchange and brokerage firms that manage these accounts are able to assure the payment of the index values indefinitely, thereby creating a perpetual security even though no individual can guarantee paying the dividend forever.

Such a market for perpetual claims could be used by individuals or corporations to hedge their income risk. A hedger would merely take a short position in his own country's perpetual claim market and invest the proceeds of that short sale in a long position in some other asset that pays a more secure income, such as a portfolio of perpetual claims on income around the world. In this way, he would have hedged that part of the income stream that depended on national income (the diversifiable income risk or "income β"). For the income perpetual claim market to work well the hedger has to have the possibility of making use of short sale proceeds. Perpetual futures are contracts that are ideally suited for that purpose.

The economic implications of GNP perpetuals are mind-boggling. Investment decisions and production plans would be unhampered by the uncertainty of the future evolution of GNP. The economic gains could be extraordinary. Any entrepreneur who is now held back from a direct investment in China, despite the excellent opportunities perceived if growth is sustained, might not be retained if the GNP risk could be hedged. And investors with general confidence in China's long-term prospects, but no specific views on sectoral developments, will participate in China's growth by going long in GNP perpetuals.

Workers in so-called "cyclical activities", that is, activities whose output has a positive correlation with GNP larger than one, are most exposed to the risk of losing their job, not for reasons of personal or firm performance, but simply because GNP may fall short of expected growth. Such workers could hedge that risk away, thereby improving their own welfare and making jobs in such activities more attractive. As such workers, at least in theory, receive in their wages a risk premium, wage costs could potentially fall with lower risk and more employment could be created in cyclical activities.

Once a GNP index is traded, it will only be a matter of time before seeing sectoral or professional indexes. There should be demand for such contracts, particularly in sectors or professions whose incomes are weakly correlated with GNP. Consider, for example, a young person contemplating studying for a higher degree in medicine or aircraft engineering. This is a substantial investment with a gestation period of up to 10 years and a potential return period of 30–40 years. The value of such an investment is highly sector-specific. (Physicians are not the best bond trackers, for example.) If, over time, excess supply arises, a substantial part of that value would therefore be lost. A professional perpetual claim (or a futures contract of the present value type) provides, on the one hand, a market view of the future earnings of a profession or of a sector ("price discovery") and a means of hedging fixed investment (education) risks. Again the potential gains for individuals and for society are large although difficult to assess quantitatively. Price discovery may induce students who are impressed by current and past earnings of physicians or aircraft engineers to change their minds when expected future professional revenue falls as embodied in the futures price below current levels. If they pursue those studies nevertheless, they can at least hedge unforeseen income deterioration.

If contracts for GNP or for sub-categories become available in many countries, then each society can hedge the risks of cyclical fluctuations and smooth the growth path so that cyclical variations would no longer imply social (and private) costs. What Keynesian demand management failed to achieve may well be realised by appropriate innovations in financial markets ("complete markets").

Furthermore, as the cycles of economic activity, long-term growth paths and external shocks are not perfectly correlated across countries, it would pay for each country to diversify risk by acquiring futures on the GDP of other countries. The outcome would be a revenue for each country that depended on its own performance and on that of others. The world economy would then become much closer to a single unified economy, a result that international trade has been unable to achieve so far, despite the theoretical prediction of the Stolper–Samuelson theorem (i.e., that with free trade incomes converge across all countries). Such a process of integration would be much more effective than forming economic areas or unions through complicated institutional build-ups.

The first to acquire futures on the GNP of other countries would be exporters whose sales depend on income (GNP) in foreign countries. But demand is not limited to exporters. Japanese workers (or their pension funds, insurance companies), confronted with meagre prospects of growth in Japan (and after years of negative stock returns after the bubble of 1990), may well wish to buy a world average performance or to bet on the United States or China or any other country.

Why has a GNP contract not yet come on the market? Perhaps the reason is simply that it is not a familiar idea. Remember from Chapter 1 that the concept of futures was known in agricultural markets for several hundreds of years and for stocks since the 17th century. It was only in the 1970s that financial futures were reborn and became a dominant species. Thriving on liquidity, a necessary precondition for a successful futures market is a widespread acceptance and familiarity with the product. As futures become a regular feature of the cultural cognisance of an ever-widening group of economic actors, contracts that were technically feasible but socially too far ahead in time to be accepted, and, therefore, could not find promoters to set up a market with the promotion costs that are required, will have a much better chance in the future.

A second possible reason is that a stock market index futures partially fulfils the functions of a GNP futures. Figure 10.2 shows, however, that stock market indexes and GNP are not strongly correlated, so that a GNP futures does provide additional value.

A third reason, as always, is that a reliable GNP indicator must be available. A practical difficulty is that these indicators, even when reliable as in the advanced countries, are subjected to periodic revisions to take account of new activities, of improvements in price deflation and to take into account qualitative changes (successive generations of computers are not the same goods and prices reflect both technological progress and decreasing production costs).

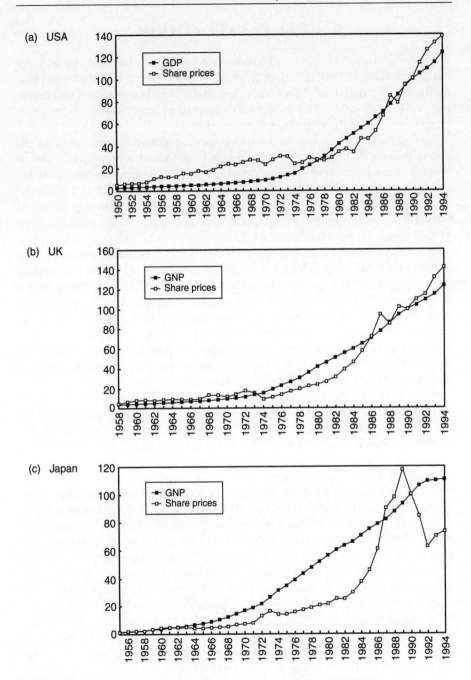

**Figure 10.2** Correlation of GNP and stock exchange indices, 1950–95
*Note*: 1990 = 100

## 6. REAL ESTATE FUTURES

In most countries real estate is the dominant value in national assets, far more important than stocks For example, in 1990 the value of US residential real estate was estimated at US$6 trillion and the value of commercial and industrial real estate at US$2.7 trillion. Together they represented about three times the value of the entire US stock market.

Real estate holdings are, furthermore, more widely distributed among the population so that changes in valuation directly affect all citizens, either as owners or as borrowers (renters). Except for the highest income quartile, expenditure on housing represents 20–30% of income and for the lower incomes housing is the most important stock of wealth. In poorer countries these relationships are even more pronounced.

Real estate is important as an asset and significantly affects the labour and loan markets. A decline of regional property markets makes it costly to sell in order to move to another location where job prospects are better but housing prices higher. Real estate is also used as a collateral for long-term loans, making both the owner and the lender heavily dependent on the evolution of property prices. In this regard it is interesting to recall that a major cause for earnings variations of banks and, in fact, the major single cause of bank failures are downturns in real estate markets (the plights of some US regional banks, UK, Scandinavian, French and Japanese banks in the 1990s are all in large part related to real estate price deflations).

It is, therefore, obvious that a real estate futures would provide a very substantial economic gain. What is the point of being able to hedge the price risk of coffee, but not the price risk of real estate? The case for a real estate futures market seems to be so obvious that one has to ask immediately why there is no liquid market in real estate futures, especially as diversification is severely limited for most owners.

In the past there have been attempts to create such futures markets. Following proposals by Miller (1989) and Gemmill (1990), futures markets in real estate were attempted by the London Futures and Options Exchange (London Fox) in 1991. There were both commercial and residential futures contracts. The commercial contract was settled on an index of appraised value. The residential contract was settled on a hedonic price index[17] derived from actual selling prices of individual homes. Unfortunately, the contracts were traded only for a brief time, from May through October. Trading volume had been very low and the Exchange had allegedly attempted to create the impression of high trading volume by false trades. Seemingly, only 7% of the reported trades were genuine. When the deception was discovered, the market was closed; officers of the Exchange resigned.[18]

The London Fox real estate contracts were launched at a time when UK real estate prices were falling slowly and steadily and there was a low turnover of real estate. This might be considered to have been an ideal time to launch such a market since price declines are what motivate hedgers. But this was a time of little excitement in the London real estate markets, with little action, and that fact may not have encouraged interest in this market.

So what is it that makes the successful creation of real estate futures so difficult? It is certainly not lack of volatility. Real estate prices show substantial autocorrelation, with small short-term volatility, but large cyclical swings. Shiller (1993) quotes recent US booms with sustained and dramatic increases in real estate prices at different times in different cities: the annual average rate of increase was 9.3% in San Francisco 1976–80, 17.7% in Boston 1983–87, 16.9% in New York 1983–87, 10.2% in Washington, DC 1986–88, 19.1% in San Francisco 1987–89, 21.2% in Honolulu 1987–90 and 22.3% in Seattle 1988–90. At the same time there have also been dramatic real estate busts: the annual average rate of change in real prices was –14.6% in Houston 1985–87, –12.2% in Oklahoma City 1986–89, –10.1% in New York 1988–91 and –13.5% in Boston 1989–91. The clear lack of synchronisation of the booms and busts suggests that any hedging markets in real estate should be defined geographically in areas much smaller than the United States.

Some real estate booms and busts outside the United States have been even bigger. In fact, the estimated appreciation of Japanese land value in 1987 alone was greater than the total Japanese gross domestic product for that year. But since the peak in 1991 prices of urban land have fallen by a third in 1995 and the price of commercial real estate by 85%. According to one estimate (Union Bank of Switzerland, Tokyo) those 5 million Japanese households who bought houses during 1987–92 have, in the meantime, suffered a fall in value of yen 50–75 trillion (US$590–890 billion). The appreciation in Korean land value exceeded the gross domestic product in that country in each year from 1988 to 1991. In 1989 alone the appreciation was over twice GDP. In contrast, at no time since 1986 has price appreciation in the stock market exceeded 34% of GDP in Korea or Japan. In both countries there has been widespread concern about the redistribution of wealth caused by these land price movements and the potential for further economic disruptions should declines in land prices turn into a landslide.

The major problem is that real estate property is not a standardised commodity and that property is held for long periods of time. Therefore sales transactions occur relatively rarely and may not be representative of the market however defined. Value depends on location, market segment (commercial vs. residential, luxury vs. lower end of the market, etc.), maintenance, architecture and so on. It is therefore difficult to define a market index and no available index is very satisfactory. Shiller (1993) shows how to construct a better benchmark index whose main ingredients are: weights that come close to the market (however defined), use of repeat-sales price series and of hedonic price estimations to account for housing characteristics.

The most useful indexes would be regional and local because, as the US examples just cited demonstrate, prices across states or cities are only weakly correlated.

Most homeowners will probably not deal directly in hedging markets, but will do so indirectly through intermediaries. Retail products that are attractive to homeowners might look like insurance policies; in fact they would be cash-settled put options on the individual homes. Such insurance policies (put options) might be attractive to homeowners who do not want to give up the upside potential for the prices of their homes, and only to insure against loss, and the products would resemble insurance policies with which homeowners are already familiar.

As shown in Technical Insight 10.3, real estate markets are notoriously inefficient so that trading is extremely costly. A futures market with its low transaction costs would make it easy to hedge against market downturns or speculate in a rising market.

---

**Technical Insight 10.3**   The inefficiency of real estate markets

A first indication of the inefficiency of real estate markets is the sizeable inertia in prices: price trends continue for months and years. That there is inertia in the US housing market has been documented by Case and Shiller (1989), Poterba (1991) and Kuo (1993). Evidence for inertia in the Tokyo housing market was found by Ito and Hirono (1993).

Strong inertia in price movements could not persist in a liquid market as it would produce a powerful profit opportunity to professional speculators. They would need only to buy when prices are rising strongly and sell when prices are declining strongly.

In illiquid markets such as this, trading to profit from serial correlation is difficult or impossible because of transaction costs. By definition, illiquid markets are markets where it is costly and difficult to trade. Brokerage costs of selling a house are often 6–8% of the value of the house and the costs of storing a house that does not sell quickly can be far greater. Purchasing a house for investment runs the risk of hidden defects, of being unrepresentative for demand trends (a "lemon"), or of high maintenance costs. Partial avoidance of such risks would increase transaction costs further. Moreover, in illiquid markets there is not the price discovery seen in liquid markets; traders may not even know when prices have been increasing in recent months. This has certainly been the case with real estate markets, where price changes are very hard to discern from casual evidence. If speculators do not know what prices have done recently, then they cannot trade on that information, and cannot do their job of reducing inertia in price movements.

To the extent that prices in liquid markets may be approximated by random walks, the variance of price changes will increase proportionally with the time interval over which the price change is measured. The variance of two-month price changes will be roughly twice the variance of the price change in one month, variance of the price change in three months will be three times the variance of the price change in one month, and so on. When prices are random walks, it does not matter over what interval the variance of price change is quoted; it can always be converted to that of a price change of another interval. People accustomed to such prices consider a measure of price-change variance over one interval as just as good as over any other interval of time. This is not the case for the positively serially correlated price changes often found in illiquid markets. For such price changes, the conditional variance may increase more than in proportion to the horizon of the forecast. For such price series, it matters over what interval the price change is measured. Taking small time intervals, there is very little variance, and it might seem that there is little uncertainty to hedge; the appearance may be quite different if longer time intervals are taken to measure price changes.

This difference in the nature of uncertainty about prices also dictates a difference in the nature of the contracts that ought to be traded and in the nature of the volume of trade. Longer horizon contracts, even perpetual claims or perpetual futures, ought to be traded with residential real estate futures, since there is little uncertainty about prices in the next few months, but there is still substantial uncertainty about the values of the index a few years on.

Futures and options markets in housing are bound to improve efficiency in the real estate market, making the cash market price look more like a random walk than it has in the past. One would also expect that basis pricing in the housing market will develop: asking prices of homes might be set in terms of futures market prices, so that the asking price adjusts automatically with the market. Sales agreements might also relate selling prices to futures market prices, reducing the risk that one of the parties will want to back out of the sales agreement if aggregate real estate prices change before the settlement date. Such practices would create a benchmark for pricing and eliminate an important reason for inefficiency in real estate markets, making them immediately responsive to conditions in the liquid futures market.

Real estate futures markets in all probability will have the effect of increasing the price of housing. If people can hedge their risks, then they will be more eager to hold housing. In other terms, the discount rate relevant to housing investments will fall as the risk premium declines.

Commercial real estate may deserve markets separate from residential real estate, since the substitution between commercial and residential real estate is not perfect, so that their prices have substantially different movements. Commercial real estate probably also shows rather dramatically different price movement across different real estate classes: apartment buildings, retail space, office space, factories and warehouses.

Future contracts for commercial real estate are even more difficult to develop than those for residential real estate. The major difficulty is to create a valid price index for commercial real estate, since there are far fewer properties sold than is the case with residential real estate. Moreover, with few sales, manipulation of the futures market via sales in the cash market is easier.[19]

To sum up: real estate is a major component of overall wealth, but real estate markets are illiquid, price information opaque and transaction costs high. As boom-and-bust cycles during the last twenty years in many countries of the world have demonstrated, the popular belief that brick-and-mortar investments are safe is unfounded. Whilst daily volatility is negligible, long-term price movements are as pronounced as those of stocks. The development of real estate derivatives would generate major social gains. They would help to make the market more liquid, to improve price information, to lower transaction costs and, of course, to hedge risks.

## 7. THE END OF BANKING?

A constant theme of this book has been the interplay between financial innovation, regulatory response and institutional adaptation. Chapter 2 provided an extensive interpretation of the recent institutional response to profound innovations in finance, under the impetus of the "Americanisation of Finance".

If regulations evolve along the path developed in Chapter 9 and if some of the future trends in financial innovation outlined in this chapter materialise, what will be the institutional response? Or, to ask the question more pointedly, will banks, as a species, survive?

The examples in Chapter 1 illustrate how difficult it is to attempt looking into the crystal ball for the future evolution of the financial system. But it is nevertheless important to attempt such a visionary exercise as policies designed today are contingent not only on past experience but also on the foreseeable future configuration of the industry.

### Agents of Change

The driving forces of change continue to be those of the past: technology, globalisation of the economy, and continued deregulation. This author expects the contours of the financial industry to evolve, possibly dramatically, not so much due to a single innovation in particular, such as new derivative products, but due to the accumulation of many significant innovations. To draw a parallel, the modern global corporation is not the result of a specific innovation such as the steam engine, electricity, the telephone, the aeroplane, the fax machine, the computer, but the result of all of these.

These changes will also have substantial repercussions on the activity of central banks and regulators of banks and capital markets (as argued in Chapter 9). Among others I shall argue that central banks will increasingly lose their ability to control the money supply, after having argued in Chapter 9 that central banks should withdraw from regulation.

Of course, I do not wish to lay down an evolutionary time path. For reference only, I consider a horizon of ten to fifteen years. For many of the predictions this may be too long, for others too short. But it is important to have a notion of directional changes.

A visible trend in the finance industry for the main institutions is to become global and universal. Knowledge generates economies of scale and, given the know-how of US and other leading institutions, they can use that superior knowledge to supply their services at low cost to clients all over the world. The initial cost of a new, complex, structured deal is many times the marginal cost of repeated applications. Moreover, continued growth of demand for customised products and contracting services suggests that, in the future, more value-added can be generated by banks acting as *principal* instead of *agent*, which again favours size. As the reason for economies of scale is knowledge and the mastery of transaction processing, globalisation is to be expected only for *knowledge-driven* business such as investment banking, *technology-driven* business such as payments systems (credit cards, securities, clearing) and not for traditional banking. Whilst the trend towards globalisation of specific financial operations is already visible, it is still hampered by national regulations and protection of domestic banking. Over time the process accelerated by the GATT's Uruguay round and entrusted to the WTO will rip away these obstacles so that globalisation will be a major phenomenon during the years to come.

Derivative products will play a major role in this process. As argued in this chapter, new types of derivatives will accelerate the integration of the world economy. The proliferation of instruments (say, futures and options on the Korean currency and government bonds) will allow global institutions to hedge their risks better in markets which so far had been considered too risky. And, advisory work on the use of derivatives is highly knowledge-intensive and will provide a major worldwide market for the leading specialists.

### Universal Banking

Another perceivable trend is the spread of universal banking, or even more, the financial conglomerate. The Second European Banking Directive, the basis for an integrated financial market in the European Union, has refrained from restricting the activities of banks to a scope inferior to that of banking in Germany. In the United States the Bank Holding Act has already made possible the regrouping of independently incorporated banks, securities houses and non-financial firms in a holding. Banks were given the authority to underwrite securities and the repeal of the Glass–Steagall Act will allow US banks to become universal, with nationwide branching.

There is a widespread belief—already challenged in Chapter 2—that universal banking is more efficient than separation of commercial and investment banking for essentially two reasons. One would be more extensive diversification. This argument should, however, lose some of its weight with the greater availability of derivatives for flexible risk management. The second advantage would consist in economies of scope.[20] At first sight, it must surely be advantageous to offer a client the whole range of financial products rather than let him drift off to other firms. From a cost point of view, more intensive staffing of a branch network may be cheaper than creating parallel networks for specialised services. But these arguments also have their limitations.[21] As supermarkets have displaced grocery shops for many retail markets, universal banks will do well in retail markets. In banking the corporate market and upper-tier private clients segments are, however, more important and growing. As wealthy consumers tend to patronise specialised gourmet shops and fashion boutiques, they will also be ready to make an extra trip (be it only to the Internet) to obtain special services from a specialised financial firm. Whilst for food a wealthy client may only spend a small multiple of an average client, his manageable assets are a high multiple and the market share of such products is correspondingly higher.

More generally, as conglomerates and large multinationals have run into difficulties in managing their operations efficiently in each market and for each production and their overall corporate strategy became unfocused, the same fate awaits the overstretched global and possibly universal bank. For pessimists the culture of commercial banks, of investment bankers and of derivative traders are too different to live harmoniously with positive synergies under one roof. This risk can be reduced by running different financial business lines as independent companies of a group. But have not conglomerates failed for lack of focus?[22]

The success of the European universal bank is based on its all-embracing house-bank relationship with corporate clients from the "cradle to the grave". Building such a relationship takes a long time and historically was cemented in markets protected against foreign competitors and competition from the capital market. Therefore, it is impossible to replicate in a global market the quintessence of the universal bank's success, namely the one-to-one relationship with a corporation where the bank is a shareholder (providing a seat on the Board of Directors), exercises proxy votes from its securities deposits, is the principal financial adviser and lender. What is possible—and this is already a visible trend—is to create conglomerates embracing all financial activities including insurance through specialised subsidiaries. Even the tightly integrated German and Swiss universal banks are separating out investment banking (Deutsche Bank transferred its investment banking to London to create Deutsche Morgan Grenfell, Credit Suisse controls CS First Boston, ING bought Barings, Swiss Bank Corporation acquired Warburg, Dillon Read and O'Connor, and Dresdner Bank Kleinwort Benson), fund management, mortgage lending, insurance and so on.

I am, therefore, certain that many major banks will strive for a conglomerate structure that federates a wide variety of financial services. Not all services will be offered on a global basis. Deutsche Bank is not a universal bank in every market, nor does Citibank offer the same products in foreign markets as those offered in New York. As illustrated by the recent concentration of investment banking activities and asset management in newly acquired London-based investment banks, the under-one-roof integrated structure of universal banks is a thing of the past. Similarly, investment banks are busy acquiring brokerage firms and asset managers so that specialised investment banking is also obsolete. The model of the future for global players is a conglomerate structure.

## Concentration vs. Specialisation

Once Glass–Steagall is repealed, US banks in their own national market will go beyond the present product and geographic restrictions and become universal banks in the form of financial conglomerates. The process of concentration through mergers and take-overs which has been underway for some years will accelerate and the atypically large number of banks in the US (still over 10 000) will dramatically diminish. The share of bank assets in megabanks (banks with assets over US$100 billion) in the United States has gone up from 9% in 1977 to 19% in 1994. Mergers, more than internal growth, have contributed to the growing shares of megabanks. Mergers also contribute to improved competitivity. It is estimated that successful mergers (i.e., where the banks involved have a similar, rather than complementary structure) save 14–16% of costs. In other countries similar merger waves have swooped over the banking industry. In Japan the banks are already of gigantic size due to mergers in the past. On economic grounds there is not much scope for further concentration. In Europe, all countries are going through intensive restructuration, often combining banking and insurance (France, Germany), banking and building societies (United Kingdom), and the formation of national banks out of regional banks (Italy).

The largest US banks will climb up on the ladder of the leading banks in the world to regain the top positions which they lost to Japanese bank giants in the 1980s and 1990s. It is, however, more likely that US banks will be the largest in terms of profitability and not necessarily in terms of balance sheet size. Securitisation is already too well developed to tempt US banks into tying their capital to low income-generating assets. The example of Citibank is telling: instead of going for asset growth with its flush capital, Citibank decided in 1995 to buy back 10% of its capital.

But, and this is perhaps more important, within the bank conglomerate, *the traditional banking business will not be the dominant source of profit or of business growth.* That role will eschew to more sophisticated subsidiaries in trading and its risk management, institutional fund management, advisory services, payments and warehousing business.

The globalisation of markets has made it possible for users of capital to lower their funding costs by tapping into multiple markets. As a result it has become much more important for banks to offer corporate borrowers products that span the global market. Those banks without global capabilities will find it difficult to offer a tailored "solution" to a corporation's financial problem. *Solutions carry far higher margins than products.*

Corporations are increasingly shopping selectively, replacing relationship banking with deal-based banking. Also the banks' ability to leverage their relationship in a one-product family, such as lending, into another, such as bond or stock underwriting, is declining as a result of the rising importance of expertise.

And around these mega-conglomerates will be a dynamic and more chaotic series of financial institutions, highly specialised, skilled, innovatory, some very profitable and others failing. Innovation has never been the strength of large organisations. If well managed they are successful in cost and quality control, mass production and keeled to successful evolution.[23] But innovations and the most spectacular profits and internal growth records will be the domain of the "boutiques", i.e., specialised institutions.

The current phenomenon of bank concentration is not entirely dictated by the underlying economics alone.[24] Certainly, there are some economies of scale and scope. But there are also diseconomies. Technological progress does not unambiguously favour scale. Expansion in the types of organised trading markets, reductions in transaction costs, and continued improvements in information-processing and telecommunications technologies will make it easier for smaller firms to offer financial services. Internet makes it possible to achieve a worldwide market presence without committing resources to a sales force or branches. Computer technology has already become such that small flexible corporations may have an advantage over mastodons. Rapid changes in regulation and increased competition award a premium to flexibility and rapid adaptations, characteristics which are more natural to smaller organisations.

Perhaps most seriously, "securitisation" and risk-management techniques definitely take away one important advantage of size, that is the advantage of a large capital base. Securitisation has allowed the splitting up of the lending processes into its components, such as originating, monitoring, risk management through diversification, quality enhancement, capital requirements, and so on. A bank with a weak capital structure but a good customer base can profitably concentrate on originating, repackaging its loans and selling them off to the capital market. Thus, and despite the Basle capital adequacy requirements, capital has become a less stringent constraint on growth of a bank. The same is true for off-balance sheet operations (derivatives) for which capital is required, but for which netting is increasingly accepted, as are collateral arrangements which diminish capital requirements.

## The Mutation of Banking

Securitisation and disintermediation will continue to undercut the lending business in its traditional form and prepare a growing role for securities markets. Something similar is going on with the liability side of banks, where money market funds are replacing deposits.

Non-bank financial intermediaries, such as credit cards, supermarkets, automatic distributors, real estate developers are, furthermore, competing successfully with banks in the loan originating business, refinancing themselves in the capital market. Their success is based on product standardisation, bundling of sales with financing, and a low cost of distribution. Table 10.3 shows the long-term evolution of the major financial intermediaries in the United States.

Looking somewhat further ahead, technological advance will not only create a global market-place for institutions but for individuals as well.

**Table 10.3**  Relative Shares of Total Financial Intermediary Assets in the United States 1960–94

|  | 1960 | 1970 | 1980 | 1990 | 1994 |
|---|---|---|---|---|---|
| Depository institutions (banks) | | | | | |
|   Commercial banks | 38.6 | 38.5 | 37.2 | 30.4 | 28.6 |
|   Savings and loans and mutual savings | 19.0 | 19.4 | 19.6 | 12.5 | 7.0 |
|   Credit unions | 1.1 | 1.4 | 1.6 | 2.0 | 2.0 |
| Mutual funds | | | | | |
|   Stock and bond | 2.9 | 3.6 | 1.7 | 5.9 | 10.8 |
|   Money market | 0.0 | 0.0 | 1.9 | 4.6 | 4.2 |
| Finance companies | 4.7 | 4.9 | 5.1 | 5.6 | 5.3 |
| Pension funds | | | | | |
|   Private | 6.4 | 8.4 | 12.5 | 14.9 | 16.2 |
|   Public (state and local government) | 3.3 | 4.6 | 4.9 | 6.7 | 8.4 |
| Insurance companies | | | | | |
|   Life insurance | 19.6 | 15.3 | 11.5 | 12.5 | 13.0 |
|   Property and casualty | 4.4 | 3.8 | 4.5 | 4.9 | 4.6 |
| Total | 100.0 | 100.0 | 100.0 | 100.0 | 100.0 |

*Source*: Board of Governors of the Federal Reserve System, Flow of Funds Accounts and Edwards and Miskkin (1995)

Multimedia superhighways will connect databases, individuals and institutions, making the place of residence both for the match of demand and supply and for regulations irrelevant. This will have profound implications for the management of institutions, income generation (as local monopolies will disappear), specialisation and, of course, for regulation also, as argued in previous chapters.

These various trends when put together suggest that banks, as traditionally defined, are a species threatened by extinction in the financial Jurassic Park. What will remain after the end of banking are financial intermediaries, but the defining elements of banks (deposits and loans) will rapidly lose importance. Deposits will increasingly be replaced by money-market funds, loans will be originated by distributors of goods themselves, or will be securitised and therefore disappear from a bank's balance sheet.

It may be worth looking at this phenomenon carefully. Intermediation is a process which in recent times has become more and more disaggregated, with its various parts carried out by different, specialised institutions. US savings banks, for example, specialise more and more in collecting deposits which they invest in growing proportions in securities rather than mortgage loans. In this way their assets are more liquid, market risk is therefore substantially reduced, credit risk is as low as desired by the choice of securities and operational costs much lower. Unfortunately, collecting savings is not what it used to be, as mutual funds provide fierce competition. Like banks, money market funds pool the savings of households and transfer these funds to borrowers by investing in their debt or equity. To do so they need neither an expensive retail net, nor a heavy lending machinery. In terms of their assets money market funds typically have operating costs of one-tenth of those of retail-oriented commercial banks. What is outsourced by mutual funds is the risk-management function. Of course, they have to manage a portfolio, but the securities they purchase are evaluated by rating agencies. In addition to a free risk assessment, they gain liquidity and save loan-monitoring costs.

In cases where banks provide the initial funding—from deposits and, more and more, with funds collected in the market—they increasingly have the option of securitising loan packages. This started with mortgages and, over time, was extended to credit cards and other homogenous loan classes and is slowly spreading to less homogenous loans. For example, securitisation of small business loans has already started. As with mortgages, at some future time, local banks may still evaluate and monitor credits, but financial market investors will take over the resource-transfer and risk functions.

Even in consumer markets, banks face stiffer competition from non-banks which have important competitive advantages. Credit cards are one example. Although often issued by banks, they are more profitable as an independent business not restricted by regional distribution limits and fully exploiting the economies of scale of the credit card technology. Credit cards serve already, and increasingly so in the future, as suppliers of credit lines. As technology reduces costs, moreover, every type of payment may be made by cards, totally replacing currency. Already today *procurement cards* with a negotiated credit line and a record-keeping system are used by companies for their purchase of goods.

Another source of competition are finance companies, associated or not with a particular distributor of goods and services. Car companies, for example, do not need a distribution network for making loans, have readily available collateral and can refinance themselves like any bank, including securitisation of their loans.

Is this trend of splitting up financial products into components which can then be delivered by specialised non-banks, some offered on the Internet, irreversible? This author believes that the classical distinction between banks and non-banks will indeed lose its importance. Some major banks will always play a role of penultimate suppliers of liquidity, but apart from this feature there is little that will differentiate a bank from a mutual fund, a credit card supplier or a finance company. In the resourcing of funds the market will assume an ever increasing weight. Institutions, the "carriers of history" will therefore change beyond the point of recognition. Certainly some financial functions may well agglomerate again when the economies of scope materialise, in forms such as Charles Sanford's vision of an integrated "wealth account". But whether one calls institutions offering widespread financial services banks, finance companies, risk managers, or asset managers, makes no material difference.

## Implications for Central Banking

It is simply a matter of time for the end of traditional banking to bring about the end of traditional money control by central banks. Banks are special because they receive deposits, have access to central bank refinancing and, as such, play a key role in the central bank's job of controlling the money supply. But if there are no longer any deposits because savers hold their liquidity in securities and make payments through their debit (credit) cards, or from their money market funds or wealth accounts, what then is there left for the central bank to control? This is an interesting question, particularly for those central banks that specialise in control of the money supply in pursuit of their single objective of price stability. One example is the German Bundesbank and it is therefore not surprising that the Bundesbank blocked introduction of money market funds in Germany until it bowed to the competitive pressure of foreign competition, in particular money-market funds set up in Luxembourg sucking savings out of the country.

In the United States, as elsewhere, there is a secular downward trend for the share of deposits in household financial assets. This trend is even more pronounced for M1 (cash and demand deposits).[25] Before 1960, M1 represented about 30% of GDP, a ratio that fell to about 15% by 1980 and has since then oscillated around that level. In relation to household financial assets which have substantially increased in relation to GDP, thanks to accumulation and appreciation of stock prices, M1 has fallen dramatically.

Even if bank deposits are not disappearing, their unique feature of "moneyness" (the constancy of its nominal value, its role as an instrument of payment) has already been challenged by perfect substitutes, such as credit cards and money-market funds. By prohibiting the private issue of bank notes, central banks enjoy a monopoly position. This monopoly is now also being challenged by electronic money ("E-money"). This new technology delivers "stored value" or "prepaid vehicles" and creates a direct competitor to government notes and coins. Since E-money is a liability of the issuing institution, similar to notes issued as liabilities of banks during the 19th century "free banking" period in the United States, it represents privately created money. If such cards are not considered as "deposits" then they could be issued by non-depository institutions who, free of regulations, would appear to have a clear competitive advantage over banks. For the time being, old habits and the "first move advantage" of ATMs are obstacles to quick adoption of E-money. With declining technological costs the long-term future seems, however, assured.

For monetarists it was essential to be able to separate money from other financial assets—a distinction that has become increasingly fuzzy. To escape that fuzziness some monetarists have recommended focusing on "base money", that is, currency in circulation and mandatory deposits with the central bank ("required reserves"). Global competition has made more and more central banks reluctant to maintain required reserves. It is likely that central banks will be forced to shift to other means of monetary control, in which case the monetary base reduces to currency in circulation—which may disappear. Figure 10.3 reproduces the evolution of M1 and currency in relation to GNP. Astonishing is the virtual constancy of currency/GDP at 5% over the last twenty-five years, despite the ever wider use of credit or payment cards. One possible explanation may be the increasing popularity of ATMs, a major technological innovation.[26] Another is the use of cash in rapidly growing global organised crime (drugs, prostitution, arms), a market estimated at over US$1 trillion in 1995, half of which was generated in the United States, and largely dollar-based across the globe (*Financial Times*, 14 February 1997). In addition, in countries with high price instability, the dollar serves as a parallel currency. According to estimates by Zurich Insurance Group for end-1996, Russians owned US$30 billion in cash or 8% of dollar cash outstanding, and some 60% of US cash is estimated to be held abroad.

No one knows how small reservable deposits must become in relation to total financial wealth, nor how small the assets of depository institutions must become in relation to total credit, before the central bank's ability to alter

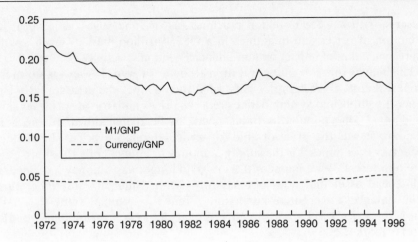

**Figure 10.3** The evolution of monetary aggregates in the United States

these institutions' behaviour by providing reserves fails to affect aspects of economic activity (interest rates, inflation). But the limiting point is certainly not zero.

To pursue the US example, in a US$7 trillion economy with more than US$30 trillion of financial claims outstanding in highly liquid markets where many of those claims change ownership frequently, why should it matter whether the Federal Reserve conducts open market policies to buy US$1 billion or US$10 billion worth of securities in the course of a year? How can such a small difference matter even for the pricing of government securities, of which there are over US$5 trillion outstanding, or for the pricing of marketable debt securities more generally, of which there are more than US$15 trillion?

For many the answer is that the Federal Reserve is a monopolist. It alone can create the reserves that, by law, depository institutions must hold. Its purchases of securities do just that. And, relative to the existing amount of bank reserves (US$54 billion at mid-year 1996), US$1 billion versus US$10 billion growth in a year is a major difference.

But being a monopolist in a market matters only if the particular market is itself important. What if banks (and other depository institutions) can just as easily carry out their activities—today extending credit and taking deposits, tomorrow managing risk and borrowing in the capital market—without incremental reserves?

If having reserves or not is no longer important to banks,[27] and if other lending and deposit creating institutions can readily take their place, then the central bank's monopoly over bank reserves no longer matters. And once it does not, no one can plausibly expect even an institution, such as the Federal

Reserve with a US$390 billion portfolio (as of June 1996), to govern the evolution of prices and quantities in a US$30 trillion market, much less to exert a meaningful impact on non-financial economic activity.[28]

This leaves one intriguing question to be answered. If there is no more money, that is, no cash or deposits, what then defines the price level?[29] The general equilibrium system defines relative prices and, for the price level to be defined, one nominal variable needs to be nailed down. In the gold standard it was the price of gold (a particular relative price). In modern monetary economies it is the supply of money or equivalently the short-term rate of interest. What happens if there is no longer any "money", defined as a financial asset that does not pay any return (interest rate) other than "convenience"? Recent research shows that the nominal value that nails down the price level could be government debt (Woodford 1995); or the futures market.[30]

# 8. CONCLUSION

The wider ramifications of the development of derivatives markets on the way business is conducted, wealth is invested and the economy is structured are a major theme of this book. I could not resist thinking a step further and extrapolating in this chapter some observable trends. This is risky business as evolution of financial structures is typically non-linear and the future full of surprises. Despite these reservations, I feel confident that the financial industry will change dramatically in its configuration and activity. The development of derivatives will turn major banks into risk-management suppliers wherever their business migrates out of traditionally defined banking.

Until now derivatives have had a major impact on the financial industry and end-users. I believe that what we have seen so far is nothing in comparison to what is to come. Derivatives techniques will be applied to a growing area of activities so far left untouched. I looked at possible applications in areas such as real estate, economic activity at aggregated and disaggregated levels and inflation. The implications are mind-boggling.

The shift of financial assets to institutional investors which started in the United States, the United Kingdom and the Netherlands, will continue in these countries and catch up in others. True pension reforms, necessary for alleviating the public sector from a heavy and growing financial responsibility in many countries, will provide sustained demand for equity over the next 20 years or so, assuring a bullish trend. The strong growth of industrial investors, the largest end-users of derivatives, will provide sustained demand for derivatives products. This chapter has discussed novel applications, such as CPI, GNP or real estate futures. Pension funds are eager to hedge against unforeseeable inflation bouts, slow growth or, as major real estate investors, declines of real estate prices.

Nor is the sacred parish of capitalist economies, the corporation, spared from dramatic transformations. The role of own funds and, hence, the cost of capital and relations between owners, managers and workers are all deeply affected by derivative-based finance. Even government actions and regulatory controls cannot escape the leverage of derivatives. What more can one wish for?

The chapter concludes with the argument that traditionally defined banks are a species condemned to extinction. Financial conglomerates will evolve, offering full financial services, some of which operating globally. This process of concentration into mega-institutions will be most pronounced in the United States, because it has the least concentrated banking system. With cash and bank chequing accounts replaced by E-money and chequable money-market funds, the role of central banks will change as well. Why would one need a central bank if there were no longer any banks?

One important issue not analysed in this chapter, because it would require too much science fiction, is the future evolution of financial market structure. But we do know that there is tremendous potential provided by Internet technology to confront demand with supply directly, possibly without intermediaries, across the globe. At least for standardised products this new technology will have a major repercussion on financial intermediation, delivery of securities and payments, and the scope and means of financial regulations. Without intermediation there is, of course, no more ground to regulate the conduct of market participants or to establish barriers against the spread of institutional failure. As deliveries and payments still have to be channelled through clearing-houses or similar institutions, the recommendations of Chapter 9 to provide the proper incentives for clearing-house self-regulation remain, however, valid.

Assuming that the hunches or provocative ideas of this chapter are worth disagreeing with, I invite the reader to "consider the contradictions".

## ENDNOTES

1 This chapter incorporates material from Shiller (1993) and Freeman (1994).
2 See, for example, Gruber (1996).
3 The number of S&P 500 Index funds grew from three in 1984 to 44 in 1994. Gruber (1996) finds that their rebalancing costs are impressively low.
4 An early identification of the conflict between management and owners is due to Berle and Means (1932).
5 Finance theory has identified the problem—without so far offering clear-cut solutions. Allen and Gale (1994, pp. 370–71) conclude their survey of the theoretical literature as follows: "Overall, the literature on the optimality of debt and equity suggests that the circumstances in which these commonly used securities are the

best are fairly restrictive. even though the securities that are issued may be optimal privately . . . no particular reason exists to believe that they are optimal from a social point of view." In other words, as far as the issue of securities is concerned, it is not immediately obvious that the "invisible hand" operates and ensures that the market structure is efficient.

6  Sanford (1993).

7  If the firm does not hedge such risks then portfolio managers can do this, presumably even more efficiently (see Chapter 4). But performance measurement is made more transparent when the firm hedges against outside events.

8  This solution corresponds, in fact, to a theoretical model elaborated by Dewatripont and Tirole (1994) to improve corporate governance.

9  Bankers have already devised ways to circumvent regulations that limit the ownership of a corporation by certain types of investors (private shareholders, foreigners, banks, etc.). The simplest are so-called "synthetic shares" issued by banks, which mimic the dividends and price movements of the underlying stock, but do not confer voting rights.

10  This would not be true of the dominant individual owner who does not opt for the incorporated structure in the first place. Both for individual shareholders and institutional investors (pension funds, equity funds), most of which are not even allowed to be represented on corporate boards, "ownership" value is close to zero.

11  Leveraged participation in the firm's profits, if desired, can be purchased individually by workers in the amounts desired by using call options. The same can be done by managers if they want to augment their bet on the firm beyond their negotiated amount in profits.

12  There is currently no futures market where the risk of inflation can be hedged directly. There do exist in some countries (for example, the United Kingdom and, more recently, in the United States) inflation-index-linked bonds and returns on such bonds are fully hedged against inflation. Index-linked bonds can also be used to construct a return on inflation, albeit at excessive costs: a portfolio short in index-linked bonds and long in non-indexed bonds is, in fact, a pure inflation portfolio. However, such markets—because of the difficulties in shorting securities, the lack of complete matching of coupons and maturities of both index-linked and non-indexed bonds and the lower liquidity of bond markets as compared to futures markets, all resulting in high costs and imperfect tracking of the CPI—are not a substitute for futures markets in the CPI.

13  If the price level were somehow correlated with other variables affecting individual well-being, then it would make sense to invest in nominal, rather than real, bonds. But such an insurance argument is hard to sustain.

14  The market was launched on 28 June 1985; 1324 contracts were traded that year. By the end of 1985, however, the contract appeared moribund: on most days no contracts were traded at all. 1986 volume was 8776 contracts, 1987 volume was two contracts, 1988 volume was zero contracts.

15  This would require, in the first instance, the construction of a reliable and representative CPI which does not exist in Mexico or China.

16  Such a contract need not be established in a local market, nor in principle does the GNP index rely on domestic concepts. Such a market could thus get around domestic manipulations of the GNP index, capital controls, regulation of domestic markets, local high transaction costs, etc.

17  A hedonic price index takes account of product attributes, such as quality, location, age, etc. Their importance is statistically determined from appropriate samples.

18  The London Fox was a small exchange without the resources to launch a major public education campaign, beyond a few seminars and mailings of brochures. It

did not seek out and develop concrete uses of the market for its best potential clients. It certainly did not pave the way for the kind of new retail institutions that would use the futures markets; there were none of the retail risk-management institutions; no mortgages with down-payment insured against real estate price declines, no home value insurance.

19 Despite such difficulties there does appear to be a nascent market in index-based real estate derivative products. In January 1993, a US$20 million real estate swap was completed by Morgan Stanley & Co. Inc. and Aldrich, Eastman and Waltch L.P., a deal touted as the first real estate swap ever. One counter-party, who agreed to pay Morgan Stanley a return based on the Russell/NCREIF (Frank Russell National Council of Real Estate Investment Fiduciaries) index of commercial real estate prices and received LIBOR (London Interbank Offered Rate), a short-term interest rate, was a corporate pension fund. The other counter-party, who paid the interest rate and received the real estate return, was a life insurance company.

20 There are economies of scope if the joint production of two goods is cheaper than producing each one separately.

21 For more details see Steinherr and Huveneers 1992 and Steinherr 1995.

22 Whilst the mega-merger waves of the 1980s spilled over into the 1990s, it is only in this decade that giant companies like AT&T, ITT, 3M, or Baxter International choose *voluntarily* to break themselves apart. As in the past, corporate raiders *force* underperformers to restructure or break up. What is new is the role played by mutual funds.

23 One business where large groups will be successful is payments transactions and securities custody. Success in these business lines is a result of economies of scale due to the high capital investment for this high technology business. But because of pervasive economies of scale only few financial groups will remain active, as suggested by the recent decision of Morgan Guarantee to sell its securities custody arm.

24 Boyd and Graham (1994) found that among the 50 largest US bank holding companies salaries and bonuses of bank managers were significantly related to size and unrelated to profitability or asset growth.

25 M1 was redefined in the Monetary Control Act of 1980 to focus on "transaction balances". Reserve requirements on savings balances were suppressed, but reserves were imposed on transaction balances with non-member banks and even with non-bank intermediaries.

26 First introduced in the United States in 1971, ATMs grew from less than 2000 in 1973 to 90 000 in 1992. They exhibit strong network externalities and economies of scale.

27 Now already banks can and regularly do fund incremental credit creation by issuing CDs or other non-reserve-bearing instruments. This situation is, of course, correctable, at least in principle, although as a practical matter difficult questions of definition among forms of obligations (direct vs. holding company, onshore vs. offshore, insured vs. uninsured, senior vs. subordinated, and so on) would inevitably arise. So, too, would problems of the competitiveness of the depository intermediary industry as a whole.

28 Central banks might attempt to regain control by imposing "reserves" in some form for financial institutions other than depository intermediaries or by centralised co-ordination of capital requirements for all lenders. But such attempts are bound to fail in the future global market.

29 The traditional concern over the indeterminacy of the price level is, however, overcome by recent research (see, for example, Woodford 1995).

30 Some elements for an answer can be sketched on the assumption that CPI futures contract exists. Its price, established in an efficient market, will deviate from the

spot market realisation only by a random element, due to news that cannot be anticipated. Such an effect will not have any repercussions on the real economy as agents have hedged their positions. The trend of the price level is therefore determined by the CPI futures market. Is there any reason for believing that this trend will be stationary, deflationary or inflationary? Not really. Certainly the anticipation of monetary policy—in the past a major ingredient for inflationary expectations—will lose its importance. The constraints of the system are: there is no outside injection of liquidity; and the supply of the productive sector and the demand are constrained by the "intertemporal budget" of the wealth accounts. If there is an inflationary shock there will be temporary inflation but no reason to anticipate a sustained inflationary trend.

# 11

# Conclusions

## THE ORIGIN OF THE SPECIES

Futures, options and other derivative products have been known and used for a remarkably long time. In the United States a futures market for agricultural commodities has existed since the early 19th century. For a variety of reasons, no futures market existed for financial products before 1972. The year 1972 is a watershed and in financial history one should really distinguish between the years before and after 1972.

Why did such markets, whose economic benefits this book has shown to be substantial, not develop earlier? Futures markets for agricultural products existed, the mathematics and economics of financial futures were known—at least enough to get something going—and large amounts of foreign-exchange forwards were offered by banks. The new element in the early 1970s was the explosion of uncertainty with the demise of the fixed exchange rate system of Bretton Woods. The new systems of flexible exchange rates gave monetary authorities increased autonomy and hence interest and inflation rates became more volatile and specific to each country. The first oil-shock in 1973 made adjustments to new equilibrium exchange rates necessary, adding further to exchange rate volatility. For the first time in post-war economic history, the earnings of firms became as much—and in many cases even more—dependent on expectational errors concerning future exchange or interest rates as on their internal management decisions.

The creation of exchanges for financial futures and options represented the beginning of a new industry—the risk-management industry—whose real significance only became plain over time. Right from the start end-users—financial and non-financial firms, asset managers, government institutions—were given the opportunity to take reasoned bets or to free themselves of unwanted risk at extremely low cost in an efficient, liquid market. Transactions were handled by associated clearing-houses that set up a risk-management structure that minimised risk through multilateral clearing, margin requirements and additional safeguards.

The first exchange-traded contracts were foreign exchange contracts, followed by contracts on bonds to hedge interest rate risk. Options on individual stocks were introduced in 1973 on the Chicago Boards Options Exchange with as much success as the futures contracts. Since the early days the span of available products and the volumes traded increased phenomenally, driven by market demand and a rapid pace of innovation. Two innovations were especially decisive. The first was "cash settlement", that is, payment or receipt of the contract's value without physical delivery. This was an efficiency gain, as most traders only wish to receive the value of their bet and not a foreign currency or a government bond. It also made the trade of non-deliverable contracts, such as "three-month interest rates", possible. The second innovation was index trading (also an example of a non-deliverable contract) which facilitated position-taking on the overall market's, or specific sub-categories', evolution. Index futures have become among the most successful contracts and indispensable ingredients for portfolio managers.

With financial deregulation and liberalisation, the need for exchange-traded derivatives led to a proliferation of exchanges around the world. From 1972 to 1982 derivative exchanges only existed in the United States. Today every developed country and some emerging countries have at least one derivative exchange.

# OTC vs. EXCHANGE-TRADED CONTRACTS

OTC derivatives contracts existed before exchange-traded products and, in recent years, have grown at an even more rapid pace. It is not immediately obvious why two totally different market organisations co-exist for essentially the same service. Why has the Darwinian struggle for survival not eliminated one form or the other? The answer is that each of these two organisations presents both clear advantages and inconveniences. OTC contracts are bilateral agreements that reflect the specific needs and wishes of the customer, whereas exchange-traded contracts are standardised. It is, therefore, easier to innovate with OTC products: a specific customer need generates a new type of contract, whereas a contract will be traded on the exchanges only when a sufficiently high level of demand can be perceived. Bilateral contracts can set amounts, maturity and other conditions exactly to customer specification, which can be an advantage over an identical traded contract with standardised terms. But the disadvantages of the specificity of the OTC contract are also quite obvious: lack of liquidity, lack of transparent and competitive pricing, and, when the contract terms are complex, the possibility of imperfect understanding by either party—but more typically the customer—of the full implications of the contract.

The advantages of the exchange-traded contracts are liquidity, transparent and competitive pricing, low cost of transactions, and risk management that exploits all possible offsets and covers residual risks to the fullest extent possible. Liquidity and transparent pricing allows timely entry and exit from the market so that contract holders can immediately react to relevant news. This already lowers the risks involved, particularly as transaction costs are extremely low—lower than in cash markets and lower than for OTC contracts. Risk management at the clearing-house of an exchange is based on multilateral netting and the clearing-house, standing in between the contracting parties, never has a net position. To protect its members, exchanges require them to post cash or safe securities with the clearing-house to cover "margins". These margins are computed with sophisticated risk-management models, taking into account the volatility of the price of the underlying cash instrument and are adjusted daily according to price movements. The exchange-traded contract appears costly because it charges users the full risk. From a public policy viewpoint this system is, therefore, attractive: full, or nearly full, risk coverage at a well-managed clearing-house makes systemic risk an extremely unlikely event. Individual customers (or members) may still fail, as Barings demonstrated in 1995, but their grave is an individual one, not a mass grave.

With OTC contracts customers do not have to pay-up for book losses and can accumulate losses over the life of the contract. For lack of liquidity, close-outs can be costly and are, therefore, often resisted. When the contract issuer forces a close-out, the financial situation of the customer is likely to take a second beating, as was illustrated by several concrete examples in this book. Because risk is not fully covered in real time, there is much more systemic risk generated by OTC contracts. Systemic risk is an "externality", not fully priced in OTC contracts, which are, therefore, more attractive from a private viewpoint and less attractive from a social viewpoint than exchange-traded products.

This book makes the case that the explanation for the success of OTC contracts must go beyond the private costs of these products. If the regulators' concern is to diminish systemic risk as much as possible, then they should impose similar conditions on both.

In fact, for reasons easy to understand, regulation of OTC markets are very different and much less rigorous and constraining than for the exchanges. The major reason is that it is difficult to localise the OTC market, identify its nationality, point at its members, or fence in its products. The exchanges, by contrast, have an address, a membership and a product range. Every element can, and is, meticulously regulated. They are like an aquarium in which the temperature, oxygen level, fish population, ratio of predators to prey and food supply can be strictly controlled. The OTC markets are like the open sea.

Both market forms also enjoy an implicit subsidy. For example, the US financial system is extremely liquidity-sensitive and derivative markets even more so. The big money-centre banks—the major derivatives dealers, which were shown to be the penultimate suppliers of liquidity—can count on the support of the Federal Reserve in case of liquidity problems and, therefore, do not hold as much liquidity (or capital for that matter) as they would in the absence of this support.

The two market forms, OTC and exchange-trade products, are alternatives, but over time their relationship has generated a substantial symbiosis. OTC dealers try to hedge their positions to the maximum possible, subject to a desired risk/cost trade-off. At the margin, after the dealers' internal offset of risk positions, the book is balanced with exchange-traded products. As a result more OTC volume also tends to generate more demands from dealers for exchange-trade products.

But, in general, the relationships are fiercely competitive. Exchanges have created products that replicate the flexibility of contract terms that are the decisive advantage of OTC products. The latter, in turn, offer standardised products on very low bid-ask spreads to offer customers a full range of products, but effectively making money mainly from the more custom-designed and often innovatory deals. With an outstanding notional amount of US$18 trillion in 1995 it would be materially impossible to reach such volumes only with custom-designed deals. It is estimated that at least three-quarters of that volume are plain vanilla deals for which there are perfect substitutes on the exchanges.

In addition, risk management of OTC products has increasingly moved closer to the way risks are managed at the exchanges. Netting is growing in importance, collateral agreements replicate the advantage of margin payments, and banks club-up to form clearing-houses or similar structures. There is, thus, some dynamics under way to bring the two market organisations more in line.

# AMERICANISATION OF GLOBAL FINANCE

One question of considerable interest is: why did it all start in the United States? The end of the Bretton Woods fixed-exchange-rate agreement affected the United States less than smaller economies. The US banking system up to 1972 was over-regulated and its performance unimpressive. Very often the Glass–Steagall segmentation of banking is seen as an unfortunate historic relic that prevents the US financial system from becoming more efficient. This book argues that, unintentionally, Glass–Steagall has made a major contribution to the emergence of the ultimately most performing financial system in the world: the American model of finance.

By separating commercial from investment banking, Glass–Steagall laid the foundations for the most competitive and innovatory investment banking in the world. It created a countervailing force to the economic and political influence of the large New York-based banks. Not enjoying the benefits of the banking franchise and not being hampered by the regulatory quid pro quo, investment banks had to innovate to be successful. Until the 1970s the innovatory rhythm was modest, but then the industry benefited from a fundamental change in financial culture: the drift from relationship-based to commoditised finance. In fact, the financing of the Vietnam War required increases in interest rates which drove savers from banks to the newly created money market funds. This was the beginning of the disintermediation process, providing new opportunities for investment banks and forcing commercial banks to innovate to make up for lower traditional incomes. Banks started to issue certificates of deposits to replace lost time deposits and the era of managed liabilities had arrived. Prime borrowers also managed to circumvent banks by issuing commercial paper so that not only liabilities but also assets became disintermediated. All this became feasible because the regulatory framework—certainly excessively cumbersome and detailed—had achieved one remarkable success: an integrity of the financial system unknown in most parts of the world, at least until very recently. The growing importance of institutional investors—money-market funds, investment funds, pension funds, insurance companies—increased the competitive pressure and built up the demand for two essential activities: risk management and liquidity services. Institutional investors developed professional asset management and became big users of derivatives to hedge or position their risks. Some particular funds—the hedge funds and index funds—became the most intensive users of risk-management instruments. The US financial industry that started to emerge in the 1970s was characterised by segmentation, commoditisation of finance, the importance of institutional investors, the intensive use of risk-management techniques and instruments, and became extremely liquidity-dependent, much more so than other financial systems. And the Federal Reserve stood ready to stabilise the Fed rate and to intervene quickly and massively when needed.

The US financial system took the lead and set the standard for other countries. The United Kingdom was particularly rapid in adopting the US model whilst other countries followed with a longer lag. In this process London benefited, of course, from its past experience as a world financial centre and had an added advantage of its own: greater internationalisation. London became the centre for the Eurodollar market and attracted, among others, US banks and securities houses. This facilitated the transfer of know-how into the Euromarket, creating a pole of attraction to financial institutions worldwide. With the emergence of an integrated European capital market, following the adoption of the Euro, London stands a good chance of becoming Europe's financial centre. Backed up by an economy comparable in size to the United

States and a strong currency, London is posed to vie with New York for financial supremacy.

The topography of the global financial landscape is far from being flat. Global means connected, but not that space or location is irrelevant. New York, London, Tokyo, Hong Kong are like skyscrapers emerging out of the global economy. The thick smog over the skyscrapers is the financial industry's network and derivatives are the heaviest particles in the cloak of smog.

Smog is not something we like. It is the, at-a-cost, avoidable residual from economic activities we need or like. Derivatives, and finance more generally, pose a number of difficulties and risks which make the job of politicians and regulators more difficult. This book has attempted to show that, from a social policy viewpoint, it is preferable to deal with these difficulties and accept some of the constraints that derivatives have created, instead of wishing derivatives away or limiting their growth one way or another.

## RISK-MANAGEMENT: ONE OF THE MOST IMPORTANT INNOVATIONS OF THE 20TH CENTURY

I consider risk-management an innovation even more significant than stock exchanges. Most people will readily agree that a well-functioning stock market is a good thing. It is, at any rate, an institution that former-socialist countries were most eager to set up to allow investors to take reasoned bets and channel resources to the most promising enterprises. Thereby any investor, whether worker, civil servant or pensioner can, over time, benefit from the growing earnings of the corporations of his choice. Economics is paying full tribute to the benefits generated by organised stock exchanges, but has problems in putting numbers on these benefits.

Risk-management finance has made possible an increasingly more precise pricing and allocation of ever more finely defined risk. Those segments of the economy that want to bear or shed a particular kind of risk can now buy/sell such risk—a prerequisite for an efficient allocation of resources. A liquidity supply mechanism ensures the smooth operation of financial markets. In essence it assures participants in financial markets that they can confidently expect to sell or buy a large amount of a security without materially affecting its price, i.e., it ensures the continuity of asset prices. Furthermore, it avoids the debilitating liquidity crises that have plagued earlier liberal financial systems in the late 19th century and early this century. This is now all the more important since the US model, particularly risk-management finance, has become crucially dependent on keeping its securitised derivative, money, and capital markets liquid, even at times when the suppliers of credit decide for precautionary reasons to shift into high-quality short-term near risk-free obligations, such as government bills.

Risk-management services cannot, of course, reduce the risks in an economy. It is even possible that, to the contrary, they increase overall risk because they create the means of engaging in high-risk activities that would have remained untouched otherwise. But these additional risks generate economic gains by expanding the horizon of the possible. The trick of risk management is to better define and structure risk and redistribute it from those unwilling to bear it to those who are happy with the proposed risk/return profile. Even if it is difficult to measure the precise gains, as is the case with most institutional innovations, it is clear, both from a theoretical and from a practical viewpoint, that the gains are very substantial. The growth of derivatives should, therefore, not be curtailed or hampered by policies motivated by concerns about increased systemic risks, consumer protection, or policy constraints. There are, indeed, problems, some artificial, some to be accepted, and the largest part containable through appropriate changes in the regulatory framework.

## WORK OF THE DEVIL OR SOCIAL BENEFIT?

To begin with, the false problems. Derivatives are often seen as the devil's instrument, upsetting market equilibria and making governments helpless in their battle against vicious speculators. It needs to be recognised that speculation is a socially useful and necessary activity. When governments try to defend an exchange rate that is out-of-line with economic fundamentals, then they fall easy prey to speculators, as illustrated with the EMS turmoil in 1992/93. Is this a social gain or loss? Governments are restrained in their actions by speculators with potent, highly leveraged derivatives. They cannot keep the welfare of their people artificially low with capital controls because swaps can easily circumvent them. Is this a loss? The leverage provided by derivatives can, of course, also be used by governments. Monetary authorities that lack foreign exchange reserves can, and do, intervene in the forward market. Their only constraint is the amount of potential loss they can accept should their strategy fail. If they are defending a fundamentally justified exchange rate, this use of derivatives is socially beneficial. If they defend an exchange rate out-of-line with basic economic factors, then the additional leverage amplifies the social cost. More generally, globalisation narrows the choice of actions in every country and derivatives are only part, albeit a very powerful part, of the overall design.

There are, of course, real problems. The first is a problem of information at various levels. This problem has been recognised and in 1997 an international task force is working on a more regular and detailed overall database for derivatives. Balance of payments have become difficult to interpret, because they do not include contingent claims or liabilities. When a crisis unfolds, as in Mexico in 1993 and in Thailand and other Asian countries in 1997, policy-makers are taken by surprise and their actions taken on the basis of incomplete and erroneous information. The same is true for financial intermediaries and corporations although progress has been made during recent years to improve their risk-accounting with new approaches, such as value-at-risk. Public disclosure of risk-accounting is at the top of regulators' priorities. But we are still far away from an international agreement on accounting standards for derivatives.

The second problem is a potential increase in systemic risk. Derivatives, by their nature, connect various markets, as they redistribute risk. Derivatives and cash markets are by design mutually interdependent; OTC and exchange markets are interactive, both are highly and irregularly liquidity-dependent; counter-parties are, more than in other financial contracts, from different currency areas, and so on. Add to this interconnection the leverage provided, the liquidity dependence, the opaqueness of OTC markets and of institutions with large positions and the high concentration within the derivatives industry, and you have a real and huge case for concern.

Policy-makers have become aware of this problem. They have also realised that little can be done in isolation as the market is global. Most of their work is, therefore, carried out in international forums and their work is progressing. In some sense they are even achieving too much and, in another, too little. Too much because within the traditional regulatory mould problems are dealt with one-by-one so that regulations become excessively heavy and the expanding patchwork lacks overall consistency. Too little because the overall outcome cannot come to grips with the main problem: systemic risk.

What tends to be forgotten in the regulatory fervour is that regulations are needed to deal with major market imperfections, not with every facet of everyday business life. And to deal with this problem in an industry whose market configuration has completely changed, a quantum jump may be necessary for the regulatory approach. This quantum jump—replacing the traditional ways with a totally new approach—has still not occurred.

This book proposes a radical change of guards, inspired by three basic facts. The first is that the financial industry possesses real-time factual knowledge and professional skills exceeding by far those of external regulators. What is needed are the right incentives for financial intermediaries to use the available knowledge and skills and to disclose their exposures. The second basic fact is that firms already operate globally, whereas regulators are national and their co-operation encounters insurmountable difficulties. The third fact is that the traditional institutional demarcation lines between banks and non-bank financial intermediaries have become blurred. As this book has tried to show, derivatives have played an important role in blowing away the demarcation lines. Regulation of particular institutions, therefore, only distorts competition and induces migration of business to less regulated institutional forms.

These basic facts suggest several constraints that any future regulatory framework has to respect. The first is that institutional regulation is no longer optimal and has to be replaced by a functional approach. Prudential regulation has to deal with activities, widely defined, and not with institutions. Codes of conduct, obviously, can only be imposed on institutions, but again they need adaptation along functional lines. The second is that incentives have to be created for self-regulation in order to exploit the superior knowledge base, skills and global reach of the market players. The consequence of greater self-regulation is that external regulation should be as parsimonious as possible, and focus strictly on market failure. The most obvious cases of market failure are systemic risk and protection of the non-professional counter-party in financial deals.

## FINANCIAL STRUCTURE IN THE 21ST CENTURY

What could the financial policy model for the next century look like? This book proposes to re-engineer the financial infrastructure in two dimensions, making it possible to considerably diminish supervision. The first, and more general, international re-engineering concerns the abolition of the banking franchise. Within each financial conglomerate the monetary services (chequing accounts, payment services) would be ring-fenced within a legally independent company with a restricted set of admissible assets in terms of credit quality and liquidity. The risk for depositors (the orphan-and-widow and classic bank run arguments) would thus be contained and minimised and deposit insurance would become largely redundant. Regulators would strictly supervise the monetary service companies to make sure that classic bank runs would stop being a matter of concern.

The activity scope of the financial conglomerate would be unlimited. For capital adequacy the internal value-at-risk model would be accepted, both for the credit and market risk exposure, much along current practices with modifications as suggested by recent innovations in credit risk assessment. The financial conglomerate, with the exception of its monetary services company, would stop being "special" and would be treated like any other corporation.

The second change in financial infrastructure would consist in generalising the risk-management of derivative exchanges to OTC markets. This could be done either by encouraging migration of OTC business to the exchanges or by setting up clearing-houses for OTC business. In fact, both features can already be observed, but to minimise systemic risk it is desirable to level the playing field further and bring costs and risks of both markets in line. With clearing-house risk-management covering at least the plain vanilla part of OTC derivatives, estimated to represent at least two-thirds of the overall OTC market, systemic risk would diminish markedly.


## SHIFTS OF POWER

With financial sector infrastructure adapted along these lines, the role of central banks would be fundamentally changed, at least in those countries where they were regulators of banks. As traditional banking accounts for a declining share of financial intermediation, it seems natural that central banks refocus on their monetary function and withdraw from regulation. Central banks will, however, retain the key role of liquidity provider of last resort. It will be important to redefine this service more narrowly than in the past where, in many countries, banks could safely assume that they would be bailed out in any circumstances. In countries where the monetary authorities have made it clear that they would be unhelpful, as, for example, in Hong Kong, banks tend to have much higher liquidity and capital ratios than, for example, in the United States. Even big banks must know that they will be allowed to fail. With the proposed ring-fencing of the monetary services, failure of a financial institution should pose fewer difficulties.

A re-engineering of the basic financial infrastructure is also the best way to cope with the loss of national regulatory control over global financial conglomerates. Markets are always a step or two ahead of policies. Sometimes policies catch up and bend markets to their objectives. In the case of global financial markets, policy-makers will have to adjust. The world will have a more or less global market, but no world regulator. Even the concept of "lead" regulator is unlikely to be accepted.

It is not only regulations that feel the powerful low tide of the financial sea change. This book has given examples of national states being unable to control their financial institutions at will, to maintain exchange controls or exchange rates at arbitrary levels or, more generally, to set policies as if financial markets and the outside world did not exist. It may be painful for policy-makers to face these constraints, but, overall, they are better for the welfare of their people. One cannot say conclusively whether globalisation is better for the poor or the rich countries. Small countries in particular suffer much more from being cut off from the rest of the world. They are necessarily more specialised and thus exposed to greater instability. For them hedging and international diversification are relatively more important than for larger countries. Before the availability of derivatives, hedging the risks of a small country would have required investments abroad. This would not have appeared attractive to a developing country. Now, as concrete examples in this book have shown, domestic resources can be invested at home and the returns swapped against world market returns.

Derivatives are the engineering device for separating investment and risk decisions.

Global markets create new opportunities and change the way nations interact. They will create an ever more integrated world economy and co-operative efforts among national policy-makers independently of their liking.

As it is easier to agree on a few basic principles rather than on detailed interventions in the market-place and its institutions, I have urged the abandonment of ever more detailed regulatory measures that regulators cannot monitor in real-time and, at any rate, are likely to exceed their means and skills. It is more promising to change the infrastructure and create the incentives for self-regulation of financial firms. This can only work under a hard-budget constraint: no firm, however important it may be to some politicians in a national economy, can hope to be bailed out when in trouble.

## CRYSTAL BALL GAZING

The last chapter attempts a look into the future. We no longer see traditional banks or central banks, or money for that matter. What we see is the exportation of the American model of finance to the rest of the world, the ascent of institutional investors, a transfer of risk management from state to the financial sector (e.g., pension plans), an imperialistic victory of US accounting and disclosure standards, greater emphasis on "shareholder value"—in short, deeper and more performing equity markets in Europe's integrated capital market, Japan, and emerging markets. Fed by a phenomenal supply of funds from pension investments that hitherto have shunned equity markets, a sustained bull market can be expected for the next generation.

We also see new forms of derivatives that allow corporations and people to make choices based on their intrinsic preferences. The resulting allocation of resources is more rational as it is unconstrained by extravagant transaction costs or unwanted groups of risk which are difficult to evaluate. At present, liquid markets exist for only a small share of household wealth and easy hedges are not available for the larger part of individuals' wealth (such as real estate, future earnings, business cycles). Until now, corporations needed excessive amounts of costly equity, because equity is a buffer for all sorts of unknown adverse events (if known, provisions could be made). Workers whose income represents about 70% of GDP at present have only the most rudimentary means of managing the risks inherent in their life-income stream. We can, therefore, safely expect much progress in the use of derivative-based hedges for the risks of corporations and their workers, fundamentally transforming the very nature of corporations and the nature of employment contracts. What we now see is the tip of the iceberg in a sea of change. What is below can already be guessed—with a wide margin of error for which this book offers no hedge.

# Glossary

**Adjustable rate mortgage (ARM)**: A mortgage agreement with interest costs tied to a short- or intermediate-term interest rate index, such as the rates on United States Treasury bills or notes. Rate adjustments are made at intervals and the premium over the index rate may vary over the term of the mortgage.

**American option**: A put or call that can be exercised at any time prior to expiration. Most listed stock options, including those on European exchanges, are US-style options. Important exceptions are certain low strike price options and/or options on shares with restricted transferability. Most listed options on other instruments are also US-style options, but a number of European-style options have been introduced in recent years, particularly on stock indexes and currencies.

**Annuity bond or note**: A fixed rate instrument which pays the investor an equal amount of cash each year over the life of the issue. Individual payments will contain increasing amounts of principal and correspondingly declining amounts of interest.

**Arbitrage**: (1) Technically, arbitrage consists of purchasing a commodity or security in one market for immediate sale in another market (deterministic arbitrage). (2) Popular usage has expanded the meaning of the term to include any activity which attempts to buy a relatively underpriced item and sell a similar, relatively overpriced item, expecting to profit when the prices resume a more appropriate theoretical or historical relationship (statistical arbitrage). (3) In trading options, convertible securities, and futures, arbitrage techniques can be applied whenever a strategy involves buying and selling packages of related instruments. (4) Risk arbitrage applies the principles of risk offset to mergers and other major corporate developments. The risk offsetting position(s) do not insulate the investor from certain event risks (such as termination of a merger agreement or the risk of completion of a transaction within a certain time) so the arbitrage is incomplete. (5) Tax arbitrage transactions are undertaken to share the benefit of differential tax rates or circumstances of two or more parties to a transaction. (6) Regulatory arbitrage transactions are designed to provide indirect access to a risk management market where one party is denied direct access by law or regulation. (7) Swap-driven arbitrage transactions are motivated by the comparative advantages which swap counter-parties enjoy in different debt and currency markets. One counter-party may borrow relatively cheaper in the intermediate- or long-term United States dollar market while the other may have a comparative advantage in floating rate sterling.

**Ask price**: The price at which a dealer will sell a security.

**Asset-backed security (ABS)**: Financial instrument collateralised by one or more types of assets, including real property, mortgages, receivables, etc.

**Asset/liability management**: Any of a variety of techniques designed to co-ordinate the management of an entity's assets with the management of its liabilities. A simple example would be a financial institution's management of the duration of its fixed income assets to match the duration of its payment liabilities.

**At-the-money option**: When the price of the underlying security equals the strike price of the option.

**Average price or rate option (APO, ARO)**: An option whose settlement value is based on the difference between the strike and the average price (rate) of the underlying on selected dates over the life of the option, or over a period beginning on some start date and ending at its expiration. The theoretical value of an average price or rate call will usually be less than the value of an otherwise identical standard option because the average price option acts like an option with a shorter expected life. The premium on an average price or rate option will also tend to be less than the combined premiums of a strip of options expiring on each measurement date, because prices or rates on the wrong side of the strike will reduce the average price or rate and, hence, the expected settlement value of the average price or rate option. With a strip, observations on the wrong side of the strike would make one piece of the strip worthless, but would not drag down the value of the others. (Also called an Asian option.)

**Barrier option**: Path-dependent options with both their payoff pattern and their survival to the nominal expiration date dependent not only on the final price of the underlying but on whether or not the underlying sells at or through a barrier (instrike, outstrike) price during the life of the option. Examples of barrier options include down-and-out and up-and-in puts and calls, early exercise trigger CAPS options and a variety of similar instruments.

**Basis point**: One hundredth of a percentage point (0.01%).

**Basis risk**: The risk that the relationship between the prices of a security and the instrument used to hedge it will change, thereby reducing the effectiveness of the hedge.

**Benchmark**: Security used as the basis for interest rate calculations and for pricing other securities. Also denotes the most heavily traded and liquid security of a particular class.

**Beta factor**: A measurement of stock price volatility *relative* to a broad market index. If a stock moves up and down twice as much as the market, it has a beta of 2. If it moves one half as much as the market, its beta is 0.5. Because it measures volatility *relatively* (to an index) rather than absolutely, the beta factor can be seriously misleading if used in stock option evaluation.

**Bid-ask spread**: The difference between the bid price and the ask price.

**Bid price**: The price at which a dealer will purchase a security.

**Book entry system**: A method for centrally registering the ownership and transfer of securities.

**Brokers**: Traders who buy and sell on behalf of customers, not for their own accounts.

**Cap**: A contract in which the buyer pays a fee to set a maximum to the flexible interest rate that it must pay on a loan. The seller agrees to pay the difference between current interest rates and an agreed rate, times the notional principal, if interest rates rise above the agreed rate.

**Capital markets**: (1) Collective term for the individual and institutional investors who invest their savings, or capital, in order to earn a return. (2) The institutions and mechanisms that channel capital from investors to investments.

**Capital standards**: Rules established by international and national regulators to keep the international financial system from collapsing as a result of bad decisions by bankers and other financiers. These rules, or standards, require financial institutions to maintain adequate capital to absorb most anticipated losses.

**Cash market**: A market for sale of a security against immediate delivery, as opposed to the futures market.

**Cash settlement**: The settlement provision on some options and futures contracts that do not require delivery of the underlying security. For options, the difference between the settlement price on the underlying asset and the option's exercise price is paid to the option holder at exercise. For futures contracts, the exchange establishes a settlement price on the final day of trading and all remaining open positions are marked-to-market at that price.

**Chaos theory**: A theory of systems that produce apparently random results which are, in fact, strictly determined.

**Chinese wall**: In United States securities regulation, a set of procedures designed to segregate some components of the information flow within an organisation to prevent non-public information held or developed in one part of the organisation from being used illegally in another part of the organisation. For example, a Chinese wall usually isolates information in an investment banking operation from trading and investment management.

**Circuit breakers**: A complex and frequently changed series of rules adopted by securities and futures exchanges in the aftermath of the 1987 market break in an attempt to slow down market activity during major stock price movements.

**Clearing corporation**: The affiliate or subsidiary of a futures or options exchange which clears, trades and holds performance bonds posted by dealers to assure performance on their own and customers' futures and options obligations. (Called a clearing house in the United Kingdom.)

**Collar**: The simultaneous purchase of a cap and sale of a floor that has the result of keeping interest rates between a desired range.

**Collateralised mortgage obligation (CMO)**: A generic term for a security backed by real estate mortgages. CMO payment obligations are covered by interest and/or principal payments from a pool of mortgages. In addition to its generic meaning, CMO usually suggests a non-governmental issue.

**Complete markets**: Markets in which investors have a full range of risk/return choices. Investment opportunities are presented in the form of basic components which the investor can assemble on a customised basis to conform to a personal utility function. One of the important contributions of derivative instruments is to increase investor utility by increasing the range of choices.

**Contingent hedge with an agreement for rebate at maturity (CHARM)**: A currency option designed for companies bidding on foreign contracts. If the company wins the contract, the option may be exercised like any other currency option. If the company loses the contract, the option is void, but the issuer rebates a portion of the premium. Consequently, the value of the payoff depends on the buyer's ability to obtain business requiring currency protection as well as on currency movements. The rebate serves the dual function of relating the net premium to the value of the hedge and facilitating the hedging position taken by the currency option dealer.

**Convergence trade**: A trade in which investors bought high-yielding European currencies and hedged themselves with lower-yielding currencies, in the expectation that a certain relationship among the currency values would be maintained.

**Convexity**: (1) In a fixed-income instrument, convexity is a measure of the way duration and price change on a particular instrument when interest rates change. A bond or note is said to have positive convexity if the instrument's value increases at least as much as duration predicts when rates drop and decreases less when rates rise. Positive convexity is desirable because it makes a position more valuable after a price change than its duration value suggests. (2) In an option position, convexity is a measure of the way the value of the position changes in response to a change in the volatility or price of the underlying instrument. A position with positive convexity (gamma) maintains or increases its value better than delta predicts when volatility increases or when prices change by a large percentage in either direction. A position with negative convexity loses value relative to delta's prediction when prices change in either direction.

**Corporate hedging**: Taking measures to protect a corporation's cash flows against currency and interest rate risks. These may be operational measures, such as purchasing materials from supplies in various countries, or financial measures, such as buying or selling financial instruments like options.

**Counter-party risk**: The risk that the other party to a contract will not fulfil the terms of a contract.

**Coupon**: Periodic interest payment on a bond. Some bonds have physical coupons that must be clipped and submitted to a bank. A *coupon rate* is the stated interest rate on the bond, equivalent to annual coupon payments as a percentage of the principal of the bond (par value).

**Cover**: To close out a position previously taken, for example, by taking a long position equal to an existing short position.

**Credit equivalent value**: The amount representing the credit risk exposure of off-balance sheet transactions. For derivatives, this represents the potential cost at current market prices of replacing the contract's cash flows if the counter-party defaults.

**Credit risk**: The risk associated with the possibility that the other party to a contract will be unwilling or unable to fulfil the terms of the contract thereby causing the holder of the claim to suffer a loss.

**Currency debasement**: Originally accomplished by mixing base metals into gold and silver coins, currency debasement is the policy of cheapening currency without acknowledging it.

**Currency swap**: A contract which commits two counter-parties to exchanging streams of *interest payments* in different currencies for an agreed period of time and to exchanging principal amounts in different currencies at a pre-agreed exchange rate at maturity.

**Daily price or trading limit**: The maximum amount that the price of a security, future, or option is permitted by an exchange to rise or fall in one day. The purpose of trading limits—much like the purpose of circuit breakers—is to impose a cooling-off period on a turbulent market.

**Dealer**: A financial intermediary that buys and sells securities or other instruments, by setting bid and offer quotes. Unlike brokers, dealers take positions in the instruments.

**Delta**: The change in the value of an option that is associated with a unit change in the price of the underlying asset.

**Delta-gamma approach:** Utilises a second-order approximation instead of a first-order approximation.

**Depository receipt**: A negotiable certificate that is issued by a US bank and that is fully backed by shares that, in turn, represent claims on the publicly traded debt or equity securities of a company. These receipts trade freely on an exchange or an OTC market. American Depository Receipts (ADRs) and Global Depository Receipts (GDRs) are identical from an operational point of view and the terms are used interchangeably, depending on the marketing strategy.

**Derivative**: (1) A contract or security whose value is closely related to and to a large extent determined by the value of a related security, commodity, or index. (2) Any bond or security that includes one or more derivatives in its structure.

**Dual currency bond**: Generically, a fixed income instrument which pays a coupon in a base currency (the currency of the investor) and the principal in a non-base currency (typically the currency of the issuer). This generic structure is subject to many variations.

**Duration**: A weighted average of the terms of all cash flows from a debt instrument. The present values of these cash flows are used as the weights with the yield to maturity used to compute the present values. Duration also represents the elasticity of the value of a bond with respect to changes in its yield to maturity. *Modified duration*: duration divided by a factor of one plus the interest rate. *Macaulay duration*: the present value weighted time to maturity of the cash flows of a fixed payment instrument or of the implicit cash flows of a derivative based on such an instrument. Originally developed as a risk measurement for bonds (the greater the duration or "average" maturity, the greater the risk), duration has proven useful in analysing equity securities and fixed income options and futures.

**Dynamic hedging**: A technique of portfolio insurance or position risk management in which an option-like return pattern is created by increasing or reducing the position in the underlying (or forwards, futures, or options on the underlying) to simulate the delta change in value of an option position. For example, a short stock index futures position may be increased or decreased to create a synthetic put on a portfolio, producing a portfolio insurance-type return pattern. Dynamic hedging relies on liquid, continuous markets with low to moderate transaction costs.

**Efficiency**: The degree to which market prices reflect all information that might affect the value of a security.

**Euromarkets**: Currency and securities markets that are beyond the jurisdiction of the government whose currency is traded. In a typical Euromarket transaction, a Japanese bank may use its US dollar deposits in London to purchase dollar-denominated securities issued in London by a corporation headquartered in Mexico City.

**European Monetary System (EMS)**: The EMS established the currency unit (European Currency Unit, or ECU) and Exchange Rate Mechanism (see below) that would lay the foundation for the European Monetary Union.

**European option**: A put or call that can be exercised only on its expiration date. The term has nothing to do with where the option is traded or what underlies it. Stock options listed on European option exchanges are usually American-style options in the sense that they can be exercised prior to the expiration date.

**Exchange**: An organised market-place for trading securities, futures contracts, or physical commodities, usually under the jurisdiction of a regulatory body.

**Exchange Rate Mechanism (ERM)**: The framework that defines the value of European currencies relative to each other.

**(Foreign) exchange risk**: The risk of an unanticipated change in the price of foreign currency that will cause the agent to suffer a loss.

**Exotic options**: Any of a wide variety of options with unusual underlyings, strike price calculations, strike price determinations, payoff mechanisms, or expiration conditions. (Also called Non-Standard Options.)

**Exposure**: The vulnerability of a portfolio to changes in asset or commodity prices.

**Firewall**: A barrier designed to prevent losses or risks taken in one part of a financial institution from weakening other parts of the institution.

**Floating currency, floating exchange rate**: A currency or exchange rate whose value is set by market forces rather than by government decisions.

**Floor**: A contract in which the buyer pays a fee to set a minimum to the flexible interest rate that it receives on a loan. The seller agrees to pay the difference between current interest rates and an agreed rate, times the notional principal, if interest rates fall below the agreed rate.

**Foreign exchange swap**: Transaction which involves the actual exchange of two currencies (principal amount only) on a specific date at a rate agreed at the time of conclusion of the contract (the short leg), and a reverse exchange of the same two currencies at a date in the future at a rate agreed at the time of the contract (the long leg). Both spot/forward and forward/forward swaps are included.

**("Outright") forward contract**: A transaction in which two parties agree to exchange a specified amount of one currency for a specified amount of another currency at some future time under conditions agreed by the two parties.

**Futures contract**: An exchange-traded contract generally calling for delivery of a specified amount of a particular financial instrument at a fixed date in the future. Contracts are highly standardised and traders need only agree on the price and number of contracts traded.

**Gamma**: The gamma of an option is the sensitivity of the option's delta to a change in the price of the underlying asset. The gamma risk is therefore the risk that the delta of an option might change.

**Gilts (or gilt-edged securities)**: Irish or UK Government medium- and long-term debt securities.

**"Good" funds**: Assets that banks are always willing to receive from other banks to represent final payment of claims. Currency and, especially, deposits at the central bank constitute good funds.

**Group of Five (G5)**: Finance ministers and central bankers of the world's five strongest economic powers: the United States, Japan, France, Germany and Great Britain.

**Group of Ten (G10)**: The G5 plus finance ministers and central bankers of Belgium, Canada, Italy, the Netherlands and Sweden.

**Haircut**: (1) The margin or, more frequently, the capital tied up when a financial intermediary takes a position. (2) A commission or fee for execution of a transaction (uncommon).

**Hammersmith and Fulham, London Borough of**: A local government in the United Kingdom that was extremely active in sterling swaps between 1986 and 1989. Swap volume was very large relative to underlying debt, suggesting large scale speculation by the borough council. The speculation was unsuccessful and a local auditor ruled that the transactions were *ultra vires*— beyond the powers of the council. The House of Lords ultimately upheld the auditor's ruling. The "legal" risk of some risk management contracts was established at considerable cost to the London financial community.

**Hedge**: An asset, liability or financial commitment that protects against adverse changes in the value of, or cash flows from, another investment or liability. An unhedged investment or liability is called an "exposure". A perfectly matched hedge will gain in value what the underlying exposure loses, or lose what the underlying exposure gains.

**Hedge funds**: Private investment pools that invest aggressively in all types of markets with managers of the fund receiving a percentage of the investment profits. Some hedge funds actually hedge, but in general a hedge fund manager makes money by taking a great deal of risk.

**Hedge ratio**: The proportion of one asset required to hedge against movements in the price of another.

**Hedging**: The process of offsetting an existing exposure by taking an opposite position in the same or a similar risk.

**Hybrid bonds**: Debt securities whose payments are determined by an equity, currency or commodity derivative incorporated in the bond's structure.

**Implied volatility (IV)**: The value of the price or rate volatility variable that would equate current option price and fair value. Alternatively, the value of the volatility variable that buyers and sellers appear to accept when the market price of an option is determined. Implied volatility is calculated by using the market price of an option as the fair value in an option model and calculating (by iteration) the volatility level consistent with that option price.

**Indexing**: Investing to mimic the performance of an index of prices rather than to beat the index.

**In-the-money**: A call (put) option contract is in-the-money when the market price of the underlying instrument exceeds (is less than) the strike price.

**Institutional investors**: Pension funds, banks, insurance companies, mutual funds and other financial institutions that accumulate savings and invest them on behalf of savers.

**Interbank market**: The market in which banks and other big investors trade currencies and securities among themselves.

**Interest rate swap**: A transaction in which two counter-parties exchange a stream of fixed rate payments for a stream of floating rate payments based on a notional principal amount which is not transferred.

**International Monetary Fund (IMF)**: An institution originally established to maintain currency values in accordance with the Bretton Woods agreements.

**Inverse floaters**: Securities designed to pay investors more when an interest rate index falls, and less when the index rate rises.

**Keiretsu**: Groups of closely related Japanese financial and industrial companies.

**Knock-out option**: A term descriptive of down-and-out or up-and-out puts and calls embedded in a structured risk management instrument or traded separately.

**Leverage** An investment or operating position subject to a multiplied effect on profit or position value from a small change in sales quantity or price. Leverage can come from high fixed costs relative to revenues in an operating situation or from debt or an option structure in a financial context.

**Limit book**: A list of traders' and dealers' limit prices.

**Limit price**: The announced price at which a trader will buy or sell a security. Also, the largest permitted price fluctuation in a futures contract during a trading session as determined by the market's rules.

**Liquidity**: The ease with which a prospective seller of a financial instrument can find a buyer at the prevailing market price.

**London Inter-Bank Offered Rates (LIBOR)**: The primary fixed income index reference rates used in the Euromarkets. Most international floating rates are quoted as LIBOR plus or minus a spread. In addition to the traditional Eurodollar and sterling LIBOR rates, yen LIBOR, DM LIBOR, Swiss franc LIBOR, etc., are also available and widely used.

**Long (short) position**: A situation in which an agent is owed (owes) or owns a positive (negative) amount of a security, and is therefore in a position to profit if the price of the security rises (falls).

**Margin**: An amount of money deposited by participants in the futures market to ensure performance of the contract. The **initial margin** is the amount that must be deposited to open either a long or a short position in a derivatives exchange, while the **maintenance margin** is the minimum amount that must remain in the account after any losses are deducted from the account as a result of marking the position to the market.

**Market-maker**: A dealer that posts ongoing quotes in a particular instrument.

**Market risk**: The risk of a change in the price of an asset that is correlated with movements in the economy as a whole and that cannot be diversified away.

**Marking-to-market**: The process of recalculating the exposure in a trading position or portfolio on the basis of current market prices.

**Medium-term notes (MTN)**: Plain vanilla debt instruments with a fixed rate and a fixed maturity (typically less than seven years, but occasionally much longer). Medium-term notes are the basic component of the debt issuance programmes of many investment grade borrowers. A medium-term note yield can serve as the base rate for a swap payment and an MTN component can be part of a hybrid security.

**Moral hazard**: The risk that a party to a transaction has not entered into a contract in good faith, has provided misleading information about its assets, liabilities, or credit capacity, or has an incentive to take unusual risks in a desperate attempt to avoid losses.

**Mortgage securities**: Securities that entitle holders to payments from a pool of mortgages.

**Natural hedge**: The shift of production facilities, working capital, or borrowing arrangements to an alternative currency area to offset undesirable cash flow exposures.

**Netting**: Substituting the amount owed by one party from the amount owed to that party and agreeing to transfer only the resulting difference.

**Notional principal**: The hypothetical amount on which swap payments are based. The notional principal in an interest rate swap is never paid or received.

**Off-balance sheet**: Financial commitments that do not generally involve booking assets or liabilities. Derivative contracts are an example.

**Open interest**: The number of contracts recorded with the exchange at the end of the day as transactions that have not been offset by an opposite trade or settled by delivery.

**Option**: The contractual right, but not obligation, to buy (*call option*) or sell (*put option*) a specified amount of the underlying security at a fixed price (strike price) before or at a designated future date (expiration date). The option *writer* is the party that sells the option.

**OTC (over-the-counter)**: A financial transaction that is not made on an organised exchange. Generally the parties must negotiate all the details of each transaction or agree to use simplifying market conventions.

**Out-of-the-money**: A call option contract is out-of-the-money when the market price of the underlying instrument is less than (exceeds) the strike price.

**Par**: The principal of a bond.

**Path-dependent option**: Whereas the value of a traditional option depends only on the price of the underlying on the day of exercise or expiration, the value of a path-dependent option depends partly or exclusively on the price pattern the underlying follows in reaching exercise or expiration. Asian (average price or rate) options, look-back options, and barrier options are all examples of path-dependent options. If early exercise could be appropriate for a US option under certain circumstances, that option is also path dependent in a sense.

**Portfolio insurance**: A programme of trading that aims to protect a portfolio against loss by buying and selling in timely response to market movements.

**Position**: A market commitment. For example, a purchaser of a futures contract has a long position, while a seller of a futures contract has a short position.

**Primary dealers**: A group of dealers in the United States with a formal, ongoing trading relationship with the Federal Reserve Bank of New York and with certain obligations in the primary and secondary market for Treasury securities. The term also applies to similar entities in other countries.

**Primary market**: A market in which a security is first sold by issuers.

**Price discovery**: A general term for the process by which financial markets attain an equilibrium price, especially in the primary market. Usually refers to the incorporation of information into the price.

**Programme trading**: (1) Originally, trading an entire portfolio in a single co-ordinated transaction, the term has come to encompass (2) index options and futures arbitrage trading designed to take advantage of temporary pricing discrepancies between index futures and/or option contracts and the underlying stocks and (3) portfolio insurance. The more specific alternative terms (1) portfolio trading, (2) index arbitrage and (3) portfolio insurance are more descriptive.

**Proprietary trading**: Trading for one's own account, rather than on behalf of customers.

**Pure discount**: A zero-coupon (see below).

**Quantity adjusting options (QUANTOS)**: (1) A fixed exchange rate foreign equity option in which the face amount of the currency coverage expands or contracts to cover changes in the foreign currency value of a designated underlying security or package of securities. Quantos are used to adjust the investor's base currency protection on an underlying position which varies in value in the non-base currency. The most common example is a cross-border, equity-linked instrument with currency protection on the value of the foreign equity position in the domestic currency. (2) An option on a percentage change in a currency pair ratio applied to a face amount denominated in a third (base) currency. Double and triple currency quantos combine or offset percentage changes in two or three currency pair ratios, none involving the base currency. The similarity of the equity and currency quantos lies in the difficulty of estimating or hedging the value of the exchange into the base currency.

**Ratio spread**: An option spread in which the number of contracts purchased and the number of contracts sold are not equal. (Also called a variable spread.)

**Replacement value**: The unrealised capital gain or loss of the contract at current market prices. That is, the amount that would have to be paid to a third party to induce them to enter into a transaction to replace the contract.

**Repurchase agreement (repo), (RP)**: A financing arrangement used primarily in the government securities markets whereby a dealer or other holder of government securities sells the securities to a lender and agrees to repurchase them at an agreed future date at an agreed price which will provide the lender with an extremely low risk return. Repos are popular because they can virtually eliminate credit problems. The repo market is enlarged and enhanced by its use in Federal Reserve Board open market operations in the United States. Repos operate slightly differently in other markets.

**Reverse floating rate note**: A popular floating rate note structure in which the rate paid increases as market floating rates decline. In a typical case, the rate paid on the note is set by doubling the swap rate (fixed rate) in effect at the time the contract is signed, and subtracting the floating reference index rate for each payment period. If floating rates fall, the result of this calculation will be a higher return on the reverse floating rate note. If floating rates rise, the payment on the reverse floating rate note will decline.

**Risk premium**: The value that investors demand in return for making risky investments; the price of risk.

**Secondary market**: A market in which a security is sold by one investor to another, as opposed to the primary market.

**Securitisation:** The process of converting assets which would normally serve as collateral for a bank loan into securities which are more liquid and can be traded at a lower cost than the underlying assets. The largest category of securitised assets is real estate mortgage loans which serve as collateral for mortgaged-backed securities. Auto loans and credit card obligations are also securitised.

**Settlement risk:** The possibility that operational difficulties interrupt delivery of funds even where the counter-party is willing and able to perform.

**Short sale:** The sale of an asset that one does not own, which results in a short position in that asset.

**Short squeeze:** A situation in which traders with short positions seeking to close their positions are required to pay an abnormally high price for the instrument because another trader has amassed a dominant long position in the instrument.

**Standard Portfolio Analysis of Risk (SPAN):** A margin calculation technique for a portfolio of futures and futures option positions. Originally developed for the Chicago Mercantile Exchange, it is now used by a growing number of futures and futures option markets as a mechanism for calculating margin requirements.

**Stop-loss trading:** A strategy in which a security is sold when its price falls below a certain level.

**Strike (exercise) price:** The price at which the holder of an option has the right to buy or sell the underlying instrument.

**Strip:** A pure-discount security created by the decomposition of a bond into separate securities for each coupon payment and for the final principal payment. The term strip comes from the US Treasury acronym for "separate trading of registered interest and principal".

**Swap:** A financial transaction in which two counter-parties agree to exchange streams of payments over time according to a predetermined rule. A swap is normally used to transform the market exposure associated with a loan from one interest rate base (fixed-term or floating) or currency of one denomination to another. A special case is a foreign exchange swap, which combines a spot transaction with an equivalent opposite forward transaction.

**Swaption:** An option to enter into a swap contract. A payer's swaption is the right to be a fixed rate payer and a receiver's swaption is the right to be a fixed rate receiver. The strike of a swaption will be the nominal exchange called for under the swap agreement.

**Syndicate**: A group of intermediaries that purchase prearranged shares of a security in the primary market and sell the security to other investors.

**Synthetic position**: A combination of securities and/or derivative instruments that produces a risk/return position equivalent to that associated with another security that may not be directly obtainable. For example, a synthetic put is a combination of spot and/or forward transaction that replicates a put option.

**Time decay**: The loss in value of an option or an instrument with an embedded option as the expiration date approaches.

**Value-at-risk**: An estimate of the maximum loss that a portfolio could generate with a given level of confidence and during a given time into the future.

**Vega risk**: The risk of a change in the value of an option due to a change in the volatility of the underlying asset.

**Volatility**: A measure of the variability of price over time; roughly, the probability of a change in price.

**Warrant**: An option to purchase or sell the underlying at a given price and time or at a series of prices and times outlined in the warrant agreement. A warrant differs from a put or call option in that it is ordinarily issued for a period in excess of one year. Warrants are issued alone or in connection with the sale of other securities, as part of a merger or recapitalisation agreement, and, occasionally, to facilitate divestiture of the securities of another corporation. Ordinarily, exercise of a common stock warrant sold by the issuer of the underlying increases the number of shares of stock outstanding, whereas a call or a covered warrant is an option on shares already outstanding. Index warrants and many put warrants are cash settled.

**Yield curve**: A graph showing the relationship of interest rates to time. In a normal yield curve, interest rates on short-term investments are lower than rates on long-term investments. In an inverted yield curve, the converse is true. In a flat yield curve, interest rates on longer-term investments are not much, if at all, higher than rates on shorter-term investments.

**Yield to maturity**: Interest rate that makes a bond's present value equal to its market price. If the price of a bond is below par, the yield to maturity is greater than the bond's coupon rate, and the bond is said to trade at a discount.

**Zero-coupon**: A bond with no coupons, only a single principal payment at maturity.

# Bibliography

Allen, F. and Gale, D. (1994) *Financial Innovation and Risk Sharing*, MIT Press, Cambridge, Mass.

Andersen, R. and Danthine, J. (1983) "Hedger Diversity in Futures Markets", *Economic Journal*, Vol. 43, pp. 370–389

Arrow, K.J. (1964) "The Role of Securities in the Optimal Allocation of Risk Bearing", *Review of Economic Studies*, Vol. 31, pp. 91–96

Arrow, K.J. and Debreu, G. (1954) "Existence of an Equilibrium for a Competitive Economy", *Econometrica*, Vol. 22, pp. 265–290

Arthur, W.B. (1989) "Competing Technologies, Increasing Returns and Lock-In by Historical Events", *The Economic Journal*, Vol. 99, March, pp. 116–131.

Arthur, W.B. (1990) "Positive Feedbacks in the Economy", *Scientific American*, February, pp. 80–85.

Artus, P. (1994) *Création d'un marché à terme, nature des imperfections financières et stabilité du prix au comptant*, Caisse des Dépôts, Doc. de travail No. 94/02F, juin.

Asquith, P. and Meulbroek, L. (1995) "An Empirical Investigation of Short Interest', *Journal of Finance* (to appear).

Bank of England (1993) *Derivatives: Report of an Internal Working Group*, Bank of England, April, London.

Bank for International Settlements (BIS) (1990) *Report of the Committee on Interbank Netting Schemes of the Central Banks of the Group of Ten Countries* ("Lamfalussy Report"), November, Basle.

Bank for International Settlements (BIS) (1992) *Recent Developments in International Interbank Relations* ("Promisel Report"), Basle.

Bank for International Settlements (BIS) (1994a) *Public Disclosure of Market and Credit Risks by Financial Intermediaries* ("Fisher Report"), September, Basle.

Bank for International Settlements (BIS) (1994b) *Macroeconomic and Monetary Policy Issues Raised by the Growth of Derivatives Markets* (main report plus compendium of annexes), November, Basle.

Bank for International Settlements (BIS) (1995) *Issues of Measurement Related to Market Size and Macroprudential Risks in Derivatives Markets* ("Brockmeijer Report"), February, Basle.

Bank for International Settlements (BIS) (1996) *Central Bank Survey of Foreign Exchange and Derivatives Market Activity 1995*, May, Basle.

Bank for International Settlements (BIS) (1996) *Proposals for Improving Global Derivatives Market Statistics*, Basle.

Bank for International Settlements (BIS) (1997) *Clearing Arrangements for Exchange-Traded Derivatives*, Basle, March.

Bank for International Settlements (BIS) *International Banking and Financial Market Developments*, various issues, Basle.

Bank for International Settlements Review (1992) *Ms. Phillips Assesses the Challenges Posed by OTC Derivatives*, December, Basle.

Basle Committee on Banking Supervision (1993a) *The Supervisory Treatment of Market Risks*, April, Basle.

Basle Committee on Banking Supervision (1993b) *Measurement of Banks' Exposure to Interest Rate Risk*, April, Basle.

Basle Committee on Banking Supervision (1993c) *The Prudential Supervision of Netting Market Risks and Interest Rate Risk*, April, Basle.

Basle Committee on Banking Supervision (1994) *Risk Management for Derivatives*, Basle.

Basle Committee on Banking Supervision (1996) *The Supervision of Cross-Border Banking*, Basle.

Basle Committee on Banking Supervision and the International Organisation of Securities Commissions (IOSCO) (1996) *Response of the Basle Committee on Banking Supervision and the International Organisation of Securities Commissions (IOSCO) to the Request of the G7 Heads of Government at the June 1995 Halifax Summit*, Basle.

Basle Committee on Banking Supervision and the Technical Committee of the International Organisation of Securities Commissions (IOSCO) (1995) *Framework for Supervisory Information about the Derivatives Activities of Banks and Securities Firms*, May, Basle.

Benston, G.J. (1973) *Bank Examination*, Bulletin of the Institute of Finance, May, New York University.

Benston, G.J. (1983) "Federal Regulation of Banking", *Journal of Bank Research*, Vol. 13, pp. 216–244.

Benston, G.J. (1996) "The Origins of and Justification for the Glass–Steagall Act", in A. Saunders and I. Walter, *Universal Banking*, Irwin, New York, pp. 31–69.

Berle, A. and Means, G.C. (1932) *The Modern Corporation and Private Property*, Macmillan, New York.

Bernstein, P.L. (1992) *Capital Ideas: The Improbable Origins of Modern Wall Street*, Free Press, New York.

Bisignano, J. (1997), "Towards an Understanding of the Changing Structure of Financial Intermediation: An Evolutionary Theory of Institutional Survival", Bank for International Settlements, mimeo.

Black, F. (1976) "The Pricing of Commodity Contracts", *Journal of Financial Economics*, Vol. 3, pp. 167–179.

Black, F. (1988) *An Equilibrium Model of the Crash, NBER Macroeconomics Annual*, Cambridge, Mass., MIT Press, pp. 269–275.

Black, F. and Jones, R. (1988) "Simplifying Portfolio Insurance for Corporate Pension Plans", *Journal of Portfolio Management*, Summer, pp. 322–326.

Black, F. and Scholes, M. (1973) "The Pricing of Options and Corporate Liabilities", *Journal of Political Economy*, Vol. 81, pp. 637–659.

Borio, C.E.V. and Van den Bergh, P. (1993) "The Nature and Management of Payment System Risks: An International Perspective", *BIS Economic Papers*, No. 36, February.

Bowman, D. and Faust, J. (1995) *Options, Sunspots and the Creation of Uncertainty*, Board of Governors of the Federal Reserve System, International Finance Discussion Papers, No. 510, June.

Boyd, J. and Graham, S.L. (1994) "Investigating the Banking Consolidation Trend", Federal Reserve Bank of Minneapolis, *Quarterly Review*, Summer.

Brennan, M. and Schwartz E. (1989) "Portfolio Insurance and Financial Market Equilibrium", *Journal of Business*, Vol. 62, pp. 455–476.

Britto, R. (1984) "Simultaneous Determination of Spot and Futures Prices in a Simple Model with Production Risk", *Quarterly Journal of Economics*, May, pp. 351–365.

Bryan, L. (1988) *Breaking Up the Bank: Rethinking an Industry Under Siege*, Dow Jones-Irwin, New York.

Carroll, M. and Lappen, A.A. (1994) "Mortgage-backed Mayhem", *Institutional Investor*, Vol. 39, July, pp. 39–54.

Caprio, G. and Klingebiel, D. (1996) "Bank Insolvencies: Cross-Country Experience", World Bank, Washington, DC.

Case, K.E. and Shiller, R.J. (1989) "The Efficiency of the Market for Single Family Homes", *American Economic Review*, Vol. 79, pp. 125–137.

Clark, J.A. (1988) "Economies of Scale and Scope at Depository Financial Institutions: A Review of the Literature", *Economic Review*, Federal Reserve Bank of Kansas City, September/October.

Coase, R.H. (1988) *The Firm, the Market and the Law*, University of Chicago Press, Chicago, Ill.

Crane, D.W. and Z. Bodie (1996) "The Transformation of Banking—Form Follows Function", *Harvard Business Review*, March–April, pp. 107–117.

Culp, C.L. and Miller, M.H. (1995) "Metallgesellschaft and the Economics of Synthetic Storage", *Journal of Applied Corporate Finance*, Vol. 7, pp. 6–21.

Cutler, D., Poterba, J. and Summers L. (1989) "What Moves Stock Prices?", *Journal of Portfolio Management*, Vol. 15, pp. 4–12.

de la Vega, J.P. (1688) *Confusion de Confusiones*, translated by H. Kellenbenz, Vol. 13 (1987). The Kress Library Series of Publications, Harvard University, Cambridge, Mass.

Dewatripont, M. and Tirole, J. (1994) *The Prudential Regulation of Banks*, MIT Press, Cambridge, Mass.

Economist, The (1993) "Stop Swapping", March.

Economist, The (1993) "European Stock Markets: Too Many Trading Places", June.

Economist, The (1993) "Bump in the Night", July.

Eckhardt, J. and Knipp, T. (1994) "Metallgesellschaft: Neue Probleme in den USA", *Handelsblatt*, 4 November.

Edwards, F. and Canter, M.S. (1995) "The Collapse of Metallgesellschaft: Unhedgeable Risks, Poor Hedging Strategy, or Just Bad Luck?", *The Journal of Futures Markets*, Vol. 15, pp. 211–264.

Edwards, F. and Ma, C.W. (1988) "Commodity Pool Performance: Is the Information Contained in Pool Prospectuses Useful?", *The Journal of Futures Markets*, Vol. 8, pp. 589–616.

Edwards, F.R. and Ma, C.W. (1992) *Futures and Options*, McGraw-Hill, New York.

Edwards, F.R. and Mishkin, F.S. (1995) "The Decline of Traditional Banking: Implications for Financial Stability and Regulatory Policy", *Federal Reserve Bank of New York Economic Policy Review*, July, pp. 27–45.

Eichengreen, B. and Wyplosz, C. (1993) "The Unstable EMS", *Brookings Papers on Economic Activity*, Vol. 1, pp. 51–143.

Eichenwald, K. (1995) *Serpent on the Rock*, Harper Business, New York.

Elton, E., Gruber, M. and Rentzler, J. (1987) "Professionally Managed, Publicly Traded Commodity Funds", *Journal of Business*, Vol. 60, pp. 175–199.

Esty, B., Tufano, P. and Headley, J. (1994) "Banc One Corporation: Asset and Liability Management", *Journal of Applied Corporate Finance*, Fall, pp. 33–51.

Fama, E.F. (1978) "The Effects of a Firm's Investment and Financing Decisions on the Welfare of its Security Holders", *American Economic Review*, Vol. 68, June, pp. 272–284.

Fama, E.F. and French, K. (1987) "Commodity Futures Prices: Some Evidence on Forecast Power, Premiums, and the Theory of Storage", *Journal of Business*, January, pp. 55–73.

Federal Reserve System Board of Governors (1993) *Derivative Product Activities of Commercial Banks*, Washington, DC, January.

Federal Reserve System Board of Governors (1993) *Remarks of S. Phillips at the Conference on Regulation of Derivative Products, Institute for International Research*, March.

Figlewski, S. (1984) "Margins and Market Integrity: Margin Setting for Stock Index Futures and Options", *The Journal of Futures Markets*, Vol. 4, pp. 385–416.

Financial Times (1995) Book Review: *Lessons from a fraud casebook*.

Finnerty, J.D. (1988) "Financial Engineering in Corporate Finance: An Overview", *Financial Management*, Vol. 17, pp. 14–33.

Finnerty, J.D. (1993) "An Overview of Corporate Securities Innovation", *Journal of Applied Corporate Finance*, Vol. 4, pp. 23–39.

Fischer, S. (1977) "Long-Term Contracts, Rational Expectations, and the Optimal Money Supply Rule", *Journal of Political Economy*, Vol. 85, pp. 191–205.

Folkerts-Landau, D. and Garber, P. (1994) "What Role for the ECB in Europe's Financial Markets?", in A. Steinherr (ed.), *30 Years of European Monetary Integration—From the Werner Plan to EMU*, Longman, London.

Folkerts-Landau, D., Garber, P. and Schoenmaker, D. (1996) *The Reform of Wholesale Payment Systems and its Impact on Financial Markets*, Group of Thirty, Washington, DC.

Folkerts-Landau, D. and Steinherr, A. (1994) "The Wild Beast of Derivatives: To Be Chained Up, Fenced In or Tamed?", First Prize, The AMEX Bank Review Awards, *Finance and the International Economy*, Vol. 8, Oxford University Press, Oxford, pp. 8-27.

Freeman, A. (1994) "The Future of Finance: Capitalism Without Owners?", in R. O'Brien (ed.), The AMEX Bank Review Awards, *Finance and the International Economy*, Vol. 8, Oxford University Press, Oxford, pp. 28–40.

French, K.R. (1986) "Detecting Spot Price Forecasts in Futures Prices", *Journal of Business*, Vol. 59, S39–S54.

Friedman, M. (1959) *A Program for Monetary Stability*, Fordham.

Froot, K.A., Scharfstein D.C. and Stein J.C. (1994) "A Framework for Risk Management", *Journal of Applied Corporate Finance*, Fall, pp. 22–32.

Garber, P. (1996) "Managing Risks to Financial Markets for Volatile Capital Flows: The Role of Prudential Regulation", *International Journal of Finance and Economics*, Vol. 1, No. 3, pp. 188–195.

Gemmill, G. (1990) "Futures Trading and Finance in the Housing Market", *Journal of Property Finance*, Vol. 1, No. 2, pp. 196–207.

General Accounting Office (GAO) of the United States (1994) *Financial Derivatives: Actions Needed to Protect the Financial System*, May, US General Accounting Office, Washington, DC.

Gennotte, G. and Leland H. (1990) "Market Liquidity, Hedging and Crashes", *American Economic Review*, Vol. 90, pp. 999–1021.

Gerschenkron, A. (1962) *Economic Backwardness in Historical Perspective*, Harvard University Press, Cambridge, Mass.

Gilibert, P.L. and Steinherr, A. (1996) "Private Capital Flows to Emerging Markets After the Mexican Crisis" in G. Calvo, M. Goldstein and E. Hochreiter (eds) *Private Capital Flows to Emerging Markets After the Mexican Crisis*, Institute for International Economics, Washington, DC.

Global Derivatives Study Group (1993) *Derivatives: Practices and Principles*, July, The Group of Thirty, Washington, DC.

Goldstein, M. (1997) "The Case for an International Banking Standard", Institute for International Economics, Washington, DC.

Goldstein, M., Folkerts-Landau, D. et al. (1993) *International Capital Markets. Part II: Systemic Issues in International Finance*, August, World Economic and Financial Surveys, IMF, Washington, DC.

Gordon, R.J. (1992) "Measuring the Aggregate Price Level: Implications for Economic Performance and Policy", Working Paper No. 3969, National Bureau of Economic Research, Cambridge, Mass.

Gros, D. and Steinherr, A. (1991) "Einigkeit macht stark—The Deutsche Mark Also?", in R. O'Brien (ed.), The AMEX Bank Review Prize Essays, *Finance and the International Economy: 5*, Oxford University Press, Oxford.

Gros, D. and Steinherr, A. (1995) *Winds of Change—Economic Reforms in Central and Eastern Europe*, Longman, London.

Grossman, S. (1988), "Program Trading and Market Volatility: A Report on Interday Relationships", *Financial Analysts Journal*, July–August, pp. 18–28.

Grossman, S. and Miller, M.H. (1988) "Liquidity and Market Structure", *Journal of Finance*, Vol. 4, July, pp. 617–637.

Grossman, S. and Sanford, J. (1988) "An Analysis of the Implications for Stock and Futures Price Volatility of Program Trading and Dynamic Hedging Strategies", *Journal of Business*, Vol. 61, July, pp. 275–298.

Group of Thirty (G30) (1994) *Derivatives: Practices and Principles*, Group of Thirty, Washington, DC.

Group of Thirty (G30) (1997) *Global Institutions, National Supervision and Systemic Risk*, Group of Thirty, Washington, DC.

Gruber, M. (1996) "Another Puzzle: The Growth of Actively Managed Mutual Funds", *Journal of Finance*, Vol. 51, July, pp. 783–810.

Hallett, H.A.J. and Yue, M. (1994) "Real Adjustment in a Union of Incompletely Converged Economies: An Example from East and West Germany", *European Economic Review*, Vol. 38, pp. 1731–1761.

Hansell, S and Muehring, K. (1992) "Why Derivatives Rattle the Regulators", *Institutional Investor*, Vol. 37, September, pp. 49–62.

Hart, O. and Kreps, D. (1986) "Price Destabilizing Speculation", *Journal of Political Economy*, Vol. 94, pp. 927–952.

Heisler, E. (1995) "Disclosure Deficits", *RISK*, Vol. 8, No. 10, October, pp. 25–32.

Hönig, T.M. (1996) "Rethinking Financial Regulation", *The Financial Regulator*, Vol. 1, No. 1, pp. 22–29.

Inquiry Report (1995) *Report of the Board of Banking Supervision Inquiry into the Circumstances of the Collapse of Barings*, July, London: HMSO.

International Monetary Fund (IMF) (1990–96) *International Capital Markets*, IMF, Washington, DC.

International Organisation of Securities' Commission (IOSCO) (1996) "Report on the Improvement of Cooperation and Coordination in the Surveillance of Securities and Futures Transactions", Montreal.

Institute of International Finance (1993) "An Integrated Bank Regulatory Approach to Derivatives Activities", May, Washington, DC.

Ito, T. and Hirono, K.N. (1993) "Efficiency of the Tokyo Housing Market", *Bank of Japan Monetary and Economic Studies*, Vol. 11, pp. 1–32.

Jarrow, R.A. and O'Hara, M. (1989) "Primes and Scores: An Essay on Market Imperfections", *Journal of Finance*, Vol. 44, pp. 1263–1287.

Jorion, P. (1995) *Big Bets Gone Bad—Derivatives and Bankruptcy in Orange County*, Academic Press, New York.

Kane, E.J. (1988) "How Market Forces Influence the Structure of Financial Regulation", in W.S. Haraf and R.M. Kushmeider (eds) *Restructuring Banking and Financial Services in America*, American Enterprise Institute for Public Policy Research, Washington, DC.

Kasman, B. (1992) "A Comparison of Monetary Policy Operating Procedures in Six Industrial Countries", *Federal Reserve Bank of New York Quarterly Review*, Vol. 17, No. 2, pp. 5–24.

Khan, B. and Ireland, J. (1993) "The Use of Technology for Competitive Advantage: A Study of Screen vs. Floor Trading", *City Research Project*, September.

Kindleberger, C.P. (1996) *World Economic Primacy 1500–1990*, Oxford University Press, Oxford.

Knight, F.H. (1921) *Risk, Uncertainty and Profit*, University of Chicago Press, Chicago, Ill.

Kuo, C–L. (1993) "Serial Correlation and Seasonality in the Real Estate Market", unpublished working paper, Yale University.

Kupiec, P. and O'Brien, J. (1995) "A Pre-Commitment Approach to Capital Requirements for Market Risk", FEDS Working Paper No. 95–34, July, Federal Reserve Board, Washington, DC.

Lakonishok, J., Shleifer A. and Vishny R. (1992) *The Structure and Performance of the Money Management Industry*, Brookings Institution, New York.

Lovell, M.C. and Vogel, R.C. (1973) "A CPI-Futures Market", *Journal of Political Economy*, Vol. 81, pp. 1009–1012.

Lucas, R.E. (1978) "Asset Prices in an Exchange Economy", *Econometrica*, Vol. 46, pp. 1429–1445.

Ma, C.W. (1989) "Forecasting Efficiency of Energy Futures Prices", *The Journal of Futures Markets*, Vol. 9, pp. 393–420.

Malz, A.M. (1995) "Currency Options Markets and Exchange Rates: A Case Study of the US Dollar in March 1995", *Current Issues in Economics and Finance*, Federal Reserve Bank of New York, Vol. 1, No. 4, July.

Markowitz, H. (1952) "Portfolio Selection", *Journal of Finance*, March, pp. 77–91.

McKinsey Company (1996), *Capital Productivity*, June, Washington DC.

Melamed, L. (1996) *Escape to the Futures*, Wiley, New York.

Merton, R.C. (1990) "The Financial System and Economic Performance", *Journal of Financial Services Research*, pp. 263–300.

Merton, R.C. (1992) "Financial Innovation and Economic Performance", *Journal of Applied Corporate Finance*, Vol. 4 (Winter) pp. 12–22.

Merton, R.C. (1995a) "Financial Innovation and the Management and Regulation of Financial Institutions", *Journal of Banking and Finance*, Vol.19.

Merton, R.C. (1995b) "A Functional Perspective of Financial Intermediation", *Financial Management*, Vol. 24, No. 2, Summer, pp. 23–41.

Miller, M.H. (1986) "Financial Innovation: The Last Twenty Years and The Next", *Journal of Financial and Quantitative Analysis*, Vol. 21, December, pp. 459–471.

Miller, M.H. (1991) *Financial Innovations and Market Volatility*, Basil Blackwell, Cambridge, Mass.

Miller, M.H. (1994) "Functional Regulation", *Pacific-Basin Finance Journal*, Vol. 2, pp. 91–106.

Miller, M.H. (1996) "The Social Cost of Some Recent Derivatives Disasters", *Pacific-Basin Finance Journal*, Vol. 4, pp. 113–127.

Miller, M.H. and Culp, C.L. (1995) "Rein In the CFTC", *The Wall Street Journal*, 17 August, p. A10.

Miller, R. (1989) "Property Price Futures and Options?", *Futures and Options World*.

Millman, G.J. (1995) *The Vandal's Crown*, Free Press, New York.

Modigliani, F. and Miller, M.H. (1958) "The Cost of Capital, Corporation Finance and the Theory of Investment", *American Economic Review*, Vol. 48, pp. 261–297.

Moody's Investor Service (1995) *Credit Risks of Clearing-houses at Futures and Options Exchanges*, June, New York.

Myers, S.C. (1984) "The Capital Structure Puzzle", *Journal of Finance*, Vol. 39, pp. 575–592.

Office of Thrift Supervision (1993) *Derivative Product Activities of Savings Associations*, March, Washington, DC.

Overdahl, J. and Schachter B. (1995) "Derivatives Regulation and Financial Management: Lessons from Gibson Greetings", *Financial Management*, Vol. 24, Spring, pp. 68–78.

Park, H. (1985) "Re-examination of Normal Backwardation Hypothesis in Futures Markets", *The Journal of Futures Markets*, pp. 505–516.

Phillips, S.M. (1993) "Clearance and Settlement of Derivative Products", June, Board of Governors of the Federal Reserve System, Washington, DC.

Pierce, J.L. (1991) *The Future of Banking*, Yale University Press, New Haven, Conn.

Poterba, J.M. (1991) "House Price Dynamics: The Role of Tax Policy and Demography", *Brookings Papers on Economic Activity*, Vol. 2, pp. 143–199.

Price Waterhouse (1995) "Corporate Treasury Control and Performance Standards", London.

Pringle, D.N. (1993) "Swaps Revisited, or, How I Learned to Stop Worrying and Love the Derivative", *Lazard Frères Equity Research*, 26 October, pp. 4–14.

Rehm, B.A. (1993) "Regulators Try to Reassure Lawmakers on Swaps", *American Banker*, 29 October, pp. 3.

Representation of Regulatory Bodies from 16 Countries (1995) *Windsor Declaration*, press release, 17 May.

Roseveare, D., Leibfritz, D., Fore, D. and Wurzel, E. (1996) "Ageing Populations, Pension Systems and Government Budgets: Simulations for 20 OECD Countries", Working Paper No.168, Paris, OECD.

Ross, S.A. (1989) "Institutional Markets, Financial Marketing and Financial Innovation", *Journal of Finance*, Vol. 44, July, pp. 541–556.

Rossi, M. (1997) *The Provision of Intraday Liquidity in Real Time Gross Settlement Systems*, Macmillan Press, London.

Rubinstein, M. (1987) "Derivative Assets Analysis", *Economic Perspectives*, Vol. 1, Fall, pp. 73–93.

Salem, G. (1993) "Rating for Banc One Reduced to Hold from Buy Based on Confusion from Heavy Exposure to Interest Rate Swaps", *Prudential Securities*, November, p. 2.

Samuelson, P.A. (1973, 1980) *Economics*, 9th and 11th edns, McGraw-Hill, New York.

Sanford, Ch. (1993) *Financial Markets in 2020*, Federal Reserve Bank of Kansas City.

Scholes, M. (1994) "Financial Infrastructure and Economic Growth, Conference on Growth and Development: The Economics of the 21st Century", June, Center for Economic Policy Research, Stanford University, Stanford, Calif.

Shaffer, S. (1988) *A Revenue-Residual Cost Study of 100 Large Banks*, Federal Reserve Bank of New York, New York.

Sharpe, W.F. (1964) "Capital Asset Prices: A Theory of Market Equilibrium under Conditions of Risk", *Journal of Finance*, Vol. 29, September, pp. 425–442.

Shiller, R.J. (1989) *Market Volatility*, MIT Press, Cambridge, Mass.

Shiller, R.J. (1993) *Macro Markets: Creating Institutions for Managing Society's Largest Economic Risks*, Oxford University Press, Oxford.

Silber, W.L. (1981) "Innovation, Competition and New Contract Design in Futures Markets", *The Journal of Futures Markets*, Vol. 1, pp. 123–155.

Silber, W.L. (1983) "The Process of Financial Innovation", *American Economic Review*, Vol. 73, pp. 89–95.

Soros, G. (1995) *Soros on Soros*, John Wiley & Sons, Inc, New York.

Stein, J.L. (1961) "The Simultaneous Determination of Spot and Futures Prices", *American Economic Review*, Vol. 51, pp. 1012–1025.

Steinherr, A. (1993) "An Innovatory Package for Financial Sector Reforms in Eastern European Countries", *Journal of Banking and Finance*, Vol. 17, pp. 1033–1057.

Steinherr, A. (1995) "Performance of Universal Banks", in A. Saunders and I. Walter (eds), *Universal Banks*, Irwin, New York, pp. 2–30.

Steinherr, A. and Huveneers, C. (1992) "Institutional Competition and Innovation: Universal Banking in the Single European Market", in A. Mullineux (ed.), *European Banking*, Blackwell, Oxford, pp. 130–147.

Steinherr, A. and Huveneers, C. (1994) "On the Performance of Differently Regulated Financial Institutions: Some Empirical Evidence", *Journal of Banking and Finance*, Vol. 18, pp. 271–306.

Steinherr, A. (1998) "European Futures and Options Markets in a Single Currency Environment", in J. Dermine and P. Hillion (eds), *European Capital Markets with a Single Currency*, Blackwell, Oxford.

Stiglitz, J.E. and Weiss, A.W. (1981) "Credit Rationing in Markets with Imperfect Information", *American Economic Review*, Vol. 71, pp. 393–410.

Stoll, H. and Whaley, R. (1988) "Volatility and Futures: Message Versus Messenger", *Journal of Portfolio Management*, Vol. 4, pp. 20–22.

Storck, E. (1995) *Euromarkt Finanz-Drehscheibe der Welt*, Schäffer-Poeschel Verlag, Stuttgart.

Swiss Bank Corporation (1994) "Understanding Derivatives", *Economic and Financial Prospects*, Special Issue.

Task Force on Conglomerate Supervision (1997) "Financial Supervision in a Global Market: A Preliminary Private Sector Perspective", February, The Institute of International Finance, Washington, DC.

Taylor, J.B. (1980) "Aggregate Dynamics and Staggered Contracts", *Journal of Political Economy*, Vol. 88, pp. 1–23.

Taylor, M. (1996) "Derivatives: An Uneven Pattern of Disclosure", *The Financial Regulator*, Vol. 1, No. 3, pp. 51–56.

Telser, L.G. (1981) "Why There Are Organised Futures Markets", *Journal of Law and Economics*, Vol. 24, April, pp. 1–23.

Tripartite Group (1995) *The Supervision of Financial Conglomerates, A Report by the Tripartite Group of Bank, Securities and Insurance Regulators*, Basle.

Tufano, P. (1989) "Financial Innovation and First-Mover Advantages", *Journal of Financial Economics*, Vol. 25, pp. 213–240.

Van Horne, J.C. (1985) "Of Financial Innovation and Excesses", *Journal of Finance*, Vol. 40, pp. 621–631.

White, L.J. (1991) *The S&L Debacle*, Oxford University Press, Oxford.

Woodford, M. (1995) "Price Level Determinacy Without Control of a Monetary Aggregate", *Carnegie-Rochester Conference Series on Public Policy*, Vol. 43, pp. 1–46.

# Index

Index compiled by Indexing Specialists